The Domestic Sources
of Ar~~~~~~~~~~icy

The Domestic Sources of American Foreign Policy

Insights and Evidence

Fourth Edition

Edited by
Eugene R. Wittkopf
and James M. McCormick

ROWMAN & LITTLEFIELD PUBLISHERS, INC.
Lanham • Boulder • New York • Toronto • Oxford

ROWMAN & LITTLEFIELD PUBLISHERS, INC.

Published in the United States of America
by Rowman & Littlefield Publishers, Inc.
A Member of the Rowman & Littlefield Publishing Group
4501 Forbes Boulevard, Suite 200, Lanham, Maryland 20706
www.rowmanlittlefield.com

P.O. Box 317, Oxford OX2 9RU, United Kingdom

British Library Cataloguing in Publication Information Available

Library of Congress Cataloging-in-Publication Data

The domestic sources of American foreign policy : insights and evidence
/ edited by Eugene R. Wittkopf and James M. McCormick.—4th ed.
    p.   cm.
Includes bibliographical references and index.
    ISBN 0-7425-2562-7 (cloth : alk. paper)—ISBN 0-7425-2563-5 (pbk. :
alk. paper)
    1. United States—Foreign relations—1945–1989.   2. United
States—Foreign relations—1989–   3. United States—Foreign
relations—Decision making.   4. United States—Foriegn relations
administration.   I. Wittkopf, Eugene R., 1943–   II. McCormick, James M.
    E840.D63 2003
    327.73—dc21   2003007488

Printed in the United States of America

⊗™ The paper used in this publication meets the minimum requirements of American
National Standard for Information Sciences—Permanence of Paper for Printed Library
Materials, ANSI/NISO Z39.48-1992.

Contents

Acknowledgments

"Beyond September 11" by Joseph S. Nye, Jr. From *The Paradox of American Power* by Joseph S. Nye, Jr. © 2002 by Joseph S. Nye, Jr. Used by permission of Oxford University Press, Inc.

"Why Don't They Like us?" by Stanley Hoffman. Reprinted with permission from *The American Prospect* Volume 12, Number 20: November 19, 2001. The American Prospect, 5 Broad Street, Boston, MA 02109. All rights reserved.

"That's Entertainment? Hollywood's Contribution to Anti-Americanism Abroad" by Michael Medved. Reprinted with permission of the author from *The National Interest* 68 (Summer 2002): 5–14.

"The Erosion of American National Interests" by Samuel P. Huntington. Reprinted by permission of *Foreign Affairs* 76 (5, September/October 1997): 28–49. © 1997 by the Council on Foreign Relations, Inc.

"Intermestic Interests and U.S. Policy toward Cuba" by Philip Brenner, Patrick J. Haney, and Walter Vanderbush. Adapted from Philip Brenner, Patrick J. Haney, and Walter Vanderbush, "The Confluence of Domestic and International Interests: U.S. Policy Toward Cuba, 1998–2001," *International Studies Perspectives* 3 (May 2002): 192–208.

"The Gap: Soldiers, Civilians, and Their Mutual Misunderstanding" by Peter D. Feaver and Richard H. Kohn. Reprinted with permission. © *The National Interest* No. 61 (Fall 2000), Washington, D.C.

"Person and Office: Presidents, the Presidency, and Foreign Policy" by Michael Nelson is an extensively revised and expanded version of the author's article "U.S. Presidency," in Joel Krieger, ed., *The Oxford Companion to the Politics of the World*, 2nd ed., pp. 690–692.

"Globalization and Diplomacy: The View from Foggy Bottom" by Strobe Talbott. Reprinted with permission from *Foreign Policy* (Fall 1997): 69–83.

"A Tale of Two Secretaries" by Eliot Cohen. Reprinted by permission of *Foreign Affairs* (81/3, May/June 2002). © 2002 by the Council on Foreign Relations, Inc.

"Smarter Intelligence" by John Deutch and Jeffrey H. Smith. Reprinted with permission from *Foreign Policy* (January/February 2002): 64–69.

"Advisors, Czars, and Councils" by Ivo H. Daalder and I. M. Destler. Reprinted with permission. © *The National Interest* no. 68 (Summer 2002), Washington, D. C.

"Trade Policy Making: The Changing Context" by Bruce Stokes and Pat Choate. From *Democratizing U.S. Trade Policy* by Bruce Stokes and Pat Choate, 2001. Council on Foreign Relations Press. Reprinted with permission.

"Law in Order: Reconstructing U.S. National Security" by William Wechsler. Reprinted with permission. © The National Interest No. 67 (Spring 2002), Washington, D.C.

"Roles, Politics, and the Survival of the V-22 Osprey" by Christopher M. Jones is adapted with permission from an article originally published in the *Journal of Political and Military Sociology*, Volume 29, No. 1 (Summer 2001).

"Policy Preferences and Bureaucratic Position: The Case of the American Hostage Rescue Mission" by Steve Smith. First appeared in *International Affairs* (London), vol. 61, no. 1, winter 1984/5, pp. 9–25. Reproduced with permission.

"NATO Expansion: The Anatomy of a Decision" by James M. Goldgeier. Reprinted with permission from *The Washington Quarterly*, 21:1 (Winter 1998), pp. 85–102. © 1998 by the Center for Strategic and International Studies (CSIS) and the Massachusetts Institute of Technology.

"Sources of Humanitarian Intervention: Beliefs, Information, and Advocacy in U.S. Decisions on Somalia and Bosnia" by Jon Western. Adapted by the author from *International Security*, 26:4 (Spring 2002), pp. 112–142. © 2002 by the President and Fellows of Harvard College and the Massachusetts Institute of Technology.

"The Changing Leadership of George W. Bush: A Pre– and Post–9/11 Comparison" by Fred I. Greenstein. Reprinted by permission of Sage Publications from *Presidential Studies Quarterly* 32 (June 2002): 387–396.

Introduction: The Domestic Sources of American Foreign Policy

On the evening of September 11, 2001, President George W. Bush wrote in his diary, "The Pearl Harbor of the 21st century took place today."[1] Indeed, the events of that day shook the moorings of American foreign policy in a way not seen in perhaps decades. They not only altered the content of American policy abroad but affected the process of foreign-policy making at home. Importantly, too, they reminded us—in a most tragic way—of the nexus between foreign and domestic policy and of the impact of globalization on Americans and their nation's place in the world.

The process of globalization—the political, economic, and social forces that are drawing peoples together regardless of state boundaries—was largely hailed and embraced by the United States in the aftermath of the Cold War. New regional and global economic organizations—the North American Free Trade Agreement, the Asia-Pacific Economic Cooperation, and the World Trade Organization—were created and expanded. Other developments were on the horizon, including a new Free Trade Area of the Americas, an expanded Association of Southeast Asian Nations, and a more encompassing European Union. New politico-military organizations were created in Asia and Europe (the ASEAN Regional Forum, the Organization for Security and Cooperation in Europe), and the North Atlantic Treaty Organization for the first time embraced as members some of its erstwhile communist foes. The information revolution exploded as well, fueled by personal computers and the expansion of global television networks, and manifest in increased transnational economic exchanges and transboundary contacts among peoples. In fact, *Foreign Policy* concluded in its "Globalization Index" that 2000 "capped a decade of dramatic expansion in global economic flows and political engagement, as well as the increased mobility of people, information, and ideas."[2]

Even as globalization proceeded apace, however, the negative side of globalizing processes became evident. Fragmentation—the political, economic, and social forces driving people apart—had pushed the world's political actors and American foreign policy in another direction. Widespread

ethnopolitical conflicts in Rwanda, Bosnia, Kosovo, East Timor, and elsewhere shifted the focus of world politics from conflicts between states to
conflicts within them, thus challenging the principle of state sovereignty.
The currency collapses in Thailand and Indonesia in the late 1990s, which
inflicted dislocations and economic hardships on people well beyond Asia,
also demonstrated the dark side of globalization. In the security sphere, too,
concerns about the proliferation of weapons of mass destruction revealed
the differences that continue to divide states and peoples. Fears of climate
change stimulated by global warming, and of social dislocations and un-
rest tied to human rights violations and growing numbers of migrants and
refugees, fragmented the global community. As a consequence, domestic
politics and foreign policy were recognized as increasingly inseparable, and
American foreign policy, especially in the latter years of the Clinton administration and the first year of the Bush administration, was compelled to
confront these complexly intertwined issues.

Still, the tragic events of September 11 brought home to Americans the
dark side of globalization more fully and more starkly then they had ever
imagined possible. Using cell phones, rapid-fire financial transfers, and open
borders—all propelled by globalization—a small band of terrorists wrought
havoc on the American homeland. The "end of geography" and the "death
of distance" took on wholly new meanings for Americans and their leaders.
No state, not even the most powerful in the world, was beyond reach,
especially by determined nonstate actors. No borders were impenetrable
for those determined to do harm. In short, the events of 9/11 demonstrated
dramatically how both globalization and fragmentation affected states and
peoples at home and abroad.

The dark side of globalization generally, and the events of September 11
in particular, have fueled a domestic debate over the appropriate U.S. world
role in the twenty-first century. Through its *National Security Strategy Statement for the United States of the America,* issued in September 2002, the Bush
administration argued that the United States ought to maintain a military sufficient to "assure our allies and friends; dissuade future military competition;
deter threats against U.S. interests, allies, and friends; and decisively defeat
any adversary if deterrence fails." Furthermore, the administration sought
to build a "coalition of the willing" to defeat terrorists and tyrants globally,
especially those with the potential to develop weapons of mass destruction. Also, it asserted that the United States reserved to itself "the option of
preemptive actions to counter a sufficient threat to our national security."
This strategy, in the words of one analyst, "could be . . . the most important
reformulation of U.S. grand strategy in over half a century."[3]

Some have taken issue with the Bush administration's reformulation of
U.S. strategy, arguing that the United States can neither go it alone nor rely
on a coalition of the willing. Instead, the United States must reformulate its
policy toward greater global cooperation. Such "cooperation can extend the

life of American primacy.... By creating international regimes and organizations, Washington can imbed its interests and values in institutions that will shape and constrain countries for decades, regardless of the vicissitudes of American power." In other words, in this view, instead of leading unilaterally or through a coalition of the willing, the United States must utilize multilateral institutions more fully, adhere to and enforce international agreements and standards more consistently, and "take the lead in creating effective international institutions and arrangements to handle new challenges, especially those arising from the downside of globalization."[4]

Much as the dark side of globalization shaped debates about the future of American foreign policy, it reshaped the potency of domestic participants in the foreign policy process. Increasingly foreign policy is viewed as a sustained domestic concern, with increased public and media attention directed toward both global issues and homeland security. The public's interest in foreign policy and in global issues generally is at a height rarely seen before. At the same time, the American people appear willing to afford the president a greater degree of latitude in shaping America's global posture. In the current domestic environment, the role of other important participants has diminished, compared with the immediate post–Cold War decade. In the immediate aftermath of 9/11, for example, Congress's foreign policy voice was muted; members evinced increased deference to presidential direction. Some interest groups, too, have lost the prominence that they had gained following the collapse of the Berlin Wall and the implosion of the Soviet Union.

At the same time, America's increasingly dense webwork of involvement in the world political economy has stimulated greater domestic pressures on the nation's foreign policies and policymaking processes. As the experience of other states confirms, interdependence compromises the sovereign autonomy of the state, blurs the distinction between foreign and domestic politics, and elevates the participation of domestically oriented government agencies in the policy process. As transnational economic exchanges accelerate, for example, they produce clear winners and losers within American society. In turn, each group vigorously appeals to government officials for either policy continuity or changes to meet its concerns. The upshot of all these components of globalization is the continuation of the "domestication" of American foreign policy, even in the aftermath of the tragic events of 2001.

DOMESTIC POLITICS AND
FOREIGN POLICY

The proposition that domestic politics explains foreign policy stands in sharp contrast to the realist tradition in the study of foreign policy. Political realism, a perspective that enjoyed widespread acceptance among policymakers and scholars during the Cold War and before, argues that foreign policy is primarily a function of what occurs outside national borders. In this tradition, states are the principal actors; power and national interests are the dominant policy considerations; and maintaining the balance of power among states is the principal policy imperative. Furthermore, all states—democratic and nondemocratic—operate on the same assumptions and respond similarly to changes in the international system. In short, from a realist perspective, domestic politics exerts little if any impact on state behavior.

While political realism provides valuable insights into the motivations and actions of states, particularly at times of heightened concern about national security, it surely underestimates the effects of the domestic environment, both historically and today. Even the Greek philosopher Thucydides, perhaps the first political realist, recognized the importance of domestic politics in shaping the external behavior of Athens and Sparta. In language with a decidedly contemporary ring, he observed that the actions leaders of Greek city-states directed toward one another often sought to affect the political climates within their own polities, not what happened between them.

Centuries later Immanuel Kant argued in his treatise *Perpetual Peace* that democracies are inherently less warlike than autocracies, because democratic leaders are accountable to the public, which restrains them from waging war. Because ordinary citizens would have to supply the soldiers and bear the human and financial costs of imperial policies, he contended, liberal democracies are "natural" forces for peace. History has been kind to Kant's thesis—democracies in fact rarely fight one another. That theme highlighted the Clinton administration's foreign policy, which held that the spread of democratic market economies is good not only for peace but also for business and prosperity. Although eclipsed since by the "war on terrorism," democratic promotion and the spread of free markets remain prominent themes in the Bush administration's larger foreign policy approach.

The impact of domestic politics on foreign policy manifested itself in new ways in the post–9/11 environment, particularly after the successful toppling of the Taliban in Afghanistan. This was evident in the responses of different states to a prospective war against Iraq. For example, it is difficult to explain France's reluctance to endorse the Bush administration's approach to Iraq without taking into account its perennial skepticism of American leadership in world affairs, grounded in its own history and experience, as well as its traditional ties with Iraq itself. Saudi Arabia's hesitance to grant access to military bases important for an attack on Iraq was closely tied to its Islamic heritage and foundations. Turkey, also with a large Muslim population, had similar concerns, with the added worry that its sizeable Kurdish minority might use the war to carve a new Kurdistan out of parts of Turkey and Iraq. The Atlantic alliance itself, of which Turkey is a member, was riven as domestic publics on both sides of "the pond" expressed serious disagreements with their leaders about a prospective war, as illustrated by the antiwar posture embraced by the chancellor of Germany as he faced reelection in 2002 and by the evident political risks that British prime minister Tony Blair ran to his own political future by supporting the United States. In another part of the world, seemingly far from the conflict, the Philippines' cautious support of U.S. policy was explained partly by its concern for the large number of overseas Filipino workers in the Middle East, including in Iraq.

DOMESTIC POLITICS AND
AMERICAN FOREIGN POLICY

America's post–Cold War and post–9/11 foreign policies are rife with examples of how domestic politics shapes its actions abroad. In the latter years of the Clinton administration, for example, the president felt constrained in dealing with various humanitarian crises abroad by an American public reluctant to support sending U.S. ground forces to cope with them. Hence, when Clinton announced his decision to bomb Serbian positions in Kosovo in response to Serbia's mistreatment of its own Albanian minority there, he explicitly excluded the option of sending ground forces from any military action. Similarly, the administration's desire to ratify the Comprehensive Test Ban Treaty was halted by a reluctant Senate, where less than a majority approved it. Congress also stymied Clinton's hopes for further expanding free trade agreements with other countries when it refused to grant him "fast track" trading authority. Also, both houses of Congress, controlled by the opposition Republican party, prodded Clinton to approve a national missile defense bill that he had originally opposed.

Upon taking office, George W. Bush too confronted a public and Congress not wholly supportive of his foreign policy plans. Early polls showed that barely a majority of Americans supported his initial foreign policy designs. An equally divided Congress also expressed skepticism about the unilateralism evident in many of the new administration's early pronouncements and actions. Opposition was voiced about the administration's reluctance to sustain the negotiations with North Korea that Clinton had initiated and about the administration's failure to take a more active role in Middle East peace efforts. September 11 changed all of that. Congressional criticism became muted, and public enthusiasm for the president's agenda blossomed. By early 2003, however, the tides once again appeared to shift as war with Iraq loomed.

Given the nation's historical roots, the constraints domestic politics impose on American foreign policy should hardly be surprisingly. Since its founding, the United States has perceived itself as a different—indeed, as an exceptional—nation, one with a foreign policy driven more by domestic values than by the vagaries of international politics. Analysts who have examined the views of Thomas Jefferson and other founders conclude that they believed that "the objectives of foreign policy were but a means to the end of posterity and promoting the goals of domestic society."[5] That belief still permeates American society and its political processes.

Still, satisfying the requirements of domestic politics arguably became more critical for foreign policy in the last decade of the twentieth century than at other times in the nation's history. Whether that is cause for concern may be debated, but it raises questions about the ability of a democratic society to pursue a successful foreign strategy. As the French political sociologist Alexis de Tocqueville observed over 150 years ago, "Foreign politics demand scarcely any of those qualities which a democracy possesses; they require, on the contrary, the perfect use of almost all those faculties in which it is deficient."

Although there may be broad agreement that domestic imperatives sometimes shape foreign policy, there is less agreement about the particulars and how they manifest themselves in the political process. For analytic purposes, we can begin our inquiry into the domestic sources of American foreign policy by grouping them into three broad categories: the nation's societal environment; its institutional setting; and the individual characteristics of its decisionmakers, and the policymaking positions they occupy.

Figure 1 illustrates the relationship between each of the domestic explanatory categories and American foreign policy and their interrelationships with one another. The figure posits that domestic policy influences are inputs into the decisionmaking process that converts policy demands into foreign policy. (We can define "foreign policy" as the goals that a nation's officials seek to realize abroad, the values that give rise to them, and the means or instruments used to pursue them.) Conceptualized as the output of the process that converts policy demands into goals and means, foreign policy is typically multifaceted, ranging from discrete behaviors linked to specific issues to recurring patterns of behavior that define the continual efforts to cope with the environment beyond a state's borders.

Although we can easily identify many of the discrete variables that make up the domestic source categories, the lines between the categories themselves are not always clear cut. To help draw these larger distinctions as well as explicate the smaller ones, it is useful to think of the explanatory categories as layers of differing size and complexity.

THE SOCIETAL ENVIRONMENT

The broadest layer is the societal environment. The political culture of the United States—the basic needs, values, beliefs, and self-images widely shared by Americans about their political system—stands out as a primary

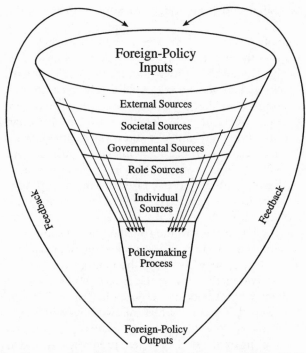

Figure 1. The Sources of American Foreign Policy. *Source:* **Charles W. Kegley Jr., and Eugene R. Wittkopf,** *American Foreign Policy: Pattern and Process,* **5th ed. (New York: St. Martin's Press, 1996), 15.**

societal source of American foreign policy. Minimally, those beliefs find expression in the kinds of values and political institutions American policy-makers have sought to export to others throughout much of its history. Included is a preference for democracy, capitalism, and the values of the American liberal tradition—limited government, individual liberty, due process of law, self-determination, free enterprise, inalienable (natural) rights, the equality of citizens before the law, majority rule, minority rights, federalism, and the separation of powers.

With roots deeply implanted in the nation's history, elements of the political culture remain potent forces explaining what the United States does in its foreign policy. But as both the positive and negative aspects of globalization are more fully recognized, the domestic roots of foreign policy may increasingly be found elsewhere. While industry, labor, and environmental interests seek to place their own stamp on U.S. responses to globalization issues (like wages, labor trafficking, and World Trade Organization dispute-settlement rulings), other entities, particularly ideological, ethnic, and single-issue groups, have expressed concern about American targets abroad in its anti-terror campaign and have sought to impose their imprint on policy positions.

Since the end of the Vietnam War, American opinion toward foreign policy issues has consistently revealed domestic divisions about what is the appropriate role of the United States in world affairs. While American opinion leaders and policymakers remain overwhelmingly internationalist in orientation, and even more so after 9/11, the question is whether the American public will become weary of its leadership against terrorism and continue to support the assertive and globalist direction outlined in the Bush administration's *National Security Strategy Statement*. Furthermore, how long the American public will be patient with, and supportive of, international institutions in dealing with the post–9/11 environment is problematic.

Historically, American leaders have been able to define the parameters of American involvement in the world and to count on public support for their choices. Especially important was the so-called Establishment, consisting of (largely male) leaders drawn from the corporate and financial world and later supplemented by faculty members from the nation's elite universities. With roots in the early twentieth century, the Establishment was a major force defining key elements of American foreign policy prior to World War II and in the decades of Cold War conflict that followed. Its role is consistent with the *elitist* model of foreign-policy making, which says that public policy is little more than an expression of elites' preferences—and the interests underlying them.

A long-standing belief that public opinion will not tolerate large losses of life in situations involving American troops is consistent with another tradition known as *pluralism*. Whereas the elitist model sees the process of policymaking as one flowing from the top downward, pluralism sees the process as an upward-flowing one. Mass public opinion, which enjoys greater weight in this model, finds expression through interest groups, whose ability to shape foreign policy has been enhanced in recent years.

The media figure prominently but quite differently in these competing policymaking models. From the elitist perspective, the media are largely the mouthpieces of elites, providing the conduit through which mass public opinion is manipulated and molded to fit elite preferences. From the pluralist perspective, on the other hand, the media comprise an independent force able to scrutinize what the government is doing and provide an independent assessment of its policies. Thus, the media appear less conspiratorial in the pluralist than in the elitist model, but their role is potent nonetheless. Indeed, to some the media *are* public opinion. Minimally, the media help to set the agenda for public discussion and often lay out for the American people the range of interpretations about foreign policy issues from which they might choose. Thus, the media help to aggregate the interests of more discrete groups in American society.

Political parties also aggregate interests. In the two-party system of the United States, political parties are broad coalitions of ethnic, religious, economic, educational, professional, working-class, and other sociodemographic groups. One of the most important functions these broad coalitions serve is the selection of personnel to key policymaking positions. They can also serve as referenda on past policy performance.

What role foreign policy beliefs and preferences play in shaping citizens' choices on these broad issues is difficult to determine. On the one hand, most citizens are motivated not by foreign policy issues but by domestic ones. Their electoral choices typically reflect those preferences, something especially evident in recent presidential elections. Still, we cannot easily dismiss the role elections play in the expression and consequences of Americans' foreign policy preferences. In the 2000 presidential campaign and election, for example, foreign policy arguably played a minor role. Because the outcome of the election was determined by a few hundred votes in many states (notably Florida), it is reasonable to hypothesize that the foreign policy preferences of only a few Americans may have been pivotal in shaping the ultimate electoral outcome. In this sense, foreign policy issues can and do matter in presidential elections.

As these ideas suggest, the political culture, the foreign policy attitudes and beliefs of leaders and masses, and the role that the media, interest groups, and elections play in shaping Americans' political preferences and transmitting them to leaders may be potent explanations of what the United States does in the world.

THE INSTITUTIONAL SETTING

As we peel away the societal environment as a source of American foreign policy, a second category is revealed: the institutional setting, consisting of the various branches of government and the departments and agencies assigned responsibility for decisionmaking, management, and implementation. The category incorporates the diverse properties related to the structure of the U.S. government—notably its presidential rather than parliamentary form—that limit or enhance the foreign policy choices made by decisionmakers and affect their implementation, thus revealing the linkages between the substance of foreign policy and the process by which it is made.

Broadly speaking, the American "foreign affairs government" encompasses a cluster of variables and organizational actors that influence what the United States does—or does not do—abroad. Most striking in this regard is the division of authority and responsibility for foreign-policy making between the Congress and the president. The Constitution embraces the eighteenth-century belief that the abuse of political power is controlled best not through centralization but by fragmenting it in a system of checks and balances. Hence, because authority and responsibility for American foreign policy is lodged in separate institutions sharing power, the Constitution is an "invitation to struggle."

The struggle for control over foreign-policy making between Congress and the president is most evident during periods when Congress and the presidency are controlled by different political parties (divided government). But even during periods when the government is not divided, conflict over foreign-policy making continues, often within the executive branch itself. There we find departments and agencies that grew in size and importance during nearly a half-century of Cold War competition with the Soviet Union. Each is populated by career professionals who fight not only for personal gain but also for what they view as the appropriate response of the United States to challenges from abroad. Not surprisingly, then, bureaucratic struggles over appropriate American policies have long been evident. They continue to leave their imprints on American foreign policy.

The growing interdependence of the United States with the world political economy reinforces these bureaucratic battles, as several executive branch departments seemingly oriented toward domestic affairs (e.g., Agriculture, Commerce, Justice, and Treasury) now also are stakeholders in the foreign policy game. This is especially evident in the fight against international terrorism. Foreign intelligence agencies (notably the CIA) and domestic law enforcement agencies (notably the FBI) are constrained by law and tradition to different policy and implementation tracks, yet today they find they must triangulate their efforts on common external threats, including not only terrorism in its physical sense but also cyberterrorism and such other challenges as trafficking in illicit drugs.

Fragmentation of authority over policymaking within the executive branch itself is a product of the complexity and competition evident within the foreign affairs government. That characterization takes on a special meaning when we consider the often overlapping roles of the White House and National Security Council staffs, the State Department, the Defense Department, the Treasury Department, the Central Intelligence Agency, and other decisionmaking units, including the new Department of Homeland Security. To be sure, the new department's charge is to integrate intelligence-gathering and law-enforcement responsibilities now spread across many different departments and agencies, but its task is a formidable one. Moreover, as more agencies have achieved places in the foreign affairs government, and as the domestic political support they enjoy has solidified, the management of policymaking by the president, whose role in the conduct of foreign affairs is preeminent, has become more difficult. To many, blame for the incoherence and inconsistency sometimes exhibited in American foreign policy lies here. Ironically, however, efforts to enhance presidential control of foreign-policy making by centralizing it in the White House have sometimes exacerbated rather than diminished incoherence and inconsistency, by encouraging competition and conflict between the presidency, on the one hand, and the executive branch departments and agencies constituting the permanent foreign affairs government, on the other.

In sum, understanding the institutional setting as a source of American foreign policy requires an examination of the responsibilities of numerous institutions and their relations with one another: the institutionalized presidency, the Congress, the cabinet-level departments, and other agencies with foreign affairs responsibilities. These, then, will be our concerns in Part II.

DECISIONMAKERS AND
THEIR POLICYMAKING POSITIONS

When we peel away the institutional setting as a domestic source of American foreign policy, the people who make the policies, their policymaking positions, and the bureaucratic environments in which they work become the focus of our attention. The underlying proposition is that the personal characteristics of individuals (personality traits, perceptions, and psychological predispositions), the role responsibilities that the individual assumes within the decision process (as president, national security adviser, or secretary of the treasury), and the differing bureaucratic environments (the Federal Bureau of Investigation versus the Central Intelligence Agency, for instance) in which individuals operate affect policy choices. Still, and despite the combination of these forces, it is important to keep in mind that the individual decisionmaker is the ultimate source of influence on policy, the final mediating force in the causal chain linking the other domestic sources to the ends and means of American foreign policy.

There are several ways in which personality and perceptual factors may impinge upon foreign-policy making. Ideas about communism and the Soviet Union instilled early in life, for example, likely affect the attitudes and behaviors of many now responsible for negotiating with the leaders of the post-Soviet states, including Russia. Similarly, policymakers' orientation toward decisionmaking may profoundly affect the nation's foreign policy strategies. It has been suggested, for example, that American leaders can be characterized as either crusaders or pragmatists. The hallmark of a crusader is a "missionary zeal to make the world better. The crusader tends to make decisions based on a preconceived idea rather than on the basis of experience. Even though there are alternatives, he usually does not see them." The pragmatist, on the other hand, "is guided by the facts and his experience in a given situation, not by wishes or unexamined preconceptions....Always flexible, he does not get locked into a losing policy. He can change direction and try again, without inflicting damage to his self-esteem."[6] Woodrow

Wilson is the preeminent twentieth-century crusader, Harry S. Truman the personification of the pragmatist. Others, including Ronald Reagan and Bill Clinton, could easily be characterized in these terms.

Personality factors also help to explain how presidents manage the conduct of foreign affairs. A president's approach to information processing, known as his or her "cognitive style," that person's orientation toward political conflict, and his or her sense of political efficacy are all important in understanding how he or she will structure the policymaking system and deal with those around the chief executive. In this case personal predispositions form a bridge between the institutional setting of American foreign-policy making and the process of decisionmaking itself.

Presidents sometimes engage in foreign-policy actions not to affect the external environment but to influence domestic politics. Foreign policy can be used to mobilize popular support at home (the "rally 'round the flag" effect), to increase authority through appeals to patriotism, and to enhance prospects for reelection using macroeconomic policymaking tools or distributing private benefits through trade policy or other mechanisms, such as defense spending distributions. Again, the connection between domestic politics and foreign policy is apparent.

Although policymakers doubtless use foreign policy for domestic purposes, it is unclear whether they do so because of who they are or because of the positions they occupy. Because of the frequency with which policymakers in the United States and other countries alike allegedly engage in this type of behavior, it seems that leaders' role requirements, not their personal predilections, explain this behavior. Policymakers' positions thus appear to stimulate certain predictable patterns of behavior. Conversely, the position an individual holds may constrain the impact of personality on policymaking behavior. Institutional roles thus reduce the influence of idiosyncratic factors on policy performance.

Individuals can, of course, interpret the roles they occupy differently. That fact blurs the distinction between decisionmakers and their policy positions as competing rather than complementary explanations of American foreign policy. Clearly, however, policymaking positions, or roles, severely circumscribe the freedom and autonomy of the particular individuals who occupy them and thus diminish the range of politically feasible choices. Hence, we must understand the relationship between the person and the position and how each separately and in combination affects policy outcomes. In no way can that conclusion be illustrated more clearly than with a simple aphorism drawn from bureaucratic politics: "Where you stand depends on where you sit."

In sum, a focus on decisionmakers and their policy positions as a category of domestic influences on American foreign policy draws attention to the capacity of individuals to place their personal imprints on the nation's conduct abroad, while simultaneously alerting us to the need to examine the forces that constrain individual initiative. Principal among these are the role-induced constraints that occur within bureaucratic settings. Because the making and execution of American foreign policy is fundamentally a group or organizational enterprise, we can surmise that these constraints are considerable. The essays in Part III will focus on these ideas and how they relate to American foreign-policy making.

NOTES

1. Bob Woodward, *Bush at War* (New York: Simon and Schuster, 2002), 37.

2. "Measuring Globalization: Who's Up, Who's Down?" *Foreign Policy* (January/ February 2003), 62–63.

3. John Lewis Gaddis, "A Grand Strategy," *Foreign Policy* (November/December 2002), 56.

4. Ivo H. Daalder and James M. Lindsay, "The Globalization of Politics: American Foreign Policy for a New Century," *Brookings Review* 21 (Winter 2003), 16–17.

5. Robert W. Tucker and David C. Hendrickson, "Thomas Jefferson and American Foreign Policy," *Foreign Affairs* 69 (Spring 1990), 139.

6. John G. Stoessinger, *Crusaders and Pragmatists: Movers of Modern American Foreign Policy* (New York: Norton, 1985), xiii–xiv.

I

THE SOCIETAL ENVIRONMENT

"Politics stops at the water's edge." That aphorism, popular during much of the Cold War, embraces the notion that domestic differences should not cloud American efforts abroad. The domestic unity implied by the phrase waned in the aftermath of the Vietnam War and, later, with the end of the Cold War, as foreign policy disputes became frequent. The tragic events of September 11 seemingly resurrected this aphorism, however, as the public rallied behind its leaders and partisan divisions were put aside to confront international terrorism. The sense of national unity was captured vividly in the hours and days immediately after 9/11, when millions of Americans flew the flag or wore it on their lapels, when members of Congress of both political parties together sang "God Bless America" on the steps of the Capitol, and when President Bush embraced the leader of the Democratic opposition, Senator Tom Daschle, in the well of the House of Representatives. In short, the societal constraints on foreign policy so readily evident during previous decades seemed to have been wiped away.

Indeed, the public's foreign policy mood shifted perceptibly after 9/11. Americans became more committed to an "active role" for the United States than at any time in recent decades, for example.[1] Not surprisingly, terrorism topped the list when people were asked to name "one of the two or three biggest problems facing the country." In addition, international terrorism was perceived as the number-one threat the United States would face over the next ten years, replacing such once-primary concerns as economic and social issues, protecting American jobs, controlling immigration, and stopping illicit trafficking in drugs.

Although the public continued to provide strong support for nonmilitary measures to address terrorism, it now also embraced a greater willingness to endorse military measures as well. American air strikes, the use of ground troops, and even assassination would be supported as antiterrorist means if accompanied by multilateral support. The public also gave strong support for more spending on defense, intelligence gathering, and homeland security.

Finally, a majority supported the maintenance of American military bases overseas. In general, then, the public was hardly a constraint on the foreign policy actions of the president; instead, it appeared to endorse the actions already under way.

The events of September 11 also altered partisan and ideological divisions on foreign policy among American policymakers, much as they had affected the public mood. While these divisions had previously constrained foreign policy actions, patriotism was now instantly reignited, and bipartisan support within Congress and between Congress and the president for an engaged American foreign policy was widely evident. Within days of 9/11, for example, Congress by overwhelming margins passed Senate Joint Resolution 23, which authorized the president to employ force "against those nations, organizations, or persons, he determines planned, authorized, committed, or aided the terrorist attacks." A month later Congress passed the USA Patriot Act, which granted even more discretion to the president in pursuing terrorist suspects, even to the extent of easing some civil liberty protections.

A year later, in October 2002, Congress continued to provide bipartisan support to the president, this time over the question of Iraq. Congress now passed a joint resolution authorizing the president to use force "as he determines to be necessary and appropriate in order to defend the national security of the United States against the continuing threat posed by Iraq and enforce all relevant United Nations Security Council Resolutions regarding Iraq." Although the creation of the Department of Homeland Security had stirred some controversy in the Senate prior to the 2002 congressional elections, after the elections and the success that the Republican Party (and hence President Bush) enjoyed in them, the Senate acted quickly. It passed the measure by a wide margin (ninety to nine), and the president later signed it into law, creating one of the largest bureaucracies in the history of the federal government. In all, then, despite occasional questioning of the administration's antiterrorist policies, both bipartisan support of the president and interbranch cooperation in shaping American foreign policy were now far more evident.

Another dimension that had contributed to greater domestic disputes in foreign policy in the immediate post–Cold War era was the emergence of a broader array of foreign policy issues (and the rise of domestic groups promoting them). That is, as the Cold War waned and finally ended, traditional security issues enjoyed less priority on the foreign policy agenda as economic and environmental issues gained greater attention. These latter issues created greater partisan, ideological, and interest conflicts, since they affected various segments of the American public differentially and thus created the conditions for more active interest-group involvement. The policy debates over granting permanent normal trading relations to China and over the Kyoto Protocol on global warming illustrate the kinds of disputes that these issues created.

In the post–9/11 environment, however, these new issues lost pride of place on the foreign policy agenda; traditional security issues once again came to the forefront. Indeed, a new "North Star," the war on terrorism, largely became the defining American foreign policy issue, much as the Soviet Union had been during the Cold War. This agenda change affected the foreign policy approach of the George W. Bush administration. The administration seeks a "distinctly American internationalism" that, as *The National Security Strategy of the United States* explains, "reflects the union of our values and our national interests." Initially the phrase "distinctly American internationalism" was a not-so-subtle emphasis on unilateralism in foreign affairs. Later, however, it came to embrace a broad security agenda that sought to involve the cooperation of the rest of the international community.

Congress also sharply altered its attention and agenda. As former representative Lee Hamilton noted shortly after 9/11, "Congress is very focused on terrorism. This is the most dramatic shift in the foreign policy agenda in a very short time that I have ever seen." Another former member, Mickey Edwards, emphasized the domestic constraints on Congress: "Members of Congress understand that politically they have to be supportive of the president and that the public is not going to put up with people playing politics."[2]

Understanding American foreign policy after September 11 thus requires a fuller understanding of the domestic political and social environment. What are the competing societal forces shaping America's responses abroad today? Which among them play pivotal roles in charting the direction of foreign policy? How are they likely to fare in the years ahead?

We begin our search for answers to these questions with three readings that discuss some domestic factors that may have contributed to the events of September 11. The readings also suggest courses of action that the United States might pursue in response to these tragic events.

In the first chapter, "Beyond September 11," noted political scientist and former Clinton administration official Joseph Nye, Jr., argues that Americans "were largely indifferent and uncertain about how to shape a foreign policy" in the 1990s. As the sole superpower, Americans did not pay much attention to foreign policy, and those that did "became arrogant about our power, arguing that we did not need to heed other nations." Nye contends that even those Americans who paid attention to foreign policy seemed to embrace the view that the United States was "both invincible and invulnerable." Indeed, through the forces of globalization America's power, especially its "soft" power (i.e., its culture and values), produced sympathy and support from many peoples and nations. But its global power and influence also produced envy and hatred. The terrorist attacks of 2001 are symptomatic of the effect that technology and communications had on "diffusing power away from governments and empowering individuals and groups to play roles in world politics."

According to Nye, American policy and how Americans view that policy need to change if the nation is to address successfully this new environment. Its policy must move away from an emphasis on unilateralism toward multilateralism. The United States, Nye argues, is "not only bound to lead, but bound to cooperate." Put differently, a major challenge for the United States is "learning to define our national interest to include global interests." That approach, he contends, "will be crucial to the longevity of [American] power and whether others see [American] hegemony as benign or not." Nye judges that the Bush administration made some strides toward multilateralism in the immediate aftermath of 9/11, but he worries about the administration's staying power. He argues that reversion to unilateralism will be harmful to the United States and to the attractiveness of America's soft power in much of the rest of the world.

In the next chapter, "Why Don't They Like Us?," political scientist Stanley Hoffmann continues this line of inquiry, arguing that the United States "lost its naivete" on September 11. Americans had believed that their nation was a benign hegemon, one that could evoke admiration in other states and peoples. Throughout history, though, "nobody—or almost nobody—ever loved a hegemon." Today two factors in particular produce envy and dislike for a hegemon: the rise within less powerful states of domestic publics that tend to constrain policymakers, and the highly unipolar nature of the current structure of international politics. The former makes the hegemon a target of disaffected states and disaffected societal groups within less powerful states, while the latter concentrates other states' attention—and criticism—on a single power more than does a multipolar system, one comprising several equally powerful states.

The United States has become a target for other reasons as well. It is disliked "by those who attack the United States for what it does (or fails to do) and [by] those who attack it for what it is." The former dislike the United States because it pursues inconsistent policies (e.g., espousing freedom but supporting dictatorships), unilateral policies (e.g., failing to support the United Nations), and perceived biased policies (e.g., supporting Israel). The latter dislike the United States because of its "values, institutions, and society—and [its] enormous impact abroad." America is viewed by some as a morally corrupt and lax society, as a society promoting globalization to the detriment of many peoples, and as a bullying society, imposing its values, culture, and democracy on others. Such charges offer a considerable challenge to the United States and its foreign policy. Hoffmann proposes a series of specific actions that the United States might pursue to reduce this global animosity.

In the third chapter, "That's Entertainment? Hollywood's Contribution to Anti-Americanism Abroad," Michael Medved discusses a broader societal factor that contributes to the dislike of the United States abroad. In particular,

Medved points to the "impact of the lurid Hollywood visions that penetrate every society on earth" and to the "anarchic and even nihilistic" nature of American pop culture, as sources of anti-Americanism. Instead of providing an accurate picture of the United States, American movies and its pop culture overemphasize sex, violence, and antisocial behavior. While some may claim that these portrayals convey the freedom that typifies American politics and society, Medved argues that they produce hatred and resentment of the United States as a lax and immoral society. Furthermore, for most Americans the excessive portrayals of sex and violence are highly inconsistent with their own experiences.

These lurid portrayals, Medved further argues, cannot be defended simply by contending that this is what the public wants. Wholesome films actually do better, he notes; the "Golden Age" of Hollywood in the 1920s and 1930s was marked by films that displayed a positive image of the United States to the rest of the world. While Hollywood has made some gestures toward a more accurate portrayal of American society in the post–9/11 period, he notes that overall "popular culture is displaying few long-term changes." Until it does, Hollywood will continue to contribute to anti-Americanism abroad.

In the next chapter, "The Erosion of American National Interests," written prior to the events of 9/11, Samuel P. Huntington, a longtime foreign policy analyst and a policy practitioner himself, worries that several challenges to the nation's traditional values threaten to undermine its global role. While the Cold War "fostered a common identity between the American people and government," he argues, its end eroded that bond.

Huntington identifies two interrelated trends as the cause of that erosion in his chapter: "changes in the scope and sources of immigration and the rise of the cult of multiculturalism." In their wake, we have witnessed "the displacement of national interests by commercial and ethnic interests" and a "foreign policy of particularism." The former reflects "the domesticization of foreign policy," while the latter reveals how powerful interest-based calculations have become in the shaping of America's foreign policy. Alarmed by these developments, Huntington calls for "a policy of restraint and reconstitution aimed at limiting the diversion of American resources to the service of particularistic subnational, transnational, and nonnational interests." Sound foreign policy, he contends, can be maintained only by looking beyond particularistic interests and focusing on the traditional values and interests of the entire nation. A question worth pondering is whether the events of September 11 created a new foreign policy consensus that overrides particularistic concerns.

The next two chapters, much in line with the kind of concern that Huntington raises, address the impacts on American foreign policy of two particular kinds of interests. One looks at policy toward Cuba in the context of the changing role of an important ethnic group in the face of growing influence exercised by competing, nonethnic groups. The second looks at the state of civil-military relations in the United States and how it might affect the United States and its foreign policy process in the future.

In "Intermestic Interests and U.S. Policy toward Cuba," Philip Brenner, Patrick J. Haney, and Walter Vandenbush analyze how interest-group activity over the Cuban embargo has changed since the end of the Cold War. During the Cold War the embargo was driven largely by external security considerations and by anti-Castro forces within the Cuban-American community; the locus of decisionmaking authority over this issue was the president. With the end of the Cold War, security considerations eroded, and the ability of business, church, and academic groups to challenge the anti-Castro forces and to reframe the issue of Cuba has increased. Now too the locus of policymaking authority has shifted from the president to the Congress, especially in light of the passage of the Cuban American Act of 1992 and the Helms-Burton Act of 1996. In the middle to late 1990s, the executive branch sought to regain control of the issue, setting off a new tug-of-war between the Congress and the president. In addition, bureaucratic politics complicated the process, as did new external pressures, principally by countries concerned by the provisions of Helms-Burton. In short, intermestic forces—forces with both international and domestic concerns—were now beginning to affect policy toward Cuba, potentially reducing the longtime influence of the anti-Castro lobby.

An important message of this chapter is that the end of the Cold War has moved policymaking away from national security concerns to incorporate domestic ones as well, with the result that more institutions are now involved in the process. That is, intermestic interest groups are now playing larger roles in foreign policy, and even traditional foreign policy actors (e.g., the Department of State) are playing enhanced roles. Importantly, in light of our earlier discussion, Brenner, Haney, and Vandenbush conclude that the events of September 11 have not fundamentally altered this pre– and post–Cold War pattern of foreign-policy making. Instead, domestic and intermestic interests groups continue to matter.

In their chapter, "The Gap: Soldiers, Civilians and their Mutual Misunderstanding," Peter D. Feaver and Richard H. Kohn report on research that investigates whether "a gap in values between the armed forces and civilian society [has] widened to the point of threatening the effectiveness of the military and impeding civil-military cooperation." The debate turns on whether the military is too ideological and conservative as compared to civilian society, too resistant to change, and too alienated from and embittered toward the civilian culture.

Feaver and Kohn begin by specifying the extent of this gap. They report that the military is more conservative than civilian elites, although less conservative than the public at large; that military officers have become more distinctly partisan and more Republican in affiliation than civilian elites or the public at large; but that civilian elites generally do not express hostility to the military, as some have argued. Still, both civilian elites and the military believe that the perceived cultural gap hurts military effectiveness.

The authors go on to discuss some factors that may account for this gap. While the demographic backgrounds of the civilians and "up-and-coming" officers do differ, Feaver and Kohn dismiss the differing backgrounds as a pivotal explanation, since "differences of opinion persist even when demographic factors are controlled, suggesting that the military may selectively attract and promote a certain profile of officers that accounts for some of these differences." Instead, they point to several other factors that may have contributed to what they call the "Republicanization" of officers: the "fallout from Vietnam, Democrats abandoning the military[,] [and] an increase during the 1980s in the proportion of young people identifying themselves as Republicans," among others. But they also argue that the military academies and war colleges have not done a good job in providing officers "with a coherent understanding of American society, its culture, and the tradition of American civil-military relations."

The implications for this continued gap could be profound for the military, for civilian control of the military, and for civil-military relations generally. For example, the gap may affect the military budget and recruitment for the military, and it may affect the public's respect and support for the military. The gap could also affect civilian control of the military, since a majority of elite military officers believe that it is proper for the military "to *insist* rather than merely to *advise* (or even advocate in private) on key matters, particularly those involving the use of force." While the civilians and the military at the highest levels often cooperate with one another, Feaver and Kohn contend, this type of elite cooperation "will not compensate for the distrust of civilians expressed at the lower ranks of the services." As a result, they propose a series of actions by both the military and the civilian sectors to rebuild the trust between the two. "Ultimately," they conclude that if the civil-military gap is to be narrowed, "the responsibility rests with civilians, partly Congress but especially the commander-in-chief."

The final two chapters in Part I take a broader look at societal influences on foreign policy by examining how the public at large affects the foreign policy process. In "The Post–9/11 Shift in Public Opinion: How Long Will It Last?" Shoon Kathleen Murray and Christopher Spinosa provide a detailed look at how public opinion has changed in light of September 11 and how it has affected the policy process. In the last chapter, "Elections and U.S. Foreign Policy," Miroslav Nincic evaluates how the electoral process and its outcomes can affect America's actions abroad.

Through a careful assessment of public opinion polls before and after 9/11, Murray and Spinosa illustrate how the public interest in, and views about, foreign policy have changed. First, while the American public largely possessed an "apathetic internationalism" prior to 9/11, after that date "public attention was riveted on international affairs." Indeed, foreign policy now ranked as the "nation's most important problem." Concerns about international terrorism displaced concerns about the economy and other issues, as we noted earlier. Second, public approval of President George W. Bush skyrocketed to 90 percent in late September 2001 and remained at extraordinarily high levels for more than a year. Indeed, as Murray and Spinosa report, after eighteen months in office, President Bush's "cumulative average [approval rating] was . . . higher than any post-Vietnam president." Third, while the public's commitment to internationalism changed little after 9/11 (including retaining a commitment to collective global leadership in world affairs), the post–9/11 public was more supportive of the use of military force (although not unilaterally). On the question of attacking Iraq, for instance, the majority of the public favored this action only in the context of support from the United Nations. Fourth, public attitudes shifted perceptibly in line with the foreign policy priorities of the Bush administration. Americans now viewed protecting the United States from terrorist attacks and preventing the spread of weapons of mass destruction as the highest foreign policy priorities. Further, they were tolerant of the Bush administration's decision to use military tribunals against suspected terrorists and to detain aliens suspected of terrorist activities.

As Murray and Spinosa note, these attitudinal changes have affected the foreign policy process, both by increasing support for the president and by focusing attention on a narrower issue agenda. With the public so supportive, the president enjoys "a degree of latitude" to conduct foreign affairs "not seen in decades." While presidents often benefit from a public "rally effect" during and following a crisis, the impact of September 11 has been longer lasting. "The result was a political climate around foreign policy issues reminiscent of the years before the breakdown of the Cold War consensus, as partisan bickering and congressional assertiveness evaporated in response to the attacks." Finally, too, the public has now turned its priorities fundamentally to the "type of hard national security issues that the Bush administration came to office wanting to pursue." In short, September 11 had a profound effect on the American public, and it remained so more than two years after those events.

In the last chapter, Nincic argues that foreign policy issues can affect the outcomes of American elections and that election results can impact foreign policy actions abroad. First of all, despite the relatively low percentage of the public that bases voting decisions on foreign policy (usually about 10 percent of the public), these voters can affect the outcome in close races, either at the presidential or congressional level. Consider the close electoral outcomes in several states in the 2000 presidential election and in the several key senate races in the 2002 congressional elections. Furthermore, in presidential elections, the foreign policy stances of presidential candidates can impact the choices of the American public in both direct and indirect ways. Indirectly, presidential candidates' foreign policy stances and attitudes may affect the image that the electorate holds of them, even when the public does not know all the specifics of the issues. That is, the image that a candidate portrays can create "an impression of leadership, decisiveness, and forcefulness." Further, the image that the public possesses about the political parties and how they will deal with international affairs may also affect voters' choices. Directly, the stances of presidential candidates may also matter. When the public is informed on foreign policy issues, cares about those issues, and sees important differences between the candidates, voters' decisions may have a direct electoral effect.

Nincic also contends that elections impact the conduct of American foreign policy in at least two ways. First, important foreign policy decisions or actions by presidents often take the electoral cycle into account. The last year of a presidential term is unlikely to be one in which the president takes new initiatives, as Nincic illustrates by looking at presidential actions toward the Soviet Union during the Cold War and various military interventions since. Interestingly, as his data illustrate, only one American intervention occurred in the fourth year of a president's term (Carter in Iran in 1980), and that with disastrous results. Second, the outcome of elections can bring abrupt change (at least for a year or two), especially when a new president takes control. Nincic catalogues a series of policy changes from president to president, including the change from the more multilateral approach of the Clinton administration to the more unilateral thrust of the Bush administration. In this sense, who gets elected president matters in the foreign policy realm. At the same time, Nincic notes, by the second or third year of a new administration "the objective realities of international politics often pull policy closer to the trends that had preceded it." On balance, then, foreign policy plays an important role in the electoral process, in terms of both the candidates that are selected by the public and of the changes in direction that an administration might undertake toward the rest of the world.

NOTES

1. The findings reported here are from the Chicago Council on Foreign Relations, "A World Transformed: Foreign Policy Attitudes of the U.S. Public after September 11," at www.worldviews.org/key_findings/us_911_report.htm (accessed September 12, 2002).

2. These former members of Congress were quoted in Miles A. Pomper, "Building Anti-Terrorism Coalition Vaults ahead of Other Priorities," *CQ Weekly*, October 27, 2001, 2552.

1

Beyond September 11

Joseph S. Nye, Jr.

The tragedy on September 11, 2001, was a wake-up call for Americans. We became complacent during the 1990s. After the collapse of the Soviet Union, no country could match or balance us. We had unsurpassed global military, economic, and cultural power. The Gulf War at the beginning of the decade was an easy victory; and at the end of the decade, we bombed Serbia without suffering a single casualty. The economy grew and the stock market boomed. We resembled Britain in its mid-Victorian glory, but with even greater global reach.

But Americans were largely indifferent and uncertain about how to shape a foreign policy to guide this power. Polls showed the American public focused on domestic affairs and paying little attention to the rest of the world. Between 1989 and 2000, the television networks closed foreign bureaus and cut their foreign news content by two-thirds. TV executives found that "young adults cared more about the Zone diet than the subtleties of Middle East diplomacy." The president of MSNBC blamed "a national fog of materialism and disinterest and avoidance."[1] And many of those Americans who did pay attention to foreign policy became arrogant about our power, arguing that we did not need to heed other nations. We seemed both invincible and invulnerable.

All that changed on September 11. The direction of the change, if not the timing, could have been foreseen. Earlier in the year, the final report of a commission on national security chaired by former senators Gary Hart and Warren Rudman warned that America's military superiority would not protect us from hostile attacks on our homeland: "Americans will likely die on American soil, possibly in large numbers."[2] The report was largely ignored. In 1997, James Woolsey and I had written that the highest priority in U.S. national security policy should be given to catastrophic terrorism, but we feared that "the very nature of U.S. society makes it difficult to prepare for this problem. Because of our 'Pearl Harbor mentality,' we are unlikely to mount an adequate defense until we suffer an attack."[3]

The terrorist attack was a terrible symptom of deeper changes that are occurring in the world. . . . A technological revolution in information and communications has been diffusing power away from governments and empowering individuals and groups to play roles in world politics—including wreaking massive destruction—that were once reserved for the governments of states. Privatization has been increasing, and terrorism is the privatization of war. Moreover, the processes of globalization have been shrinking distances, and events in faraway places—such as Afghanistan—are having a greater impact on American lives. The world has been changing from the Cold War era to the global information age, but until very recently, American attitudes and policies were not keeping pace.

Where do we go from here? Americans are still wrestling with how best to combine our power and our values while reducing our vulnerabilities. As the largest power in the world, we excite both longing and hatred among some, particularly in the Muslim world. As one Pakistani physician and religious leader put it, "You are blind to anyone beyond your borders. . . . America is the world's biggest bully. Is it any wonder that so many cheer when the bully finally gets a bloodied nose?"[4] At the same time, the tragedy also produced an enormous upwelling of sympathy for the United States in most parts of the world.

Some Americans are tempted to believe that we could reduce these hatreds and our vulnerability if we would withdraw our troops, curtail our alliances, and follow a more isolationist foreign policy. But isolationism would not remove our vulnerability. Not only are the terrorists who struck on September 11 dedicated to reducing American power, but in the words of Jordan's King Abdallah, "they want to break down the fabric of the U.S. They want to break down what America stands for."[5] Even if we had a weaker foreign policy, such groups would resent the power of the American economy, which would still reach well beyond our shores. American corporations and citizens represent global capitalism, which is anathema to some.

Moreover, American popular culture has a global reach regardless of what we do. There is no escaping the influence of Hollywood, CNN, and the Internet. American films and television express freedom, individualism, and change (as well as sex and violence). Generally, the global reach of American culture helps to enhance our soft power—our cultural and ideological appeal. But not for everyone. Individualism and liberties are attractive to many people but repulsive to some, particularly fundamentalists. American feminism, open sexuality, and individual choices are profoundly subversive of patriarchal societies. One of the terrorist pilots is reported to have said that he did not like the United States because it is "too lax. I can go anywhere I want and they can't stop me."[6] Some tyrants and fundamentalists will always hate us because of our values of openness and opportunity, and we will have no choice but to deal with them through more effective counterterrorism policies. But those hard nuggets of hate are unlikely to catalyze broader hatred unless we abandon our values and pursue arrogant and overbearing policies that let the extremists appeal to the majority in the middle.

What policies should guide our power, and can we preserve it? The United States has been compared to the Roman Empire, but even Rome eventually collapsed. A decade ago, the conventional wisdom lamented an America in decline. Best-seller lists featured books that described our fall. The cover of a popular magazine depicted the Statue of Liberty with a tear running down her cheek. Japan was eating our lunch and would soon replace us as number one. That view was wrong at the time, and I said so. When I wrote *Bound to Lead* in 1989, I predicted the continuing rise of American power. But power has its perils.

In his election campaign, President George W. Bush said, "If we are an arrogant nation, they'll view us that way, but if we're a humble nation, they'll respect us." He was right, but unfortunately, many foreigners saw the United States in 2001 as arrogantly concerned with narrow American interests at the expense of the rest of the world. They saw us focusing on the hard power of our military might rather than our soft power as we turned our backs on many international treaties, norms, and negotiating forums. In their eyes, the United States used consultations for talking, not listening. Yet effective leadership requires dialogue with followers. American leadership will be more enduring if we can convince our partners that we are sensitive to their concerns. September 2001 was a start toward such sensitivity, but only a start.

The problem is more than a partisan one. President Bush has declared that he is not a unilateralist, and President Clinton originally touted "assertive multilateralism" but subsequently backed away from United Nations peacekeeping efforts. Nor was he able to follow through on many of his multilateral initiatives. One reason was that Americans were internally preoccupied and relatively indifferent to our extraordinary role in the world. Both Republicans and Democrats in Congress responded largely to domestic special interests and often treated foreign policy as a mere extension of domestic politics. Congress tried to legislate for the rest of the world and imposed sanctions when others did not follow American law—for example, on trade with Iran or Cuba. Not only did Congress refuse to ratify more than a dozen treaties and conventions over the last decade, but it reduced foreign aid, withheld our dues to the United Nations and other international agencies, slashed spending at the State Department, and abolished the U.S. Information Agency. We must do better than that.

I am not alone in warning against the dangers of a foreign policy that combines unilateralism, arrogance, and parochialism. A number of American adherents of realist international relations theory have also expressed concern about America's staying power. Throughout history, coalitions of countries have arisen to balance dominant powers, and the search for new state challengers is well under way. Some see China as the new enemy; others envisage a Russia-China-India coalition as the threat. Still others see a uniting Europe becoming a nation-state that will challenge us for primacy. But... while the realists have a point, they are largely barking up the wrong tree.

In fact, the real challenges to our power are coming on cat's feet in the night, and ironically, our desire to go it alone may ultimately weaken us. The contemporary information revolution and its attendant brand of globalization are transforming and shrinking our world. At the beginning of this new century, these two forces have increased American power, including our ability to influence others through our attractive or "soft" power. But with time, technology spreads to other countries and peoples, and our relative preeminence will diminish. For example, today our twentieth of the global population represents more than half of the Internet. Many believe that in a decade or two, Chinese will be the dominant language of the Internet. It will not dethrone English as a lingua franca, but at some point the Asian market will loom larger than the American market. Or to take other examples, in international trade and antitrust matters the European Union already balances American economic power, and Europe's economic and soft power is likely to increase in years to come.

Even more important, the information revolution is creating virtual communities and networks that cut across national borders. Transnational corporations and nongovernmental actors (terrorists included) will play larger roles. Many of these organizations will have soft power of their own as they attract our citizens into coalitions that ignore national boundaries. As one of America's top diplomats observed, NGOs are "a huge and important force... In many issues of American policy, from human rights to the environment, NGOs are in fact the driving force."[7] By traditional measures of hard power, compared to other nations, the United States will remain number one, but being number one ain't gonna be what it used to.

Globalization—the growth of networks of worldwide interdependence—is putting new items on our national and international agenda whether we like it or not. Many of these issues we cannot resolve by ourselves. International financial stability is vital to the prosperity of Americans, but we need the cooperation of others to ensure it. Global climate change, too, will affect Americans' quality of life, but we cannot manage the problem alone. And in a world where borders are becoming more porous than ever to everything from drugs to infectious diseases to terrorism, we are forced to work with other countries behind their borders and inside ours.... We are not only bound to lead, but bound to cooperate.

How should we guide our foreign policy in a global information age? Some in the current foreign policy debates look at our preponderance in power and see a modern empire. For example, self-styled neo-Reaganites advocate a foreign policy of "benign American hegemony." Since American values are good and we have the military power, we should not feel restrained by others. In their eyes, "Americans should understand that their support for American pre-eminence is as much a boost for international justice as any people is capable of giving. It is also a boon for American interests and for what might be called the American spirit."[8]

But many conservative realists as well as liberals believe that such views smack of hubris and arrogance that alienate our friends. Americans have always viewed our nation as exceptional, but even our Declaration of Independence expressed "a decent respect for the opinions of mankind." If we are truly acting in the interests of others as well as our own, we would presumably accord to others a substantial voice and, by doing so, end up embracing some form of multilateralism.[9] As our allies point out, even well-intentioned Americans are not immune to Lord Acton's famous warning that power can corrupt.... Learning to define our national interest to include global interests will be crucial to the longevity of our power and whether others see the hegemony as benign or not.

Americans are divided over how to be involved with the rest of the world. At the end of the Cold War, many observers were haunted by the specter of the return of American isolationism. The debate today, however, is not only between isolationists and internationalists but also within the internationalist camp, which is split between unilateralists and multilateralists. Some urge a new unilateralism in which we refuse to play the role of docile international citizen, instead unashamedly pursuing our own ends. They speak of a unipolar world because of our unequaled military power. But ... military power alone cannot produce the outcomes we want on many of the issues that matter to Americans.

... I would be the last to deny the continuing importance of military power. Our military role is essential to global stability. And the military is part of our response to terrorism. But we must not let the metaphor of war blind us to the fact that suppressing terrorism will take years of patient, unspectacular work, including close civilian cooperation with other countries. On many of the key issues today, such as international financial stability, drug smuggling, or global climate change, military power simply cannot produce success, and its use can sometimes be counterproductive. As President Bush's father said after the September tragedy, "Just as Pearl Harbor awakened this country from the notion that we could somehow avoid the call of duty and defend freedom in Europe and Asia in World War II, so, too, should this most recent surprise attack erase the concept in some quarters that America can somehow go it alone in the fight against terrorism or in anything else for that matter."[10]

The initial American response followed this advice. Congress suddenly approved a big dues payment and confirmed our ambassador to the United Nations. The president sought UN support and stressed coalition building. The Treasury and White House, which earlier had undercut international cooperation on money-laundering tax havens, rapidly became proponents of cooperation. But unilateralism is far from banished. "At first, the Pentagon was even unwilling to have NATO invoke the alliance's mutual-defense clause. The allies were desperately trying to give us political cover and the Pentagon was resisting it. Eventually Secretary of Defense Donald Rumsfeld understood it was a plus, not a minus, and was able to accept it."[11] Other officials, however, worried that coalitions would shackle the United States and that invoking the international authority of the UN or NATO would set a bad precedent. Internal debates about how to implement the Bush doctrine of eliminating the scourge of terrorism raised concerns in other countries that the United States would be the unilateral judge of whether a country is supporting terrorism and the appropriate methods of response.[12] In the Congress, at the same time that our ally Britain was ratifying the treaty creating an international criminal court, Senator Jesse Helms was pressing legislation that would authorize "any necessary action to free U.S. soldiers improperly handed over to the court, a provision dubbed by some delegates as 'the Hague invasion clause.' "[13] How long the new multilateralism will last and how deep it goes remains an open question.

Any retreat to a traditional policy focus on unipolarity, hegemony, sovereignty, and unilateralism will fail to produce the right outcomes, and its accompanying arrogance will erode the soft power that is often part of the solution. We must not let the illusion of empire blind us to the increasing importance of our soft power.

How should we act in this time of unparalleled power and peril? Can we learn how to use our hard and soft power in productive combination to not only defeat terrorism but deal with the other issues of a global information age? Can we wisely use our lead during these years early in the century to build a framework for the long term? Can we promote and ensure our basic values of freedom and democracy? Are our domestic attitudes and institutions up to the challenge, or will we fritter away our advantage through inattention or arrogance? Why are we having such a hard time defining our national interest in this global information age?

... We ... need to determine how to use the current decades of our pre-eminence to advance long-term national and global interests. Our historical test will be to develop a consensus on principles and norms that will allow us to work with others to create political stability, economic growth, and democratic values. American power is not eternal. If we squander our soft power through a combination of arrogance and indifference, we will increase our vulnerability, sell our values short, and hasten the erosion of our preeminence....

NOTES

1. Jim Rutenberg, "Networks Move to Revive Foreign News," *New York Times,* September 24, 2001, C10.

2. Gary Hart and Warren Rudman, cochairmen, United States Commission on National Security/21st Century, *New World Coming: American Security in the 21st Century, Phase I Report* (Washington, D.C.: U.S. Commission on National Security/21st Century, 1999), 4.

3. Joseph S. Nye Jr. and R. James Woolsey, "Perspective on Terrorism," *Los Angeles Times,* June 1, 1997, M5.

4. Anwar ul-Haque quoted in Colin Nickerson, "Some in Region See a Robin Hood Story," *Boston Globe,* September 24, 2001, 1.

5. King Abdallah quoted in Thomas Friedman, "The Big Terrible," *New York Times,* September 18, 2001, 31.

6. Jim Yardley, "Training Site Is Questioned About Links to Hijackers," *New York Times,* September 13, 2001, A4.

7. Thomas Pickering quoted in "The FP Interview," *Foreign Policy,* July-August 2001, 38.

8. Robert Kagan and William Kristol, "The Present Danger," *The National Interest,* Spring 2000, 58, 64, 67.

9. Robert W. Tucker, "American Power—For What?" (symposium), *Commentary,* January 2000, 46.

10. Patrick Tyler and Jane Perlez, "World Leaders List Terms to Join U.S. in Coalition and Press Multilateralism," *New York Times,* September 19, 2001, 1.

11. Elaine Sciolino and Steven Lee Meyers, "U.S., Preparing to Act Largely Alone, Warns Taliban That Time Is Running Out," *New York Times,* October 7, 2001, A1.

12. Karen DeYoung, "Allies Are Cautious on Bush Doctrine," *Washington Post,* October 16, 2001, 1.

13. Associated Press, "Britain Ratifies Treaty Creating Criminal Court," *International Herald Tribune,* October 5, 2001.

2

Why Don't They Like Us?

How America Has Become the Object of Much of the Planet's Genuine Grievances—and Displaced Discontent

Stanley Hoffmann

It wasn't its innocence that the United States lost on September 11, 2001. It was its naivete. Americans have tended to believe that in the eyes of others the United States has lived up to the boastful clichés propagated during the Cold War (especially under Ronald Reagan) and during the Clinton administration. We were seen, we thought, as the champions of freedom against fascism and communism, as the advocates of decolonization, economic development, and social progress, as the technical innovators whose mastery of technology, science, and advanced education was going to unify the world.

Some officials and academics explained that U.S. hegemony was the best thing for a troubled world and unlike past hegemonies would last—not only because there were no challengers strong enough to steal the crown but, above all, because we were benign rulers who threatened no one.

But we have avoided looking at the hegemon's clay feet, at what might neutralize our vaunted soft power and undermine our hard power. Like swarming insects exposed when a fallen tree is lifted, millions who dislike or distrust the hegemon have suddenly appeared after September 11, much to [Americans'] horror and disbelief. America became a great power after World War II, when we faced a rival that seemed to stand for everything we had been fighting against—tyranny, terror, brainwashing—and we thought that our international reputation would benefit from our standing for liberty and stability (as it still does in much of Eastern Europe). We were not sufficiently marinated in history to know that, through the ages, nobody—or almost nobody—has ever loved a hegemon.

Past hegemons, from Rome to Great Britain, tended to be quite realistic about this. They wanted to be obeyed or, as in the case of France, admired. They rarely wanted to be loved. But as a combination of high-noon sheriff and proselytizing missionary, the United States expects gratitude and affection. It was bound to be disappointed; gratitude is not an emotion that one associates with the behavior of states.

THE NEW WORLD DISORDER

This is an old story. Two sets of factors make the current twist a new one. First, the so-called Westphalian world has collapsed. The world of sovereign states, the universe of Hans Morgenthau's and Henry Kissinger's Realism, is no longer. The unpopularity of the hegemonic power has been heightened to incandescence by two aspects of this collapse. One is the irruption of the public, the masses, in international affairs. Foreign policy is no longer, as Raymond Aron had written in *Peace and War,* the closed domain of the soldier and the diplomat. Domestic publics—along with their interest groups, religious organizations, and ideological chapels—either dictate or constrain the imperatives and preferences that the governments fight for. This puts the hegemon in a difficult position: It often must work with governments that represent but a small percentage of a country's people—but if it fishes for public support abroad, it risks alienating leaders whose cooperation it needs. The United States paid heavily for not having had enough contacts with the opposition to the shah of Iran in the 1970s. It discovers today that there is an abyss in Pakistan, Saudi Arabia, Egypt, and Indonesia between our official allies and the populace in these countries. Diplomacy in a world where the masses, so to speak, stayed indoors, was a much easier game.

The collapse of the barrier between domestic and foreign affairs in the state system is now accompanied by a disease that attacks the state system itself. Many of the "states" that are members of the United Nations are pseudostates with shaky or shabby institutions, no basic consensus on values or on procedures among their heterogeneous components, and no sense of national identity. Thus the hegemon—in addition to suffering the hostility of the government in certain countries (like Cuba, Iraq, and North Korea) and of the public in others (like, in varying degrees, Pakistan, Egypt, and even France)—can now easily become both the target of factions fighting one another in disintegrating countries and the pawn in their quarrels (which range over such increasingly borderless issues as drug trafficking, arms trading, money laundering, and other criminal enterprises). In addition, today's hegemon suffers from the volatility and turbulence of a global system in which ethnic, religious, and ideological sympathies have become transnational and in which groups and individuals uncontrolled by states can act on their own. The world of the nineteenth century, when hegemons could impose their order, their institutions, has been supplanted by the world of the twenty-first century: Where once there was order, there is now often a vacuum.

What makes the American Empire especially vulnerable is its historically unique combination of assets and liabilities. One has to go back to the Roman Empire to find a comparable set of resources. Britain, France, and Spain had to operate in multipolar systems; the United States is the only superpower.

But if America's means are vast, the limits of its power are also considerable. The United States, unlike Rome, cannot simply impose its will by force or through satellite states. Small "rogue" states can defy the hegemon (remember Vietnam?). And chaos can easily result from the large new role of nonstate actors. Meanwhile, the reluctance of Americans to take on the Herculean tasks of policing, "nation building," democratizing autocracies, and providing environmental protection and economic growth for billions of human beings stokes both resentment and hostility, especially among those who discover that one can count on American presence and leadership only when America's material interests are gravely threatened. (It is not surprising that the "defense of the national interest" approach of Realism was developed for a multipolar world. In an empire, as well as in a bipolar system, almost anything can be described as a vital interest, since even peripheral disorder can unravel the superpower's eminence.) Moreover, the complexities of America's process for making foreign-policy decisions can produce disappointments abroad when policies that the international community counted on—such as the Kyoto Protocol and the International Criminal Court—are thwarted. Also, the fickleness of U.S. foreign-policy making in arenas like the Balkans has convinced many American enemies that this country is basically incapable of pursuing long-term policies consistently.

None of this means, of course, that the United States has no friends in the world. Europeans have not forgotten the liberating role played by Americans in the war against Hitler and in the Cold War. Israel remembers how President Harry Truman sided with the founders of the Zionist state; nor has it forgotten all the help the United States has given it since then. The democratizations of postwar Germany and Japan were huge successes. The Marshall Plan and the Point Four Program were revolutionary initiatives. The decisions to resist aggression in Korea and in Kuwait demonstrated a commendable farsightedness.

But Americans have a tendency to overlook the dark sides of their course (except on the protesting left, which is thus constantly accused of being un-American), perhaps because they perceive international affairs in terms of crusades between good and evil, endeavors that entail formidable pressures for unanimity. It is not surprising that the decade following the Gulf War was marked both by nostalgia for the clear days of the Cold War and by a lot of floundering and hesitating in a world without an overwhelming foe.

STRAINS OF ANTI-AMERICANISM

The main criticisms of American behavior have mostly been around for a long time. When we look at anti-Americanism today, we must first distinguish between those who attack the United States for what it does, or fails to do, and those who attack it for what it is. (Some, like the Islamic fundamentalists and terrorists, attack it for both reasons.) Perhaps the principal criticism is of the contrast between our ideology of universal liberalism and policies that have all too often consisted of supporting and sometimes installing singularly authoritarian and repressive regimes. (One reason why these policies often elicited more reproaches than Soviet control over satellites was that, as time went by, Stalinism became more and more cynical and thus the gap between words and deeds became far less wide than in the United States. One no longer expected much from Moscow.) The list of places where America failed at times to live up to its proclaimed ideals is long: Guatemala, Panama, El Salvador, Chile, Santo Domingo in 1965, the Greece of the colonels, Pakistan, the Philippines of Ferdinand Marcos, Indonesia after 1965, the shah's Iran, Saudi Arabia, Zaire, and, of course, South Vietnam. Enemies of these regimes were shocked by U.S. support for them—and even those whom we supported were disappointed, or worse, when America's cost-benefit analysis changed and we dropped our erstwhile allies. This Machiavellian scheming behind a Wilsonian facade has alienated many clients, as well as potential friends, and bred strains of anti-Americanism around the world.

A second grievance concerns America's frequent unilateralism and the difficult relationship between the United States and the United Nations. For many countries, the United Nations is, for all its flaws, the essential agency of cooperation and the protector of its members' sovereignty. The way U.S. diplomacy has "insulted" the UN system—sometimes by ignoring it and sometimes by rudely imposing its views and policies on it—has been costly in terms of foreign support.

Third, the United States' sorry record in international development has recently become a source of dissatisfaction abroad. Not only have America's financial contributions for narrowing the gap between the rich and the poor declined since the end of the Cold War, but American-dominated institutions such as the International Monetary Fund and the World Bank have often dictated financial policies that turned out to be disastrous for developing countries—most notably, before and during the Asian economic crisis of the mid-1990s.

Finally, there is the issue of American support of Israel. Much of the world—and not only the Arab world—considers America's Israel policy to be biased. Despite occasional American attempts at evenhandedness, the world sees that the Palestinians remain under occupation, Israeli settlements continue to expand, and individual acts of Arab terrorism—acts that Yasir Arafat can't completely control—are condemned more harshly than the killings of Palestinians by the Israeli army or by Israeli-sanctioned assassination squads. It is interesting to note that Israel, the smaller and dependent power, has been more successful in circumscribing the United States' freedom to maneuver diplomatically in the region than the United States has been at getting Israel to enforce the UN resolutions adopted after the 1967 war (which called for the withdrawal of Israeli forces from then-occupied territories, solving the refugee crisis, and establishing inviolate territorial zones for all states in the region). Many in the Arab world, and some outside, use this state of affairs to stoke paranoia of the "Jewish lobby" in the United States.

ANTIGLOBALISM AND ANTI-AMERICANISM

Those who attack specific American policies are often more ambivalent than hostile. They often envy the qualities and institutions that have helped the United States grow rich, powerful, and influential.

The real United States haters are those whose anti-Americanism is provoked by dislike of America's values, institutions, and society—and their enormous impact abroad. Many who despise America see [it] as representing the vanguard of globalization—even as they themselves use globalization to promote their hatred. The Islamic fundamentalists of al-Qaeda—like Iran's Ayatollah Khomeini [more than] 20 years ago—make excellent use of the communication technologies that are so essential to the spread of global trade and economic influence.

We must be careful here, for there are distinctions among the antiglobalist strains that fuel anti-Americanism. To some of [America's] detractors, the most eloquent spokesman is bin Laden, for whom America and the globalization it promotes relentlessly through free trade and institutions under its control represent evil. To them, American-fueled globalism symbolizes the domination of the Christian-Jewish infidels or the triumph of pure secularism: They look at the United States and see a society of materialism, moral laxity, corruption in all its forms, fierce selfishness, and so on. (The charges are familiar to [Americans] because [they] know them as an exacerbated form of right-wing anti-Americanism in nineteenth- and twentieth-century Europe.) But there are also those who, while accepting the inevitability of

globalization and seeming eager to benefit from it, are incensed by the contrast between America's promises and the realities of American life. Looking
at the United States and the countries [it supports], they see insufficient social
protection, vast pockets of poverty amidst plenty, racial discrimination, the
large role of money in politics, the domination of the elites—and they call
[Americans] hypocrites. (And these charges, too, are familiar, because they
are an exacerbated version of the left-wing anti-Americanism still powerful
in Western Europe.)

On the one hand, those who see themselves as underdogs of the world
condemn the United States for being an evil force because its dynamism
makes it naturally and endlessly imperialistic—a behemoth that imposes
its culture (often seen as debased), its democracy (often seen as flawed),
and its conception of individual human rights (often seen as a threat to
more communitarian and more socially concerned approaches) on other
societies. The United States is perceived as a bully ready to use all means,
including overwhelming force, against those who resist it: Hence, Hiroshima,
the horrors of Vietnam, the rage against Iraq, the war on Afghanistan.

On the other hand, the underdogs draw hope from their conviction that
the giant has a heel like Achilles'. They view America as a society that cannot
tolerate high casualties and prolonged sacrifices and discomforts, one whose
impatience with protracted and undecisive conflicts should encourage its
victims to be patient and relentless in their challenges and assaults. They
look at American foreign policy as one that is often incapable of overcoming
obstacles and of sticking to a course that is fraught with high risks—as with
the conflict with Iraq's Saddam Hussein at the end of the Gulf War; as in the
flight from Lebanon after the terrorist attacks of 1982; as in Somalia in 1993;
as in the attempts to strike back at bin Laden in the Clinton years.

Thus America stands condemned not because [its] enemies necessarily
hate [its] freedoms but because they resent what they fear are [its] Darwinian
aspects, and often because they deplore what they see as the softness at [its]
core. Those who, on [the] side [of the United States], note and celebrate
America's power of attraction, its openness to immigrants and refugees, the
uniqueness of a society based on common principles rather than on ethnicity
or on an old culture, are not wrong. But many of the foreign students, for
instance, who fall in love with the gifts of American education return home,
where the attraction often fades. Those who stay sometimes feel that the
price they have to pay in order to assimilate and be accepted is too high.

WHAT BRED BIN LADEN

This long catalog of grievances obviously needs to be picked apart. The complaints vary in intensity; different cultures, countries, and parties emphasize
different flaws, and the criticism is often wildly excessive and unfair. But we

are not dealing here with purely rational arguments; we are dealing with emotional responses to the omnipresence of a hegemon, to the sense that many people outside this country have that the United States dominates their lives.

Complaints are often contradictory: Consider "America has neglected us, or dropped us" versus "America's attentions corrupt our culture." The result can be a gestalt of resentment that strikes Americans as absurd: [Americans] are damned, for instance, both for failing to intervene to protect Muslims in the Balkans and for using force to do so.

But the extraordinary array of roles that America plays in the world—along with its boastful attitude and, especially recently, its cavalier unilateralism—ensures that many wrongs caused by local regimes and societies will be blamed on the United States. [Americans] even end up being seen as responsible not only for anything bad that [its] "protectorates" do—it is no coincidence that many of the September 11 terrorists came from America's proteges, Saudi Arabia and Egypt—but for what [its] allies do, as when Arabs incensed by racism and joblessness in France take up bin Laden's cause, or when Muslims talk about American violence against the Palestinians. Bin Laden's extraordinary appeal and prestige in the Muslim world do not mean that his apocalyptic nihilism . . . is fully endorsed by all those who chant his name. Yet to many, he plays the role of a bloody Robin Hood, inflicting pain and humiliation on the superpower that they believe torments them.

Bin Laden fills the need for people who, rightly or not, feel collectively humiliated and individually in despair to attach themselves to a savior. They may in fact avert their eyes from the most unsavory of his deeds. This need on the part of the poor and dispossessed to connect their own feeble lot to a charismatic and single-minded leader was at the core of fascism and of communism. After the failure of pan-Arabism, the fiasco of nationalism, the dashed hopes of democratization, and the fall of Soviet communism, many young people in the Muslim world who might have once turned to these visions for succor turned instead to Islamic fundamentalism and terrorism.

One almost always finds the same psychological dynamics at work in such behavior: the search for simple explanations—and what is simpler and more inflammatory than the machinations of the Jews and the evils of America—and a highly selective approach to history. Islamic fundamentalists remember the promises made by the British to the Arabs in World War I and the imposition of British and French imperialism after 1918 rather than the support the United States gave to anticolonialists in French North Africa in the late 1940s and in the 1950s. They remember British opposition to and American reluctance toward intervention in Bosnia before Srebrenica, but they forget about NATO's actions to save Bosnian Muslims in 1995, to help Albanians in Kosovo in 1999, and to preserve and improve Albanians' rights in Macedonia in 2001. Such distortions are manufactured and maintained by the controlled media and schools of totalitarian regimes, and through the religious schools, conspiracy mills, and propaganda of fundamentalism.

WHAT CAN BE DONE?

Americans can do very little about the most extreme and violent forms of anti-American hatred—but they can try to limit its spread by addressing grievances that are justified. There are a number of ways to do this:

- First—and most difficult—drastically reorient U.S. policy in the Palestinian-Israeli conflict.
- Second, replace the ideologically market-based trickle-down economics that permeate American-led development institutions today with a kind of social safety net. (Even *New York Times* columnist Thomas Friedman, that ur-celebrator of the global market, believes that such a safety net is indispensable.)
- Third, prod [U.S.] allies and protegés to democratize their regimes, and stop condoning violations of essential rights (an approach that can only, in the long run, breed more terrorists and anti-Americans).
- Fourth, return to internationalist policies, pay greater attention to the representatives of the developing world, and make fairness prevail over arrogance.
- Finally, focus more sharply on the needs and frustrations of the people suffering in undemocratic societies than on the authoritarian regimes that govern them.

America's self-image today is derived more from what Reinhold Niebuhr would have called pride than from reality, and this exacerbates the clash between how [Americans] see [themselves] and foreign perceptions and mis-perceptions of the United States. If [Americans] want to affect those external perceptions (and that will be very difficult to do in extreme cases), [they] need to readjust [their] self-image. This means reinvigorating [Americans'] curiosity about the outside world, even though [their] media have tended to downgrade foreign coverage since the Cold War. And it means listening carefully to views that [Americans] may find outrageous, both for the ker-nel of truth that may be present in them and for the stark realities (of fear, poverty, hunger, and social hopelessness) that may account for the excesses of these views.

Terrorism aimed at the innocent is, of course, intolerable. Safety pre-cautions and the difficult task of eradicating the threat are not enough. If [Americans] want to limit terrorism's appeal, [they] must keep [their] eyes and ears open to conditions abroad, revise [their] perceptions of [themselves], and alter their world image through [their] actions. There is nothing un-American about this. [Americans] should not meet the Manichaeanism of [their] foes with a Manichaeanism of self-righteousness. Indeed, self-examination and self-criticism have been the not-so-secret weapons of America's historical success. Those who demand that [Americans] close ranks not only against murderers but also against shocking opinions and emotions, against dissenters at home and critics abroad, do a disservice to America.

3

That's Entertainment?

Hollywood's Contribution to Anti-Americanism Abroad

Michael Medved

"THINK AMERICA: WHY THE HOLE WORLD
HATES YOU?"

This message, proudly proclaimed in a hand-lettered sign held aloft by a
scowling, bearded Pakistani protestor during one of the angry demonstrations that followed September 11, continues to challenge the world's dominant power. In responding to such disturbing questions about the origins
of anti-Americanism, glib commentators may cite the imperial reach of U.S.
corporations, or Washington's support for Israel, or sheer envy for the freedom and prosperity of American life. But they must also contend with the
profound impact of the lurid Hollywood visions that penetrate every society
on earth. The vast majority of people in Pakistan or Peru, Poland or Papua
New Guinea, may never visit the United States or ever meet an American
face to face, but they inevitably encounter images of L.A. and New York in
the movies, television programs and popular songs exported everywhere by
the American entertainment industry.

Those images inevitably exert a more powerful influence on overseas
consumers than they do on the American domestic audience. If you live
in Seattle or Cincinnati, you understand that the feverish media fantasies
provided by a DMX music video or a *Dark Angel* TV episode do not represent everyday reality for you or your neighbors. If you live in Indonesia
or Nigeria, however, you will have little or no first-hand experience to balance the negative impressions provided by American pop culture, with its

intense emphasis on violence, sexual adventurism, and every inventive variety of anti-social behavior that the most overheated imagination could concoct. No wonder so many Islamic extremists (and so many others) look upon America as a cruel, Godless, vulgar society—a "Great Satan", indeed.

During violent anti-American riots in October 2001, mobs in Quetta, Pakistan specifically targeted five movie theaters showing U.S. imports and offered their negative review of this cinematic fare by burning each of those theaters to the ground. "Look what they did!" wailed Chaudary Umedali amid the smoking ruins of his cinema. He said that a thousand rioters smashed the doors of his theater and threw firebombs inside because "they didn't like our showing American films." Ironically, the last movie he had offered his Quetta customers was *Desperado*—a hyper-violent, R-rated 1995 shoot-em-up with Antonio Banderas and Salma Hayek, specifically designed by its Texas-born director Robert Rodriguez for export outside the United States (in this case, to worldwide Hispanic audiences).

Even the President of the United States worries publicly about the distorted view of this embattled nation that Hollywood conveys to the rest of the world. In his eloquent but uncelebrated address to students at Beijing's Tsinghua University on February 22 [2002], George W. Bush declared: "As America learns more about China, I am concerned that the Chinese people do not always see a clear picture of my country. This happens for many reasons, and some of them of our own making. Our movies and television shows often do not portray the values of the real America I know."

Ironically, the President assumed in his remarks that the Beijing students he addressed felt repulsed by the messages they received from American entertainment—despite abundant evidence that hundreds of millions of Chinese, and in particular the nation's most ambitious young people, enthusiastically embrace our pop culture. During the tragic Tiananmen Square rebellion more than a decade ago, pro-democracy reformers not only seized on the Statue of Liberty as a symbol of their movement, but indulged their taste for the music and fashions identified everywhere as part of American youth culture. American conservatives may abhor the redoubtable Madonna and all her works, but the youthful activists who brought about the Velvet Revolution in Prague reveled in her cultural contributions.

This contradiction highlights the major dispute over the worldwide influence of Hollywood entertainment. Do the spectacularly successful exports from the big show business conglomerates inspire hatred and resentment of the United States, or do they advance the inevitable, End-of-History triumph of American values? Does the near-universal popularity of national icons from Mickey Mouse to Michael Jackson represent the power of our ideals of free expression and free markets, or do the dark and decadent images we broadcast to the rest of the world hand a potent weapon to America-haters everywhere?

TELLING IT LIKE IT ISN'T

Of course, apologists for the entertainment industry decry all attempts to blame Hollywood for anti-Americanism, insisting that American pop culture merely reports reality, accurately reflecting the promise and problems of the United States, and allowing the worldwide audience to respond as they may to the best and worst aspects of our society. During a forum on movie violence sponsored by a group of leading liberal activists, movie director Paul Verhoeven (author of such worthy ornaments to our civilization as *Robocop* and *Basic Instinct*) insisted: "Art is a reflection of the world. If the world is horrible, the reflection in the mirror is horrible." In other words, if people in developing countries feel disgusted by the Hollywood imagery so aggressively marketed in their homelands, then the problem cannot be pinned on the shapers of show business but rather arises from the authentic excesses of American life.

This argument runs counter to every statistical analysis of the past twenty years on the distorted imagery of American society purveyed by the entertainment industry. All serious evaluations of movie and television versions of American life suggest that the pop culture portrays a world that is far more violent, dangerous, sexually indulgent (and, of course, dramatic) than everyday American reality. George Gerbner, a leading analyst of media violence at the Annenberg School of Communications at the University of Pennsylvania, concluded after thirty years of research that characters on network television fall victim to acts of violence *at least fifty times more frequently* than citizens of the real America.

If anything, the disproportionate emphasis on violent behavior only intensifies with the export of American entertainment. For many years, so-called action movies have traveled more effectively than other genres, since explosions and car crashes do not require translation. This leads to the widespread assumption abroad that the United States, despite the dramatically declining crime rate of the last decade, remains a dangerous and insecure society. On a recent trip to England, I encountered sophisticated and thoughtful Londoners who refused to travel across the Atlantic because of their wildly exaggerated fear of American street crime—ignoring recent statistics showing unequivocally that muggings and assaults are now more common in London than in New York. On a similar note, a recent traveler in rural Indonesia met a ten-year old boy who, discovering the American origins of the visitor, asked to see her gun. When she insisted that she didn't carry any firearms, the child refused to believe her: he knew that all Americans carried guns because he had seen them perpetually armed on TV and at the movies.

The misleading media treatment of sexuality has proven similarly unreliable in its oddly altered version of American life. Analysis by Robert and

Linda Lichter at the Center for Media and Public Affairs in Washington, DC reveals that on television, depictions of sex outside of marriage are nine to fourteen times more common than dramatizations of marital sex. This odd emphasis on non-marital intercourse leads to the conclusion that the only sort of sexual expression frowned upon by Hollywood involves physical affection between husband and wife. In reality, all surveys of intimate behavior (including the famous, sweeping 1994 national study by the University of Chicago) suggest that among the more than two-thirds of American adults who are currently married, sex is not only more satisfying, but significantly more frequent, than it is among their single counterparts. One of pop culture's most celebrated representatives of the "swinging singles" lifestyle today, Kim Cattrall of *Sex and the City,* recently published a best-selling book full of revealing confessions. In *Satisfaction: The Art of the Female Orgasm,* Cattrall describes a life dramatically different from the voracious and promiscuous escapades of the character she portrays on television. In the intimate arena, she felt frustrated and unfulfilled—as do nearly half of American females, she maintains—until the loving ministrations of her husband, Mark Levinson, finally enabled her to experience gratification and joy.

Even without Cattrall's revelations, anyone acquainted with actual unattached individuals could confirm that *Friends* and *Ally McBeal* hardly represent the common lot of American singles. On television and at the movies, the major challenge confronted by most unmarried characters is trying to decide among a superficially dazzling array of sexual alternatives. The entertainments in question may suggest that these explorations will prove less than wholly satisfying, but to most American viewers, single or married, they still look mightily intriguing. To most viewers in more traditional societies, by contrast, they look mightily decadent and disrespectful.

Consider, too, the emphasis on homosexuality in contemporary television and movies. In less than a year between 2001 and 2002, three major networks (NBC, HBO, MTV) offered different, competing dramatizations of the murder of Matthew Shepherd—the gay Wyoming college student beaten to death by two thugs. No other crime in memory—not even the murder of Nicole Brown Simpson—has received comparable attention by major entertainment companies. The message to the world at large not only calls attention to homosexual alternatives in American life, but focuses on our brutal and criminal underclass.

The Gay and Lesbian Alliance Against Defamation (GLAAD) publishes an annual scorecard in which it celebrates the number of openly gay characters who appear regularly on national television series, and recently counted more than thirty. This trendy fascination with homosexuality (as illustrated by the worshipful attention given to Rosie O'Donnell's hugely publicized "coming out") obviously overstates the incidence of out-of-the-closet gay identity; all scientific studies suggest that less than 3 percent of adults unequivocally see themselves as gay.

For purposes of perspective, it is useful to contrast the pop culture focus on gay orientation with media indifference to religious commitment. A handful of successful television shows such as *Touched By An Angel* and *Seventh Heaven* may invoke elements of conventional faith, if often in simplistic, childlike form, but ardent and mature believers remain rare on television and at the movies. The Gallup Poll and other surveys suggest that some 40 percent of Americans attend religious services on a weekly basis—more than four times the percentage who go to the movies on any given week. Church or synagogue attendance, however, hardly ever appears in Hollywood or television portrayals of contemporary American society, while mass media feature gay references far more frequently than religious ones. This is hardly an accurate representation of mainstream America, and the distortion plays directly into the hands of some of our most deadly enemies. In October 2001, an "official" press spokesman for Osama bin Laden's Al-Qaeda terror network summarized the struggle between Islamic fanatics and the United States as part of the eternal battle "between faith and atheism." Since the United States represents by far the most religiously committed, church-going nation in the Western world, this reference to the nation's godlessness gains credibility abroad only because of Hollywood's habitual denial or downplaying of the faith-based nature of our civilization.

The ugly media emphasis on the dysfunctional nature of our national life transcends examples of widely decried, tacky and exploitative entertainment, and pointedly includes the most prodigiously praised products of the popular culture. In recent years, some 1.5 billion people around the world watch at least part of Hollywood's annual Oscar extravaganza, and in April 2000 they saw the Motion Picture Academy confer all of its most prestigious awards (Best Picture, Best Actor, Best Director, Best Screenplay) on a puerile pastiche called *American Beauty.* This embittered assault on suburban family life shows a frustrated father (Kevin Spacey) who achieves redemption only through quitting his job, lusting after a teenaged cheerleader, insulting his harridan wife, compulsively exercising and smoking marijuana. The only visibly loving and wholesome relationship in this surreal middle class nightmare flourishes between two clean-cut gay male neighbors. The very title, *American Beauty,* ironically invokes the name of an especially cherished flower to suggest that all is not, well, rosy with the American dream. If the entertainment establishment chooses to honor this cinematic effort above all others, then viewers in Kenya or Kuala Lumpur might understandably assume that it offers a mordantly accurate assessment of the emptiness and corruption of American society.

EXPLAINING MEDIA MASOCHISM

This prominent example of overpraised artistic ambition suggests that the persistent problems in Hollywood's view of America go far beyond the normal pursuit of profit. While *American Beauty* director Sam Mendes and screenwriter Alan Ball might well aspire to critical acclaim, the movie's producers always understood that this tale of suburban dysfunction probably would not be a slam-dunk box office blockbuster (though the Oscars ensured that it did quite well commercially). The most common excuse for the ferocious focus on violence and bizarre behavior—the argument that the "market made me do it" and that public demands leave entertainment executives with no choice—falls apart in the face of the most rudimentary analysis.

Every year, the American movie industry releases more than 300 films, with a recent average of 65 percent of those titles rated "R"—or adults only—by the Motion Picture Association of America. Conventional wisdom holds that the big studios emphasize such disturbing, edgy R-rated releases precisely because they perform best at the box office, but an abundance of recent studies proves that the public prefers feel-good, family fare....

The other argument in defense of the entertainment emphasis on troubled aspects of American life involves the inherently dramatic nature of social dysfunction. According to the celebrated Tolstoyan aphorism, "All happy families are the same; every unhappy family is unhappy in its own way." This logic suggests an inevitable tendency to highlight the same sort of unpleasant but gripping situations so memorably brought to life by eminent pre-cinematic screenwriters like Sophocles and Shakespeare. Divorce and adultery offer more obvious entertainment value than marital bliss; criminality proves more instantly compelling than good citizenship. In an intensely competitive international marketplace, the dark—even deviant—obsessions of the present potentates of pop culture may seem to make a crude sort of sense.

This approach, however, ignores the striking lessons of Hollywood's own heritage and the wholesome basis on which our star-spangled entertainment industry came to conquer the world. In the 1920s and 1930s, the American movie business faced formidable competition from well-developed production centers in Italy, France, Germany, England and even Russia. Obvious political disruptions (including the brutal intrusion of fascist and communist tyranny) helped U.S. corporations triumph over their European rivals, and drove many of the most talented individuals to seek refuge across the Atlantic. But even more than the historic circumstances that undermined America's competitors, Hollywood managed to dominate international markets because of a worldwide infatuation with the America it both exploited and promoted. Without question, iconic homegrown figures such as Jimmy Stewart, Mae West, Henry Fonda, Shirley Temple, Clark Gable, Jimmy Cagney and John Wayne, in addition to charismatic imports like Charlie Chaplin, Cary Grant and Greta Garbo, projected qualities on screen that came to seem quintessentially, irresistibly American. As film critic Richard Grenier aptly commented during a March 1992 symposium:

> Aside from the country's prominence, there seems to have been an irresistible magnetism about a whole assemblage of American attitudes—optimism, hope, belief in progress, profound assumptions of human equality, informality—often more apparent to foreigners than to Americans themselves, that the outside world has found compelling. Over many decades these attitudes became so entrenched in world opinion as "American" that in recent times, when certain Hollywood films have taken on a distinctly negative tone, America has still retained its dramatic power, Hollywood, as it were, living on its spiritual capital.

In other words, in its so-called Golden Age, the entertainment industry found a way to make heroism look riveting, even fashionable, and to make decency dramatic. In contrast to the present day, when most of the world watches American pop culture with the sort of guilty fascination we might lavish on a particularly bloody car crash, people in every corner of the globe once looked to our entertainment exports as a source of inspiration, even enlightenment. As the English producer David Puttnam revealed in an eloquent 1989 interview with Bill Moyers, he cherished the days of his childhood when

> the image that was being projected overseas was of a society of which I wanted to be a member. Now cut to twenty years later—the image that America began projecting in the 1970s, of a self-loathing, very violent society, antagonistic within itself—that patently isn't a society that any thinking person in the Third World or Western Europe or Eastern Europe would wish to have anything to do with. America has for some years been exporting an extremely negative notion of itself.

The change came about in part because of a change in the people running the major studios and television networks. As movie historian Neal Gabler perceptively observed in his influential book, *An Empire of Their Own,* Hollywood's founding generation consisted almost entirely of East European immigrant Jews who craved American acceptance so powerfully that they used celluloid fantasies to express their ongoing adoration for their adopted country. Their successors, on the other hand, came from far more "respectable" backgrounds—in some cases as the privileged children and grandchildren of the founders themselves. In the 1960s and 1970s, they sought to establish their independence and artistic integrity by burnishing their countercultural credentials. To illustrate the magnitude and speed of the change, the 1965 Academy Award for Best Picture went to the delightful and traditionally romantic musical, *The Sound of Music*. A mere four years later, that same coveted Oscar went to *Midnight Cowboy*—the gritty story of a down-and-out male hustler in New York City, and the only X-rated feature ever to win Best Picture.

From the beginning and through to the present day, the leaders of the entertainment community have felt a powerful need to be taken seriously. The creators of the industry were born outsiders who earned that respect by expressing affection for America; the moguls of the later generations have been for the most part born insiders who earned their respect by expressing their alienation. This negativity naturally found an eager international audience during the Vietnam War era and in the waning years of the Cold War with the widespread dismissal of the "cowboy culture" of Reaganism. Even after the collapse of the Soviet Empire, anti-Americanism remained fashionable among taste-setting elites in much of the world, appealing with equal fervor to critics from the Right and the Left. In Afghanistan in the 1980s, for example, the beleaguered Russian Communists and the indefatigable *mujaheddin* might agree on very little—but they both felt powerful contempt for the freewheeling and self-destructive mores of American culture as promoted everywhere by the Hollywood entertainment machine.

Even as post-Cold War globalization enhanced the economic power and political influence of the United States, it helped the entertainment industry sustain its anti-American attitudes. With the removal of the Iron Curtain, vast new markets opened up for Hollywood entertainment, with developing economies in Asia and Latin America, too, providing hundreds of millions of additional customers. Between 1985 and 1990, inflation-adjusted revenues from overseas markets for U.S. feature films rose 124 percent at a time when domestic proceeds remained relatively flat. As a result, the portion of all movie income derived from foreign distribution rose from 30 percent in 1980 to more than 50 percent in 2000. James G. Robinson, influential chairman of Morgan Creek Productions, was right to have predicted to the *Los Angeles Times* in March 1992: "All of the real growth in the coming years will be overseas."

The fulfillment of his forecast has served to further detach today's producers from any sense of patriotic or parochial identification, encouraging their pose as Americans who have nobly transcended their own Americanism. A current captain of the entertainment industry need not ask whether a putative project will "play in Peoria"—so long as it plays in Paris, St. Petersburg and Panama City. As I argued in the pages of *Hollywood Vs. America* in 1992: "While the populist products of Hollywood's Golden Age most certainly encouraged the world's love affair with America, today's nihilistic and degrading attempts at entertainment may, in the long run, produce the opposite effect, helping to isolate this country as a symbol of diseased decadence."

WHY DO THEY WATCH IT?

With that isolation increasingly apparent after the unprecedented assault of 9/11, the question remains: Why does so much of the world still seem so single-mindedly obsessed with American entertainment, for all its chaotic and unrepresentative elements?

The most likely answer involves what might be described as the "*National Enquirer* appeal" of Hollywood's vision of life in the United States. While waiting in the supermarket checkout lines, we turn to the scandal-ridden tabloids not because of our admiration for the celebrities they expose, but because of our uncomfortable combination of envy and resentment toward them. The tabloids compel our attention because they allow us to feel superior to the rich and famous. For all their wealth and glamor and power, they cannot stay faithful to their spouses, avoid drug addiction, or cover up some other guilty secret. We may privately yearn to change places with some star of the moment, but the weekly revelations of the *National Enquirer* actually work best to reassure us that we are better off as we are.

In much the same way, Hollywood's unpleasant images of America enable the rest of the world to temper inevitable envy with a sense of their own superiority. The United States may be rich in material terms (and movies and television systematically overstate that wealth), but the violence, cruelty, injustice, corruption, arrogance and degeneracy so regularly included in depictions of American life allow viewers abroad to feel fortunate by comparison. Like the *Enquirer* approach to the private peccadilloes of world-striding celebrities, you are supposed to feel fascinated by their profligate squandering of opportunity and power.

In this sense, American pop culture is not so much liberating as it is anarchic and even nihilistic. Our entertainment offerings do not honor our freedom and liberty as political or cultural values so much as they undermine all restraints and guidelines, both the tyrannical and the traditional. As Dwight Macdonald wrote in his celebrated 1953 essay, "A Theory of Mass Culture": "Like 19th century capitalism, Mass Culture is a dynamic, revolutionary force, breaking down the old barriers of class, tradition, taste, and dissolving all cultural distinctions." Amplifying Macdonald's work, Edward Rothstein of the *New York Times* wrote in March 2002: "There is something inherently disruptive about popular culture. It undermines the elite values of aristocratic art, displaces the customs of folk culture and opposes any limitation on art's audiences or subjects. It asserts egalitarian tastes, encourages dissent and does not shun desire." It should come as no surprise, then, that even those who embrace the symbols and themes of American entertainment may feel little gratitude toward a force that casts them loose from all traditional moorings, but offers no organized system of ideas or values by way of replacement.

PATRIOTISM AND PROFIT

In 1994, I participated in an international conference on the family in Warsaw and listened to the plaintive recollections of a troubled Polish priest. He recalled the days of the Cold War, "when we listened in basements to illegal radios to Radio Free Europe so we could get a little bit of hope, a little bit of truth, from the magical land of America." After the collapse of Communism, however, America's message seemed dangerous and decadent rather than hopeful. "All of a sudden, we're struggling against drugs and free sex and AIDS and crime—and all of that seems to be an import from America. It's like the message of freedom that we heard before was only the freedom to destroy ourselves."

On a similar note, an American businessman of my acquaintance traveling in Beirut struck up a conversation with the proprietor of a falafel stand who announced himself an enthusiastic supporter of the radical, pro-Iranian terrorist group, Hizballah. Ironically, his small business featured a faded poster showing a bare-chested, machine-gun toting Sylvester Stallone as Rambo. My friend asked about the place of honor provided to an American movie hero. "We all like Rambo," the Hizballah supporter unblushingly declared. "He is a fighter's fighter." But wouldn't that make the Lebanese dissident more favorably inclined toward the United States, the visitor inquired. "Not at all," was the response. "We will use Rambo's methods to destroy the evil America."

This love-hate relationship with Hollywood's twisted imagery also characterized the 19 conspirators who made such a notable attempt to "destroy evil America" with their September 11 atrocities. During their months and years in the United States, Mohammed Atta and his colleagues savored the popular culture—renting action videos and visiting bars, peep shows, lap dancing parlors and Las Vegas—immersing themselves in Western degradation to stiffen their own hatred (and self-hatred?) of it.

In response to the terrorist attacks and to the onset of the war that followed, leaders of the Hollywood community expressed some dawning awareness that they may have indeed contributed to some of the hatred of America expressed around the world. Beyond a brief flurry of flag-waving, and the generous contributions to the 9/11 fund by leading celebrities from Julia Roberts to Jim Carrey, members of the entertainment elite showed a new willingness to cooperate with the defense establishment. Working through the Institute for Creative Technologies at USC (originally created to enlist Hollywood talent for shaping virtual reality simulators for military training), creators of movies like *Die Hard, Fight Club* and even *Being John Malkovich* brain-stormed with Pentagon brass. Their purpose, according to several press reports, involved an attempt to concoct the next possible plot that might be launched against the United States, and then to devise strategies to counteract it.

In a sense, this unconventional program acknowledged the fact that violent, demented, anti-social and conspiratorial thinking has come to characterize a major segment of the entertainment establishment. How else could an objective observer interpret the idea that the military turned first to millionaire screenwriters in order to understand the thought processes of mass-murdering terrorists?

Beyond this strange collaboration, top show business executives met with Karl Rove, political representative of President Bush, in an attempt to mobilize Hollywood creativity to serve America in the war against terror. The well-publicized "summit" discussed public service ads to discourage bigotry against Muslims in America and additional productions to give the United States a more benign image in the Islamic world. A handful of top directors, including William Friedkin (*The French Connection, The Exorcist* and the excellent *Rules of Engagement*) expressed their willingness to drop all their pressing projects and enlist full-time to help the American war effort. In this determination, these pop culture patriots hoped to follow the example of the great Golden Age director Frank Capra, who served his country during World War II through the creation of the epic *Why We Fight* series.

Alas, the White House and the Pentagon failed to take advantage of the self-sacrificing spirit of the moment, or to pursue the entertainment industry opportunities that presented themselves after September 11. As the trauma of terrorist attacks gradually recedes into memory and the nation loses focus on its sense of patriotic purpose, the popular culture is displaying few long-term changes. Perhaps a more positive attitude toward the military may be the chief legacy of the deadly attacks—an attitude publicly celebrated so far in a handful of movies (*Behind Enemy Lines, Black Hawk Down, We Were Soldiers*), incidentally, all produced before the September 11 catastrophe. More significant changes, involving a new sense of responsibility for the images of America that pop culture transmits around the world, never even merited serious discussion in Hollywood. For the top entertainment conglomerates, this may count as an unseized opportunity for public service, but also a missed chance for corporate profit.

In his February [2002] speech in Beijing, President Bush held the Chinese students transfixed with a picture of America that departed dramatically from the visions they had received from made-in-USA music, movies and television. "America is a nation guided by faith", the President declared. "Someone once called us 'a nation with the soul of a church.' This may interest you—95 percent of Americans say they believe in God, and I'm one of them." Bush went on to appeal to the family priorities that have characterized Chinese culture for more than 3,000 years: "Many of the values that guide our life in America are first shaped in our families, just as they are in your country. American moms and dads love their children and work hard and sacrifice for them because we believe life can always be better for the next generation. In our families, we find love and learn responsibility and character."

If Hollywood's leaders placed themselves within the context of the wider American family, they might also learn responsibility and character—and discover that a more wholesome, loving and balanced portrayal of the nation they serve could enhance rather than undermine their worldwide popularity.

4

The Erosion of American National Interests

Samuel P. Huntington

THE DISINTEGRATION OF IDENTITY

The years since the end of the Cold War have seen intense, wide-ranging, and confused debates about American national interests. Much of this confusion stems from the complexity of the post–Cold War world. The new environment has been variously interpreted as involving the end of history, bipolar conflict between rich and poor countries, movement back to a future of traditional power politics, the proliferation of ethnic conflict verging on anarchy, the clash of civilizations, and conflicting trends toward integration and fragmentation. The new world is all these things, and hence there is good reason for uncertainty about American interests in it. Yet that is not the only source of confusion. Efforts to define national interest presuppose agreement on the nature of the country whose interests are to be defined. National interest derives from national identity. We have to know who we are before we can know what our interests are. Historically, American identity has had two primary components: culture and creed. The first has been the values and institutions of the original settlers, who were Northern European, primarily British, and Christian, primarily Protestant. This culture included most importantly the English language and traditions concerning relations between church and state and the place of the individual in society. Over the course of three centuries, black people were slowly and only partially assimilated into this culture. Immigrants from western, southern, and eastern Europe were more fully assimilated, and the original culture evolved and was modified but not fundamentally altered as a result. In *The Next*

Note: Notes have been deleted.

55

American Nation, Michael Lind captures the broad outlines of this evolution when he argues that American culture developed through three phases: Anglo-America (1789–1861), Euro-America (1875–1957), and Multicultural America (1972–present). The cultural definition of national identity assumes that while the culture may change, it has a basic continuity. The second component of American identity has been a set of universal ideas and principles articulated in the founding documents by American leaders: liberty, equality, democracy, constitutionalism, liberalism, limited government, private enterprise. These constitute what Gunnar Myrdal termed the American Creed, and the popular consensus on them has been commented on by foreign observers from Crevecoeur and Tocqueville down to the present. This identity was neatly summed up by Richard Hofstadter: "It has been our fate as a nation not to have ideologies but to be one."

These dual sources of identity are, of course, closely related. The creed was a product of the culture. Now, however, the end of the Cold War and social, intellectual, and demographic changes in American society have brought into question the validity and relevance of both traditional components of American identity. Without a sure sense of national identity, Americans have become unable to define their national interests, and as a result subnational commercial interests and transnational and nonnational ethnic interests have come to dominate foreign policy.

LOSS OF THE OTHER

The most profound question concerning the American role in the post–Cold War world was improbably posed by Rabbit Angstrom, the harried central character of John Updike's novels: "Without the cold war, what's the point of being an American?" If being an American means being committed to the principles of liberty, democracy, individualism, and private property, and if there is no evil empire out there threatening those principles, what indeed does it mean to be an American, and what becomes of American national interests?

From the start, Americans have constructed their creedal identity in contrast to an undesirable "other." America's opponents are always defined as liberty's opponents. At the time of independence, Americans could not distinguish themselves culturally from Britain; hence they had to do so politically. Britain embodied tyranny, aristocracy, oppression; America, democracy, equality, republicanism. Until the end of the nineteenth century, the United States defined itself in opposition to Europe. Europe was the past: backward, unfree, unequal, characterized by feudalism, monarchy, and imperialism. The United States, in contrast, was the future: progressive, free, equal, republican. In the twentieth century, the United States emerged on the world scene and increasingly saw itself not as the antithesis of Europe but rather as the leader of European-American civilization against upstart challengers to that civilization, imperial and then Nazi Germany.

After World War II the United States defined itself as the leader of the democratic free world against the Soviet Union and world communism. During the Cold War the United States pursued many foreign policy goals, but its one overriding national purpose was to contain and defeat communism. When other goals and interests clashed with this purpose, they were usually subordinated to it. For 40 years virtually all the great American initiatives in foreign policy, as well as many in domestic policy, were justified by this overriding priority: the Greek-Turkish aid program, the Marshall Plan, NATO, the Korean War, nuclear weapons and strategic missiles, foreign aid, intelligence operations, reduction of trade barriers, the space program, the Alliance for Progress, military alliances with Japan and Korea, support for Israel, overseas military deployments, an unprecedentedly large military establishment, the Vietnam War, the openings to China, support for the Afghan mujahideen and other anticommunist insurgencies. If there is no Cold War, the rationale for major programs and initiatives like these disappears.

As the Cold War wound down in the late 1980s, Gorbachev's adviser Georgiy Arbatov commented: "We are doing something really terrible to you—we are depriving you of an enemy." Psychologists generally agree that individuals and groups define their identity by differentiating themselves from and placing themselves in opposition to others. While wars at times may have a divisive effect on society, a common enemy can often help to promote identity and cohesion among people. The weakening or absence of a common enemy can do just the reverse. Abraham Lincoln commented on this effect in his Lyceum speech in 1837 when he argued that the American Revolution and its aftermath had directed enmity outward: "The jealousy, envy, avarice incident to our nature, and so common to a state of peace, prosperity, and conscious strength, were for a time in a great measure smothered and rendered inactive, while the deep-rooted principles of hate, and the powerful motive of revenge, instead of being turned against each other, were directed exclusively against the British nation." Hence, he said, "the basest principles of our nature" were either dormant or "the active agents in the advancement of the noblest of causes—that of establishing and maintaining civil and religious liberty." But he warned, "this state of feeling must fade, is fading, has faded, with the circumstances that produced it." He spoke, of course, as the nation was starting to disintegrate. As the heritage of World War II and the Cold War fades, America may be faced with a comparable dynamic.

The Cold War fostered a common identity between American people and government. Its end is likely to weaken or at least alter that identity. One possible consequence is the rising opposition to the federal government, which is, after all, the principal institutional manifestation of American national identity and unity. Would nationalist fanatics bomb federal buildings and attack federal agents if the federal government was still defending the country against a serious foreign threat? Would the militia movement be as strong as it is today? In the past, comparable bombing attacks were usually the work of foreigners who saw the United States as their enemy, and the first response of many people to the Oklahoma City bombing was to assume that it was the work of a "new enemy," Muslim terrorists. That response could reflect a psychological need to believe that such an act must have been carried out by an external enemy. Ironically, the bombing may have been in part the result of the absence of such an enemy. [Note that this article was first written before 9/11. *–Eds.*]

Georg Simmel, Lewis A. Coser, and other scholars have shown that in some ways and circumstances the existence of an enemy may have positive consequences for group cohesion, morale, and achievement. World War II and the Cold War were responsible for much American economic, technological, and social progress, and the perceived economic challenge from Japan in the 1980s generated public and private efforts to increase American productivity and competitiveness. At present, thanks to the extent to which democracy and market economies have been embraced throughout the world, the United States lacks any single country or threat against which it can convincingly counterpose itself. Saddam Hussein simply does not suffice as a foil. Islamic fundamentalism is too diffuse and too remote geographically. China is too problematic and its potential dangers too distant in the future.

Given the domestic forces pushing toward heterogeneity, diversity, multiculturalism, and ethnic and racial division, however, the United States, perhaps more than most countries, may need an opposing other to maintain its unity. Two millennia ago in 84 B.C., after the Romans had completed their conquest of the known world by defeating the armies of Mithradates, Sulla posed the question: "Now the universe offers us no more enemies, what may be the fate of the Republic?" The answer came quickly; the republic collapsed a few years later. It is unlikely that a similar fate awaits the United States, yet to what extent will the American Creed retain its appeal, command support, and stay vibrant in the absence of competing ideologies? The end of history, the global victory of democracy, if it occurs, could be a most traumatic and unsettling event for America.

IDEOLOGIES OF DIVERSITY

The disintegrative effects of the end of the Cold War have been reinforced by the interaction of two trends in American society: changes in the scope and sources of immigration and the rise of the cult of multiculturalism. Immigration, legal and illegal, has increased dramatically since the immigration laws were changed in 1965. Recent immigration is overwhelmingly from Latin America and Asia. Coupled with the high birth rates of some immigrant groups, it is changing the racial, religious, and ethnic makeup of the United States. By the middle of [this] century, according to the Census Bureau, non-Hispanic whites will have dropped from more than three-quarters of the population to only slightly more than half, and one-quarter of Americans will be Hispanic, 14 percent black, and 8 percent of Asian and Pacific heritage. The religious balance is also shifting, with Muslims already reportedly outnumbering Episcopalians.

In the past, assimilation, American style, . . . involved an implicit contract in which immigrants were welcomed as equal members of the national community and urged to become citizens, provided they accepted English as the national language and committed themselves to the principles of the American Creed and the Protestant work ethic. In return, immigrants could be as ethnic as they wished in their homes and local communities. At times, particularly during the great waves of Irish immigration in the 1840s and 1850s and of the southern and eastern European immigration at the turn of the century, immigrants were discriminated against and simultaneously subjected to major programs of "Americanization" to incorporate them into the national culture and society. Overall, however, assimilation American style worked well. Immigration renewed American society; assimilation preserved American culture.

Past worries about the assimilation of immigrants have proved unfounded. Until recently immigrant groups came to America because they saw immigration as an opportunity to become American. To what extent now, however, do people come because they see it as an opportunity to remain themselves? Previously immigrants felt discriminated against if they were not permitted to join the mainstream. Now it appears that some groups feel discriminated against if they are not allowed to remain apart from the mainstream.

The ideologies of multiculturalism and diversity reinforce and legitimate these trends. They deny the existence of a common culture in the United States, denounce assimilation, and promote the primacy of racial, ethnic, and other subnational cultural identities and groupings. They also question a central element in the American Creed by substituting for the rights of individuals the rights of groups, defined largely in terms of race, ethnicity, gender, and sexual preference. These goals were manifested in a variety of statutes that followed the civil rights acts of the 1960s, and in the 1990s the Clinton administration made the encouragement of diversity one of its major goals.

The contrast with the past is striking. The Founding Fathers saw diversity as a reality and a problem: hence the national motto, *e pluribus unum*. Later political leaders, also fearful of the dangers of racial, sectional, ethnic, economic, and cultural diversity (which, indeed, produced the biggest war of the century between 1815 and 1914), responded to the need to bring us together, and made the promotion of national unity their central responsibility.

"The one absolutely certain way of bringing this nation to ruin, of preventing all possibility of its continuing as a nation at all," warned Theodore Roosevelt, "would be to permit it to become a tangle of squabbling nationalities..." Bill Clinton, in contrast, [was] almost certainly the first president to promote the diversity rather than the unity of the country he [led]. This promotion of ethnic and racial identities means that recent immigrants are not subject to the same pressures and inducements as previous immigrants to integrate themselves into American culture. As a result, ethnic identities are becoming more meaningful and appear to be increasing in relevance compared with national identity.

If the United States becomes truly multicultural, American identity and unity will depend on a continuing consensus on political ideology. Americans have thought of their commitment to universal values such as liberty and equality as a great source of national strength. That ideology, Myrdal observed, has been "the cement in the structure of this great and disparate nation." Without an underlying common culture, however, these principles are a fragile basis for national unity. As theories of cognitive dissonance suggest, people can change their ideas and beliefs relatively quickly and easily in response to a changed external environment. Throughout the formerly communist world, elites have redefined themselves as devoted democrats, free marketeers, or fervent nationalists.

For most countries, ideology bears little relation to national identity. China has survived the collapse of many dynasties and will survive the collapse of communism. Absent communism, China will still be China. Britain, France, Japan, Germany, and other countries have survived various dominant ideologies in their history. But could the United States survive the end of its political ideology? The fate of the Soviet Union offers a sobering example for Americans. The United States and the Soviet Union were very different, but they also resembled each other in that neither was a nation-state in the classic sense of the term. In considerable measure, each defined itself in terms of an ideology, which, as the Soviet example suggests, is likely to be a much more fragile basis for unity than a national culture richly grounded in history. If multiculturalism prevails and if the consensus on liberal democracy disintegrates, the United States could join the Soviet Union on the ash heap of history.

IN SEARCH OF NATIONAL INTERESTS

A national interest is a public good of concern to all or most Americans; a vital national interest is one which they are willing to expend blood and treasure to defend. National interests usually combine security and material concerns, on the one hand, and moral and ethical concerns, on the other. Military action against Saddam Hussein [in 1991] was seen as a vital national interest because he threatened reliable and inexpensive access to Persian Gulf oil and because he was a rapacious dictator who had blatantly invaded and annexed another country. During the Cold War the Soviet Union and communism were perceived as threats to both American security and American values; a happy coincidence existed between the demands of power politics and the demands of morality. Hence broad public support buttressed government efforts to defeat communism and thus, in Walter Lippmann's terms, to maintain a balance between capabilities and commitments. That balance was often tenuous and arguably got skewed in the 1970s. With the end of the Cold War, however, the danger of a "Lippmann gap" vanished, and instead the United States appears to have a Lippmann surplus. Now the need is not to find the power to serve American purposes but rather to find purposes for the use of American power.

This need has led the American foreign policy establishment to search frantically for new purposes that would justify a continuing U.S. role in world affairs comparable to that in the Cold War. The Commission on America's National Interests put the problem this way in 1996: "After four decades of unusual single-mindedness in containing Soviet Communist expansion, we have seen five years of ad hoc fits and starts. If it continues, this drift will threaten our values, our fortunes, and indeed our lives."

The commission identified five vital national interests: prevent attacks on the United States with weapons of mass destruction, prevent the emergence of hostile hegemons in Europe or Asia and of hostile powers on U.S. borders or in control of the seas, prevent the collapse of the global systems for trade, financial markets, energy supplies, and the environment, and ensure the survival of U.S. allies.

What, however, are the threats to these interests? Nuclear terrorism against the United States could be a near-term threat, and the emergence of China as an East Asian hegemon could be a longer-term one. Apart from these, however, it is hard to see any major looming challenges to the commission's vital interests. New threats will undoubtedly arise, but given the scarcity of current ones, campaigns to arouse interest in foreign affairs and support for major foreign policy initiatives now fall on deaf ears. The [Clinton] administration's call for the "enlargement" of democracy does not resonate with the public and is belied by the administration's own actions. Arguments from neoconservatives for big increases in defense spending have the same air of unreality that arguments for the abolition of nuclear weapons had during the Cold War.

The argument is frequently made that American "leadership" is needed to deal with world problems. Often it is. The call for leadership, however, begs the question of leadership to do what, and rests on the assumption that the world's problems are America's problems. Often they are not. The fact that things are going wrong in many places in the world is unfortunate, but it does not mean that the United States has either an interest in or the responsibility for correcting them. The National Interests Commission said that presidential leadership is necessary to create a consensus on national interests. In some measure, however, a consensus already exists that American national interests do not warrant extensive American involvement in most problems in most of the world. The foreign policy establishment is asking the president to make a case for a cause that simply will not sell. The most striking feature of the search for national interests has been its failure to generate purposes that command anything remotely resembling broad support and to which people are willing to commit significant resources. [Since this was written, public opinion polls repeatedly show that Americans broadly embrace dealing with international terrorism as a foreign policy priority. –Eds.]

COMMERCIALISM AND ETHNICITY

The lack of national interests that command widespread support does not imply a return to isolationism. America remains involved in the world, but its involvement is now directed at commerical and ethnic interests rather than national interests. Economic and ethnic particularism define the current American role in the world. The institutions and capabilities—political, military, economic, intelligence—created to serve a grand national purpose in the Cold War are now being suborned and redirected to serve narrow subnational, transnational, and even nonnational purposes. Increasingly people are arguing that these are precisely the interests foreign policy should serve.

The Clinton administration [gave] priority to "commercial diplomacy," making the promotion of American exports a primary foreign policy objective. It was successful in wringing access to some foreign markets for American products. Commercial achievements have become a primary criterion for judging the performance of American ambassadors. President Clinton may well [have spent] more time promoting American sales abroad than doing anything else in foreign affairs. If so, that would be a dramatic sign of the redirection of American foreign policy. In case after case, country after country, the dictates of commercialism . . . prevailed over other purposes including human rights, democracy, alliance relationships, maintaining the balance of power, technology export controls, and other strategic and political considerations described by one [Clinton] administration official as "stratocrap and globaloney." "Many in the administration, Congress, and the broader foreign policy community," a former senior official in the Clinton Commerce Department argued . . . , "still believe that commercial policy is a tool of foreign policy, when it should more often be the other way around—the United States should use all its foreign policy levers to achieve commercial goals." The funds devoted to promoting commercial goals should be greatly increased; the personnel working on these goals should be upgraded and professionalized; the agencies concerned with export promotion need to be strengthened and reorganized. Landing the contract is the name of the game in foreign policy.

Or at least it is the name of one game. The other game is the promotion of ethnic interests. While economic interests are usually subnational, ethnic interests are generally transnational or nonnational. The promotion of particular businesses and industries may not involve a broad public good, as does a general reduction in trade barriers, but it does promote the interests of some Americans. Ethnic groups promote the interests of people and entities outside the United States. Boeing has an interest in aircraft sales and the Polish-American Congress in help for Poland, but the former benefits residents of Seattle, the latter residents of Eastern Europe.

The growing role of ethnic groups in shaping American foreign policy is reinforced by the waves of recent immigration and by the arguments for diversity and multiculturalism. In addition, the greater wealth of ethnic communities and the dramatic improvements in communications and transportation now make it much easier for ethnic groups to remain in touch with their home countries. As a result, these groups are being transformed from cultural communities within the boundaries of a state into diasporas that transcend these boundaries. State-based diasporas, that is, trans-state cultural communities that control at least one state, are increasingly important and increasingly identify with the interests of their homeland. "Full assimilation into their host societies," a leading expert, Gabriel Sheffer, has observed in *Survival,* "has become unfashionable among both established and incipient state-based diasporas... many diasporal communities neither confront overwhelming pressure to assimilate nor feel any marked advantage in assimilating into their host societies or even obtaining citizenship there." Since the United States is the premier immigrant country in the world, it is most affected by the shifts from assimilation to diversity and from ethnic group to diaspora.

During the Cold War, immigrants and refugees from communist countries usually vigorously opposed, for political and ideological reasons, the governments of their home countries and actively supported American anti-communist policies against them. Now, diasporas in the United States support their home governments. Products of the Cold War, Cuban-Americans ardently support U.S. anti-Castro policies. Chinese-Americans, in contrast, overwhelmingly pressure the United States to adopt favorable policies towards China. Culture has supplanted ideology in shaping attitudes in diaspora populations.

Diasporas provide many benefits to their home countries. Economically prosperous diasporas furnish major financial support to the homeland, Jewish-Americans, for instance, contributing up to $1 billion a year to Israel. Armenian-Americans send enough to earn Armenia the sobriquet of "the Israel of the Caucasus." Diasporas supply expertise, military recruits, and on occasion political leadership to the homeland. They often pressure their home governments to adopt more nationalist and assertive policies towards neighboring countries. Recent cases in the United States show that they can be a source of spies used to gather information for their homeland governments.

Most important, diasporas can influence the actions and policies of their host country and co-opt its resources and influence to serve the interests of their homeland. Ethnic groups have played active roles in politics throughout American history. Now, ethnic diaspora groups proliferate, are more active, and have greater self-consciousness, legitimacy, and political clout. In recent years, diasporas have had a major impact on American policy towards Greece and Turkey, the Caucasus, the recognition of Macedonia, support for Croatia, sanctions against South Africa, aid for black Africa, intervention in Haiti, NATO expansion, sanctions against Cuba, the controversy in Northern Ireland, and the relations between Israel and its neighbors. Diaspora-based policies may at times coincide with broader national interests, as could arguably be the case with NATO expansion, but they are also often pursued at the expense of broader interests and American relations with long-standing allies. Overall, as James R. Schlesinger observed in a 1997 lecture at the Center for Strategic and International Studies, the United States has "less of a foreign policy in a traditional sense of a great power than we have the stapling together of a series of goals put forth by domestic constituency groups... The result is that American foreign policy is incoherent. It is scarcely what one would expect from the leading world power."...

The displacement of national interests by commercial and ethnic interests reflects the domesticization of foreign policy. Domestic politics and interests have always inevitably and appropriately influenced foreign policy. Now, however, previous assumptions that the foreign and domestic policymaking processes differ from each other for important reasons no longer hold. For an understanding of American foreign policy it is necessary to study not the interests of the American state in a world of competing states but rather the play of economic and ethnic interests in American domestic politics. At least in recent years, the latter has been a superb predictor of foreign policy stands. Foreign policy, in the sense of actions consciously designed to promote the interests of the United States as a collective entity in relation to similar collective entities, is slowly but steadily disappearing....

PARTICULARISM VS. RESTRAINT

...The alternative to particularism is... not promulgation of a "grand design," "coherent strategy," or "foreign policy vision." It is a policy of restraint and reconstitution aimed at limiting the diversion of American resources to the service of particularistic subnational, transnational, and nonnational interests. The national interest is national restraint, and that appears to be the only national interest the American people are willing to support at this time in their history. Hence, instead of formulating unrealistic schemes for grand endeavors abroad, foreign policy elites might well devote their energies to designing plans for lowering American involvement in the world in ways that will safeguard possible future national interests.

At some point in the future, the combination of security threat and moral challenge will require Americans once again to commit major resources to the defense of national interests. The *de novo* mobilization of those resources from a low base, experience suggests, is likely to be easier than the redirection of resources that have been committed to entrenched particularistic interests. A more restrained role now could facilitate America's assumption of a more positive role in the future when the time comes for it to renew its national identity and to pursue national purposes for which Americans are willing to pledge their lives, their fortunes, and their national honor.

5

Intermestic Interests and U.S. Policy toward Cuba

Philip Brenner, Patrick J. Haney, and Walter Vanderbush

INTRODUCTION

At the start of Bill Clinton's second term, U.S. policy toward Cuba seemed frozen in a Cold War time warp. The president recently had signed the Helms-Burton Act, also known as LIBERTAD, codifying all the existing executive orders on the embargo and ostensibly closing off the possibility of any new initiatives. Only Congress could change the embargo by writing new legislation, and it was hardly in a conciliatory mood toward Cuba. Explanations for the impressive stability of the embargo policy often emphasize the importance of Cuban-American voters in the electorally strategic states of Florida and New Jersey. Their contribution to Bush's Florida success in the 2000 election reinforces a single-factor analysis that focuses on this ethnic group in explaining U.S. policy toward Cuba. At the end of 2002, the policy freeze seemed as cold as ever: the embargo was still in force, the two countries continued to hurl harsh invective at each other, and Cuba remained on the short U.S. list of allegedly "terrorist" nations. Superficially, U.S. policy toward Cuba after Clinton signed Helms-Burton appeared to be as unchanging as one would expect an iceberg to be.

In reality, there is considerable movement today beneath the iceberg of American Cuba policy. The House and Senate have voted separately several times to permit the sale of food and medicine to the island, and even the Bush administration relaxed some rules on the sale of food to Cuba. Across the political spectrum, editorial writers, academic associations, business and labor leaders, farm associations, and even Cuban-American groups have called for a change in U.S. policy. Despite the seemingly firm resolve of President Bush to maintain a tough embargo against Cuba, the compelling momentum that developed after 1998 to lift U.S. sanctions on food and medicine and to engage rather than to confront this longtime adversary makes change rather than stability more likely. The apparent continuity of the general embargo policy thus obscures changes in the relative importance of the factors that shape Cuba policy. Similarly, a singular focus on the political power of Cuban-Americans in analyzing Cuba policy obscures the actual dynamics of the process in this case.

We propose that a multifactor analysis better captures this dynamic. It follows from Rockman's observation in the foreign-policy making process, the "central players of the past no longer exclusively determine the agenda." He argues that this is due to the increased importance of "trade, commercial, financial, economic, and even regulatory issues" (Rockman 1997, 36). A multifactor analysis directs our attention to Congress as well as the executive, to groups that have been traditionally excluded from studies about Cuba policy, and even to agencies within the executive branch that were ignored previously. Congress is both more engaged and also more open to political forces in foreign policy than perhaps ever before, and the executive is today more fragmented.

While resistance to change among active Cuban-Americans certainly continues to influence U.S. policy toward Cuba, we focus here on four other important factors that emerged in recent years: (1) the relatively new entry of business and farm interests into the Cuba policy process; (2) the executive's constitutionally based interests; (3) bureaucratic interests; and (4) pressure from outside the United States. The multifaceted nature of the forces—mostly domestic but some foreign—shaping the policy now makes this case a useful model for understanding more generally the politics of U.S. foreign-policy making since the end of the Cold War. The study here first provides an overview of the policy steps that the Clinton administration took following passage of the Helms-Burton Act and the wrangling over Cuba policy that played out in the White House and in Congress during this period. It then examines U.S.-Cuba policy by describing each of the four factors in isolation and then by looking at the interaction among them, showing how they are linked together. Ultimately, we argue, the case demonstrates that the largely discarded concept of *intermestic* policy—which addresses interests with both domestic or international elements—deserves renewed attention.

BACKGROUND: (N)EVER CHANGING CUBA POLICY

When the Soviet Union effectively pulled out from Cuba in 1991, U.S. domestic antagonists of the communist regime reasoned that increased economic pressure on the island could topple the Cuban government. Senator Connie

Mack (R-Fla.) sponsored legislation that would have restored a pre-1975 regulation that barred third-country subsidiaries of U.S. corporations from trading with Cuba. President George H. W. Bush vetoed the bill that included the "Mack amendment," in part because it angered U.S. allies who saw the law as an extraterritorial infringement on their sovereignty. But the restriction reemerged in 1992 in the Cuban Democracy Act (CDA), sponsored by then Rep. Robert Torricelli (D-N.J.). The CDA also included "Track II" provisions designed, as Torricelli envisioned it, to "wreak havoc" on the Cuban society through means other than the embargo, by fomenting discord through dissident organizations and media. The Bush administration initially opposed it, but when presidential candidate Bill Clinton endorsed the CDA, President Bush signed it into law.

The CDA did exacerbate the deteriorating economic conditions in Cuba, which led to a "rafter" crisis in August and September 1994, when more than twenty-five thousand people used makeshift crafts in efforts to reach U.S. territory. To stem this flow, the Clinton administration abruptly changed the long-standing U.S. policy of allowing Cuban exiles to gain asylum if they were rescued in international waters. The president ordered that rafters be housed at Guantanamo Naval Base on Cuba, and he declared that they would not be permitted to enter the United States. In 1995, in the wake of near riots at the base, the émigrés there were allowed to come to the United States. But a new order stipulated that Cubans rescued in international waters would thereafter be returned to Cuba. At the same time, internal reviews in the executive branch began to examine whether the United States should begin a new course in its relations with Cuba.

Anti-Castro stalwarts saw these moves by the Clinton administration as the first steps toward a U.S.-Cuban rapprochement. Prompted in part by that assessment, Senator Jesse Helms (R-N.C.), the new chair of the Senate Foreign Relations Committee, and Rep. Dan Burton (R-Ind.), the new chair of the House Subcommittee on Western Hemispheric Affairs, began drafting legislation to tighten the embargo (Vanderbush and Haney 1999, 397–401; Blight and Brenner 2002, 166–68). The Helms-Burton legislation was awaiting House-Senate conference action in February 1996 when two planes from a Cuban exile group, Brothers to the Rescue, violated Cuban airspace and were then shot down in international waters in March 1996.

Until Helms-Burton, the various U.S. trade sanctions against Cuba that constituted the embargo derived from several grants of authority the Congress had handed to the president. President Dwight Eisenhower used this authority in 1960 to impose a partial embargo that prohibited the export of most goods to Cuba. Subsequent presidents issued executive orders that altered particular sanctions pursuant to this authority. The Helms-Burton Act codified all executive orders in effect on March 1, 1996, and thus appeared to diminish executive power by denying the president any ability to modulate the embargo in pursuit of U.S. foreign policy goals (LeoGrande 1998, 80–81). But in 1998 and 1999 President Clinton announced several steps that attempted to ease some parts of the embargo while reasserting presidential authority in this domain.

Clinton's actions shifted the ground under the embargo, weakening its foundation. Perhaps most important, Clinton made the changes without any demand that the Cuban government meet conditions or reciprocate. In contrast, Clinton policy in his first term had called for "calibrated responses" by the United States in reaction to demands that the Cuban government improve its human rights record. In fact, reciprocity had governed U.S. policy since the 1970s. The new rules the president announced seemingly were modest. They permitted increased cultural exchanges, and sales of food to private restaurants (which had proliferated in Havana) and of farm equipment, seed, and fertilizer to private farmers. Still, this crack in the sanctions created a rationale that corporations could use to lobby the administration for further relaxations of the embargo, and it provided legitimacy for those efforts. The announcement thus opened the door to new pressure.

Cuban officials strongly rejected the opening, perhaps blinded by the Track II rhetoric Clinton used in his announcements, which included references to hastening regime change. They claimed it was a new form of "imperial aggression." Because of Cuba's tepid response to them, Clinton's moves had little practical impact beyond increasing the legitimacy of embargo opponents. The momentum had begun to move in the direction of dismantling sanctions, but it had not yet coalesced around a viable vehicle.

In 1999 then Senator John Ashcroft (R-Mo.) offered one such vehicle. The Ashcroft amendment to an agricultural spending bill would have lifted food and medicine sanctions against Cuba and prohibited the president from imposing unilateral restrictions on international trade in agricultural or medical products. While usually influential organizations such as the U.S. Chamber of Commerce supported the Ashcroft amendment, the House, prodded by its Republican leaders, was able to strike it from the final bill. Then, in the spring of 2000, the House Appropriations Committee approved a similar (though ultimately weaker) measure offered by George R. Nethercutt (R-Wash.). Throughout that summer, House Republican leaders attempted to prevent passage of the Nethercutt amendment. They were responding largely to two "entrepreneurial" members, Lincoln Diaz-Balart (R-Fla.) and Ileana Ros-Lehtinen (R-Fla.), who were devoted to maintaining the Cuban embargo. The House expressed its frustration in passing (by a vote of 301 to 116) an unconventional measure that would have left the embargo in place while prohibiting the executive branch from enforcing it with respect to food and medicine. The Republican leadership heard the message, and just before adjournment in September it brokered a deal to pass the Nethercutt amendment as part of the Trade Sanctions Reform and Export Enhancement Act of 2000, but with a prohibition that U.S. entities could not extend credit to Cuba (as is the normal process in international transactions) for the sale of food and medicine. The agreement came on the same day that eight prominent Republicans, including former secretary of defense Frank Carlucci and former U.S. Trade Representative and Republican National Committee Chairman Clayton Yeutter, issued a public call for an end to the embargo on food and medicine.

During the first eight months of 2001, the momentum to relax the U.S. embargo continued apace. Rice growers and several members of Congress traveled to Cuba in April, hoping to encourage President Fidel Castro to purchase food under the terms of the 2000 Trade Act. Three months later the House approved legislation to lift nearly all restrictions on travel to Cuba, by a vote of 240 to 186, and the Senate was expected to take up that measure in September. The September 11 terrorist acts halted the momentum for a policy change. Not only did the new war on terrorism absorb legislators' energies, but they were wary of getting out in front on Cuba, because it had been one of the seven countries on the State Department's "terrorism list." This concern was reinforced two weeks after September 11, when the FBI arrested the Pentagon's principal Cuba analyst on charges that she was a Cuban spy.

However, the demonization of Cuba was short-lived. Nature contributed to a softening of the U.S. position when Hurricane Michelle devastated Cuba's harvest in November 2001. The Bush administration offered disaster relief. The Cuban government rejected the offer; instead, it sought to purchase food from the United States using expedited procedures that would avoid the restrictions in the Nethercutt amendment. Under pressure from humanitarian groups, and as the UN General Assembly by now had voted 167-3 for a resolution condemning the U.S. embargo, the Bush administration relented and permitted the sales. Though the initial deals were small, U.S. agricultural sales to Cuba in the six months after the hurricane exceeded a hundred million dollars.

The State Department's rationale for keeping Cuba on the terrorism list also was flimsy. Its *Patterns of Global Terrorism 2001* report charged that the Cuban government provided safe haven to members of certain terrorist groups. But Cuba had taken in alleged Basque terrorists under an agreement with the Spanish government, and until recently, the FARC (Revolutionary Armed Forces of Colombia) had maintained offices in many Latin American countries. In May 2002, John R. Bolton, Under Secretary of State for Arms Control, accused Cuba of developing a capability for biological terrorism. But Bolton's charges quickly lost currency when former president Jimmy Carter challenged them during a much-publicized visit to Cuba. Carter had been briefed on the matter by the State Department, and Bolton's move was interpreted as a transparent ploy to undermine any impact Carter's trip might have against the embargo policy.

Carter, who would receive the Nobel Peace Prize a few months later, attacked the embargo during his trip in an unprecedented, nationally televised address to the Cuban nation. Speaking in Spanish, the former president called for both improved U.S.-Cuban relations and an adherence to democratic processes in Cuba. The positive reception he received contributed to a growing sense of inevitability in the U.S. Congress that the embargo's days were numbered. On May 15, the day after Carter's address, thirty-four members of Congress formally announced a bipartisan Cuba Working Group (CWG) to promote an end to the embargo. Two months later the House passed an amendment to the Treasury Department appropriations bill—sponsored by Jeff Flake (R-Arizona), one of the organizers of the CWG—that would have prohibited the use of any funds to enforce the embargo on travel to Cuba by U.S. citizens, even though the trade sanctions themselves remained in place. The 262-167 vote included seventy-three Republicans on the majority side. Though Senate conferees on the Treasury appropriations bill were prepared to accept the Flake amendment, it was ultimately cast aside in the face of a threatened presidential veto and due to the members' eagerness to finish business and begin full-time campaigning for the fall 2002 election.

Thus by the end of 2002, U.S. policy toward Cuba had changed only modestly. But the pieces were in place to begin a major transformation, because the most important shift already had occurred in the politics behind Cuba policy. The confluence of forces that determined the policy had become far more complex than is sometimes recognized. Below, we try to sort through and identify the important actors and forces involved in this process.

FACTORS SHAPING CUBA POLICY

New Groups Join the Fray

For nearly two decades the Cuban American National Foundation (CANF) was a central force in crafting Cuba policy. Founded in 1981 at the urging of Reagan administration officials, it quickly built a web of relationships in the executive branch and developed bipartisan ties with several influential members of Congress who sponsored CANF-backed legislation (Haney and Vanderbush 1999; Kiger 1997). But CANF's influence began to wane during the early part of Clinton's first term. After the November 1997 death of CANF's powerful founder, Jorge Mas Canosa, and a 1998 *New York Times* story about CANF links to terrorist Luis Posada Carriles and other exiles indicted for plotting to assassinate Castro (Bardach and Rohter 1998), the organization began to lose much of its clout on Capitol Hill. Infighting among members of CANF's board of directors in 2001 furthered weakened the organization's influence. As CANF's importance declined, however, new Cuban-American members of Congress picked up the slack on the Hill— Ileana Ros-Lehtinen and Lincoln Diaz-Balart are Republicans from Florida, and Robert Menendez is a Democrat from New Jersey. Lincoln's younger brother Mario joined him in Congress following the 2002 election. This bloc of "entrepreneurial" members of Congress (Tierney 1994) has been very powerful in holding the line on the embargo on the hill. Proof of its influence can be seen in the comments of retiring House majority leader Dick Army (R-Tex.) that his support for the embargo was rooted in his friendship with the Cuban-American House members from Florida; he described his support as "loyalty to friends" (quoted in Richter 2002).

Meanwhile, business, church, and academic groups opposed to the embargo became more actively involved in this area, as did Cuban-Americans who supported a dialogue with Cuba (LeoGrande 2000, 38–41). When the pope openly criticized U.S. sanctions during his January 1998 visit to Cuba, these groups increased their efforts. The U.S. Catholic Conference called on the U.S. government to take a fresh look at its Cuba policy. Americans for Humanitarian Trade with Cuba, an organization founded in January 1998 by prominent former U.S. officials and corporate leaders, gained former House Ways and Means Committee chair Sam Gibbons (D-Fla.) as a member soon after the pope's visit. USA*Engage, a group of more than six hundred companies founded in 1997 to promote engagement and trade in place of economic sanctions with rival nations, demanded a reappraisal of U.S. policy toward Cuba. In the academic and journalistic communities, a wave of anti-embargo rhetoric and activity continued to grow. Editorials from newspapers across the political spectrum criticized the embargo.

In October 1998 former Republican secretaries of state Henry Kissinger, George P. Shultz, and Lawrence Eagleburger and Senators John Warner (R-Va.) and Christopher Dodd (D-Conn.) led a bipartisan group in proposing that Clinton create a commission to review U.S. policy toward Cuba. In the background, the Council on Foreign Relations had organized a task force that was expected to issue a report with recommendations for significantly relaxing the embargo. On the other side, Senator Helms, Reps. Diaz-Balart, Ros-Lehtinen, and Robert Menendez (D-N.J.), and CANF condemned the call for a commission. Supporters of the embargo reportedly feared that a commission would provide a cover for Clinton to relax the embargo. Clinton reportedly rejected the commission proposal in deference to Vice President Al Gore, who argued that it would harm his presidential campaign in Florida (Brenner 1999).

By rejecting the commission and offering a relaxed embargo to business and political leaders, the president simultaneously tried to satisfy pro-embargo interests while mollifying critics of Cuba policy. But his January 1999 announcement itself opened the door to more interest group pressure on both the legislative and executive branches. In a sense, the Clinton administration did what the Reagan administration had done in fostering the power of CANF—it tried to expand the scope of conflict to change the balance of political power (Schattschneider 1960, chap. 1). By focusing on trade, Clinton brought new and powerful groups into the process of shaping Cuba policy and made the administration itself vulnerable to lobbying. This enabled the administration, and the Congress, to assert that it was responding to "legitimate pressures" as it changed the policy. For example, twenty members of the American Farm Bureau, which came out against the embargo for the first time in January 1999, received permission to visit Cuba in May of the same year. Upon their return, the group's president, Dean Kleckner, testified before the Senate that the "embargo or sanction does long-term harm to farmers and the agricultural economy" (Alvarez 2000).

In reframing the issue as one of trade instead of national security or ethnic politics, Clinton helped anti-embargo forces acquire a significant new source of influence—farm-state senators and representatives. Republican farm-state senators such as Sam Brownback (Kansas), Chuck Grassley (Iowa), and Don Nickles (Oklahoma), among others, provided key support for the Ashcroft amendment. The Nethercutt amendment similarly garnered support from farm-state House Republicans. After a July 2002 meeting with President Bush's senior adviser, Karl Rove, Congressman Jeff Flake (R-Ariz.) explained his resistance to presidential pressure by commenting, "I feel at some point that the farm state politics will overwhelm the Florida politics" (Marquis 2002). In the wake of falling global commodity prices and the growing U.S. trade deficit, the agro-industry case for trade with Cuba became increasingly difficult to refute.

Nethercutt's success in 2000 was fueled by the conjunction of several events. House passage of permanent normal trading relations with China—a communist country with a human rights record worse than Cuba's—vitiated the logic of some arguments put forth by embargo proponents. Pharmaceutical companies had added their voice to the chorus against the embargo. And now Elián González had entered the picture, literally. When the six-year-old boy was saved off the Florida coast in November 1999, the American public attached his face to its image of Cuba instead of Castro's. The seeming irrationality of Cuba policy was now personified by the difficulty of reuniting an appealing little boy with his father. In addition, the stalemate further damaged the credibility of the anti-Castro lobby, which defied public sentiment in trying desperately to keep the six-year-old from returning to Cuba.

The end of the Cold War generated a relative decline in the importance of traditional security interests and opened the door to greater interest group activism over foreign policy (Uslander 1995). As Cuba ceased to be a security issue, the farm lobby felt comfortable in advocating an end to the embargo.

It combined with former government officials who represented global corporations to transform much of the debate about the Cuban trade sanctions from one of Cold War themes articulated through ethnic politics to one focused on international trade. But when security concerns reemerged as a result of the September 11 terrorist acts, these new groups were forced to retreat temporarily. The security issue vis-à-vis Cuba was, however, short-lived, and trade was soon restored as the fulcrum of the congressional debate.

The Executive's Interests

Since at least World War II, presidents have zealously guarded the executive's preeminence in foreign policy. Clinton's signing of LIBERTAD was a significant departure from usual presidential behavior—he not only approved a tightened embargo but appeared to give away a large measure of presidential prerogative to Congress at the same time. Senator Helms made this clear in asserting that he meant LIBERTAD to be "Clinton Proof." The president's steps after 1996 can be seen in part as an effort to regain institutional power, not just as a domestic actor but as an international actor who must negotiate with foreign governments and implement trade policy. Here the president's domestic political standing and international standing are intimately linked. In suspending the controversial Title III, which gave to U.S. nationals the right to sue in U.S. courts companies who do business in Cuba involving property seized after the revolution ("trafficking in stolen property"), the president had to report that his action was in the national interest of the United States *and* would expedite a transition to democracy in Cuba. The bill's drafters had calculated that Clinton could not invoke the suspension provision of the law, because it would be difficult to show that Cuba was transitioning toward democracy (Vermillion 1999). That Clinton invoked it at each six-month interval spoke to his institutional interest in regaining lost ground for the presidency.

This institutional interest reportedly led Attorney General Janet Reno to suggest "a review of the bill's constitutionality" as a prelude to a veto (Nuccio 1999, 27, fn 9). For similar reasons the Clinton administration later opposed the Nethercutt amendment, although the president ultimately did not veto the agriculture appropriations bill in which the amendment resided. One official, who asked to remain anonymous, explained in an interview with the authors in 2000 that "Nethercutt would take away the president's freedom to use trade sanctions. For example," he said, "Clinton would have been prevented from sanctioning Pakistan after it exploded a nuclear device in 1998."

In order to understand the variety of Cuba policy decisions Clinton made—from waiving Title III to his 1999 initiatives, to his position against the Nethercutt amendment—one must take more than just policy preferences into account and also see the institutional interests that are at stake. As evidence of this, note that President Bush continued the Clinton practice of suspending Title III, despite his outspoken championing of the Helms-Burton Act and pressure from Cuban-Americans, to whom he owed a debt because of their strong support in the 2000 election and its aftermath in Florida. In part he signed the suspensions in 2001 and 2002 because he too sought to retain the limited prerogative for the executive that the act afforded with Title III.

Bureaucratic Interests

Inside the administration, opinions on Cuba varied from one agency to another, and at times within an agency. In some instances, these differences reflected the interests of a particular agency, and so the conflict over Cuba policy might be described as a classic case of bureaucratic politics. In general, though, the battle lines reflected other factors not neatly encompassed by that model. One fault line occurred within the State Department itself. While Secretary of State Albright reportedly supported the idea of a presidential commission, she also was sensitive to the predilections of Senator Helms. Thus her comments to the press in January 1999 nearly scuttled the proposal for baseball games between the Cuban national team and the Baltimore Orioles. In subsequent negotiations to finalize the games, State Department officials took their cue from her and were so rigid that only the last-minute intervention of Assistant to the President for National Security Affairs Sandy Berger saved the games (Armstrong 1999). The Office of Cuban Affairs had had numerous conflicts over U.S. policy toward Cuba in prior years with the State Department's Bureau of Human Rights and Humanitarian Affairs. The Human Rights bureau had sought to relax the embargo as a way of promoting greater openness in Cuba; Cuban Affairs tended to take a hard-line stance, seemingly in deference to Helms. At the same time, Under Secretary of State for Economic Affairs Stuart Eizenstat sought to maintain a consistent anti-Cuban position inside the government, because it strengthened his hand in negotiations with the allies—a task with which he was charged in order to form a common front with European allies over sanctions against Cuba. This had become an important mission, because U.S. trading partners had expressed anger over the extraterritorial provisions of the Helms-Burton Act.

The allies' concerns, though, highlighted an important disagreement within the administration over the general direction of U.S. foreign policy, a disagreement that could not be neatly compartmentalized along agency lines. While there was general support in the Clinton administration for the promotion of free trade, many disagreed over the nature of the world order that was necessary to achieve this goal. For example, Treasury Secretary Robert Rubin emphasized the primacy of stable markets and advocated intervention mainly for that purpose. But the Office of Foreign Assets Control in the Treasury Department supported sanctions as a weapon in the U.S.

arsenal, even when they destabilized trade regimes. The Commerce Department generally pursued its traditional role of promoting trade for U.S. corporations, but Eizenstat began his campaign for Cuba sanctions while he was Under Secretary of Commerce for International Trade. Within the national security community there were conflicts over whether Cuba was a security threat that could justify larger budgets or a potential partner in the fight against drug trafficking, which some saw as one of the most important threats to the United States.

Bureaucratic fights over Cuba policy declined once Bush took office. The president had advanced a strong anti-Castro position as a way of distinguishing himself from Vice President Al Gore in the 2000 campaign. Nearly all the officials appointed to key positions relating to Cuba were Cuban-Americans who had ties to domestic anti-Castro groups. Others had worked previously to tighten the embargo. In 2002 the informal leader of the anti-Castro clique in the administration was Otto Reich, a former U.S. ambassador to Venezuela and lobbyist for Bacardi who had helped to craft Helms-Burton and who had a long association with the Cuban-American members of the House. Nominated by Bush to be Assistant Secretary of State for Western Hemispheric Affairs, he was unable to obtain Senate confirmation in 2001 because of illegal activities undertaken by the State Department Office of Public Diplomacy, which he had directed in the early 1980s, and his alleged support for anti-Castro terrorists. He was given a "recess" appointment in January 2002. Reich's deputy responsible for Cuba was Dan Fisk, the architect of Helms-Burton as the principal Latin American aide to Senator Helms. Reich's recess appointment having expired, he moved to a position in the White House that does not require Senate confirmation, and President Bush tapped Roger Noriega, ambassador to the Organization of American States and a former Helms staffer, for the post.

Yet even this lineup did not always produce consistency. Two weeks after Under Secretary of State Bolton charged that Cuba was developing a bioterrorism capability, the annual report from the State Department's Office of Counterterrorism made no mention of bioterrorism in its case against Cuba. In short, under both Clinton and Bush, actors within the executive branch promoted Cuba policies that reflected at varying times narrow personal goals, agency interests, or particular constructions of U.S. global interests in the face of increasing globalization. These constructions in part resulted from accommodations officials made to satisfy both domestic and international interests inside and outside the agencies.

External Pressures

The forty-year attempt of the United States to isolate Cuba had the perverse effect of isolating the United States. Even before the extraterritorial provisions of the 1992 Cuban Democracy Act generated annual UN General

Assembly votes against the U.S. embargo, allies had voted with their feet by trading with Cuba. Their criticism only escalated with the Helms-Burton Act.

International forces put pressure on the administration to change U.S. policy throughout 1998. In a series of masses across the island in January, Pope John Paul II found common ground with Castro in a critique of global capitalism's blind market forces, and he pointedly called for an end to "oppressive economic measures—unjust and ethically unacceptable—imposed from outside the country." The pontiff's remarks had U.S. domestic implications because of its impact on the American Catholic community, including members of Cuban descent.

Cuba reacted to the pope's plea for greater freedom by releasing more than three hundred political prisoners, relaxing travel restrictions on priests, and permitting some church broadcasts. The pope's visit further undermined international acquiescence in the embargo, and several South American countries signed trade pacts with Cuba over the following months. Caribbean countries gave Castro a hero's welcome at a summit in which the region's leaders signed a free trade agreement.

Meanwhile, Cuba's economic performance undermined the rationale of the unilateral sanctions. The small country was most vulnerable from 1989 to the mid-1990s, when its gross domestic product declined by nearly 40 percent, after it lost Soviet subsidies and favorable trade arrangements with Soviet bloc countries. But in 1996 the economy began to grow again, as it opened up to international capital and found new trading partners. The largest of these, Mexico, Canada, and Spain, were making investments that had the potential of closing out U.S. corporations from future opportunities in the Cuban market.

Mexican and Canadian trade with Cuba also had the potential of undermining either the North American Free Trade Agreement (NAFTA) or the embargo itself. Thorough enforcement of LIBERTAD, which Senator Helms was demanding, required the U.S. denial of visas to officials of Canadian corporations "trafficking" in Cuban property that had been nationalized away from U.S. citizens. Such denials would conflict with NAFTA provisions that prohibited restraints on trade. While Mexico and Canada largely limited themselves to rhetorical denunciations of LIBERTAD, the Canadian parliament passed a law in 1996 making it illegal for a Canadian corporation to adhere to the terms of Helms-Burton. (The law has never been invoked.) One reason both Clinton and Bush suspended Title III of Helms-Burton was to assuage the anger of U.S. trading partners, and Clinton did not vigorously enforce Title IV provisions that required him to deny visas to officers of such corporations.

U.S. allies did not criticize Helms-Burton solely because it interfered with trading opportunities for European companies; they were concerned about its possible effect on the World Trade Organization (WTO). Sensitive to this criticism, the Clinton administration agreed in 1997 to seek changes in the law—to eliminate its extraterritorial provisions—in return for a European Union (EU) promise to curtail trade with Cuba. But the administration's failure to obtain congressional approval of the changes renewed the EU's criticisms of U.S. policy (Smith 1999). At stake was the very basis of the WTO. Clinton administration officials asserted that the WTO charter allowed countries to impose unilateral trade sanctions for "national security" reasons. This stratagem opened a potentially fatal loophole for the organization and U.S. trade objectives, because it gave any country an excuse to ignore WTO restraints when doing so suited its interests.

The views of several European trade partners—that the extraterritorial elements of Helms-Burton and the 1992 Torricelli bill conflicted with the free trade goals of the WTO—were articulated by such corporate leaders in the United States as retired Chrysler chairman Lee Iacocca and real estate developer Mort Zuckerman, and the major corporations that supported Americans for Humanitarian Trade with Cuba and USA*Engage. It was thus prominent Americans with stakes in U.S.-based global corporations who conveyed international pressures. Critical articles and editorials in business-oriented publications such as *The Economist* and the *Wall Street Journal* also reflected a frustration with what corporate leaders saw as an outmoded policy.

UNDERSTANDING CUBA POLICY

In the immediate aftermath of the Cold War, Cuba policy was shaped largely by domestic U.S. politics. At times during the Cold War, too, domestic interests rivaled national security concerns in shaping the policy. When more than a hundred thousand Cubans arrived in Florida during the 1980 Mariel boatlift, for example, the U.S. relationship with the Castro regime was infused with concerns related to immigration. But typically international interests shaped the policy from 1960 to 1990.

Once Cuba lost its security policy significance, the votes and campaign contributions from the Cuban-American community gained greater prominence. This relationship between domestic politics and foreign policy was quite straightforward. Candidates understood they would gain votes and funding in Florida or New Jersey if they supported a hard-line policy toward Cuba (see Morley and McGillion 2002). It would be foolish to assert, with Florida's importance in the 2000 presidential election still fresh in everyone's mind, that this simple calculation has disappeared. But by the end of the 1990s the confluence of domestic and international interests involved in making Cuba policy had become more complicated than a simple electoral model suggests, and today this intersection of multiple factors has given Cuba policy a quality of indeterminacy that passage of the Helms-Burton Act would seem to have precluded.

A central aspect of the complexity is enhanced congressional involvement in foreign-policy making. The domestic political interests of members of Congress in areas that might benefit from the export of agricultural products to Cuba are new additions to a field that already included senators and representatives with large Cuban-American constituencies. Declining global commodity prices helped to prompt new efforts to find markets for products ranging from rice to apples. The role of international forces also included U.S. economic and political relationships with allies in Europe and the Americas, although that pressure seemed most evident within the executive branch. For business groups in the United States, the Cuban embargo represents an opportunity to challenge the wider use of economic sanctions as a foreign policy tool. Within a context shaped by global developments and domestic political pressures, the executive and legislative branches are engaged in an ongoing struggle to protect their respective institutional interests with regard to policy toward Cuba.

Congressional activism on Cuba policy should not come as a total surprise. Tierney (1994) alerts us to congressional policy entrepreneurialism. Lindsay and Ripley observe that Congress tends to leave decision making on "strategic" issues to the executive (1993, 18–22), but by the 1990s the Cuba case had largely ceased to be a strategic issue as Cuba had withdrawn its forces from Africa and the Soviet Union (and later Russia) ended its support for Cuba. Moreover, in the 1990s Congress was more willing than before to involve itself in even strategic issues. Nevertheless, the scope of congressional involvement in this case is striking, and the fact that Capitol Hill is now perhaps the important locus of Cuba policy is similarly noteworthy.

This suggests that it is time to resurrect the notion of "intermestic" politics that Bayless Manning (1977) introduced twenty-five years ago. Manning argued that the idea highlighted the blurring of lines between policies that had previously been categorized as exclusively international or domestic in nature. The phenomenon he described was just emerging then. Today it is rare that a policy can be contained only in one category.

Contrary to Manning's formulation, though, our findings suggest that it is not the issue that is intermestic but rather the factors shaping a policy. That is, U.S. presidents act simultaneously as domestic political actors and as international figures. In the Cuba case, President Clinton acted as a domestic player (how do I respond to Congress and interest groups and hold onto presidential power in this policy area?) and as an international figure (how do I work with allies and respond to the pope's visit to Cuba?). Congress and the myriad of interest groups involved were similarly "intermestic" actors, balancing domestic and global interests simultaneously.

The intermestic nature of the multiple factors shaping Cuba policy suggests two conceptual problems with a framework that has been used to explain foreign policy decisionmaking, the "two-level game" model

(Putnam 1988; LeoGrande 1998). The idea behind a two-level game is that a chief of government (COG) must deal simultaneously with foreign and domestic audiences when crafting policy, and often the two cannot be simultaneously satisfied. In the Cuba case, a policy change became stalemated when Clinton attempted to mollify his domestic audience with harsh rhetoric aimed at Cuba while he was attempting to relax the embargo in order to reach out to Cuba. Cuban officials focused on his rhetoric and slammed the door on him.

The first problem with the two-level game model that our review of Cuba policy unearths is related to a simplifying assumption of the model. Clinton's dilemma was more complicated than the game suggests, because it was being played at more than two levels. The president needed to satisfy at least two sets of international actors (the U.S. antagonist, Cuba, and U.S. allies who sought an end to the embargo) whose interests were not identical, and at least two sets of domestic actors (Cuban-Americans, and the new groups we described) with opposing agendas. The two-level game construct tends to focus on only one external actor and one unified internal actor. It also emphasizes the centrality of the COG in policymaking. But in this case Congress was at least an equally important actor, especially after Helms-Burton. As constituents become more aware of the way that foreign policy impacts their daily lives—that is, as globalization integrates domestic and international factors—members of Congress will increasingly acquire electoral incentives to become involved in foreign policy. A model such as the two-level game, which assumes the COG determines policy alone, will accordingly become less relevant.

But, it may be argued, the Cuba case describes a unique process that is not relevant to other foreign policy issues. To be sure, the complicated dynamics underlying Cuba policy may be more pronounced than in other cases. But its main elements appear to be more norms than outliers. In foreign policy cases ranging from those involved with classic security issues like arms control to "new" issues like human rights and global economics, new actors have become increasingly important in the policy process, particularly Congress and interest groups. This trend began before the end of the Cold War, and it intensified after 1991 across the spectrum of U.S. foreign policy.

We would argue that it is likely to endure, and key to its endurance is the recognition that these trends began *before* the end of the Cold War. Vietnam, Watergate, and the civil rights movement contributed to a fairly new American policy landscape that forms the backdrop of U.S. foreign policy. Congress and interest groups became increasingly engaged in foreign policy during the late 1970s and the 1980s. The end of the Cold War served to buttress this trend, not start a new one. Thus it is unlikely that even a new threat such as global terrorism could dampen the level of activity around foreign-policy making. However dangerous the world may be after September 11, 2001, these dangers are unlikely to shut down entirely this new world of American foreign-policy making.

That is not to say that there cannot be temporary setbacks for the "new" actors; the foreign policy process since the attacks of September 11, 2001, would seem to suggest that at least in terms of waging the "war" on terrorism the presidency has a strong hold on power—and is seeking to strengthen that hold. Yet as the president tries to claim extraordinary wartime powers, a wide range of actors continues to challenge his prerogatives. Even the war effort seems porous and open to influence deep inside the bureaucracy and outside the executive. So while the president may enjoy some temporary pockets of relative power over foreign-policy making, we argue that the "new normal" looks a lot like the dynamics behind the Cuba policy we have presented. Today policymakers find themselves continuously trying to balance their domestic and international interests, and they do so in an increasingly complex political environment. Cuba policy provides a useful case on which to base further efforts to probe this reality.

REFERENCES

Alvarez, L. 2000. "U.S. Farm Groups Join Move to Ease Cuba Embargo." *New York Times*. May 24, A8.

Armstrong, S. 1999. Remarks to the Cuba Project, Georgetown University. April 26.

Bardach, A. L., and L. Rohter. 1998. "A Bomber's Tale: Decades of Intrigue, Life in the Shadows, Trying to Bring Down Castro." *New York Times*. July 13, A1.

Blight, J. G., and Brenner, P. 2002. *Sad and Luminous Days: Cuba's Struggle with the Superpowers after the Missile Crisis*. Lanham, Md.: Rowman & Littlefield.

Brenner, P. 1999. "Washington Loosens the Knot (a Little Bit)." *NACKA Report on the Americas* (March/April): 41–47.

Haney, P. J., and W. Vanderbush. 1999. "The Role of Ethnic Interest Groups in U.S. Foreign Policy: The Case of the Cuban American National Foundation." *International Studies Quarterly* 43: 341–61.

Kiger, P. J. 1997. *Squeeze Play: The United States, Cuba, and the Helms-Burton Act* Washington, D.C.: Center for Public Integrity.

LeoGrande, W. M. 1998. "From Havana to Miami: U.S. Cuba Policy as a Two-Level Game." *Journal of Interamerican Studies and World Affairs* 40: 67–86.

———. 2000. "A Politics-Driven Policy: Washington's Cuba Agenda Is Still in Place— For Now." *NACKA Report on the Americas* (November/December).

Lindsay, J. M., and R. B. Ripley. 1993. "How Congress Influences Foreign and Defense Policy." In *Congress Resurgent: Foreign and Defense Policy on Capitol Hill*. Edited by Randall B. Ripley and James M. Lindsay, 17–36. Ann Arbor: University of Michigan Press.

Manning, B. 1977. "The Congress, the Executive and Intermestic Affairs: Three Proposals." *Foreign Affairs* 55: 306–24.

Marquis, C. 2002. "It's Republican vs. Republican on Cuba." *New York Times.* July 28, I18.

Morley, M. and C. McGillion. 2002. *Unfinished Business: American and Cuba after the Cold War, 1989–2001.* New York: Cambridge University Press.

Nuccio, R. A. 1999. "Cuba: A U.S. Perspective." In *Transatlantic Tension: The United States, Europe, and Problem Countries.* Edited by Richard N. Haass. Washington, D.C.: Brookings Institution Press.

Putnam, R. D. 1988. "Diplomacy and Domestic Politics: The Logic of Two-Level Games." *International Organization* 42: 427–69.

Richter, P. 2002. "Army Urges End to Cuba Sanctions." *Los Angeles Times.* August 9, 1.

Rockman, B. A. 1997. "U.S. Foreign Policy in a Changing World." In *U.S. Foreign Policy after the Cold War.* Edited by Randall B. Ripley and James M. Lindsay, 21–41. Pittsburgh: University of Pittsburgh Press.

Schattschneider, E. E. 1960. *The Semi-Sovereign People.* New York: Holt, Rinehart, and Winston.

Smith, W. S. 1999. "European Union–U.S. Understanding Fails to Resolve Dispute over Helms-Burton Act." *International Policy Report* (March).

Tierney, J. T. 1994. "Congressional Activism in Foreign Policy: Its Varied Forms and Stimuli." In *The New Politics of American Foreign Policy.* Edited by D. A. Deese, 102–29. New York: St. Martin's Press.

Uslander, E. 1995. "All Politics Are Global: Interest Groups in the Making of Foreign Policy." In *Interest Group Politics.* Edited by A. J. Cigler and B. A. Loomis. 4th ed. Washington, D.C.: CQ Press.

Vanderbush, W., and P. J. Haney. 1999. "Policy toward Cuba in the Clinton Administration." *Political Science Quarterly* 114: 387–408.

Vermillion, S. 1999. From the office of Lincoln Diaz-Balart, telephone interview with one of the authors, February 8.

6

The Gap

Soldiers, Civilians, and their Mutual Misunderstanding

Peter D. Feaver and Richard H. Kohn

In A 1997 speech at Yale University, Secretary of Defense William Cohen claimed to see "a chasm developing between the military and civilian worlds, where the civilian world doesn't fully grasp the mission of the military, and the military doesn't understand why the memories of our citizens and civilian policy makers are so short, or why the criticism is so quick and so unrelenting." Cohen was voicing an age-old concern about America's relations with its military, one echoed in recent years by policymakers who fear that, absent an urgent threat to the nation's security, a democratic society will not nurture and support an adequate military, and that the military's loyalty to civilian authority will diminish accordingly.

The question at the end of the 1990s was said to be a "cultural" one: Has a "gap" in values between the armed forces and civilian society widened to the point of threatening the effectiveness of the military and impeding civil-military cooperation? To answer this question, we directed a comprehensive study, The Project on the Gap Between the Military and Civilian Society, sponsored by the Triangle Institute for Security Studies . . . with a grant from the Smith Richardson Foundation. Specifically, the project sought to answer three questions: *What is the character of the civil-military gap today? What factors are shaping it? What are the implications for military effectiveness and civil-military cooperation?*

To assess these questions, we, in cooperation with roughly two dozen experts, surveyed some 4,900 Americans drawn from three groups: military

Note: Some footnotes have been deleted; others have been renumbered.

officers identified for promotion or advancement, influential civilians, and the general public.[1] The questions we posed addressed many topics: defense and foreign policy, social and moral issues, and relations between civilian policymakers and military officers. Our team then analyzed the answers and combined them with other political, sociological and historical studies to draw conclusions and offer specific recommendations.

We discovered that, while the concerns of the secretary of defense and others should not be exaggerated, numerous schisms and disturbing trends have emerged in recent years, which, if not addressed, may further undermine civil-military cooperation and in certain circumstances harm military effectiveness.

NOT A NEW CONCERN

Concerns about a troublesome divide between the armed forces and the society they serve are hardly new and in fact go back to the beginning of the Republic. Writing in the 1950s, Samuel Huntington argued that the divide could best be bridged by civilian society tolerating, if not embracing, the conservative values that animate military culture. Huntington also suggested that politicians allow the armed forces a substantial degree of cultural autonomy. Countering this argument, the sociologist Morris Janowitz argued that in a democracy military culture necessarily adapts to changes in civilian society, adjusting to the needs and dictates of its civilian masters.[2] The end of the Cold War and the extraordinary changes in American foreign and defense policy that resulted have revived the debate.

The contemporary heirs of Janowitz see the all-volunteer military as drifting too far away from the norms of American society, thereby posing problems for civilian control. They make four principal assertions. First, the military has grown out of step ideologically with the public, showing itself to be inordinately right-wing politically, and much more religious (and fundamentalist) than America as a whole, having a strong and almost exclusive identification with the Republican Party. Second, the military has become increasingly alienated from, disgusted with and sometimes even explicitly hostile to civilian culture. Third, the armed forces have resisted change, particularly the integration of women and homosexuals into their ranks, and have generally proved reluctant to carry out constabulary missions. Fourth, civilian control and military effectiveness will both suffer as the military—seeking ways to operate without effective civilian oversight and alienated from the society around it—loses the respect and support of that society.

By contrast, the heirs of Huntington argue that a degenerate civilian culture has strayed so far from traditional values that it intends to eradicate healthy and functional civil-military differences, particularly in the areas of gender, sexual orientation and discipline. This camp, too, makes four key claims. First, its members assert that the military is divorced in values from a political and cultural elite that is itself alienated from the general public. Second, it believes this civilian elite to be ignorant of, and even hostile to, the armed forces—eager to employ the military as a laboratory for social change, even at the cost of crippling its warfighting capacity. Third, it discounts the specter of eroding civilian control because it sees a military so thoroughly inculcated with an ethos of subordination that there is now *too much* civilian control, the effect of which has been to stifle the military's ability to function effectively. Fourth, because support for the military among the general public remains sturdy, any gap in values is inconsequential. The problem, if anything, is with the civilian elite.

The debate has been lively (and inside the Beltway sometimes quite vicious), but it has rested on very thin evidence—competing anecdotes, claims and counterclaims about the nature of civilian and military attitudes. Absent has been a body of systematic data exploring opinions, values, perspectives and attitudes inside the military compared with those held by civilian elites and the general public. Our project provides some answers.

THE REAL GAP

The military officers in our survey are indeed much more conservative than the civilian elite, but not more conservative than the general public. On social values, the military diverges from both the elite and the public, fitting somewhere between the two—considerably more conservative than the former but not as conservative as the latter. On the issue of personal and political freedoms, for example, the military responses were unambiguously on the side of civil liberty. Very strong majorities of the officers we surveyed responded that they opposed removing from public libraries anti-religious books (89 percent), pro-communist books (94 percent) or pro-homosexuality books (82 percent)—higher support for free speech than one would find in a random sample of the public at large. Intriguingly, one of the largest gaps between our military sample and that of the general public concerns views on human nature. On the classic question of whether most people can be trusted, a strong majority in both our elite samples—civilian (60 percent) and military (65 percent)—responded affirmatively, but an equally strong majority of our mass sample responded that "you can't be too careful." Still, military officers express great pessimism about the moral health of civilian society and strongly believe that society would be better off if it adopted military mores. While civilian elites share such pessimism, they strongly disagree that the military has a role to play in civic renewal.

Military officers are more "religious" than civilian elites, although not as dramatically as some have claimed. If "religious" is measured by the frequency of attending religious services or of engaging in religious activity, the difference is slight. For instance, roughly comparable percentages of officers and civilian elites report that they pray anywhere from several times a day to once a week (roughly a fifth in all instances). The opinion divide is somewhat greater if the gauge is taken to be the degree to which faith plays a role in everyday life. Servicemen are more likely than civilian elites to agree that "the Bible is the inspired word of God, true, and to be taken word for word" (18 versus 11 percent); more likely to agree that "the Bible is the inspired word of God, true, but not to be taken word for word" (48 versus 34 percent); and less likely to agree that "the Bible is a book of myths and legends" (3 versus 7 percent). In any case, the differences are not strikingly large. Except for a larger proportion of Roman Catholics and a smaller proportion of Jews, religious identification in the armed forces is congruent with that of the broader American population.

Despite common assumptions to the contrary, civilian elites, while having relatively little personal connection with the military, do not express a great deal of hostility to the warrior culture. Only 7 percent (compared with 1 percent of servicemen) believe that a so-called "social engineering role"—that is, redressing historical discrimination—is a "very important" role for the military, although somewhat more (23 percent, versus 14 percent of the military) say it is at least "important." However, on the question of whether the cultural gap hurts military effectiveness, roughly a third of civilian elites who have never served in the military think so, and, interestingly, slightly more than a third of the military agrees. Elite civilians do not have an inflated view (relative to the military) of the military's ability to perform effectively in constabulary missions, although they are somewhat more eager to use the military for humanitarian operations. The military officers we surveyed criticized the quality of political leadership and expressed a pervasive hostility toward the media; yet at the same time, both rising officers and the rank and file possess more trust and confidence in government institutions than do their civilian counterparts.

The officers we surveyed also express little dissatisfaction (about the same as the public and civilian elites) with the current extent of gender integration in the military, although they oppose expanding combat roles for women. But by a very large margin (76 percent) the military officers we surveyed oppose gays and lesbians serving openly, an idea that more than 50 percent of both the civilian elites and the mass public favor.

While officers still consider themselves to be neutral servants of the state, the officer corps has developed a more distinctive partisan affinity. Over the last generation, the percentage of officers that identifies itself as independent (or specifies no party affiliation) has gone from a plurality (46 percent) to a minority (27 percent), and the percentage that identifies itself as Republican has nearly doubled (from 33 percent to 64 percent).[3] While elite civilians and the mass public are split about evenly, for every Democrat in our sample of officers there are eight Republicans. Their political views are not, however, the "hard right" Republican positions some observers expected to see.

WHAT FACTORS SHAPE THE GAP?

Most students of these issues, no matter what side they take in the debate, assert the following: the media are hostile to the military and portray it negatively, encouraging civilian hostility toward it; popular culture (films and novels) caricatures and disparages the military; the media influence civilian attitudes toward the use of force (the "CNN effect"); the gap between military personnel and civilians is widening, due to factors such as the decline in veterans as a percentage of civilian society, the downsizing of the armed forces since the Cold War, and the self-selection of the all-volunteer force; and professional military education is the key arena in which the professional values and norms of the officer are shaped, and, hence, where civil-military concerns should be addressed.

Our team's findings challenge many of these assumptions. The media play a complex role in shaping civilian and military perspectives. But contrary to views widely held among elite military officers, the major daily newspapers do not generally portray the armed forces in a harsh light. Content analyses over a period of six months discovered ratios of positive to negative stories in excess of two to one. While popular fiction and film do stereotype both the military and civilian society, the effect is not uniform. Some action thrillers (*Executive Orders, Rules of Engagement*) have depicted tough realists in uniform with higher moral standards, greater loyalty and more competence than civilians—and have disparaged politicians, political institutions, and a hedonistic and greedy civilian culture. High-brow fiction and film (*Catch-22*, Stanley Kubrick's war films) tend to do the reverse.

Our military and civilian samples did differ in background, suggesting that demographics may partly exacerbate differences between the two groups. The up-and-coming officers in our sample were disproportionately male, white, Catholic and highly educated. Nevertheless, differences of opinion persist even when demographic factors are controlled, suggesting that the military may selectively attract and promote a certain profile of officer that accounts for some of these differences. Thus, opinion gaps between officers and civilian elites are narrower at the lowest ranks than at the more senior levels. Numerous factors have contributed to the "Republicanization" of the officer corps. They include: the fallout from Vietnam; Democrats abandoning the military and Republicans embracing it; an increase during the 1980s in the proportion of young people identifying themselves as Republican and expressing an interest in joining the military; and the Reagan-era military build-up. Lastly, the curricula at military academies and war colleges fail to provide officers with a coherent understanding of American society, its culture, and the tradition of American civil-military relations. In some cases military education accentuates civil-military differences.

THE STAKES

Unquestionably, this gap in viewpoints affects national defense, but not always in the way observers of civil-military relations seem to believe. So far the defense budget has not been hurt by the gap and the divide does not appear to be the principal factor driving the current crisis of recruiting and retaining people in uniform. Yet while much is made of the public's respect for and confidence in the military, this confidence is brittle and shallow, and may not endure. Personal connections to the military among civilians are declining. And because the gap in opinion tracks closely with the presence or absence of such contacts, support for national defense could diminish in the future.

For the first seventy-five years of the twentieth century, there was always a higher percentage of veterans in Congress than in the comparable age cohort in the general population. This "veteran's advantage" preceded the introduction of the draft but began to decline with the end of conscription. Indeed, beginning in the mid-1990s, the percentage of veterans in Congress has dropped below that in the population at large. Thus far this has not affected congressional voting patterns, but, if the general gap is indicative, the change in veterans' representation will diminish congressional understanding of the military and may affect agenda-setting and support.

The experience gap is partly counterbalanced by the military's significance as an institution in American society, which remains very high. The material presence of the military remains strong; it consumes a large, if shrinking, portion of the GDP; its reach is geographically distributed in rough proportion to regional population share (although sparse in the Midwest); and it is prominent on the public stage and especially in the media. There are trends, however—such as the downsizing of the armed forces, which reduces social connections to the military—that will inevitably diminish its institutional presence.

Emerging professional norms within the officer corps promise more friction in civil-military relations. As Eliot Cohen points out in his article in [*The National Interest* (Fall 2000)], the principle of civilian control is well entrenched in the United States, but the military officers we surveyed showed some reluctance to accept one of its basic premises: namely, that civilian leaders have a right to be wrong. Contrary to the traditional understanding of civilian control, a majority of elite military officers today believes that it is proper for the military to *insist* rather than merely to *advise* (or even advocate in private) on key matters, particularly those involving the use of force—for instance, "setting rules of engagement," developing an "exit strategy," and "deciding what kinds of military units (air vs. naval, heavy vs. light) will be used to accomplish all tasks." Most likely a result of the Vietnam debacle—which the military still blames on civilian micromanagement, failed strategies and "go along" military leaders—this assertiveness has already caused friction among policymakers and will continue to do so. It may lead in some instances to unprofessional behavior. Many military officers we briefed disagree with our interpretation of this finding. Ironically, many of them invoked a reading of *Dereliction of Duty*, H.R. McMaster's widely read and influential analysis of civil-military relations under President Johnson and Secretary McNamara, to justify a norm that military officers ought to insist that their advice be followed, and resign in protest if the senior civilian leadership seems to be pursuing a reckless policy.[4]

The so-called "Republicanization of the force" finding has received considerable attention and in some cases has been misunderstood. While we discovered a remarkably high percentage of partisan association, we did not ask other questions on our survey about partisanship and therefore have no systematic evidence of a correlation between party identification and intensity of partisan activity. But there is anecdotal evidence that the old taboos are weakening: senior officers, for example, have identified their party affiliation in talks with junior subordinates or written letters to the editor critiquing one party or another. To dismiss this partisan gap with the explanation that the military is simply "identifying with the GOP out of self-interest" is to miss the point entirely. Developing a partisan identity harms the U.S. military and national defense. Viewed as "just another interest group," the armed forces would lose public and financial support. Uniformed advice would be less trusted by the civilian leadership, and, eventually, military professionalism would deteriorate.

Another of our findings is that the presence of veterans in the national political elite has a profound effect on the use of force in American foreign policy. At least since 1816, the greater the presence of veterans in this elite, the less likely the United States has been to initiate the use of force in the international arena. This effect is statistically stronger than many other factors known to influence the use of force. The trend of declining veterans in the national political elite suggests, all other things being equal, a continuing high rate of military involvement in conflicts in the coming years.

Finally, the notion that the American public is unusually casualty shy—widely believed by policymakers, civilian elites and military officers—is sheer myth. The American public will accept casualties if they are deemed necessary to accomplish a mission that has its support. Concerning the constabulary interventions that have become a staple of the post-Cold War era, the public is much more accepting of casualties than the military officers we surveyed. The military's casualty aversion is not a mere expression of self-preservation, but is more likely grounded in a lack of confidence in the political leadership, or a belief by senior officers that casualties will spell failure no matter what the outcome of the operation.

IMPLICATIONS

Three main critiques have been offered by those who think that the civil-military gap is much ado about nothing. First, divides of this sort have been around since the beginning of the Republic. Second, the principal challenges facing national security today are recruiting, retention, modernization, organization, and the growing mismatch between military missions and the resources devoted to defense—none of which is chiefly caused by this gap. Third, such divergences do not really matter because, at the highest policy levels, civilian and military elites have "fused"—that is, suppressed their differences to cooperate and work together amicably.

But the gap and the tensions related to it are real, and they may have serious and lasting consequences for U.S. national security—consequences that could shackle future administrations. To begin with, the post-Cold War era is the first period in American history in which a large professional military has been maintained in peacetime. The lack of an urgent and immediate threat to the nation's existence, of the kind that during the Cold War forced military and civilian elites to reconcile their differences, may now foster a much higher level of civil-military conflict. And if, as we foresee, support for the armed forces and understanding of their needs diminish, they will be less capable and effective.

Then, too, while the gap is not the principal cause of recruiting and retention problems, it is likely to exacerbate them in the future. The public's respect and admiration for the military no longer translates into a willingness to join the armed forces. The narrowing of personal connections to the military means that recruiters today must persuade doubtful prospects with less help from family and friends who have served themselves. Moreover, since expressions of support for the armed forces derive partly from personal connections to them, the reservoir of public confidence may shrink as the war generations die off.

Finally, the fusion between civilian and soldier at the most senior policymaking levels will not compensate for the distrust of civilians expressed in the lower ranks of the services. In fact, the divergence of opinion between the senior and junior ranks has created a troubling divide within the officer corps itself. In suggesting that the military has a responsibility not merely to advise but to insist on policy, field grade officers believe that their leaders, under certain circumstances, should resist civilian direction or resign in protest. In our follow-on exchanges with hundreds of military officers, a two-part rationale has been offered: civilian leaders are increasingly ignorant about military matters and so cannot be trusted to make wise decisions; and, in any case, the greatest disasters in U.S. history (Vietnam being the exemplar) could have been averted had senior officers spoken out against misguided, even duplicitous, politicians.[5] Mid-level officers who endorse this thesis express frustration with their senior leaders for not resisting more vigorously political pressure and perceived civilian mismanagement. Many complain about readiness, gender integration and declining standards of discipline and training. Nearly half of the officers we surveyed said they would leave the service if "senior uniformed leadership [did] not stand up for what is right in military policy."[6]

The implications for civil-military cooperation, civilian control and indeed American democracy are profound. The senior-most military officers we briefed understand that civil-military relations in a democracy do not and cannot operate this way. "The mid-level officers seem to think," one told us, "that we can 'insist' on things in the Oval Office. That is not how it works at that level." The military advises and even advocates strongly in private, but, once a decision is made, its duty is to execute official policy. In the U.S. military there is no tradition of resignation in protest of dubious or unwise policies. In fact, the American military rejected individual and mass resignation—which can be indistinguishable from mutiny—at Newburgh, New York in 1783 when dissident officers tried to sway the army to march on Congress or go on strike, and were only dissuaded by a dramatic confrontation with their commander, George Washington. Union officers could not say in 1862, "We signed on to save the Union, not to free the slaves; we quit." George C. Marshall did not consider resigning in 1942 over the decision to invade North Africa, which he opposed. Resignation accompanied by protest undermines civilian control by giving a whip to the military ("do it our way or else")—and, paradoxically, leads to an *increase* in the politicization of the force. For if civilians fear a resignation in the event of a serious policy dispute, they will vet the military leadership for pliability and compliance and promote only "yes-men."

To address these troubling trends, the Department of Defense must undertake a series of initiatives to improve civilian understanding of military affairs. [Clinton's] Secretary of Defense Cohen's . . . "Public Outreach Initiative" web site is a good but modest step. The Marine Corps' new "One Year Out" program, which places promising officers in civilian work places, should be expanded to more officers and broadened to the other services. ROTC must be expanded without regard to "yield" until such time as the entire officer accession process can be revised. Congress should fund expanded outreach to the media and community leaders through such programs as the

Joint Civilian Orientation Course and through cooperation with Hollywood. Tinkering with the civilian side will fail, however, unless accompanied by change on the military side, and the place to begin is officer education. Civil-military relations need thorough coverage at every level, from Academy and ROTC through Staff and War College and flag officer short courses.

For the longer term, systemic change will be needed, particularly a re-view from the ground up of the military and civilian personnel systems in order to assure the quantity and quality of people in national defense. The way we recruit, promote and manage the precious human resources of the armed forces has changed remarkably little over the last half century, and the system has in any event been a response to two world wars and the Cold War—an industrial age system now trying to field an information age force. Likewise, the quality of civilian policymakers has too long been neglected. And, because national defense spending depends so heavily on professional and personal relationships among the uniformed and civilian leaderships, fu-ture administrations should institutionalize procedures for team-building be-tween political appointees and their military counterparts and subordinates.

Ultimately, however, responsibility for the relationship, as with everything else in military affairs, lies with civilians: partly Congress, but especially the commander-in-chief. . . . The American public should judge its politicians accordingly—and in the coming years hold them accountable for their stew-ardship of the nation's security.

NOTES

1. For greater detail on the project, see our web site, www.poli.duke.edu/civmil.

2. Huntington, *The Soldier and the State: The Theory and Politics of Civil-Military Relations* (Cambridge, MA: Harvard University Press, 1957); Janowitz, *The Profes-sional Soldier: A Social and Political Portrait* (Glencoe, IL: Free Press, 1960).

3. Ole R. Holsti, "A Widening Gap Between the U.S. Military and Civilian Society? Some Evidence, 1976–1996," *International Security* (Winter 1998/99), p. 11; Holsti, "A Widening Gap," TISS project paper.

4. The book argues that the civilians lied to the service Chiefs and misrepresented their views to Congress and the public—and the Chiefs went along with it, thus contributing to a disastrous military strategy. Officers interpret the book as saying that the Chiefs ought to have resisted the strategy and to have resigned over it—a rendering congruent with the "received wisdom" in the officer corps for the last quarter century. According to the author, the book does not argue that the Joint Chiefs of Staff (JCS) should have insisted that the administration follow its advice, but, rather, that the JCS failed to give its best military advice to the national command authority. McMaster, *Dereliction of Duty: Lyndon Johnson, Robert McNamara, the Joint Chiefs of Staff, and the Lies that Led to Vietnam* (New York: HarperCollins, 1997).

5. In contrast, Eliot Cohen has argued that the success of democracies at war has involved effective questioning, oversight and on occasion intervention by civilian leaders into the technical aspects of military affairs. Cohen, "The Unequal Dialogue," TISS project paper.

6. This is much higher than the opposition expressed with regard to other hot-button issues about which officers have strong views: slightly more than a quarter said they would leave if "homosexuals were allowed to serve openly in the military," and only 6 percent said they would leave if "women were allowed to serve in ground combat units."

7

The Post–9/11 Shift in Public Opinion

How Long Will It Last?

Shoon Kathleen Murray and Christopher Spinosa

The coordinated attack by nineteen terrorists who hijacked four commercial airline flights and crashed two of them into the World Trade Center and a third into the Pentagon, killing approximately three thousand people, profoundly shocked Americans. This was the first major attack on the continental United States since the War of 1812. The collective emotional response was remarkable. American flags and patriotic messages suddenly appeared everywhere—outside homes, on cars and trucks, and on highway overpasses. The stock market plunged. Seven in ten Americans reported feeling depressed, and many had trouble sleeping or concentrating (Huddy, Khatib, and Capelos 2002, 439). One in three Americans said that the attacks had been a "life-altering experience" for them (Moore 2002). On the basis of analysis of poll data more than a year later, this chapter documents how much public opinion changed as a result of this horrific event and how that change has affected the political climate within the United States.

PUBLIC OPINION BEFORE THE ATTACKS

What was the public mood before September 11? Americans began the new millennium having just lived through a decade of great prosperity with relatively little concern about international threats. At the start of the 1990s, some scholars thought that the public would "return to the womb" of isolationism (Schlesinger 1995). Many political leaders in Congress, in the executive branch, and in the media concurred, perceiving the public to be against most foreign commitments and involvement in multinational organizations (Kull and Destler 1999). Even poll-savvy President Clinton agreed, stating that the public "[doesn't] want us to waste any money overseas. Nothing is more unpopular than doing that right now" (quoted in Kull 1995, 102).

However, a careful analysis of public responses to poll questions does not support this depiction of public attitudes. To be sure, the public was wary of the nation's taking on a role as the predominant world leader. But survey research consistently found a strong majority of the public agreeing that the United States must stay active in the world and cooperate fully with the United Nations (Richman 1993, 1996; Kull 1995; Kull and Destler 1999). Essentially, the public wanted the United States to share the burden of world leadership.

While Americans did not want to disengage from the world, they did place a greater priority on domestic issues than on foreign policy (Richman 1993; Kull and Destler 1999). One political observer aptly coined the term "apathetic internationalism" to describe the state of public opinion in the 1990s (Lindsay 2000).

An apathetic public, in turn, affected the politics of foreign-policy making. Lindsay (2000) observed that "politicians worry less about what the public thinks about an issue than about how intensely it cares." The public's inattention "encourage[d] politicians, who naturally gravitate[d] toward issues that matter to the public, to neglect foreign policy" or to "cater to groups with narrow but intense preferences." Congress could take anti–United Nations positions (withholding U.S. dues to the organization, attempting to restrict American involvement in peacekeeping operations, and insisting upon internal UN restructuring) despite widespread public support for the institution (Kull and Destler 1999). Likewise, the Republican-controlled Senate could deny ratification of the Comprehensive Test Ban Treaty—a major foreign policy objective of President Clinton and one that a strong majority of the public backed—without repercussions (Destler 2001, 83).

As Lindsay (2000) observes, "in the 1990s, with no major threat to U.S. security on the horizon and with public interest waning, the costs of challenging the president plummeted." Even though most of the public agreed with President Clinton's liberal internationalist agenda, it was difficult within this partisan context for the president to lead the country (Destler 2001).

THE NEW BIPARTISAN POLITICAL CLIMATE

September 11 shattered Americans' indifference. Suddenly, public attention was riveted on international affairs and the dangers posed by the Al Qaeda terrorist network. The president's public approval rating soared, and with it his political capital vis-à-vis other political actors in Washington, D.C.

When faced with a direct threat, the public strongly favored commitments of money and troops abroad to pursue the Al Qaeda network, to punish the Taliban regime for harboring Osama Bin Laden, and even to remove Saddam Hussein from power in Iraq, because of his pursuit of weapons of mass destruction (WMD). The public's top foreign policy priorities focused more on hard national security issues, in line with President George W. Bush's agenda, and less on liberal internationalist causes, such as reducing global warming, combating world hunger, or fighting the AIDS pandemic.

Even the opposition party in Congress stood behind the president's foreign policy objectives. A new bipartisan consensus among party leaders (that the United States faces immediate threats from terrorism to which it must respond), along with a supportive public, created a political climate in Washington reminiscent of the late 1960s. President Bush enjoyed political latitude not seen since the North Vietnamese and Vietcong 1968 Tet offensive stimulated widespread opposition to the Vietnam War (Hallin 1984).

The question no one can answer, however, is how long this new political climate will last. Was September 11 a watershed event that united Americans around new long-term foreign policy goals? Or did the shock of a homeland attack create an unusually long "rally around the flag phenomenon," a hyper-rally, so to speak, that will soon dissipate?

This chapter documents the public's reaction to September 11 through the fall of the following year and puts pertinent polling results into broad historical perspective.

GEORGE W. BUSH'S APPROVAL RATINGS TOP OTHER POST-VIETNAM PRESIDENTS

"Rally around the flag" events, defined as surges in public approval for presidential job performance, sometimes occur when the nation faces an international crisis. For example, John F. Kennedy got a twelve-point boost in approval ratings from the Cuban missile crisis (to 74 percent), and George H. W. Bush got a twenty-point boost (to 83 percent) at the start of the 1991 Gulf War.

Public approval of George W. Bush skyrocketed following the terrorist attacks. His approval rating, which had stood at 51 percent in early September 2001, surged to 90 percent later that month—a thirty-nine-point boost. This is the highest recorded presidential approval rating since Gallup began asking the question in 1945. It is also the largest measured "rally" in approval for a president in response to a crisis.[1]

Equally important, public approval remained at an elevated level more than a year later. By mid-September 2002, 70 percent of the public still approved of the way Bush was handling his job as president. It stood at a

Table 7.1. Comparative Presidential Approval Ratings at Selected Time Intervals, Cumulative Average

President	6 months	12 months	18 months
Truman[a]	87.0	68.8	58.3
Eisenhower	69.2	68.2	67.5
Kennedy	75.4	75.7	75.3
Johnson	76.5	75.3	72.5
Nixon	63.0	61.8	59.8
Ford	50.8	47.5	46.2
Carter	66.7	61.8	55.8
Reagan	61.3	57.2	52.9
Bush	61.5	66.4	67.1
Clinton	50.0	51.4	49.8
Bush	56.8	69.3	71.8

[a]Fewer polls are included in the averages for the Truman presidency (one at six months, four at twelve months, six at eighteen months).
Source: Ragsdale 1998, 194–97 and *Gallup Poll Monthly.*

healthy 63 percent going into the midterm congressional elections and then rose again, to 68 percent, immediately following the November vote.[2]

Table 7.1 puts Bush's approval ratings into historical perspective. Six months into his term, Bush's approval rating, a cumulative monthly average of 57 percent, was low compared to past presidents; only Clinton and Ford had lower public approval ratings so early in their term. But eighteen months into his administration, the picture was very different: Bush's cumulative average was now higher than that of any post-Vietnam president.

Bush's public image got a sustained boost from the terrorist attacks and his administration's subsequent tough response. Public approval is thought to be an important element of presidential power, in that it increases a president's ability to mobilize the executive branch and persuade the legislative branch to follow his agenda (Neustadt 1990; Kernell 1997). The combination of Bush's popularity and heightened public fear about international dangers gives the president latitude to take international action without much congressional interference.

LITTLE EFFECT ON BASIC VIEWS ABOUT AMERICA'S ROLE IN THE WORLD

The attacks on September 11 did not fundamentally challenge Americans' basic internationalist beliefs. Figure 7.1 shows Americans' responses to the question of whether "it is best for the future of the country if we take an active part in world affairs, or if we stay out of world affairs." A strong majority consistently answers that the United States should take an active

Percent of those who believe the U.S. should take an active role in the world

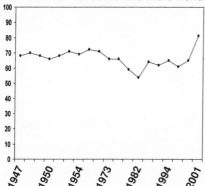

Percent of those who think the U.S. should "fully" cooperate with the U.N.

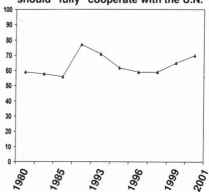

Question: "Do you think it will be best for the future of the country if we take an active part in world affairs, or if we stay out of world affairs?" *Source: The Gallup Monthly,* June 1999 and Roper online. *Note:* Two poll dates in 1999, the April (61%) and June (69%) results were averaged for this figure.

Question: "Do you agree or disagree with the following statement . . . The United States should cooperate fully with the United Nations." *Source:* Richman (1996) for data 1980–1995; Roper On-Line for data 1996–2001.

Figure 7.1. The U.S. in Foreign Affairs

role, but that sentiment became even more widespread after the terrorist attacks. When the Program on International Policy Attitudes (PIPA) asked the question in early November 2001, it found that 81 percent agreed with this position—the highest percentage since the question was first asked in 1947. Likewise, when Americans were asked in November 2001 whether the United States should "cooperate fully with the United Nations," 70 percent agreed, a high point matched only by the surge of optimism felt for the multilateral institution following the Gulf War in 1991 (also shown in figure 7.1).

Nor has the public changed its view about the type of leadership role the United States should play in world affairs. As discussed above, in the post–Cold War era the public consistently has favored solving problems by sharing power and responsibility with other nations and multilateral institutions. This basic orientation has not changed in response to the attacks. As shown in table 7.2, when asked whether they favor a leadership role in which the United States is the primary actor or one in which the United States shares power with other nations, a strong majority of Americans preferred, both before and after September 11, that the burden for international activism be shared.

In stark contrast to public sentiment, the Bush administration has shown a penchant for unilateralism. Early in his administration, Bush repudiated the Kyoto Protocol, a multilateral treaty meant to reduce the pace of global

Table 7.2. Americans' Views about What Role the U.S. Should Play

Type of Role	June 1996 (PIPA)	June 2000 (PIPA)	June 2002 (CCFR)
Continue to be the preeminent world leader	13%	11%	17%
Solve problems together with other nations	74	72	71
Withdraw from most efforts to solve international problems	12	15	9
Don't know	1	2	3

Source: PIPA polls through Roper On-Line; Chicago Council on Foreign Relations, "American Public Opinion & Foreign Policy," 2002, 27 (a portion of the *Worldviews 2002* study conducted jointly with the German Marshall Fund). Question wording: "Which statement comes closer to your position?
A. As the sole remaining superpower, the U.S. should continue to be the preeminent world leader in solving international problems.
B. The U.S. should do its share in efforts to solve international problems together with other countries.
C. The U.S. should withdraw from most efforts to solve international problems."

warming. He "unsigned" the Rome Statute, a treaty that created an International Criminal Court to try soldiers and political leaders accused of genocide, war crimes, and crimes against humanity. Likewise, in September 2002, Bush made a speech at the United Nations, calling on the Security Council to write a resolution that would force renewed arms inspections in Iraq, but left little doubt that the United States would act alone to disarm Iraq of WMD if necessary. Only American public opinion could serve as a constraint on high-profile unilateral action.

INCREASED SUPPORT FOR MILITARY INTERVENTION

After the loss of the Vietnam War, the American public became more reticent to send troops to fight in foreign wars. The "Vietnam syndrome" has caused post-Vietnam American leaders to be relatively restrained in the use of ground troops. The United States committed significant military personnel only in operations, like Grenada, where the power disparity was so lopsided as to ensure quick success; or in Bosnia, where a peace agreement had been negotiated; or in Kosovo, where most of the fighting would be done from the air. The Gulf War was a more risky military intervention. Still, the Iraqi military was forced to retreat from Kuwait largely by means of a high-tech aerial war; President George H. W. Bush made the decision not to pursue a ground war to remove Saddam Hussein from power. As a result, the United States incurred only 148 combat casualties (Kull and Ramsey 2001, 215). One important feature of the post–September 11 public reaction, therefore, concerns public support for the use of ground troops.

Table 7.3 presents poll data about actual and prospective military interventions since the early 1990s. The questions included in the table have several

Table 7.3. Comparisons across Interventions in Public Support for Use of Ground Troops

Intervention and Question Wording:	Date	Polling Sponsor	Favor	Oppose
Bosnia: Do you favor or oppose the United	7/92	NBC/WSJ	27	65
States sending troops to Yugoslavia to	12/92	NBC/WSJ	26	62
try to help stop the fighting there?	4/93	NBC/WSJ	35	52
Haiti: In order to remove the military and	7/94	CBS	21	64
restore the elected president of Haiti,	8/94	CBS/NYT	31	58
Jean-Bertrand Aristide, to his position,				
would you favor or oppose the U.S.				
sending in ground troops?				
Rwanda: In order to stop the killing in	6/94	CBS	28	61
Rwanda, do you favor or oppose the				
United States sending in ground troops?				
Kosovo: Should the U.S. send ground	5/99	Fox News	27	59
troops into combat against the Serbian	6/99	Fox News	27	60
Army in Kosovo?[a]				
If the current NATO air and missile strikes	3/99	Gallup	31	65
are not effective in achieving United				
States' objectives in Kosovo, would you				
favor or oppose President Clinton				
sending U.S. ground troops into the				
region to stop Serbian attacks on				
Kosovo?				
Afghanistan: Do you favor or oppose the	9/01	Harris	64	28
use of U.S. ground troops in	10/01	Harris	71	21
Afghanistan?				
Would you support or oppose sending a	10/01	ABC	76	21
significant number of U.S. ground				
troops into Afghanistan to overthrow the				
Taliban government?				
Iraq: Would you favor or oppose sending	4/02	Gallup	59	36
U.S. ground troops to invade Iraq in				
order to remove Saddam Hussein from				
power?				
Would you favor or oppose invading Iraq	9/02	Gallup	57	38
with U.S. ground troops in an attempt to	10/02	Gallup	54	40
remove Saddam Hussein from power?				

[a] This sample included registered voters.
Source: Roper On-Line.

features in common. First, they all refer specifically to sending ground troops to accomplish a large goal. This is important because the public, in general, exhibits more support for limited humanitarian actions, retaliatory air strikes, and rescue missions, all of which suggest quick operations, than for more open-ended combat (Sobel 1998; Klarevas 1999). Second, the questions make no reference to the United Nations, allies, or NATO. Past studies have shown that public support for an intervention increases if the question refers to multinational cooperation (Kelleher 1994; Sobel 1998; Kull and Destler 1999).[3] Third, the poll question had to be asked before ground troops were actually committed, an action that could potentially invoke a "rally" and skew comparisons across interventions. In Haiti, for example, we did not use polls after Clinton announced that the introduction of troops was imminent. We do include questions about ground troops if the United States has initiated only air strikes, as in Kosovo after March 1999. Finally, the polls selected are illustrative, not comprehensive; we have not attempted to show all possible poll questions of which dates or wording might fit the above criteria.

The pattern of public support is striking. Responding to similar question types, the public exhibited majority support for sending troops to topple the Taliban in Afghanistan and Saddam Hussein in Iraq, but it showed majority opposition to sending troops for earlier military interventions in Bosnia, Haiti, or Kosovo. Note, however, that none of the military interventions from the 1990s addressed a direct threat to the United States. A case can be made that rooting out the Al Qaeda network from Afghanistan or stopping Saddam Hussein from acquiring WMD are actions that serve immediate national interests. Past studies have shown that the "principal policy objectives" or stakes involved in a military operation affect public support for it (Jentleson 1992; Larson 1996). As such, it is possible that the change in the nature of operations being pursued, away from humanitarian interventions, has in itself lifted public support. In this regard, it is helpful to note that when Gallup asked in February 2001, well before the terrorist attacks, whether respondents would favor or oppose "sending American troops back to the Persian Gulf in order to remove Saddam Hussein from power in Iraq," 52 percent favored such an action, with 42 percent against.

Even after September 11, however, the public remained opposed to unilateral military intervention. A series of questions asked by Gallup in September 2002 clearly illustrate this point. Respondents were first asked the general question (included in table 7.3) about whether they favored invading Iraq to remove Hussein from power, and 57 percent said they did. Next, respondents were asked if they would favor an invasion with the question wording making it clear that the United Nations supported the operation. The percentage favoring invasion swelled to 79 percent (see table 7.4). But when asked about their support if the United Nations opposed an invasion, only 37 percent favored an invasion. When asked whether they would support an invasion if the United States had to act alone, only 38 percent favored it.[4]

Overall, President Bush appears to have more latitude to commit ground troops to pursue his particular international agenda than has been seen in decades (e.g., retaliating against or crushing the Al Qaeda terrorist network and preventing circumstances that could cause even worse attacks on

Table 7.4. Americans Oppose an Invasion of Iraq without U.N. Support

Question Wording: Some people say they would support invading Iraq with U.S. ground troops only if certain conditions were true. For each of the following conditions, please say if you would favor or oppose invading Iraq with U.S. ground troops if it were true. How about if . . .	*Favor*	*Oppose*
The United Nations supported invading Iraq?	79	19
The United Nations opposed invading Iraq?	37	58
Congress supported invading Iraq?	69	28
Congress opposed invading Iraq?	37	59
Other countries participated in invading Iraq?	79	18
The United States had to invade Iraq alone?	38	59

Source: Roper On-Line; Gallup, September 20–22, 2002.

America if an unfriendly party acquired WMD). However, public skepticism would likely rise if he did so unilaterally.

POPULAR FOREIGN POLICY PRIORITIES SHIFT TOWARD ALIGNMENT WITH BUSH'S AGENDA

Polls show that Americans shifted their policy priorities somewhat in response to the September 11 attacks. As shown in table 7.5, the Pew Research Center asked respondents in early September, before the attacks, and again

Table 7.5. Shift in Foreign Policy Priorities, Percentage Considering Each Goal a "Top Priority"

Foreign Policy Goals	Sept. 2001 (Prior to Attacks)	Oct. 2001	Change
Protect U.S. from terrorist attacks	80	93	+13
Prevent spread of weapons of mass destruction	78	81	+3
Insure adequate energy supplies for U.S.	74	69	−5
Reduce spread of AIDS and other infectious diseases	73	59	−14
Combat international drug trafficking	64	55	−9
Protect groups or nations threatened with genocide	49	48	−1
Strengthen the United Nations	42	46	+4
Deal with problem of world hunger	47	34	−13
Deal with global warming	44	31	−13

Source: Pew Research Center for People and the Press, "America's New Internationalist Point of View," released October 24, 2001, pp. 3, 14.

in October 2001 "how much priority" should be given to particular "long-range foreign policy goals." The data reveal how markedly public attitudes shifted. Even before the attacks, 80 percent of respondents considered "taking measures to protect the U.S. from terrorists attacks" to be a top priority; that percentage swelled to 93 percent after September 11. Public attitudes about "preventing the spread of weapons of mass destruction" moved in the same direction. At the same time, Americans appear to have downgraded other issues in importance, such as reducing the spread of AIDS, addressing world hunger, or dealing with global warming. These results suggest that the public had shifted its priorities, adding emphasis on hard security issues and reducing emphasis on welfare-related international issues.[5]

The public appears to have focused more on hard security concerns as the nation's top priorities, a shift in attitude that is in line with George W. Bush's post–September 11 political agenda. In the words of one analyst, "The shift in public opinion has created a new foreign policy consensus precisely where the administration has taken U.S. foreign policy. The Bush's administration's own approach to the crisis . . . appears perfectly in accord with public attitudes" (Pollack 2001).

ALTHOUGH FOREIGN POLICY INCREASES IN PRIORITY, IT REMAINS SECOND TO DOMESTIC ISSUES

In terms of federal spending, public attitudes have shifted to favor a greater allocation of resources toward international security. The Chicago Council on Foreign Relations (CCFR) asked respondents in 1998 and 2002 whether we are spending enough on a wide variety of federal programs. As shown in table 7.6, the areas of greatest change, presumably in response to September 11, are intelligence gathering (a thirty-nine-point increase, from 27 percent in 1998 to 66 percent in 2002) and defense spending (a fourteen-point increase, from 30 percent to 44 percent).

Still, domestic issues continue to top Americans' lists of where they believe money needs to be spent. True, support for increased spending on health care, education, and crime prevention has dropped off slightly since 1998; nonetheless, significantly more Americans still believe that federal money needs to be spent on these issues than on intelligence gathering, the defense budget, homeland security, or foreign and military aid. In short, a greater percentage of Americans support spending more on national security after the attack, but even more respondents continue to want higher spending to address domestic problems. These results are reaffirmed by a May 2002 Gallup poll, which found that "53 percent of Americans think the U.S. government is spending the right amount to fight the war on terrorism. . . .

Table 7.6. Change in Attitudes about Government Spending (Percentage Who Want to Expand Spending)

Federal Government Program	1998	2002	Change
Health care	78	77	−1
Aid to education	79	75	−4
Programs to combat violence and crime	76	70	−6
Gathering intelligence information about other countries	27	66	+39
Homeland security	NA	65	NA
Social security	66	64	−2
Defense spending	30	44	+14
Economic aid to other nations	13	14	+1
Military aid to other nations	8	10	+2

Source: CCFR, "American Public Opinion and Foreign Policy," 2002, 14 (a portion of the *Worldviews 2002* study conducted jointly with the German Marshall Fund). "NA" means not available. Question wording: "Now I am going to read a list of present federal government programs. For each, I'd like you to tell me whether you feel it should be expanded, cut back, or kept about the same."

When asked a separate question about domestic spending, just 27 percent of Americans said the United States is spending the right amount when it comes to such issues as education, healthcare and Social Security. In fact, a majority (63 percent) says that there is too little spending in these areas" (Carlson 2002a, 1).

Domestic issues still remain a high priority among the American public and, as such, a source of political vulnerability for the White House. The Pew Research Center released a June 2002 study entitled *Domestic Concerns Will Vie with Terrorism in Fall,* in which it reported that "the President's standing appears to hinge largely on evaluations of his handling of foreign policy and terrorist threats. The public is far more critical when it comes to a number of domestic policies, particularly health care and Social Security." Scholars have shown that the media agenda has a "priming" effect, spurring the public to evaluate presidential performance according to issues highlighted in the evening news or daily paper (Iyengar and Kinder, 1987). If the sense of threat from abroad were to subside, and the public debate as reflected in the media were to switch back to domestic problems, Bush's political standing could slip.

MILITARY TRIBUNALS, ALIEN DETAINEES, ASSASSINATIONS BY THE CIA, AND SURVEILLANCE

Historically, Americans have reacted permissively toward their leaders' actions in times of threat or crisis, even if basic liberties are rescinded. "Presidents frequently realize their widest freedom of action in such circumstances, because the American people typically acquiesce in and support the decisions of their leaders" (Wittkopf, Kegley and Scott 2003, 261).

The Bush administration declared the devastating terrorist attacks of September 11 to be an act or war—not a crime. Accordingly, the U.S. reaction was characterized as a wartime response, justifying extreme action. Just six weeks after the attack, on October 26, the president signed new legislation, the USA Patriot Act, which gave "the government a freer hand to conduct searches, detain or deport suspects, eavesdrop on Internet communications, monitor financial transactions and obtain electronic records on individuals" (Larden 2001). A few weeks later, on November 13, President Bush signed a military order declaring that noncitizens linked to terrorism could be detained by military authorities and tried in military courts. In the following months, the government rounded up and detained more than a thousand aliens who had been living within the United States; deported hundreds of immigrants after holding secret, closed hearings; announced new rules permitting the government to eavesdrop on conversations between suspects held in custody and their lawyers; imprisoned hundreds of combatants captured in Afghanistan at the U.S. base at Guantanamo Bay, in Cuba; designated a few U.S. citizens as "enemy combatants" and then held them without charges or access to lawyers; and assassinated six terrorist suspects, including one American, in Yemen, using a CIA-operated Predator, an unmanned aerial vehicle.

Survey research reveals public support for most of these actions. To begin with, when asked a general question about whether the Bush administration's response to terrorism had gone "too far in restricting civil liberties," most disagreed. During the fall of 2001, seven in ten Americans responded that the administration had handled the "situation just about right"; almost six in ten Americans continued to think so by the summer of 2002.[6] Table 7.7 offers a sample of "typical" responses to poll questions about recent government actions.[7] Regarding the detention and deportation of aliens, a strong majority of Americans—over 70 percent—expressed support for "allowing the government to deport or indefinitely detain any foreigner in this country who is suspected of supporting any organization involved in terrorism." The public was not disturbed by Attorney General John Ashcroft's announcement that attorney-client privacy did not apply to suspected terrorists. A majority of the public was supportive of the administration's stance on military tribunals; when the president's name was invoked, support rose even higher.[8] The public likewise supported the policy of imprisoning at Guantanamo Bay combatants captured in Afghanistan and favored CIA assassinations against "known terrorists."

The public showed more wariness about increased surveillance at home. As one study concluded: "Americans were . . . moderately supportive of the government monitoring communications when the target of investigation remained vague but were less supportive of broad communications monitoring

Table 7.7. Public Perceptions of Government Treatment toward Non-American Terrorist Suspects or Combatants

Sample Questions	Date	Survey House	Response Options	
As part of the effort to combat terrorism, would you support or oppose allowing the government to deport or indefinitely detain any foreigner in this country who is suspected of supporting any organization involved in terrorism?	9/01 9/02	WP Gallup	Favor 87% 77	Oppose 12% 20
Do you think it should be legal or illegal for the federal government to wiretap conversations between people who are being held on terrorism charges and their lawyers?	11/01	WP	Legal 73	Illegal 24
Would you favor or oppose the following measures to curb terrorism?.... Allowing the CIA (Central Intelligence Agency) to conduct assassinations overseas when pursuing suspected enemies of the U.S.	9/01	PSRA/PEW	Favor 67	Oppose 22
If suspected terrorists are captured and put on trial by the U.S., would you rather see that happen in—a regular court of law in which evidence would be presented in a public trial, or a military tribunal in which U.S. officers would examine evidence in secret hearings?	12/01	Gallup	Regular Court 42	Military Tribunal 53
From what you've seen or heard in the news, do you approve or disapprove of the Bush administration's plan to put non-U.S. citizens charged with terrorism on trial in special military tribunals rather than in the regular court system?	11/01	PSRA/NW	Approve 68	Disapprove 22
Based on what you have heard or read, would you consider the way the U.S. is treating the Taliban soldiers being held at the U.S. base at Guantanamo Bay in Cuba to be acceptable or unacceptable treatment, or don't you know enough to say?	1/02	Gallup	Acceptable 72	Not Acceptable 4

Source: Roper On-Line; Gallup Organization; American Enterprise Institute, "American Public Opinion on the War on Terrorism," available online. The September 2001 data in the table were gathered after the attacks.

Table 7.8. Public Attitudes about Surveillance at Home

Sample Questions	Date	Survey House	Response Options	
Here are some increased powers of investigation that law enforcement agencies might use when dealing with people suspected of terrorist activity, which would also affect our civil liberties. For each please say if you would favor or oppose it. Law enforcement monitoring of Internet discussions in chat rooms and other forums.	9/01 3/02 8/02	Harris Interactive	Favor 63 55 42	Oppose 32 41 45
Here are some increased powers of investigation that law enforcement agencies might use when dealing with people suspected of terrorist activity, which would also affect our civil liberties. For each please say if you would favor or oppose it. Expanded government monitoring of cell phones and e-mail, to intercept communications.	9/01 3/02 8/02	Harris Interactive	Favor 54 44 32	Oppose 41 51 55
Next, please tell me if you favor or oppose taking each of the following actions in the United States for at least several years. How about—Making it easier for legal authorities to read mail, e-mail, or tap phones without a person's knowledge?	10/01	Gallup	Favor 37	Oppose 60
Would you favor or oppose the following measures to curb terrorism—Allowing the U.S. government to monitor your credit card purchases?	9/01 8/02	PSRA/PEW	Favor 40 32	Oppose 55 63
Would you favor or oppose the following measures to curb terrorism—Allowing the U.S. government to monitor your personal telephone calls and e-mails?	9/01 8/02	PSRA/PEW	Favor 26 22	Oppose 70 76

Source: Roper On-Line; Gallup Organization; American Enterprise Institute, "American Public Opinion on the War on Terrorism," available online; Huddy, Khatib, and Capelos (2002). The September 2001 data in the table were gathered after the attacks.

when the target was the phone, e-mail message, or regular mail of ordinary Americans, including themselves" (Huddy, Khatib, and Capelos 2002, 419). As shown in table 7.8, when the question wording mentioned that surveillance focused on terrorist suspects, the public response was mixed. But when asked about increased government ability to monitor the activities of ordinary citizens, a majority was opposed, and the level of opposition increased notably as time passed.

One Gallup question captured the rising concern about violations of civil liberties: "What comes closer to your view: the government should take all steps necessary to prevent additional acts of terrorism in the U.S. even if it means your basic civil liberties would be violated, or the government should take steps to prevent additional acts of terrorism but not if those steps would violate your basic civil liberties?" In January 2002, 47 percent of respondents answered that government should take all necessary steps, while 49 percent drew the line at violating civil liberties. By September 2002, only 33 percent picked the former option (a drop of 14 percentage points) and 62 percent chose the latter (an increase of 13 percentage points) (Carlson 2002b).

IMPLICATIONS FOR GOVERNANCE

The terrorist attacks on September 11, 2001, followed soon after by anthrax-filled letters mailed to network news anchors and congressional leaders, left Americans feeling vulnerable. People realized that even more destructive attacks could occur—that a network of fanatical anti-American Islamists willing to die for their cause could explode a radioactive "dirty bomb" in an urban area or release a deadly virus on a major metropolitan subway. Facing such new threats, the political climate changed within Washington; partisan differences receded, allowing the president a degree of latitude not seen in decades to conduct foreign affairs.

It is well known that international crises can create "special moments" or "rally 'round the flag" phenomena during which the public's approval of the president's performance surges. Scholars have linked this increase in popular support to the unusually bipartisan mix of commentary about the president that is conveyed through the media at such times. Brody (1984, 42) delineates the process:

> When events are breaking at an unusually rapid pace, and the administration has a virtual monopoly on information about the situation, opposition political leaders tend to refrain from comment or make cautiously supportive statements. Presidential critics change their positions in response to their patriotism and outrage at the threat to the country, and from a desire not to appear intemperate. Until the situation becomes clearer, opposition political leaders have a substantial incentive to remain silent or to be vaguely supportive . . . and almost no incentive to criticize the president. . . . If opposition political leaders are silent or supportive of presidential action, reporters and editors will either have to carry an usually uncritical mix of news about presidential performance or risk the appearance of searching out negative comment for its own sake. . . . As a

result, press and television accounts of the "politics" surrounding crises will be unusually full of bipartisan support for the president's actions. The public responds accordingly.[9]

Most rallies do not last long, typically a month or two, and then presidents' ratings return to a more normal range. But the "special moment" created by the terrorist attacks lingered. More than a year later, the opposition party continued to be politically supportive of (or at least timid about opposing) Bush's foreign policy agenda; the White House kept the "War on Terrorism" and a possible war with Iraq high on the public agenda, and the public responded in kind. To be sure, George W. Bush's approval ratings dropped significantly from their high point in the fall of 2001, but his performance ratings still remained elevated. The result was a political climate around foreign policy issues reminiscent of the years before the breakdown of the Cold War consensus, as partisan bickering and congressional assertiveness evaporated in response to the attacks. The exceptional outcome of the 2002 midterm election may have reflected this political dynamic. All midterm elections, going back to Herbert Hoover, resulted either in no change in the overall control of the House and the Senate or in a loss of one or both houses for the sitting president's party. However, in the 2002 midterm election, the Republican Party made gains in the House and, more importantly, won back control of the Senate.

Further, events have reshaped popular priorities such that they are more in line with the president's agenda. The public's foreign policy priorities have narrowed, becoming more focused on the type of hard national security issues that the Bush administration came into office wanting to pursue. The horror of September 11 and the realization that more attacks were likely moved the public discussion away from divisive foreign policy topics like the U.S. rejection of the Kyoto Protocol and toward unifying issues, namely the need to pursue the "War on Terrorism" abroad and to enhance preparedness at home. The military operations Bush wants to pursue are popularly seen as worth the sacrifice of lives and treasure. Not only does Bush have the support of an interested public that agrees with his muscular internationalist agenda, but the Republican Party now has control of the White House and both houses of Congress.

It is impossible to foresee how long this remarkable political climate can be sustained. The Pew Research Center reported that the top news story in 2002, judging by viewer interest, was the possibility of war with Iraq.[10] However, measures of public confidence about the economy have been low; if media attention were to refocus on domestic problems and the public began to evaluate the president's performance based on those criteria, George W. Bush's political capital could evaporate. The fortunes of George H. W. Bush in 1992 illustrate how quickly a president's popularity can fade once talk of war victories is replaced by talk of poor economic performance (Ansolabehere, Behr, and Iyengar 1993, 148–49). Likewise, an adverse war in Iraq, with many U.S. lives lost and the larger goal (removing Saddam Hussein without causing massive regional instability) not met, could lead opposition elites and the public to turn their ire onto the administration. Then again, another terrorist attack could occur within the United States, refueling the crisis and the drive for political unity. If the collective sense of threat stays high, Bush's political latitude will most likely remain wide; if it fades, partisanship may reemerge and public support decline.

Finally, a comparison of the political climate before and after September 11 raises a troubling question. During the Clinton presidency, the liberal internationalist agenda of the Democratic Party—which is more sympathetic to such multilateral agreements as the Kyoto Protocol, the Comprehensive Test Ban Treaty, the International Criminal Court, as well as to the use of American power for humanitarian goals like the prevention of genocide— was attacked and obstructed by the opposition party, even when it garnered majority public support (Destler 2001). But as illustrated by the political reaction to September 11, the more hard-line realpolitik tendencies of the Republican Party have received the support of both the opposition party and public, because of a credible threat. Is the American party system capable of producing unity for bold international action only when faced with an immediate threat? Can an American president pursue an energetic international agenda only if it is militarist and responds to direct national threats?

NOTES

1. Gains and losses in the president's approval rating range from −13 points to +13 points following major uses of force between 1950 and 1984 (Lian and Oneal 1993, 284). Brody (1991, 56–58) counts sixty-five events that are potential rally points between 1948 and 1986; the opinion movement in presidential approval ranges from −21 (Iran-contra scandal) to +16 (Vietnam peace agreement).

2. These are Gallup poll results for the question "Do you approve or disapprove of the way George W. Bush is handling his job as president?"

3. The reader should note that the public support for intervention in Bosnia and Kosovo, for example, was much higher when the question wording mentioned sending troops in cooperation with NATO allies.

4. These findings are supported by surveys conducted by PIPA and the Pew Research Center as well.

5. The Chicago Council on Foreign Relations (CCFR) sponsored polls about foreign policy in 1998 and 2002. It also found a shift in perceptions of "critical threats," such that more people named terrorism, chemical and biological weapons, and "the possibility of unfriendly nations becoming nuclear powers" as such; fewer people named "AIDS, the Ebola virus and other potential epidemics," or economic competition from low-wage countries, Japan, or Europe. However, a slightly greater

percentage of people named global warming as a threat in 2002 than in 1998. Also, they find that the threat perceived from China and Russia has been downgraded as well. See CCFR, 2002, "American Public Opinion & Foreign Policy," 16 (a portion of the *Worldviews 2002* study conducted jointly with the German Marshall Fund).

6. The exact question wording was "Based on what the Bush administration has done so far and proposes to do in response to terrorism, do you think they are going too far in restricting civil liberties in this country, not far enough, or are handling this situation just about right?" The polls were conducted November 29–30, 2001, and August 28–29, 2002, by Princeton Survey Research Associates for *Newsweek*.

7. There are too many possible variations of poll questions to illustrate all of them here. For a more comprehensive review, see American Enterprise Institute, "American Public Opinion on the War on Terrorism," available online, and Huddy, Khatib, and Capelos (2002).

8. Public response is affected by question wording on this topic, such that in a few instances majority opinion was against military tribunals. But these are exceptions. In almost all question variations, a majority of the public supports military tribunals.

9. Lian and Oneal (1993) found that other variables matter as well: how prominently the crisis is reported, the president's initial popularity, war weariness.

10. The study, entitled "Americans Thinking about Iraq, but Focused on the Economy," was released October 10, 2002.

REFERENCES

Ansolabehere, Stephen, Roy Behr, and Shanto Iyengar. 1993. *The Media Game.* New York: Macmillan.

Brody, Richard A. 1984. "International Crises: A Rallying Point for the President?" *Public Opinion* 6: 41–43, 60.

Brody, Richard A. 1991. *Assessing the President: the Media, Elite Opinion, and Public Support.* Stanford, Calif.: Stanford University Press.

Carlson, Darren K. 2002a. "Americans Eye Price of Post-9/11 Spending." Gallup Organization (June 25).

———. 2002b. "One Year Later, Concern for Civil Liberty Rising." Gallup Organization (September 10).

Destler, I. M. 2001. "The Reasonable Public and the Polarized Policy Process." In *The Real and the Ideal: Essays on International Relations in Honor of Richard H. Ullman,* chap. 5, 75–90. Lanham, Md.: Rowman & Littlefield.

Hallin, Daniel C. 1984. "The Media, the War in Vietnam, and Political Support: A Critique of the Thesis of an Oppositional Media." *Journal of Politics* 46: 2–24.

Huddy, Leonie, Nadia Khatib, and Theresa Capelos. 2002. "The Polls-Trends: Reactions to the Terrorist Attack of September 11, 2001." *Public Opinion Quarterly* 66: 418–50.

Iyengar, Shanto, and Donald Kinder. 1987. *News That Matters.* Chicago: University of Chicago Press.

Jentleson, Bruce W. 1992. "The 'Pretty Prudent Public': Post Post-Vietnam American Opinion and the Use of Military Force." *International Studies Quarterly* 36: 49–74.

Kelleher, Catherine M. 1994. "Soldiering On." *Brookings Review* 12: 26–29.

Kernell, Samuel. 1997. *Going Public: New Strategies of Presidential Leadership.* 3rd ed. Washington, D.C.: Congressional Quarterly.

Klarevas, Louis J. 1999. *American Public Opinion on Peace Operations: The Cases of Somalia, Rwanda, and Haiti.* Ph.D. dissertation, School of International Service, American University.

Kull, Steven. 1995. "What the Public Knows That Washington Doesn't." *Foreign Policy* 101: 102–15.

Kull, Steven, and Clay Ramsey. 2001. "The Myth of the Reactive Public: American Public Attitudes on Military Fatalities in the Post–Cold War Period." In *Public Opinion and the Use of Force,* ed. Philip Everts and Pierangelo Isernia, 205–28. New York: Routledge.

Kull, Steven, and I. M. Destler. 1999. *Misreading the Public: The Myth of the New Isolationism.* Washington, D.C.: Brookings Institution Press.

Larden, George Jr. 2001. "U.S. Will Monitor Calls to Lawyers: Rule on Detainees Called 'Terrifying.'" *Washington Post,* November 9, A1.

Larson, Evic V. 1996. *Casualties and Consensus.* Santa Monica, Calif.: RAND.

Lian, Bradley, and John R. Oneal. 1993. "Presidents, the Use of Military Force, and Public Opinion." *Journal of Conflict Resolution* 37: 277–300.

Lindsay, James M. 2000. "The New Apathy: How an Uninterested Public Is Reshaping Foreign Policy." *Foreign Affairs* 79: 2–8.

Moore, David W. 2002. "For One-Third of Americans, 9/11 Was a 'Life-Altering' Experience." *Gallup Poll Monthly,* no. 436 (January 2): 2–3.

Neustadt, Richard E. 1990. *Presidential Power and the Modern Presidents: The Politics of Leadership from Roosevelt to Reagan.* New York: Free Press.

Pollack, Kenneth. 2001. "Hard Times and Hard Policies." In *America's New Internationalist Point of View.* Pew Research Center for the People and the Press. Survey Report, October 24.

Ragsdale, Lyn. 1998. *Vital Statistics on the Presidency: Washington to Clinton.* Washington, D.C.: Congressional Quarterly.

Richman, Alvin. 1993. "The Polls-Trends: American Support for International Involvement." *Public Opinion Quarterly* 57: 264–76.

Richman, Alvin. 1996. "The Polls-Trends: American Support for International Involvement: General and Specific Components of Post–Cold War Involvement." *Public Opinion Quarterly* 60: 305–21.

Saad, Lydia. 2002. "Have Americans Changed? Effects of September 11th Have Largely Faded." Gallup Organization (September 11).

Schlesinger, Arthur Jr. 1995. "Back to the Womb? Isolationism's Renewed Threat." *Foreign Affairs* 74 (July/August): 2–8

Sobel, Richard. 1998. "The Polls-Trends: United States Intervention in Bosnia." *Public Opinion Quarterly* 62: 250–78.

Wittkopf, Eugene R., Charles W. Kegley, Jr., and James M. Scott. 2003. *American Foreign Policy,* 6th ed. Thomson Wadsworth.

8

Elections and U.S. Foreign Policy

Miroslav Nincic

Although competitive elections and political partisanship are principal pillars of democracy, politics, it is often said, should stop at water's edge. The claim is that effective foreign policy requires national unity and that a disinterested pursuit of the national, not parochial, interests should guide government's dealings with the outside world. The sentiment seems reasonable but in fact reflects neither a sound conception of what democracy requires nor a realistic view of what it allows. The meaning of the national interest is not self-evident; except for the most extreme and obvious common needs, its content can emerge only from a vigorous debate on the country's priorities and the costs that may be accepted in their pursuit.[1] Moreover, actual and aspiring leaders cannot be expected to neglect the possibilities offered by foreign policy for gaining an edge over their opponents. Campaigning on foreign affairs allows politicians to take lofty positions on dramatic international issues, enabling them to draw clear lines between themselves and their rivals. In any case, sensible people can differ on the best course in foreign policy, and it is unreasonable to wish or expect that these differences should be muted. Therefore, the conduct of international relations is and should be, like other facets of policy, part of the rough-and-tumble of electoral politics. With this in mind, two broad questions will be addressed here. First, just how important is foreign policy to the outcome of national elections? Second, what are the consequences for external affairs of their involvement in the electoral process? The answer to the first question illuminates an interesting facet of U.S. politics; the answer to the second may help account for the foreign policies the nation pursues.

Miroslav Nincic

Table 8.1. The Impact of Issue Categories on Voting Decisions: 1988

Type of Issue	Percent considering the Issue Most Important
Economic	55
Social	13
Foreign Affairs	10
All Equally Important	13
Don't Know/No Opinion	1

Source: Media General Associate Press, 1988.

FOREIGN POLICY AND ELECTORAL CHOICES

Apart from party identification, two broad influences on a person's electoral choices have been identified: voter feeling about candidates' positions on important issues, and more subjective considerations involving their character and personality.[2] Candidates' foreign policy stances affect perceptions of both sorts, but it appears that where voting on the issues is concerned, domestic affairs carry more weight than international issues (see table 8.1). This is natural, since most voters know more about the former than the latter and see fewer direct connections between external policy and their own interests. Still, national polls indicate that while foreign policy does not rank at the top of most voters' concerns, it cannot be ignored. A survey conducted in 1988 asked respondents whether economic, social, or foreign policy issues were most important to their votes. Although foreign policy came in last of the three, 10 percent considered it the most important issue.

More recently, a slightly different survey confirmed that foreign policy was not the "major factor" prompting the voting decisions of most Americans but that, again, for 10 percent of the public it was the single most important issue (see table 8.2).

Ten percent may not seem much, but in a country where national elections are often decided by paper-thin margins, an issue deemed *most* important by a tenth of the electorate cannot be neglected—especially by presidential candidates. Moreover, the proportion of those considering foreign affairs among the issues affecting their voting decisions is quite large. For example, one poll conducted before the 2000 election revealed that 21.5 percent of the respondents considered this to be "one" of the issues most important to their vote for president, while a whopping 60.4 percent said it was "somewhat important."[3] Under the circumstances, it is not astonishing that foreign policy should figure prominently in most presidential campaigns.

Table 8.2. The Impact of Issue Categories on Voting Decisions: 2000

Type of Issue	Percent Considering the Issue Most Important
Education	20
The Economy	16
Taxes	15
Social Security	15
Health Care	12
Foreign Policy	10
Prescription Drugs	5
Other	5
Don't know	2

Source: Washington Post Tracking Poll, October 2000.

Since it is generally appreciated that most Americans are not very well informed about international politics, we must ask how foreign policy manages to shape their electoral preferences. I suggest that this happens in two manners—one indirect, the other direct.

The Indirect Effect

Even if voters are not much concerned with the specifics of the issues, a candidate's stance on international matters can create an impression of leadership, decisiveness, and forcefulness—attributes most voters seek in a leader, independently of policy specifics. Candidates' foreign policy attitudes shape the images the electorate has of them, and thus, indirectly, voting decisions. According to Robert Strauss, one of the deans of American party politics, "If the electorate does not always understand the nuances of a foreign policy issue, it can readily sense a candidate's ability to deal with a difficult situation, project command bearing, and articulate a sense of national purpose."[4] These perceptions, in turn, are often influenced by the manner in which a candidate proposes to deal with foreign challenges.

In any case, the public's evaluation of a president's foreign policy record predicts his overall approval ratings. Statistical analysis suggests that its impact is comparable to that of public perceptions of his economic performance—in either case, a president's overall approval rating is expected to increase by 1 percent for every 2 percent increase in public endorsement of his economic or foreign policy.[5] As a first-term president's popularity is key to his reelection, so, by extension, is approval of his handling of foreign affairs.

There is another indirect manner by which a person's thinking on foreign policy may influence his or her vote: via a *political party effect*. Even if a voter is unacquainted with the specifics of many foreign policy issues or with candidate positions on these issues, that person may hold a general opinion, based on his or her overall opinion of the leading parties, of their respective ability to deal with foreign nations and international institutions. Thus, for example, thinking that the Democratic Party is compassionate or that the GOP is tough could, depending on a person's characterization of and feelings about the outside world, convince that person that either Democrats or Republicans can more effectively handle external issues.

Interestingly, foreign policy appears to influence voting even in congressional elections. For example, in 1998, 34 percent of those asked announced that "handling foreign affairs" would be "very important" in deciding who they would support for Congress, while 48 percent said it would be "somewhat important."[6] Since at most half of all Americans can identify their congressional representatives, and since few know much about the specifics of foreign policy, it can be assumed that only a very small fraction of the electorate could identify their congresspersons' positions on international affairs and vote accordingly. How, then, can voters evaluate the ability of the congressional candidates to handle external affairs? The answer, one suspects, is that while they are unable to link foreign policy directly to candidates, they use the latters' party affiliation as a cognitive shortcut. Thus, a voter who feels that international affairs should matter at the ballot box is most likely to consider which party does a better job at foreign policy and choose the candidate representing that party, knowing little else about the candidate or the issues.

The relative attractiveness of the two major parties has shifted over time—with Democrats enjoying a slight edge until the 1980s, Republicans surging ahead in the nineties, and the situation becoming indeterminate around the turn of the millennium. As importantly, the number of Americans perceiving no major difference in the abilities of the two parties to handle international policy has decreased significantly since the early post–world war period, along with the decline in the bipartisanship of that period (see figure 8.1). This implies that for voters who care about foreign affairs, partisanship is more likely to sway their vote now than once was the case.

The Direct Effect

When voters are sufficiently aware of the issues, when these issues matter to them, and when they perceive relevant differences between parties or candidates, foreign policy can have a direct impact on electoral outcomes. During the Cold War, America's Soviet policy injected itself into most presidential elections of the postwar period, with candidates striving to prove their uncompromising toughness toward Moscow. By the 1970s public perceptions of the Soviet Union had mellowed, the electorate no longer seemed comfortable with the anti-Soviet rhetoric and militance of earlier decades, and a number of other foreign policy issues began competing for political attention.

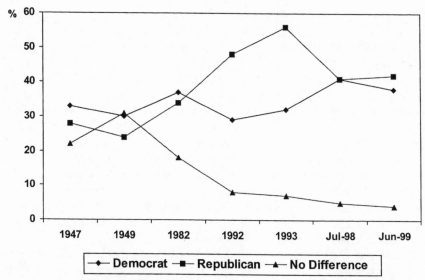

Figure 8.1. Which Political Party Americans Think Can Best Handle Foreign Affairs.
Data for 1947, 1949, 1982, 1992, and 1993 are from the *Gallup Poll.* Data for other
years is from the *Washington Post.*
For 1982, the answer was "neither party." For 1998 and 1999, the answer was "both
equally."

The greatest electoral resonance has been associated with decisions to
commit U.S. forces to foreign combat; the political impact has hinged both
on their success and their cost.[7] Quick and relatively costless intervention
usually bolsters the political fortunes of incumbents. Thus, the intervention that, while claiming very few U.S. casualties, appeared to defeat the Al
Qaeda terrorist network in Afghanistan and toppled the pro-terrorist Taliban
government boosted George W. Bush's popularity immensely, increased
popular support for the Republican Party, and, quite conceivably, helped
Republicans to their midterm electoral victory in 2002. Similarly, the wave
of popular enthusiasm accompanying the short and successful intervention
in Grenada may well have contributed to President Reagan's strong showing
in the 1984 election. Nevertheless, the surge in incumbent support associated with such actions may not always have great longevity, as indicated by
George H. W. Bush's inability to sustain into the 1992 election the surges in
approval that followed the 1991 Gulf War.

When an intervention drags on longer than expected, and when it is associated with significant U.S. casualties, presidential support declines rapidly,
and challengers benefit from a perception that they will bring the conflict
to an earlier end than will the incumbents. Even as far back as August 1952,
67 percent of those surveyed thought that Dwight Eisenhower would do a
better job of bringing the Korean War to a successful conclusion than Adlai

Stevenson, and this probably affected the outcome of that year's election.[8] Similarly, in September 1972, 58 percent of the public reckoned that Richard Nixon would do a better job of terminating the Vietnam entanglement, while less than half that number felt that George McGovern would.[9] Like Eisenhower, Nixon won by a large margin. It has been pointed out that despite Vietnam's salience at the time, the issue did little to affect the outcome of the 1968 presidential election, but this seems to be because voters failed to see much of a difference between Nixon's and Humphrey's Vietnam policies. In 1971 more than twice as many Americans said they would vote for a candidate who favored removing all U.S. forces from Vietnam than for one who would leave a residual force to assist the South Vietnamese.[10] By the second half of 1993, most Americans were weary of the intervention in Somalia, and the Clinton administration withdrew U.S. forces—fortunately for the president, the unsuccessful intervention was terminated long enough before the 1996 election not to affect its outcome.

There are, therefore, strong grounds for asserting that candidate stances on international affairs can have a direct impact on voter choices, and in the cases of the U.S. Soviet policy and military intervention, they did. Other issues, such as terrorism or international environmental challenges, may in the future matter enough to Americans to influence their electoral behavior. Under the circumstances, it is not surprising that foreign policy may be twisted to produce short-term political benefits. How might this be so?

THE FOREIGN POLICY CONSEQUENCES
OF ELECTIONS

There are at least two ways in which electoral logic affects the conduct of U.S. foreign policy. First, it affects the timing of important decisions, which often follow an electoral rhythm rather than one dictated by international challenges. Second, it creates discontinuities in the substance of foreign policy, which sometimes undermine the ability of other nations to adjust their own policies to those of the United States.

Electoral Cycles and Periodicities in Policy

Attentive to the electoral implications of their foreign policy positions, politicians often adjust their stances according to expected political benefits—a tendency implying that the conduct of U.S. international affairs is, in part at least, shaped by domestic political and electoral logic. This is reflected in how incumbents and challengers divide their attention between international and domestic matters. When foreign relations are going well, incumbents try to focus voters' attention on international relations, while challengers seek to draw that attention toward domestic matters. By contrast, when foreign policy is more problematic, challengers turn the spotlight on the incumbents' conduct of external relations, while the latter try to focus attention on the domestic realm.[11]

One of the most obvious ways in which elections influence foreign policy is by the periodicity they impart to its conduct. This has been apparent within a number of foreign policy areas. Because of their electoral impact, I will focus on U.S. policy toward the Soviet Union and on decisions to use military force abroad. The Cold War is behind us, but Washington's Soviet policy illustrates how even the most consequential policies have been, and may again be, tethered to electoral logic. Furthermore, because, benefiting from its unchallenged power, the United States has since then resorted to military force more frequently than ever before, it is important to see how these decisions are affected by the election cycle.

Cold War Politics. During the Cold War, presidential contenders tended to compete in asserting uncompromising toughness toward Moscow while questioning the wisdom of their rivals' positions. At the same time, the unease of much of the electorate with excessive saber rattling and inflammatory rhetoric, as well as the objective need to curb the escalatory risks associated with the rivalry, meant that constructive policies had to coexist with firmness. The result was a cyclical quality in U.S.-Soviet relations. In the fourth year of a typical four-year cycle, the need to establish staunch anti-Soviet credentials for electoral purposes made it unlikely that cooperative gestures would be made toward the Kremlin, producing some of the most bellicose Cold War rhetoric. Because of the uncompromising attitudes adopted in election years, a movement toward cooperation was not usually possible very soon thereafter, either; little progress in U.S.-Soviet relations could be expected during the first year of the next four-year cycle. Accordingly, the first constructive steps often were witnessed during the cycle's second year, and because such initiatives rarely bear immediate fruit, tangible achievements were not likely before the third year. After this, election year pressures typically precluded further progress in the near term, and so on.[12]

This pattern was illustrated in a number of ways. Average increases in U.S. strategic spending (almost all of which was directed against the Soviet Union) were highest during the fourth and first years of the cycle, lower during the second, and lowest during the third year. By far the greatest number of arms control agreements were signed during the third year, the fewest in the first and fourth years. Also, most superpower summits—occasions for improving bilateral relations—occurred during third years.[13] It is also significant that U.S. policy toward the Soviet Union was considerably more cooperative during second presidential terms than during first terms; arms control agreements were more frequent, summits were more often held, and strategic spending was more likely to decline than to increase. A credible explanation is that second-term presidents worried less about the electoral implications of important foreign policy decisions.

Thus, even the most momentous aspect of U.S. postwar foreign policy was, in the periodicities it exhibited and perhaps in its overall tenor, driven by the rhythms of electoral politics. This demonstrates that even the most important aspects of U.S. foreign policy are not immune to the pressures of electoral politics.

Military Intervention. We have seen that voters are very attentive to the risks of armed involvements abroad and that while surges in presidential popularity may accompany short and successful actions, inconclusive and costly military undertakings—such as, for example, the intervention in Lebanon in the early 1980s and the Somalia imbroglio a decade later—can dissolve popular support and magnify electoral risks. The problem is that it is not always possible to anticipate how successful military force will be. Interventions often acquire dynamics of their own, and costs and duration may far exceed what initially had been expected. Under the circumstances, a very different impact of the electoral cycle on military intervention would be expected depending on how risk acceptant or risk averse political leaders were thought to be. If risk acceptant, incumbents might wish to benefit from the expected surge in public approval associated with brief and successful intervention, and so time armed incursions to coincide with the fourth year of the election cycle, when the incumbent (if a first-term president) or his party's designated successor might derive the most electoral benefit from the action. If leaders are risk averse, the fear of a costly and inconclusive venture might make intervention less likely in close proximity to election years and relatively more so at the beginning of the four-year cycle (when the chances of extrication before the next election are better).

As not every show of force or bit of saber rattling is of interest to us, our standard of military "intervention" here will be the employment in combat of U.S. force over a period of at least twenty-four hours and involving at least one American casualty. Fourteen interventions since World War II satisfy this definitional requirement. Table 8.3 lists these interventions along with the year within the electoral cycle when the action was initiated.

The evidence supports the hypothesis of risk-averse politicians. Although the incidence of U.S. military engagement is fairly evenly spread across the first three years of the cycle, a *single* instance of an intervention is encountered during a fourth year; intervention is four or five times more likely in any one of the other three years (see table 8.4). It is also worth noting that the only example of a fourth-year intervention—the Iran hostage-rescue attempt in 1980—was an unambiguous failure that contributed to President Carter's electoral defeat. Again, and other things being equal, electoral considerations shape the timing by which a principal instrument of U.S. foreign policy is used. This is pretty much in line with what occurs in other

Table 8.3.   U.S. Military Interventions and the Electoral Cycle

Intervention	Year in Cycle
Korea 1950	2
Lebanon 1958	2
Vietnam 1965	1
Dominican Republic 1965	1
Mayaguez rescue 1975	3
Iran hostage rescue 1980	4
Lebanon 1982	2
Grenada 1983	3
Libya 1986	2
Panama 1989	1
Persian Gulf 1991	3
Somalia 1993	1
Yugoslavia 1999	3
Afghanistan 2001	1

democracies. As the best available study of the election-war relation observes, "When elections are approaching, Democratic states have avoided wars. After elections, they have tended to enter more wars."[14] At the same time, the outcome of the presidential election—whether a Republican or Democrat is elected—may not make very much difference, as the frequency of intervention is only slightly higher in the former case.

Elections and Policy Discontinuity

Apart from the periodicities that electoral cycles sometimes impart to external affairs and that shape the timing of policy, electoral campaigns and the resulting leadership transitions (especially when accompanied by party transitions) often cause sharp discontinuities in the actual substance of U.S. foreign policy. Significant departures from current policy promised in campaigns, and the need to live up to promises, create large gaps between the policies of the past and the future, making it harder both for adversaries and friends to anticipate the course of America's international activity and to adjust their own behavior accordingly.

The lack of a domestic constituency with interests identifiably affected by foreign policy allows candidates considerable latitude in their campaign

Table 8.4.   Distribution of Military Interventions Across the Electoral Cycle

Year 1	Year 2	Year 3	Year 4
5	4	4	1

stances in this area—in any case, more than in the realm of domestic policy, where the structure of domestic interests and norms of compromise between competing interests keep action within predictable boundaries. For the same reasons, even between elections there is less ballast, in the form of domestic interests, to keep foreign policy in the middle of the road. Accordingly, the foreign policy of one presidential administration may mark an abrupt change from that which preceded it, especially when a party transition is involved.

Thus, President Eisenhower's relative indifference to the Third World was replaced by President Kennedy's virtual obsession with it as an arena of East-West conflict. Whereas the Nixon and Ford administrations' pragmatic approach to geopolitics left little room for concern with human rights, President Carter initially made that a cornerstone of his foreign policy. The Carter administration's step-by-step approach to a Middle East settlement was dropped in the Reagan administration's unsuccessful attempt to sweep regional differences under the carpet and to create an anti-Soviet alliance of pro-Western states in the region. George H. W. Bush's hands-off attitude vis-à-vis the conflicts in the Balkans was replaced by President Clinton's interventionism in the region.

An especially stark discontinuity characterized the transition from the Clinton to the George W. Bush administration, bringing a sharp change in the nation's entire approach to its relations with the international community. Commitment to joint international progress toward commonly elaborated goals, at least among the world's developed democracies, was abandoned in favor of a largely unilateralist approach to international relations. Thus, the new administration pulled out of the 1997 Kyoto Protocol, designed to reduce global emissions of greenhouse gases—the major source of global warming. It declined to adhere to a treaty establishing an International Criminal Court to deal with crimes against humanity, a project resulting from a growing international commitment during the 1990s to make governments as well as individuals accountable for such crimes. It abandoned the prior administration's policy of negotiations with North Korea—a nation believed to have the capability to produce nuclear weapons and to possess the means of delivering them. It altered U.S. policy toward the Middle East conflict—showing far greater support for Israeli military measures in the region. And so forth.

The sharpest departures from a predecessor's policies often are recorded during the first (and sometimes second) year of a presidential transition; beyond that, the objective realities of international politics often pull policy closer to the trends that had preceded it. Yet when Republicans replace Democrats and vice versa, U.S. foreign policy often exhibits a lurching, and generally ineffectual, quality, especially during the early phase of the new administration.

CONCLUSION

Despite the sentiment that politics should stop at water's edge, electoral gamesmanship and foreign policy march in an intimate embrace. How external affairs are handled does matter to electoral outcomes, both in an indirect and direct manner, and politicians naturally seek to draw what benefits they can from this fact. U.S. foreign policy bears the traces. While reasonable people may disagree on the extent to which the long-term essence of this policy is shaped by domestic political competition, it is hard to deny its impact on the periodicities and discontinuities that this policy often exhibits.

NOTES

1. See Miroslav Nincic, "The National Interest and Its Interpretation," *Review of Politics* (January 1999): 76–94.

2. For an overview of thinking on American voting behavior, see Richard G. Niemi and Herbert F. Weisberg, *Classics in Voting Behavior,* 4th ed. (Washington D.C.: Congressional Quarterly Press, 2001).

3. Program on International Public Attitudes (PIPA), Center for International and Security Studies, University of Maryland, October 2000.

4. Robert Strauss, "What's Right with U.S. Campaigns," *Foreign Policy* (Fall 1982): 34.

5. See Miroslav Nincic, *Democracy and Foreign Policy: The Fallacy of Political Realism* (New York: Columbia University Press, 1992), 94–96.

6. *Washington Post* survey, July 9–12, 1998.

7. See Eric V. Larson, *Casualties and Consensus: The Historical Role of Casualties in Domestic Support for U.S. Military Operations* (Santa Monica, Calif.: RAND, 1966).

8. See, for example, Herbert B. Asher, *Presidential Elections and American Politics,* 3rd ed. (Homewood, Ill.: Dorsey Press, 1984), 199–200.

9. George H. Gallup, *The Gallup Poll: Public Opinion 1972–1977* (Wilmington, Del.: Scholarly Resources, 1978), 64.

10. Gallup, *The Gallup Poll,* 2136.

11. Kurt Taylor Gaubatz, "Elections and Foreign Policy: Strategic Politicians and the Domestic Salience of International Issues," unpublished manuscript, Graduate School in International Studies, Old Dominion University, Norfolk, Virginia, 2002.

12. This is developed in Miroslav Nincic, "U.S. Soviet Policy and the Electoral Connection," *World Politics* 42 (April 1990): 370–96.

13. See Nincic, "U.S. Soviet Policy and the Electoral Connection."

14. Kurt Taylor Gaubatz, *Elections and War: The Electoral Incentive in the Democratic Politics of War and Peace* (Stanford, Calif.: Stanford University Press, 1999), 147.

II

THE INSTITUTIONAL SETTING

Foreign policy is a product of the actions officials take on behalf of the nation. Because of this, the way the government is structured for policymaking also arguably affects the conduct and content of foreign affairs. Thus, we can hypothesize that a relationship exists between the substance of policy and the institutional setting from which it derives. The proposition is particularly compelling if attention is directed not to the foreign policy goals the nation's leaders select but to the means they choose to satisfy particular objectives.

A salient feature of the American institutional setting is that the president and the institutionalized presidency—the latter consisting of the president's personal staff and the Executive Office of the President—are preeminent in the foreign-policy making process. This derives in part from the authority granted the president in the Constitution and in part from the combination of judicial interpretation, legislative acquiescence, personal assertiveness, and custom and tradition that have transformed the presidency into the most powerful office in the world. The crisis-ridden atmosphere that characterized the Cold War era also contributed to the enhancement of presidential authority by encouraging the president to act energetically and decisively when dealing with global challenges. The widely shared consensus among American leaders and the American public that the international environment demanded an active world role also contributed to the felt need for strong presidential leadership. Although this viewpoint was sometimes vigorously debated in the years following American involvement in Vietnam, the perceived need for strong presidential leadership was generally accepted throughout the Cold War.

Because of the president's key role in foreign-policy making it is useful to consider the institutional arrangements that govern the process as a series of concentric circles that effectively alter the standard government organization chart so as to draw attention to the core, or most immediate source of the action (see figure II.1). Thus, the innermost circle in the policymaking

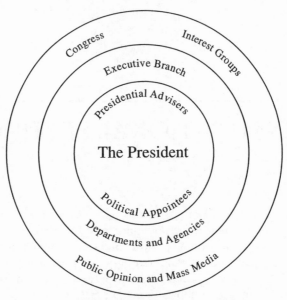

Figure II.1. The concentric circles of policy making. *Source:* **Adapted from Roger Hilsman,** *To Move a Nation* **(New York: Doubleday, 1967), 541–544.**

process consists of the president, his immediate personal advisors, and such important political appointees as the secretaries of state and defense, the director of central intelligence, and various under, deputy, and assistant secretaries who bear responsibility for carrying out policy decisions. Here, in principle, is where the most important decisions involving the fate of the nation are made.

The second concentric circle comprises the various departments and agencies of the executive branch. If we exclude from that circle the politically appointed heads of agencies and their immediate subordinates, who are more properly placed in the innermost circle, we can think of the individuals within the second circle as career professionals who provide continuity in the implementation of policy from one administration to the next. Their primary tasks—in theory—are to provide top-level policymakers with the information necessary for sound decisionmaking and to carry out the decisions policymakers reach. As noted in the introduction to this book, the involvement of the United States in a complex webwork of interdependent ties with other nations in the world has led to the involvement in foreign affairs of many organizations the primary tasks of which are seemingly oriented toward the domestic environment. The Treasury Department has become especially visible in recent years, as the globalization of the world political economy has increased the salience of economic issues as foreign policy issues. The Departments of Agriculture, Commerce, and Justice (including the Federal Bureau of Investigation [FBI]) have also figured prominently as globalization and international terrorism have blurred the distinction between foreign and domestic politics and policy. Congress's creation in November 2002 of the Department of Homeland Security especially epitomizes the linking of the domestic and international arenas within one organization. While the new department, as its name implies, has the explicit duty of protecting citizens at home, it also has the responsibility to gather and analyze intelligence information about foreign threats and to deter and protect against such attacks as occurred on September 11, 2001.

The Departments of State and Defense and the intelligence community continue to command center stage among the dozens of executive-branch departments and agencies now involved in foreign affairs. The State Department's role derives from being the only department charged (in theory at least) with responsibility for the whole range of America's relations with other nations. The Defense Department and the intelligence community, especially the Central Intelligence Agency (CIA), on the other hand, in the Cold War years derived their importance from the threatening and crisis-ridden atmosphere; they often had ready alternatives from which top-level policymakers could choose when diplomacy and negotiation seemed destined to fail. While both bureaucracies played a diminished role in the post–Cold War world, both appear to have especially important parts to play in the post–9/11 world.

Moving beyond the departments and agencies of the executive branch, the third concentric circle consists of Congress. Although technically a single institutional entity, Congress often appears to embrace many different centers of power and authority—ranging from the House and Senate leadership to the various coalitions operative in the legislative branch, and from the various committees and subcommittees in which Congress does its real work to the individual senators and representatives, who often vie with one another for publicity as well as power. Of all the institutions involved in foreign-policy making, Congress is least engaged in the day-to-day conduct of the nation's foreign relations, as reflected in its placement in the outermost circle.

Does this stylized description of the relative influence of various institutions and actors involved in foreign-policy making continue to hold in the wake of September 11? Roger Hilsman, who first suggested this institutional conceptualization some four decades ago in his *To Move a Nation,* even then cautioned against a too facile reliance upon this description. Although the institutional setting may affect the form and flow of policy, the politicking inherent in the process by no means conforms to the neatly compartmentalized, institutionalized paths implied by Hilsman's framework. What the nation chooses to do abroad is more often the product of an intense political struggle among the prominent players in the policymaking process, the policymaking positions or roles occupied by the key decisionmakers, and the characteristics of those individuals. The changed and changing nature of the international system is also pertinent to the contemporary institutional setting. As the constraints and opportunities in the twenty-first century unfold, the character and responsiveness of institutions largely formed during the decades of Cold War can be expected to change. It is a viewpoint we examine in the chapters in Part II.

Beginning with the innermost concentric circle, a case can be made that the post–9/11 changes in the global environment have strengthened the presidency and increased its centrality in the governmental setting. Indeed, *The Economist* proclaimed shortly after September 11 that "the United States is witnessing the most dramatic expansion in presidential power for a generation."[1] In effect, we seem to be witnessing a return of the "imperial presidency" of the Vietnam era. Yet as Michael Nelson argues in the first chapter in Part II, "Person and Office: Presidents, the Presidency, and Foreign Policy," it is really a study of the combination of the characteristics of the presidency and characteristics of the individual occupying the presidency that provides the fullest understanding of that institution.

Nelson begins by noting that the presidency possesses several important constitutional powers, although their exact operation was never made clear by the framers. Indeed, "it took well over a century for parchment to become practice" and "for all the constitutionally enumerated powers of the presidency to come to life." The activation of these powers, Nelson notes, actually came sooner in foreign policy than in domestic policy with Washington's proclamation of neutrality in the war between France and England and the declaration of the Monroe Doctrine. These, and other early unilateral actions by presidents, were defended by citing the nature of the presidency, with its unity of office and its election by the entire country. In the modern era, these arguments for presidential leadership were strengthened with the emergence of the Cold War and with the reluctance of Congress to challenge executive prerogatives in foreign affairs. Despite congressional passage of the War Powers Resolution in the aftermath of the Vietnam War, for example, succeeding presidents have not "complied with the letter, much less the spirit," of that law. Throughout much of the history of the Republic, too, the Supreme Court has routinely backed the executive's prerogatives in foreign affairs.

Another dimension of the office that aids presidential dominance is the president's dual role as chief of state and chief of government. The former role allows the president to represent the nation externally; the latter allows the president to lead the nation internally. Importantly, both roles afford the president the opportunity to lead the public, thus enhancing his ability to use his popularity to promote his policy.

The experiences, the personality, and the skills that an individual brings to the office are also important for understanding presidents' conduct of foreign policy. Some presidents served as secretary of state prior to assuming office, but recent ones more often come with backgrounds as state governors. As a result, recent presidents have had less experience in foreign affairs than as chief executives. The degree of self-confidence and the degree of consistency in their actions, Nelson points out, may also be helpful in understanding presidents' behavior. Finally, the leadership skills of a president—his management of authority within his own staff, his tactical political skills in dealing with Congress, and his presentation of self to the public—appear to be crucial in making the presidency function effectively as an institution.

In "Presidential Wars," Louis Fisher is pessimistic about the prospects of altering the balance of executive-legislative influence in foreign policy, even on issues involving the use of American force abroad. In this critical policy arena, presidents continue to act unilaterally. "Instead of coming to Congress for authority," as the Constitution calls for, "presidents are more likely to justify military actions either on the commander in chief clause . . . or on decisions reached by the UN Security Council and NATO."

President Truman encouraged this process early in the Cold War by first promising to obtain congressional approval for any use of U.S. troops as part of a United Nations operation, but then ignoring Congress when he sent American troops to Korea in June 1950. Presidents George H. W. Bush and Bill Clinton continued that tradition in the immediate post–Cold War years. "Instead of seeking authority from Congress [to prosecute war against Saddam Hussein], Bush created a multinational alliance and encouraged the [United Nations] Security Council to authorize the use of military force." Even when Bush finally asked Congress to vote on the use of force in the Gulf, "he was asking for 'support,' not authority."

In sending American forces to Haiti and Bosnia and using American air power in Kosovo, Clinton followed a similar strategy. To deal with Haiti, he sought and obtained a Security Council resolution authorizing an invasion and explicitly denied that he needed congressional support: "I have not agreed that I was constitutionally mandated to obtain the support of Congress." In Bosnia, he invoked authority under Article II of the Constitution and the NATO Treaty to deploy American forces as part of the Dayton Accords of November 1995, and he again denied that he needed congressional approval for his actions. Before the Kosovo campaign, Clinton again looked to NATO to authorize action, and he made that decision unilaterally ("I decided that the United States would vote to give NATO the authority to carry out military strikes against Serbia").

In early 2002 when George W. Bush first began discussing war against Iraq, there was little mention of going to Congress to request its support— or even going to an international forum, as his father and Clinton had done to justify earlier interventions. By the fall of that year, the administration had changed its mind and asked the Congress to pass a resolution on Iraq prior to the 2002 congressional elections. In this highly partisan atmosphere, and because of the popularity of the president, Bush easily succeeded in obtaining a resolution to use force against Iraq at his discretion.

In all of these cases—Korea, the Persian Gulf, Haiti, Bosnia, Kosovo, and Iraq—Congress acquiesced in presidential encroachment on its powers. Indeed, Fisher argues that "Congress . . . not only fails to fight back but even volunteers fundamental legislative powers, including the war power and the power of the purse." While partisan politics partially explains Congress's acquiescence, members of both political parties often support presidential prerogatives. In the end, Fisher worries that the process "undermines public control, the system of checks and balances, and constitutional government."

Another important institutional mechanism within the first concentric circle of foreign-policy making is the National Security Council (NSC) system. It consists of the formal National Security Council, the complex of interagency committees that carry on its work, and the NSC staff, which serves the president, his advisers, and the committees making up the NSC system. The NSC staff is headed by the president's assistant for national security affairs, who has assumed a position of prominence in recent decades. Similarly, the NSC system and staff have become crucial mechanisms within the institutionalized presidency used by the White House to ensure its control of policymaking and to enhance prospects for policy coherence and consistency with presidential wishes.

Often the visibility and power of the national security assistant has been cause for conflict with other key participants in the process, notably the secretary of state. That was especially apparent during the Nixon and Carter presidencies. During the Reagan presidency, the role of the NSC staff became more contentious—indeed, infamous—as the staff engaged in the abuse of power: Lieutenant Colonel Oliver L. North undertook covert operational activities designed to divert profits from the sale of arms to Iran to the Contras fighting the Sandinista regime in Nicaragua, in apparent contravention of congressional prohibitions.

Steps were later taken to ensure that the NSC staff would no longer engage in operational activities, and both the first Bush and Clinton presidencies were marked by the absence of public squabbles between their respective secretaries of state (James A. Baker for Bush, Warren Christopher and later Madeleine Albright for Clinton) and national security advisers (Brent Scowcroft for Bush, Anthony Lake and then Samuel Berger for Clinton). Still,

Scowcroft, Lake, and Berger were powerful players in the policy process, exercising decisive influence in supporting Bush's determination to evict Iraqi forces from Kuwait and pressing Clinton to intervene in Haiti and to support the expansion of NATO. Under President George W. Bush, the pattern of a strong and influential national security adviser continues. Condoleezza Rice, according to one assessment, plays "a critical, if largely hidden, role in the overall direction of the president's foreign policy." She possesses extraordinary influence with Bush because she is personally close and reassuring to the president, and he trusts her judgment on foreign policy matters.

In the next chapter, Ivo H. Daalder and I. M. Destler provide a closer look at the role of the national security adviser in the foreign policy process. In their "How National Security Advisers See Their Role," they draw directly on the results of two recent roundtables with individuals who served in this position over the past forty years.

Daalder and Destler begin their analysis by identifying the reasons the role of the national security adviser has expanded since its inception. The primary reason is what they call "the president's need for close-in foreign policy support," but other factors have aided this expansion as well. As the NSC staff increased and became institutionalized, it assumed new functions in the policy process (e.g., crisis management). As the foreign policy agenda expanded, the NSC adviser and staff also took on more intermestic issues. As "U.S. politics no longer ends at the water's edge," the NSC, acting as the White House's surrogate, assumed responsibility to monitor the political aspects of foreign policy actions.

Within the context of these expanded responsibilities, Daalder and Destler identify three principal roles that the national security adviser undertakes: managing the foreign policy decisionmaking process, undertaking operational matters, and assuming public responsibilities. The most important of these is the first one, managing the decision process. In this role, the adviser needs "to ensure both that those with strong stakes are involved and that all realistic policy options are fully considered." He or she must also make certain that choices are made in a "timely manner" and must oversee "the implementation of the decisions made by the president and his or her advisers."

The operational and public roles of the national security advisers have less importance than the managerial one, but they have become increasingly used in recent years. As we have seen, in the aftermath of the Iran-Contra scandal in the mid-1980s, the NSC and its staff formally rejected an operational role. In practice, as Daalder and Destler point out, the national security adviser and the NSC staff continue to play an operational role. This role occurs for several reasons: other governments have counterparts to the adviser and require this kind of direct interaction, the traditional foreign policy bureaucracies have not been responsive to the president's directives, or the president wants to signal a fundamental shift in foreign policy through the adviser's action. The public role of the national security adviser has largely emerged with the increased politicization of foreign policy over the past three or four decades and with the expansion of media outlets, which have required that an administration have "all the bases . . . covered" in addressing foreign affairs. With this public role, demands for more accountability of the advisers have increased, including requiring Senate confirmation of these appointments, which is not currently done.

If the institutions in the innermost (presidential) concentric circle have seemingly become more powerful since 9/11, that decidedly is not the case with Congress. Instead, it has reverted to a foreign policy role reminiscent of the early years of the Cold War. In "From Deference to Activism and Back Again: Congress and the Politics of American Foreign Policy," James M. Lindsay surveys the changes in congressional attitudes toward the foreign policy process during the past decade. In 1995, Congress was accused by then Secretary of State Warren Christopher of waging "an extraordinary onslaught on the president's authority to manage foreign policy." In 2002, Lindsay notes, the concern was that Congress "had abdicated any foreign policy role." His explanation for this congressional *volte face* lies not within "the realm of law" but within "the realm of politics." As he notes, "times of peace [such as 1995] favor congressional activism," but "times of war [such as 2002] favor congressional deference."

While the Constitution provides the framework for both Congress and president to exercise influence in the conduct of foreign policy, the political arena has often been the determinant of whether the Congress actually exercises its authority. Lindsay argues that the ebbs and flows of congressional actions in foreign affairs largely turn on the perceived threat from abroad. Congressional deference was particularly evident in the immediate post–World War II years, for example, but it came "to a crashing halt" with the Vietnam War. Later, "the end of the Cold War accelerated and exacerbated the trend toward congressional activism." Indeed, the Clinton administration faced a series of congressional foreign policy challenges, and, more often than not, Congress prevailed.

September 11 changed that again, as "the pendulum of power swung sharply back toward the White House." Not only did members of Congress promptly provide the president with sweeping authority to retaliate against terrorism, but they reversed policy stances that they had previously adopted. They quickly agreed to pay overdue UN dues to facilitate coalition building through that body, they lifted sanctions against Pakistan that had been imposed since the military coup in that country in 1999, and they were prepared to increase defense spending sharply. Congressional criticism of the war on terrorism was muted, and criticism that did arise was quickly challenged on patriotic grounds.

What, Lindsay asks, is the "proper balance between activism and deference?" His judgment is that both have costs and benefits. Congressional activism forces the president and his advisers to think through their policy options, and it affords the Congress the opportunity to debate and legitimate the chosen course with the American public. Yet such activism has its downside. It makes the process more cumbersome and time consuming, and it may also lead to an incoherent policy if the two branches differ on the direction of policy. While congressional deference may avoid such problems, it may contribute to presidential "overreach" on policy. Because "presidents and their advisers are not infallible," congressional checks and balances can aid in their choices of the best policies for the nation.

According to the Constitution, the president and Congress are coequal partners in foreign-policy making. Both are elected by the American people. In practice, however, the bureaucratic organizations of the permanent foreign affairs government depicted in the second concentric circle in figure II.1 provide continuity from one administration to the next and through the continuing presidential and congressional electoral cycles. Not surprisingly, then, the organizations constituting the foreign affairs government are often described as "the fourth branch of government."

People who work in the "fourth branch" often spend their entire careers managing the routine affairs that constitute America's relations with other countries. Indeed, these career professionals and the organizations they work for are expected to be the government's "eyes and ears," searching for incipient global changes and assessing American needs and interests abroad. Thus these key institutions can be expected to change as global challenges and opportunities change. As the last five chapters in Part II suggest, organizations central to American diplomatic, military, intelligence, and economic policymaking are in fact responding to the post–9/11 world. How well they have adapted is, however, a matter of sometimes contentious political dispute, as the previous chapters dealing with congressional-executive relations suggest.

Strobe Talbott, deputy secretary of state in the Clinton administration and the political appointee with primary responsibility for managing the internal operations of the Department of State, writes persuasively about the need for organizational change in his "Globalization and Diplomacy: The View from Foggy Bottom." Globalization—propelled by "the powerful technological forces of the Information Age [that] have helped to stitch together the economic, political, and cultural lives of nations, making borders more permeable to the movement of people, products, and ideas"—has already begun to transform the lives of people around the world in both positive and negative ways. The challenge for American foreign policy is to respond to globalization in a positive way. According to Talbott, the State Department, America's foreign policy organization responsible for the conduct of U.S. foreign affairs, has an important role to play in shaping this response.

As Talbott notes, the State Department has already undertaken some important changes that are transforming the nature of America's diplomatic operations. New bureaus have been created and others consolidated; greater interactions on global issues are taking place between the State Department and the Departments of Defense, Commerce, and Justice in Washington and abroad. Most importantly, the State Department has sought to implement a strategy of working "multi-multilaterally." That is, its personnel have cooperated with other American agencies, other countries, and numerous governmental and nongovernmental institutions to address issues that cannot be resolved by a single agency, country, or institution—whether it be to help resolve issues of water resources in the Middle East or to implement the Dayton Accords in Bosnia. In this way, Talbott argues, the United States and other governments can "leverage scarce resources and improve their ability to address transnational threats."

The American military as a foreign and national security policy institution has hardly been immune from the impact of recent events, and it has not been immune from calls for change over the past decade or more. Indeed, George W. Bush campaigned for the presidency on a commitment to remake and strengthen the military. Just after Bush took office, *The U.S. Commission on National Security/Twenty-first Century* (the Hart-Rudman Commission) argued that the Pentagon "needs to be overhauled" and that "strategy should once again drive the design and implementation of U.S. national security policies."

In "A Tale of Two Secretaries," Eliot A. Cohen discusses the difficulties in transforming the Department of Defense and the difficult task that Secretary of Defense Donald Rumsfeld faces in carrying out such a mission. When Rumsfeld assumed office in 2001, there was considerable discussion of a "defense transformation," but during his early months in office there was "little evidence of it." Instead, complaints were heard about Rumsfeld's treatment of senior military officers and the relatively meager proposed increase in the defense budget. The events of September 11, however, dramatically changed that portrait, giving Rumsfeld as a "Secretary of War" a better prospect for making significant changes. In this sense, the Pentagon may now be poised for significant transformation, but Cohen warns that no one should be under an illusion about the nature of the task.

In fact, Cohen begins his analysis by noting that the secretary of defense has "an impossible job—if one hopes to change quickly the institutions of the armed forces rather than merely preside over them." The reasons turn on the fact that the secretary must rely on political appointees; it takes time to attract candidates to staff the key offices, since the mediocre "compensation packages" and the extensive "vetting" of potential appointments may discourage many high-quality candidates. As a result, the secretary of defense has to rely upon the military bureaucracy that is already in place. While the military personnel occupying those positions may be highly qualified individuals, they are also committed to existing operating procedures. In such an environment, fundamental change remains difficult.

Despite bureaucratic resistance to change, Cohen argues that forces within the Pentagon may precipitate change, and that the effects of 9/11 may well aid that process. One force is the sheer size of the budget. Within such a budget, there exist opportunities to innovate with the development of new weapon systems, including several that proved very useful in Afghanistan in 2001 and 2002. A second force is "a cadre of energetic young officers" who have "operational experience and advanced technical education" and who "are slowly but surely dragging the system along with them." A third factor is the "American eagerness to change, experiment, and modernize"; these qualities will inevitably permeate the military as well.

Still, addressing America's defense needs after 9/11 remains a substantial challenge. The procurement of new weaponry and the maintenance of an adequate infrastructure are two unmet needs, as the limited actions in Afghanistan in 2001 and 2002 also revealed. That engagement demonstrated the problems that shortages of precision-guided weapons can produce, but it also confirmed the benefits of unmanned aerial vehicles. Both areas need attention, but America's will to address them—and to open its wallet to do so—remains unclear. Furthermore, the array of existing American engagements abroad will not be easy to undo, further eroding the possibility of significant military transformation.

The intelligence community is the third major foreign policy institution in the second concentric circle of policymaking. It too has been buffeted by recent changes in world politics. While the intelligence community has long come under criticism for its failures in intelligence estimates, the impact of September 11 produced a firestorm of criticism within the Congress; calls were heard for investigations of the presumed failures that had allowed the events to happen.

In "Smarter Intelligence," former Clinton administration director of central intelligence John Deutch, and a former CIA general counsel, Jeffrey H. Smith, provide a critique of the intelligence community, offering a series of prescriptions for improving America's counterterrorism intelligence. They begin by considering the constraints that have operated on the intelligence community and intelligence sharing within the government. The intelligence community, initially the CIA but including other agencies later, was created to monitor foreign threats and collect and analyze information before foreign policy actions were taken. The Federal Bureau of Investigation, on the other hand, was founded to collect evidence after a crime had occurred and to prosecute and convict the accused. Neither agency is inclined to share information with the other; there has been little cooperation between them. The CIA strives to protect "its sources and methods," and the FBI seeks to prevent "future court action." Nonetheless, as Deutch and Smith note, the key to successful intelligence reform revolves around "the proper balance between national security and law enforcement goals."

Deutch and Smith outline several changes in structure, authority, and process within the intelligence community that they believe will produce the needed reforms. For example, they recommend that the authority of the director of central intelligence (DCI) over all components of the intelligence community (the CIA, National Security Agency, Defense Intelligence Agency, FBI, and others) and over all foreign-intelligence organizations working with these agencies "be clarified and strictly enforced." Further, currently responsibility for the collection and analysis of human and technical intelligence on which the United States relies is fragmented among different agencies. This kind of "fragmentation makes no sense when considering the global terrorist threat," and it should be changed. Deutch and Smith also recommend that serious consideration be given to separating the position of the head of the CIA and that of the DCI, currently held by the same individual, but that this change occur only "if the DCI is given budgetary, planning, and management authority over the agencies that are responsible for national-level intelligence." Finally, they note that as covert operations are increasingly used "to destroy terrorist cells and facilities that may produce or store weapons of mass destruction," the distinction between covert actions taken by the CIA and special operations led by the military will become increasingly blurred. The former, however, require presidential findings that are shared with Congress, while the latter do not. Thus congressional strictures on covert actions should be rethought.

Although Deutch and Smith recommend that these and other important changes be made in the intelligence community, they endorse rules that have been put in place in recent decades to make CIA operations more accountable. One concerns the need to gain approval from the CIA's covert-action division, the Directorate of Operations, before recruiting agents with serious criminal and poor human rights backgrounds. A second is President Ford's executive order prohibiting assassination as an instrument of American foreign policy—an appropriate international norm that the United States should not violate in its effort to win the war on terrorism. The third concerns wiretaps on foreigners in the United States and on American citizens who may be associated with terrorists. Deutch and Smith note that recent congressional changes have clarified which wiretaps are permissible; they believe that "it is possible to devise a system to collect large amounts of information without compromising the privacy and rights of American citizens." They conclude that while the American people can be better protected than in the past, the public "should be under no illusion that the intelligence community can remove all risk.... [I]t is unreasonable to expect 100 percent success."

While intelligence reform is an important component for enhancing America's security, the Hart-Rudman Commission in early 2001, prior to 9/11, recommended that a "new, cabinet-level National Homeland Security Agency" be established. Immediately after September 11, President Bush created by executive order an Office of Homeland Security, but he initially balked at a separate cabinet post for this function. Prodded by members of Congress, Bush changed his mind and embraced the idea of a new cabinet agency, which became the Department of Homeland Security in late 2002. The new department consolidates twenty-two agencies and nearly 170,000 workers into the third-largest bureaucracy in the federal government, with responsibilities in the areas of border and transportation security, emergency preparedness, science and technology, and information analysis related to terrorist threats. With such a broad mandate and an uncertain structure, the department was immediately criticized "as a management challenge without precedent." Fears were also raised about whether its unwieldy nature may "divert [it] from its central mission of safeguarding the American public from terrorist attacks."[2]

In "Advisors, Czars, and Councils: Organizing for Homeland Security," Ivo H. Daalder and I. M. Destler share these concerns, arguing that a centralized institutional structure will not be the most efficacious approach to increasing the safety of Americans in the post–9/11 world. Writing shortly before the new Homeland Security Department was created, they agreed that while some reorganization may be necessary, it would not be crucial to success. After all, as they note, "the diffusion of responsibility is inherent in providing homeland security because success depends on a multitude of unconnected individuals making good decisions. It is inherently a decentralized operation." The border guard or airport security guard must make good decisions about possible threats and report them to their immediate superiors, who in turn notify state and federal authorities. A top-down structure will not be able to perform these functions. "Even with full Cabinet status, the secretary of a new Department of Homeland Security will not be able to coordinate the activities and actions of his many cabinet colleagues who have an interest in and share responsibility for protecting the American homeland."

Daalder and Destler suggest that the homeland security adviser (now secretary) could draw upon the lessons of the National Economic Council (NEC) and the National Security Council operations to develop organizational arrangements and policy processes so as to foster cooperation throughout the various levels of government. As head of the NEC during the Clinton administration, for example, Robert Rubin was able to gain influence by proposing new initiatives and fostering cooperation among a myriad of different organizations and departments. Similarly, the NSC system of committees and interagency working groups also provides some guidance for operating procedures (e.g., the use of both formal and informal channels of cooperation).

In addition, and more importantly for the homeland security adviser (now secretary), is the need to coordinate activities from the bottom up and to make certain "how the system operates at ground level." This means that the head of the agency would need to ensure that other cabinet agencies with security responsibilities are in the loop and that other levels of government (and even the private sector) are also brought into the process. While this is a "daunting task," it can be accomplished if the adviser (secretary) sees his role as "cross-government collaborator and mobilizer," but "not as [that of] a 'czar' issuing orders."

An important foreign policy legacy of the Clinton administration was the expansion of American trade through the completion of several bilateral and multilateral trade agreements (e.g., the North American Free Trade Agreement [NAFTA] and the World Trade Organization [WTO]) and the placement of economic policymaking at the center of American foreign policy. The Bush administration came to office with a similar commitment to free trade policymaking. Trade, however, can be controversial, as both the Clinton and Bush administrations learned. In December 1999 at a WTO meeting in Seattle, Clinton faced massive demonstrations by environmental, labor, and antiglobalization groups protesting against international trade regulations that allegedly were eroding domestic standards designed to protect the environment and workers. At a meeting in Quebec City, Canada, over the Free Trade Area in the Americas (FTAA) in April 2001, Bush faced similar protests. Furthermore, demonstrations occurred later at other international economic forums on global-trade policymaking.

In their chapter "Trade Policy Making: The Changing Context," Bruce Stokes and Pat Choate discuss the U.S. trade policymaking process and explain how it has affected American trade decisions. In particular, they trace the organizational context of trade policy making domestically since the founding of the Republic. They also briefly discuss policymaking at the international level and illustrate how that has affected the domestic policy process.

Because the Constitution is ambiguous about the trade policy process, giving ultimate trade authority to the Congress but directing the president to negotiate with other nations, these two institutions have historically relied upon three approaches to deal with this ambiguity. The first, roughly from the beginning of the present constitutional government in 1789 until the 1930s, saw the Congress in charge of trade policy, with debates confined to that institution. The second, roughly from the passage of the Reciprocal Trade Agreements Act of 1934 through the Kennedy Round of multilateral negotiations in the late 1960s, saw the Congress grant the president greater authority to initiate trade policy and conduct negotiations.

The third phase, largely a reaction to the second, dates from the passage of the Trade Act of 1974 to the present. That legislation "recast the balance of power between Congress and the executive branch . . . and opened up the trade policy making process to new actors." Specifically, that act established the "fast track" procedure (which granted the president authority to negotiate trade agreements without congressional interference), expanded the trade agenda to include tariff and nontariff barriers in the negotiating process, and incorporated private-sector advisory groups into the negotiating process. At the same time, the legislation reserved to Congress "a degree of consultation and oversight not included in past extensions of trade-negotiating authority." Despite these innovations, the process has not worked well. Increasingly there has been a decline in support across party lines for the executive-directed trade policy, as evidenced by the cautious support for trade agreements like NAFTA in 1993 and the African Growth and Opportunity Act in 2000 and the difficulty of renewing fast-track authority during the Clinton years. (That authority was renewed during the Bush administration by only one vote in the House.) The important message that Stokes and Choate leave about the trade policy making process is "the need to constantly re-equilibrate the policymaking process to accommodate changing substantive interests in the hope that the process can continue to produce a consensus on trade policy."

At the international level, the "trade rule-making and dispute settlement" processes have largely been post–World War II phenomena. Near the end of that war, three international institutions were proposed: the International Monetary Fund (IMF), the World Bank, and the International Trade Organization (ITO). Only the first two became realities. In lieu of the ITO, a weaker trading organization, the General Agreement on Tariffs and Trade (GATT), "became the principal global forum for multilateral trade negotiations." Although GATT negotiations produced a number of tariff reductions over the years, the system had no firm enforcement mechanism. In 1995, GATT was replaced by the World Trade Organization, an organization that not only had a broader trade agenda but also included a dispute-settlement mechanism.

The mandate of the WTO has sparked considerable domestic debate. Some in the business community seek to use international commitments to enforce particular standards and principles, while some labor, consumer, and environmental groups oppose WTO standards that may override domestic regulation. As result, Stokes and Choate argue, "trade negotiations and international commercial agreements are less and less about tariffs, quotas, and other formal at-the-border impediments to foreign commerce and more and more about domestic regulatory environments and how they impede or enhance international competition." Such regulatory questions expand the policymaking process on trade to new issues and new actors at both the domestic and international levels. The question of which set of standards and rules will prevail—international or domestic ones—will likely be the key trade concern for some time. As Stokes and Choate conclude, "some way must be found to minimize this friction and maximize the benefits of high standards and liberalized trade."

NOTES

1. "The Imperial Presidency," *The Economist,* November 3, 2001, 39.

2. Philip Senon, "Establishing New Agency Is Expected to Take Years and Could Divert It from Mission," *New York Times,* November 20, 2002, A12.

9

Person and Office

Presidents, the Presidency, and Foreign Policy

Michael Nelson

Henry Jones Ford, in his classic work *The Rise and Growth of American Government,* quoted Alexander Hamilton's prediction to a friend that the time would "assuredly come when every vital question of the state will be merged in the question, 'Who shall be the next president?'" Ford cited this remark to support his argument that in creating the presidency, the Constitutional Convention of 1787 had "revived the oldest political institution of the race, the elective kingship."

Although there is much truth in Ford's evaluation of the presidency, it also displays a certain measure of ambivalence on a fundamental issue. Is the presidency best understood as a person ("Who shall be the next president?") or an office (an "elective kingship")?

Political scientists in the twentieth, and now the twenty-first, centuries have continued to grapple with Ford's conundrum. Most of them probably would agree that the best answer to the person-or-office question is some combination of both: person and office, president and presidency. The office has become important mostly because its constitutional design suited it well for national leadership in the changing circumstances of history. But because the Constitution invested so much responsibility in the person who is the president, that person's background, personality, and leadership skills are consequential as well.

Modern political scientists also tend to agree on a second matter—namely, that the presidency and the presidents who occupy the office are never more important than in the making of foreign policy. This is especially true of issues and challenges that concern the national security.

OFFICE

The Constitutional Convention created a government marked less by separation of powers than, in political scientist Richard Neustadt's apt phrase, by "separated institutions sharing powers." Institutional separation meant that in stark contrast to parliamentary governments, which typically draw their executive leaders from the legislature, the president was forbidden by Article I, Section 6 of the Constitution to appoint any sitting member of Congress to the cabinet or White House staff. These severely separated branches were, however, constitutionally enjoined to share in the exercise of virtually all the powers of the national government. Congress is empowered to "make all laws," but the president may veto them. The Senate may (or may choose not to) give "Advice and Consent" concerning presidential appointments to the executive branch and the judiciary. In matters of war, the president is "Commander in Chief of the Army and Navy," but Congress has the power to "declare war," to "raise and support Armies," and to "provide and maintain a Navy." In matters of peace, no treaty proposed by a president can take effect unless two-thirds of the Senate votes to ratify it.

Powers alone do not define power. Through history, the presidency has become much more powerful than at its inception, even though the formal powers of the office have remained the same. A second cluster of constitutional decisions, those concerning the number and selection of the executive, provides much of the explanation for the presidency's expanding influence. The framers of the Constitution, after much debate, created the presidency as a unitary, not a plural or committee-style, office and provided that the president would be elected by the entire nation, independently of Congress and the state governments. In doing so, they made the president the only national officer who can plausibly claim both a political mandate to speak for the people and their government, and an institutional capacity to lead with what the Pennsylvania delegate James Wilson described as "energy, unity, and responsibility."

Lead, that is, when and in such areas of public policy as national leadership is sought—which, during the nineteenth century, it usually was not in the domestic realm. Historically, it took well over a century for parchment to become practice—that is, for all of the constitutionally enumerated powers of the presidency to come to life. Congress seized the lion's share of the government's shared powers in domestic policy nearly from the beginning, dominating even the executive appointment process. When it came to legislation, members of Congress treated with scorn most early presidential efforts to recommend or influence their consideration of bills and resolutions. Nor, until Andrew Jackson in the 1830s, were presidents able to exercise the veto power without provoking a politically disabling storm of opposition on Capitol Hill.

Although presidential disempowerment was long-lived, it was not eternal. The weakness of the presidency in domestic matters was a function of the weak national government that generally prevailed during the nineteenth century. The country, then a congeries of local economies and cultures, was not seeking what the presidency was constitutionally designed to provide, namely, energetic leadership on behalf of national initiatives. But the conditions that sustained weak government began to change around the turn of the century. The widespread dissemination of railroads and telegraph lines made all but inevitable the development of a national economy, and with this transformation came demands that the national government take measures to facilitate the spread (while taming the excesses) of the new and massive corporations. Early twentieth-century presidents Theodore Roosevelt and Woodrow Wilson roused a popular mandate for the president to make full use of the office's constitutional powers to lead Congress and the executive branch. Franklin D. Roosevelt, during the Great Depression of the 1930s, and more recent presidents such as Lyndon B. Johnson and Ronald Reagan also played the role of chief legislator on a grand scale.

In contrast to the slow awakening of the presidency's constitutional powers concerning domestic policy, on matters of foreign policy the powers of the office were activated early. In 1793, George Washington issued the Proclamation of Neutrality on his own authority, declaring that the United States would not take sides in the war between England and France. Critics declared that he lacked that authority. Because a declaration of war must be approved by Congress, they argued, so must a declaration not to go to war. Secretary of the Treasury Alexander Hamilton, writing as "Pacificus," replied in a series of pseudonymous newspaper articles that the president's constitutional powers were sufficient. Unlike the vesting clause of Article I, which states that "All legislative Powers herein granted shall be vested in a Congress of the United States," the vesting clause for the president lacks the words "herein granted," stating instead: "The executive Power shall be vested in a President of the United States of America." The omission of these two words, Hamilton claimed, meant that the president had constitutional powers beyond those specified by name, especially in foreign policy. Washington's proclamation stood.

Although presidents had to struggle to invigorate the domestic powers of their office during the nineteenth and early twentieth century, they usually were able to get their way when deciding how the United States should deal with other countries. In 1823 an otherwise weak president, James Monroe, issued the Monroe Doctrine on his own authority. The doctrine declared that the Americas were off limits to any attempts at European colonization. James K. Polk secretly negotiated for the annexation of Texas during the mid-1840s and, by sending troops into disputed territory, provoked war with Mexico. Without congressional consultation, Presidents William McKinley, William Howard Taft, Woodrow Wilson, and Calvin Coolidge dispatched American forces into foreign countries.

Similarly, beginning with the Washington administration, presidential decisions about which foreign governments to recognize have gone uncontested as a proper exercise of the president's constitutional authority to "receive Ambassadors." Treaties gradually gave way to executive agreements as the main form of contract between the United States and other countries.

When criticized for their assertiveness in foreign policy, presidents invariably invoked the institutional nature of their office, especially its unitary character and election by the entire country. In his book *The Decline and Resurgence of Congress,* James Sundquist summarized the standard (and politically persuasive) response of presidents to their critics: "Quick decision was imperative; . . . the move had to be made, or negotiations conducted, in secret, and only the executive could maintain confidentiality; . . . only the president has the essential information; . . . effective intercourse with other nations requires the United States to speak with a single voice, which can only be the president's."

Arguments such as these became especially compelling in the post–World War II era. As in previous wars, vast temporary powers had been granted to the president during the Second World War. What made this war different was its aftermath. Instead of lapsing into relative isolation from world political affairs, the United States entered into a Cold War with the Soviet Union. New technologies of warfare, especially nuclear weapons and intercontinental delivery systems, raised the specter of instant and global destruction.

These developments made the president's number and selection-based constitutional strengths appear even more significant than during past wars. Increased reliance not only on executive agreements but also on secrecy in all diplomacy made the conduct of postwar foreign policy a shared power with Congress in only the most nominal sense. The Republican Eightieth Congress (1947–1949) was angrily partisan on domestic issues, but it readily assented to Democratic president Harry S. Truman's far-reaching foreign policy initiatives, including the Marshall Plan and the North Atlantic Treaty Organization (NATO). Congress supported the American intervention in the Korean War, which it was never asked to declare, with annual military appropriations. It provided similar support for the war in Vietnam during the 1960s and early 1970s. In the years between these two wars, Congress wrote virtual blank checks in advance support of whatever actions the administrations of

Dwight D. Eisenhower and John F. Kennedy might decide to take in the Middle East, Berlin, Cuba, and elsewhere.

Much was made in the post-Vietnam era of Congress's newfound assertiveness in foreign policy. In 1973, for example, Congress enacted the War Powers Resolution over President Richard Nixon's veto. The resolution requires the president to consult with Congress "in every possible instance" before sending American forces into hostile or dangerous situations. After committing the armed forces, the president is then charged to remove them within sixty (or, by special presidential request, ninety) days unless Congress votes to authorize their continued involvement.

Every president since the War Powers Resolution was enacted has questioned its constitutionality. A number of military operations have been undertaken—by Presidents Gerald Ford (the *Mayaguez* rescue), Jimmy Carter (the attempted Iranian hostage rescue), Ronald Reagan (the Grenada invasion), George H. W. Bush (the Panama invasion and the Persian Gulf War), Bill Clinton (the stationing of peacekeeping troops in Somalia, Haiti, and Bosnia), and George W. Bush (the war on terrorism). In few instances have these presidents complied with the letter, much less the spirit, of the War Powers Resolution. Yet Congress has seldom voted to start the sixty-day clock, and never when it mattered. The main lesson of three decades of experience under the resolution is that law cannot substitute for political will if Congress is to curb the president's role in war making.

Congress's weakness in foreign-policy making can be partially explained by its institutional character: large, diverse, unwieldy, and slow. As Sundquist observed, Congress can "disrupt the policy that the president pursues, but it cannot act affirmatively to carry out a comprehensive substitute policy of its own." Congress also is constrained by the public's expectations of its members. Voters want their representatives and senators to concern themselves more with local than national interests, which leaves out most foreign policies. Not surprisingly, Congress is most assertive on those few global issues that have a clear domestic policy coloration, such as trade policy and support for nations, especially Israel, that have large and well-organized domestic lobbies.

As for the Supreme Court, on the whole it has defended presidents' expansive interpretations of their constitutional powers in foreign policy. In its most important case, *United States v. Curtiss-Wright Export Corp.* (1936), the Court echoed Pacificus in declaring that "the President is the sole organ of the federal government in the field of international relations." The president, the Court continued, "not Congress, has the better opportunity of knowing the conditions which prevail in foreign countries, and especially is this true in time of war." The Court's strong defense of presidential power in foreign affairs was all the more remarkable because at the time of the decision, the justices were reining in the president's powers in domestic policy.

One other aspect of the presidential office merits special attention. In making the presidency a unitary office elected by its own national constituency, the framers of the Constitution unwittingly combined the normally separate executive leadership roles of chief of government and chief of state into one office. As chief of government, the president is called on to act as a partisan political leader in the manner of, for example, the British prime minister. As chief of state, the president is the equivalent of the British monarch—the ceremonial leader of the nation and the living symbol of national unity.

The significance of the chief of state role has little to do with the insignificant formal powers that accompany it or the activities it requires. Rather it lies in the emotions the role arouses in citizens. Long before they have any knowledge of what the president does, young children already have positive feelings about the president's seemingly boundless power and benevolence. The death of a president causes adults to react in an equally emotional way. Surveys taken shortly after the Kennedy assassination found Americans displaying symptoms of grief that otherwise appear only at the death of a close friend or family member. Similar outpourings seem to have accompanied the deaths in office, whether by assassination or natural causes, of all presidents, whether they were young or old, popular or unpopular. In Great Britain, it is royal deaths, such as King George V's in 1936 and Princess Diana's in 1997, that occasion such deep emotions. It is the monarch whom children think of as powerful and good, not the prime minister.

The public's attachment to the president as chief of state sometimes has strong implications for the president's powers as chief of government, especially in foreign policy. In particular, the often-observed "rally 'round the flag effect" is a way in which the president benefits politically from being the nation's living symbol of unity. A rally effect is the sudden and substantial increase in public approval of the president that occurs in response to dramatic international events involving the United States. These include sudden military interventions, major diplomatic actions, and attacks on the United States. Richard Nixon's public approval rating rose twelve percentage points after his October 1969 "Vietnamization" speech. Gerald Ford's jumped eleven points after he dispatched troops to rescue the *Mayaguez*. Carter added twelve points to his approval rating as a result of the Camp David summit that achieved peace between Israel and Egypt. Reagan's approval rating leaped eight points when he invaded Grenada. George H. W. Bush's rating soared higher than any previous president's after the American victory against Iraq in the Gulf War. His record was broken by his son, George W. Bush, after he launched the war on terrorism in September 2001. The younger Bush's approval rating rose from 51 percent to 90 percent and remained above 75 percent for nearly a year, strengthening his hand as he directed the course of American policy toward Afghanistan and Iraq.

PERSON

Because the presidency is important, so is the person who is president. What kinds of experience do presidents typically bring with them into office? What manner of personality? What skills of leadership?

Concerning experience, presidents almost always have been drawn from the ranks of high governmental officials: vice presidents, members of Congress, governors, cabinet members, or generals. Yet in more recent elections, the roster of presidential candidates has largely been confined to governors and vice presidents.

The disappearance of cabinet members, generals, and members of Congress from the presidential talent pool has reduced the likelihood that the president will be experienced in foreign policy before taking office. Early in the nation's history, service as secretary of state was the main stepping stone to the presidency. Four of the first six presidents—Thomas Jefferson, James Madison, James Monroe, and John Quincy Adams—had previously served as secretary of state. Generals in successful wars, such as Andrew Jackson (War of 1812), Zachary Taylor (Mexican-American War), Ulysses S. Grant (Civil War), and Dwight D. Eisenhower (World War II) sometimes have been elected president, but not in the modern era of warfare. In the four elections from 1960 to 1972, every major party nominee was a senator or a former senator. But in the anti-Washington political climate that has dominated presidential elections since the Vietnam War and Watergate scandal, not a single senator has been elected president.

Instead of secretaries of state, generals, and senators, state governors have dominated the ranks of the presidency in recent years. Of the five presidents elected since the mid-1970s, four were governors: Jimmy Carter of Georgia in 1976, Ronald Reagan of California in 1980 and 1984, Bill Clinton of Arkansas in 1992 and 1996, and George W. Bush of Texas in 2000. (The only exception was Vice President George H. W. Bush in 1988.) Although international concerns came to dominate the administrations of all four of these presidents, nearly everything they knew about foreign policy came from election-year cramming and on-the-job experience.

The personality, or psychological character, that a president brings to the White House is, considering the power of the office and the pressures that weigh upon its occupant, of obvious importance. In 1972, James David Barber drew scholarly attention to this concern. In his book *The Presidential Character,* Barber offered a theory that places each president into one of four character types. The most dangerous of these is the "active negative," the president who is attracted to politics by a lack of self-esteem that can only be compensated for psychologically by dominating others through the wielding of official power. When active-negative presidents feel that their hold on power is threatened, they react in rigidly defensive ways, persisting in ineffective and destructive courses of action and treating critics as enemies. In Barber's view, Wilson's failure to compromise with Senate critics on the League of Nations treaty and Johnson's unwillingness to change course in Vietnam were the products of active-negative psychological characters.

Critics have taken Barber to task for a number of fundamental weaknesses in his theory. At root, the psychological study of personality is still too murky a field to explain, much less to predict, the presidential character. But public concern remains high. For example, in 2000 doubts about character went a long way toward explaining the outcome of the presidential election. Democratic candidate Al Gore carried a reputation into the campaign as an aggressive, experienced, and skillful debater, a reputation that his Republican opponent, George W. Bush, lacked. Yet Bush ended up benefiting considerably more from their three nationally televised debates than Gore did. In the first debate, Gore treated his opponent with disdain, often speaking condescendingly when it was his turn and sighing and grimacing while Bush spoke. Chastened by the adverse public response, Gore was deferential, almost obsequious during the second debate. He hit his stride in the third debate, but the inconsistency of his behavior from one debate to the next fed voters' doubts about who Gore really was. Bush was not strongly impressive in any of the debates, but voters saw the same person in all three of them. Gore, who had entered the debate season leading Bush by around five percentage points in the polls, left it trailing by five points.

The skills of leadership that a president requires may be more confidently described than the presidential character. In relations with the rest of the executive branch, the president is called upon to be an adroit *manager of authority,* both of lieutenants on the White House staff (whose chronic sycophancy toward the president and hostility toward the president's critics perennially threaten to overwhelm the good effects of their loyalty, talent, and hard work) and of the massive departments and agencies of the bureaucracy, whose activities lie at the heart of the president's role as chief executive. For example, George W. Bush went a long way toward reassuring foreign policy experts who doubted his understanding of international issues by appointing experienced Washington hands to important executive positions, especially Richard Cheney as vice president, Colin Powell as secretary of state, and Donald Rumsfeld as secretary of defense.

Presidential leadership of Congress requires different, more *tactical political skills.* Senators and representatives, no less than the president, are politically independent and self-interested. No one has described the challenge of leading them more pithily and precisely than Neustadt in his book *Presidential Power.* To lead, Neustadt argued, is to persuade; to persuade is to bargain; and to bargain is to convince members of Congress that their interests and the president's are (or can be made to be) the same.

Ultimately, a president's standing with Congress and the bureaucracy rests on the bedrock of public opinion, which makes the *presentation of self* (a phrase invented by the sociologist Erving Goffman) to the American people an important category of leadership skills. Presentation of self involves not just speech making, press conferences, and other forms of rhetoric but dramaturgy as well. During Richard Nixon's first term, for example, he reinforced a televised speech appealing for the support of the "silent majority" of blue-collar workers and their families by dramatically donning a hard hat before a cheering crowd (and a battery of cameras) at a New York City construction site. Bill Clinton, concerned that neither the military nor the American people regarded him as a confident commander in chief, learned from studying videotapes of Ronald Reagan how to transform limp, offhand salutes on ceremonial occasions into shoulders-back posture and crisp salutes. George W. Bush used rhetoric and dramaturgy to reassure a worried nation two days after the September 11 attacks. Standing in the midst of New York's Ground Zero with his arm around a rescue worker, Bush answered listeners who said they could not hear him by declaring, "I can hear *you.* The rest of the world hears you. And the people who knocked these buildings down will hear all of us soon."

Perhaps a president's most important leadership skill involves a *strategic sense* of the historical possibilities of the time. These possibilities are defined both by objective conditions (the international situation, the budget, the health of the economy, and so on) and by the public mood. Above all, the president must have a highly developed aptitude for what Woodrow Wilson called "interpretation"—that is, the ability to understand and articulate the varying, vaguely expressed desires of the American people for change or quiescence, material prosperity or moral challenge, isolation from or intervention in the problems of the world, and so on.

In the end, the background, personality, and leadership skills of the president are important because of the ways in which the Constitution and changing historical circumstances have made the presidency important. Person and office, although defined and often discussed separately, are in essence one.

10

Presidential Wars

Louis Fisher

From 1789 to 1950, all major military initiatives by the United States were decided by Congress, either by a formal declaration of war or by a statute authorizing the president to use military force. There were some notable exceptions, such as the actions by President James Polk that led to hostilities between the United States and Mexico. Presidents also used military force for various "life and property" actions, but they were typically limited, short-term engagements. By and large, the first century and a half followed the framers' expectations that matters of war and peace would be vested in the government's representative branch—Congress.

The record since 1950 has been dramatically different. Presidents over the past half century have felt increasingly comfortable in acting unilaterally when using military force against other countries. Instead of coming to Congress for authority, they justify military actions either on the commander in chief clause in the Constitution or on decisions reached by the UN Security Council and NATO. Even with these departures, however, only two major U.S. wars have been entered into without a congressional declaration or authorization of war—Korea in 1950 and Yugoslavia in 1999.

CONSTITUTIONAL PRINCIPLES

When the American Constitution was drafted in 1787, the framers were aware that existing models of government placed the war power and foreign affairs solely in the hands of the king. Thus, matters of treaties, appointment of ambassadors, the raising and regulation of fleets and armies, and the initiation of military actions against other countries had been vested in the king. Accordingly, John Locke and William Blackstone, whose writings deeply influenced the framers, assigned war powers and foreign affairs exclusively to the executive branch.

This monarchical model was expressly rejected at the Philadelphia convention. As revealed in the historical records of the Constitutional Convention,[1] Charles Pinckney said he was for "a vigorous Executive but was afraid the Executive powers of [the existing] Congress might extend to peace & war &c which would render the Executive a Monarchy, of the worst kind, to wit an elective one." Although John Rutledge wanted the executive power placed in a single person, "he was not for giving him the power of war and peace." James Wilson supported a single executive but "did not consider the Prerogative of the British Monarch as a proper guide in defining the Executive powers. Some of these prerogatives were of a Legislative nature. Among others that of war & peace &c." Edmund Randolph worried about executive power, calling it "the foetus of monarchy."

The framers recognized that the president would need unilateral power in one area: defensive actions to repel sudden attacks when Congress was not in session to legislate. The early draft of the Constitution empowered Congress to "make war." Charles Pinckney objected that legislative proceedings "were too slow" for the safety of the country in an emergency, since he expected Congress to meet but once a year. James Madison and Elbridge Gerry moved to insert "declare" for "make," leaving to the president "the power to repel sudden attacks."

Debate on the Madison-Gerry amendment underscored the limited grant of authority to the president. Pierce Butler wanted to give the president the power to make war, arguing that he "will have all the requisite qualities, and will not make war but when the Nation will support it." Roger Sherman objected: "The Executive shd. be able to repel and not to commence war." Gerry said he "never expected to hear in a republic a motion to empower the Executive alone to declare war." George Mason spoke "agst giving the power of war to the Executive, because not [safely] to be trusted with it; . . . He was for clogging rather than facilitating war."

Similar statements were made at the state ratifying conventions. In Pennsylvania, James Wilson expressed the prevailing sentiment that the system of checks and balances "will not hurry us into war; it is calculated to guard against it. It will not be in the power of a single man, or a single body of men, to involve us in such distress; for the important power of declaring war is vested in the legislature at large."[2] The framers also took great pains to separate the purse and the sword. They were familiar with the efforts of English kings to rely on extraparliamentary sources of revenue for military expeditions. After a series of monarchical transgressions, England lurched into a bloody civil war. The origin of democratic government is directly related to legislative control over the purse.

The U.S. Constitution states that "No Money shall be drawn from the Treasury, but in Consequences of Appropriations made by Law." In

Federalist No. 48, Madison explained that "the legislative department alone has access to the pockets of the people." The Constitution empowers Congress to lay and collect taxes, duties, imposts, and excises; to borrow money on the credit of the United States; and to coin money and regulate its value. The power of the purse, Madison said in *Federalist* No. 58, represents the "most compleat and effectual weapon with which any constitution can arm the immediate representatives of the people, for obtaining a redress of every grievance, and for carrying into effect every just and salutary measure."

In making the president the commander in chief, Congress retained for Congress the important check over spending. Madison set forth this tenet: "Those who are to *conduct a war* cannot in the nature of things, be proper or safe judges, whether *a war ought* to be *commenced, continued,* or *concluded.* They are barred from the latter functions by a great principle in free government, analogous to that which separates the sword from the purse, or the power of executing from the power of enacting laws." At the Philadelphia convention, George Mason counseled that the "purse & the sword ought never to get into the same hands (whether Legislative or Executive.)"

Throughout the next century and a half, major military actions were either declared by Congress (the War of 1812, the Mexican War of 1846, the Spanish-American War of 1898, World War I, and World War II) or authorized by Congress (the Quasi-War against France from 1798 to 1800 and the Barbary Wars during the administrations of Thomas Jefferson and James Madison). In either case, presidents came to Congress for authority to take part in offensive actions.

The record since 1950 has been fundamentally different. In that year President Harry Truman sent American troops to Korea, without ever coming to Congress for authority. He based his actions in part on resolutions adopted by the UN Security Council, but nothing in the history of the UN Charter implies that Congress ever contemplated placing in the hands of the president the unilateral power to wage war. Truman's initiative became a model for President George H. W. Bush in going to war against Iraq in 1991 and President Bill Clinton in threatening to invade Haiti in 1994. In addition, Clinton cited NATO as authority for air strikes in Bosnia and sending ground troops to that region. In 1999, he relied on NATO to wage war against Yugoslavia. But the legislative histories of the UN and NATO show no intent on the part of Congress to sanction independent presidential war power.

THE UNITED NATIONS AND NATO

In 1945, during Senate debate on the UN Charter, President Truman sent a cable from Potsdam stating that all agreements involving U.S. troop commitments to the United Nations would first have to be approved by both houses of Congress. He pledged without equivocation: "When any such agreement or agreements are negotiated it will be my purpose to ask the Congress for appropriate legislation to approve them."[3] By "agreements" he meant the procedures that would permit UN military force in dealing with threats to peace, breaches of the peace, and acts of aggression. All UN members would make available to the Security Council, "on its call and in accordance with a special agreement or agreements," armed forces and other assistance for the purpose of maintaining international peace and security.

The UN Charter provided that these agreements, concluded between the Security Council and member states, "shall be subject to ratification by the signatory states in accordance with their respective constitutional processes." Each nation would have to adopt its own procedures for meeting their international obligations.

After the Senate approved the UN Charter, Congress had to decide the meaning of "constitutional processes." What procedure was necessary, under the U.S. Constitution, to bring into effect the special agreements needed to contribute American troops to UN military actions? That issue was decided by the UN Participation Act of 1945, which stated without the slightest ambiguity that the agreements "shall be subject to the approval of the Congress by appropriate Act or joint resolution." The agreements between the United States and the Security Council would not result from unilateral executive action, nor would they be brought into force only by the Senate acting through the treaty process. Action by both houses of Congress would be required.

At every step in the legislative history of the UN Participation Act— hearings, committee reports, and floor debate—these elementary points were underscored and reinforced. Executive officials repeatedly assured members of Congress that the president could not commit troops to UN military actions unless Congress first approved.

During this time the Senate also approved the NATO treaty of 1949, which provides that an armed attack against one or more of the parties in Europe or North America "shall be considered an attack against them all." In the event of an attack, member states could exercise the right of individual or collective self-defense recognized by Article 51 of the UN Charter and assist the country or countries attacked by taking "such action as it deems necessary, including the use of armed force." However, Article 11 of the treaty states that it shall be ratified "and its provisions carried out by the Parties in accordance with their respective constitutional processes." The Southeast Asia Treaty (SEATO) of 1954 also stated that the treaty "shall be ratified and its provisions carried out by the Parties in accordance with their respective constitutional processes."

Do these treaties grant the president unilateral power to use military force against other nations? First, it is well recognized that the concept in mutual security treaties of an attack on one nation being an attack on all does not require from any nation an immediate response. Each country maintains the sovereign right to decide such matters by itself. As noted in the Rio Treaty of 1947, "no State shall be required to use armed force without its consent." In the U.S. system, who decides to use armed force?

During hearings in 1949 on NATO, Secretary of State Dean Acheson told the Senate Foreign Relations Committee that it "does not mean that the United States would automatically be at war if one of the other signatory nations were the victim of an armed attack. Under our Constitution, the Congress alone has the power to declare war." Of course he was merely saying what is expressly provided for in the Constitution. However, nothing in the legislative history of NATO gives the president any type of unilateral authority in the event of an attack. That the president lacks unilateral powers under the UN Charter or NATO should be obvious from the fact that both are international treaties entered into by way of a presidential proposal and Senate advice and consent. The president and the Senate cannot use the treaty process to strip the House of Representatives of its prerogatives over the use of military force.

In the words of one scholar, the provisions in the NATO treaty that it be carried out according to constitutional processes was "intended to ensure that the Executive Branch of the Government should come back to the Congress when decisions were required in which the Congress has a constitutional responsibility." The NATO treaty "does not transfer to the President the Congressional power to make war."[4] Those predictions would be eroded by practices during the Clinton administration.

TRUMAN IN KOREA

With these treaty and statutory safeguards supposedly in place to protect legislative prerogatives, President Truman nonetheless sent U.S. troops to Korea in 1950 without ever seeking or obtaining congressional authority. How could this happen? How could so many explicit executive assurances to Congress be ignored and circumvented?

On June 26, Truman announced that the UN Security Council had ordered North Korea to withdraw its invading forces to positions north of the thirty-eighth parallel and that "in accordance with the resolution of the Security Council, the United States will vigorously support the effort of the Council to terminate this serious breach of the peace." The next day he ordered U.S. air and sea forces to provide military support to South Korea. It was not until the evening of June 27 that the Security Council actually called for military action. In his memoirs, *Present at the Creation,* Dean Acheson admitted that "some American action, said to be in support of the resolution of June 27, was in fact ordered, and possibly taken, prior to the resolution."

Truman violated the statutory language and legislative history of the UN Participation Act, including his own assurance from Potsdam that he would first obtain the approval of Congress before sending U.S. forces to a UN action. How was this possible? He simply ignored the special agreements that were supposed to be the guarantee of congressional control. Indeed, no state has ever entered into a special agreement with the Security Council—and none is ever likely to do so.

Truman exploited the UN machinery in part because of a fluke: the Soviet Union had absented itself from the Security Council during two crucial votes taken during the early days of the crisis. It is difficult to argue that the president's constitutional powers vary with the presence or absence of Soviet (or other) delegates to the Security Council. As Robert Bork noted in 1971, "the approval of the United Nations was obtained only because the Soviet Union happened to be boycotting the Security Council at the time, and the president's Constitutional powers can hardly be said to ebb and flow with the veto of the Soviet Union in the Security Council."[5]

Truman tried to justify his actions in Korea by calling it a UN "police action" rather than an American war. That argument was suspect from the start and deteriorated as U.S. casualties mounted. The UN exercised no real authority over the conduct of the war. Other than token support from a few nations, it remained an American war—measured by troops, money, casualties, and deaths—from start to finish. The euphemism "police action" was never persuasive. As a federal court concluded in 1953, "We doubt very much if there is any question in the minds of the majority of the people of this country that the conflict now raging in Korea can be anything but war."[6]

BUSH IN IRAQ (1990–1991)

Truman's initiative in Korea became a precedent for actions taken in 1990 by President George H. W. Bush. In response to Iraq's invasion of Kuwait on August 2, Bush sent several hundred thousand troops to Saudi Arabia for defensive purposes. Over the next few months, the size of the American force climbed to 500,000, giving Bush the capability for mounting an offensive strike.

Instead of seeking authority from Congress, Bush created a multinational alliance and encouraged the UN Security Council to authorize the use of military force. The strategic calculations have been recorded by James A. Baker III, who served as secretary of state in the Bush administration. In his book *The Politics of Diplomacy,* Baker says he realized that military initiatives by Presidents Reagan in Grenada and Bush in Panama had reinforced in the international community the impression that American foreign policy followed a "cowboy mentality." In response to those concerns, Bush wanted to assemble an international political coalition. Baker notes: "From the very beginning, the president recognized the importance of having the express approval of the international community if at all possible." It is noteworthy that Bush would seek the express approval of other nations but not the express approval of Congress.

On November 20, Bush said he wanted to delay asking Congress for authorization until after the Security Council considered a proposed resolution supporting the use of force against Iraq. About a week later, on November 29, the Security Council authorized member states to use "all necessary means" to force Iraqi troops out of Kuwait. "All necessary means" is code language for military action. To avoid war, Iraq had to withdraw from Kuwait by January 15, 1991. Although the Security Council "authorized" each member state to act militarily against Iraq, the resolution did not compel nor obligate them to participate. Instead, member states were free to use (or refuse) force pursuant to their own constitutional systems and judgments about national interests.

What procedure would the United States follow in deciding to use force? When Secretary of Defense Dick Cheney appeared before the Senate Armed Services Committee on December 3, 1990, he said that President Bush did not require "any additional authorization from the Congress" before attacking Iraq. Through such language he implied that authorization from the UN was sufficient. The UN action, he said, made congressional action not only unnecessary but counterproductive:

> As a general proposition, I can think that the notion of a declaration of war to some extent flies in the face of what we are trying to accomplish here. And what we are trying to accomplish is to marshal an international force, some 26, 27 nations having committed forces to the enterprise, working under the auspices of the United Nations Security Council.

In other words, once presidents assembled an international force and obtained support through a Security Council resolution, Congress had no role except perhaps to pass a resolution indicating its support. According to this position, whether Congress acted or not had no bearing on the president's freedom to move ahead with the multinational force.

The Justice Department argued in court that President Bush could order offensive actions against Iraq without seeking advance authority from Congress. On December 13, 1990, in *Dellums v. Bush,* the court expressly and forcefully rejected the sweeping interpretation of presidential war power advanced by the Justice Department. If the president had the sole power to determine that any offensive military operation, "no matter how vast, does not constitute war-making but only an offensive military attack, the congressional power to declare war will be at the mercy of a semantic decision by the Executive." But, having dismissed the Justice Department's interpretation, the court then held that the case was not ripe for adjudication.

On January 8, 1991, President Bush asked Congress to pass legislation supporting the UN position. Clearly he was asking for "support," not authority. The next day reporters asked whether he needed authority from Congress. His reply: "I don't think I need it. . . . I feel that I have the authority to fully implement the United Nations resolutions." The legal crisis was avoided on January 12 when Congress authorized offensive actions against Iraq. In signing the bill, Bush indicated that he could have acted without legislation: "As I made clear to congressional leaders at the outset, my request for congressional support did not, and my signing this resolution does not, constitute any change in the longstanding positions of the executive branch on either the president's constitutional authority to use the Armed Forces to defend vital U.S. interests or the constitutionality of the War Powers Resolution." Despite his comments, the bill expressly authorized the action against Iraq. A signed statement does not alter the contents of a public law.

In one of his last addresses as president, Bush used a speech at West Point to explain his theory of presidential war power. Referring to President Washington's warning of the dangers of "entangling alliances," and saying that Washington was correct at that point in history, Bush noted that what was "entangling" in Washington's day "is now essential." Congress had a constitutional role in these involvements, but apparently more to offer support rather than to grant authority. Presidential leadership "involves working with the Congress and the American people to provide the essential domestic underpinning if U.S. military commitments are to be sustainable." "Authority" seems to come only from international organizations. In both Iraq and Somalia, Bush said, U.S. forces were "acting under the full authority of the United Nations."

CLINTON IN HAITI

During the 1992 presidential campaign, Bill Clinton projected himself as a strong leader in foreign affairs and indicated a willingness to resort to military action. Criticizing Bush's foreign policy, he said he would be willing to use military force—in concert with other nations—to bring humanitarian aid to the citizens of Bosnia and Herzegovina. While saying he did not relish the prospect of sending Americans into combat, "neither do I flinch from it."[7] He accused the Bush administration of "turning its back" on "those struggling for democracy in China and on those fleeing Haiti."

Once in office, Clinton's position on what to do about the military regime in Haiti fluctuated from month to month, depending on shifting political pressures. Jean-Bertrand Aristide, the island's first democratically elected president, had been overthrown in a military coup on September 30, 1991.

Political repression by the military rulers produced a flood of refugees trying to reach the United States. President Bush maintained that the Haitians were fleeing because of economic conditions, not political persecution, and refused to qualify them for asylum. Refugees were returned to Haiti. Although Clinton had criticized this policy during the 1992 campaign, he reversed course the next year and accepted the policy of the Bush administration.

As the flood of refugees continued, pressure mounted on Clinton to intervene militarily. In October 1993 he sent a contingent of six hundred U.S. soldiers to Haiti to work on roads, bridges, and water supplies. A group of armed civilians, opposed to U.S. intervention, prevented them from landing. Lightly armed, the U.S. troops were instructed by their commanders not to use force but to leave the area. The retreat in the face of tiny Haiti was widely interpreted as a humiliation of the United States.

Clinton soon began threatening to use military force. By late July 1994, rumors began to circulate about an imminent Security Council resolution that would authorize the invasion of Haiti. Dante Caputo, the United Nations envoy to Haiti, wrote a "confidential" memo to UN Secretary General Boutros Boutros-Ghali describing the political calculations within the Clinton White House. This memo, which found its way into the *Congressional Record,* states that Clinton's advisers believed that an invasion of Haiti would be politically desirable because it would highlight for the American public "the president's decision making capability and the firmness of leadership in international political matters."[8]

On July 31 the UN Security Council adopted a resolution "inviting" all states, particularly those in the region of Haiti, to use "all necessary means" to remove the military leadership in that island. At a news conference on August 3, Clinton denied that he needed authority from Congress to invade Haiti: "Like my predecessors of both parties, I have not agreed that I was constitutionally mandated to obtain the support of Congress." In a nationwide television address on September 15, Clinton told the American people that he was prepared to use military force to invade Haiti, referring to the Security Council resolution and expressing his willingness to lead a multilateral force "to carry out the will of the United Nations." No mention at all of the will of Congress.

The public and a substantial majority of legislators assailed the planned invasion. Criticized in the past for currying public favor and failing to lead, Clinton now seemed to glory in the idea of acting against the grain. He was determined to proceed with the invasion: "But regardless [of this opposition], this is what I believe is the right thing to do. I realize it is unpopular. I know it is unpopular. I know the timing is unpopular. I know the whole thing is unpopular. But I believe it is the right thing." Apparently there was no consideration of doing the legal thing, the authorized thing, or the constitutional thing.

Clinton emphasized the need to keep commitments: "I'd like to mention just one other thing that is equally important, and that is the reliability of the United States and the United Nations once we say we're going to do something." But who is the "we"? It was not Congress or the American public. It was a commitment made unilaterally by the executive branch acting in concert with the United Nations.

An invasion of Haiti proved unnecessary. Clinton sent former President Jimmy Carter to negotiate with the military leaders in Haiti. They agreed to step down to permit the return of Aristide. Initially, nearly twenty thousand U.S. troops were dispatched to occupy Haiti and provide stability. Both houses passed legislation stating that "the president should have sought and welcomed Congressional approval before deploying United States Forces to Haiti."

INTERVENTION IN BOSNIA

In concert with the United Nations and NATO, the Bush and Clinton administrations participated in humanitarian airlifts in Sarajevo and helped enforce a "no-fly zone" (a ban on unauthorized flights over Bosnia-Herzegovina). In 1993 Clinton indicated that he would have to seek support and authorization from Congress before ordering air strikes. On May 7 he stated: "If I decide to ask the American people and the United States Congress to support an approach that would include the use of air power, I would have a very specific, clearly defined strategy." He anticipated asking "for the authority to use air power from the Congress and the American people."

Later in the year he began to object to legislative efforts to restrict his military options. Instead of seeking authority from Congress, Clinton now said he would seek from Congress advice and support. He was "fundamentally opposed" to any statutory provisions that "improperly limit my ability to perform my constitutional duties as Commander-in-Chief." He would operate through NATO, even though NATO had never used military force during its almost half-century of existence.

In 1994, Clinton announced that decisions to use air power would be taken in response to UN Security Council resolutions, operating through NATO's military command. There was no more talk about seeking authority from Congress. Curiously, by operating through NATO, Clinton would seek the agreement of England, France, Italy, and other NATO allies, but not Congress. NATO air strikes began in February 1994 and were followed by additional strikes throughout the year and into the next. The authorizing body was a multinational organization, not Congress.

The next escalation of U.S. military action was Clinton's decision to introduce ground troops into Bosnia. When reporters asked him on October 19,

1995, if he would send the troops even if Congress did not approve, he replied: "I am not going to lay down any of my constitutional prerogatives here today." On the basis of what he considered sufficient authority under Article II of the Constitution and under NATO, he ordered the deployment of twenty thousand American ground troops to Bosnia without obtaining authority or support from Congress. In an address on November 27, 1995, he said that deployment of U.S. ground troops to Bosnia was "the right thing to do," paralleling his justification for invading Haiti. It was the right thing, even if not the legal thing.

On December 21, Clinton expected that the military mission to Bosnia "can be accomplished in about a year." A year later, on December 17, 1996, he extended the troop deployment for another eighteen months. At the end of 1997 he announced that the deployment would have to be extended again, but this time without attempting to fix a deadline. In 2003, U.S. troops were still in Bosnia.

THE WAR IN YUGOSLAVIA

In October 1998, the Clinton administration was again threatening the Serbs with air strikes, this time because of Serb attacks on the ethnic Albania majority in Kosovo. At a news conference on October 8, Clinton stated: "Yesterday I decided that the United States would vote to give NATO the authority to carry out military strikes against Serbia if President Milosevic continues to defy the international community." An interesting sentence—"*I* decided that the United States . . ." Whatever Clinton decided would be America's policy.

Clinton's chief foreign policy advisers went to Capitol Hill to consult with lawmakers, but not to obtain their approval. Although Congress was to be given no formal role in the use of force against Serbs, legislatures in other NATO countries took votes to authorize military action in Yugoslavia. The Italian Parliament had to vote approval for the NATO strikes, and the German Supreme Court ruled that the Bundestag, which had been dissolved with the election that ousted Chancellor Kohl, had to be recalled to approve deployment of German aircraft and troops to Kosovo.

With air strikes imminent in March 1999, the Senate voted fifty-eight to forty-one in support of military air operations and missile strikes against Serbia. On April 28, after the first month of bombing, the House took a series of votes on war in Yugoslavia. A vote to authorize the air operations and missiles strikes lost on a tie vote, 213 to 213. Several resolutions were offered in the Senate, to either authorize or restrict the war, but they were tabled. The Senate chose procedural remedies rather than voting on the merits.

During the bombing of Serbia and Kosovo, Representative Tom Campbell (R-Cal.) went to court with twenty-five other House colleagues to seek a declaration that President Clinton had violated the Constitution and the War Powers Resolution by conducting the air offensive without congressional authorization. A district judge held that Campbell did not have standing to raise his claims. Although each House had taken a number of votes, Congress had never as an entire institution ordered Clinton to cease military operations. In that sense, there was no "constitutional impasse" or "actual confrontation" for the court to resolve.[9]

THE IRAQ RESOLUTION IN 2002

When the Bush administration first began talking about war against Iraq in 2002, the White House cautioned that President George W. Bush was carefully studying a number of options. On August 21, stating that "we will look at all options," he said the country was too preoccupied with military action against Iraq. Yet five days later Vice President Dick Cheney delivered a forceful speech that implied that only one option existed: going to war. He warned that Saddam Hussein would "fairly soon" have nuclear weapons and that it would be useless to seek a Security Council resolution requiring Iraq to submit to weapons inspectors. Newspaper editorials concluded that Cheney's speech left little room for measures short of destroying Hussein's regime through preemptive military action. What happened to the options carefully being weighed by Bush?

The meaning of "regime change" shifted with time. On April 4, 2002, Bush said that he had made up his mind "that Saddam needs to go.... The policy of my Government is that he goes." Yet when Bush addressed the United Nations on September 12, he laid down five conditions (including inspections) that could lead to a peaceful settlement. If Hussein complied with those demands, he could stay in power.

What had happened to the policy of regime change?

After the September 12 speech, Iraq agreed four days later to unconditional inspections. At that point, the administration began to belittle the importance of inspections. If they were of little use, why have Bush go to the UN and place that demand on Iraq and the Security Council?

Initially, the White House concluded that Bush did not need authority from Congress. However, for one reason or another, Bush decided in early September to seek authorization from Congress. There was pressure on lawmakers to complete action on the authorizing resolution before they adjourned for the elections, inviting partisan exploitation of the war issue. Several Republican nominees in congressional contests made a political weapon out of Iraq, comparing their "strong stand" on Iraq to "weak" positions by Democratic campaigners.

The administration released various accounts to demonstrate why Iraq was an imminent threat. On September 7, Bush cited a report by the International Atomic Energy Agency (IAEA) that the Iraqis were "six months away from developing a weapon. I don't know what more evidence we need." However, the report did not exist. The administration promoted a story about Mohamed Atta, the 9/11 leader, meeting with an Iraqi intelligence officer in Prague in April 2001. Yet Czech president Vaclav Havel was convinced that there was no evidence that the meeting ever took place.

The administration tried to make a link between Iraq and Al Qaeda, but the reports could never be substantiated. There was some evidence of Al Qaeda in the northern part of Iraq, but that is Kurdish territory made semi-autonomous because of American and British fighter planes that police the no-fly zones. Besides, members of Al Qaeda are present in some sixty countries. Presence alone in not a basis for using military force.

There was little doubt that Bush would gain House support. The question was whether the vote would divide along party lines. The partisan issue blurred when House Minority Leader Dick Gephardt (D-Mo.) broke ranks with many in his party and announced support for a slightly redrafted resolution. He said: "We had to go through this, putting politics aside, so we have a chance to get a consensus that will lead the country in the right direction." Of course, politics could not be put aside. The vote on the resolution was inescapably and legitimately a political decision. Lawmakers would be voting on whether to commit as much as $100 billion or $200 billion to the war, stretching over a period of years. Their actions would stabilize or destabilize the Middle East, strengthen or weaken the war against terrorism, enhance or debase the nation's prestige.

Why were Democrats so worried about being labeled "antiwar"? There was no evidence that the public, in any broad sense, supported war against Iraq. A *New York Times* poll published on October 7 indicated that 69 percent of Americans believed that Bush should be paying more attention to the economy. On the question "Should the U.S. take military action against Iraq fairly soon or wait and give the U.N. more time to get weapons inspectors into Iraq?," 63 percent wanted to wait. A *Washington Post* story on October 8 noted that the public's enthusiasm for war against Iraq "is tepid and declining."

On October 10, the House passed the Iraq resolution, 296-133. That evening, the Senate voted seventy-seven to twenty-three for the resolution. It would have been better for Congress as an institution, and for the country as a whole, to have Bush request the Security Council to authorize inspections in Iraq, and then to come to Congress after the elections (as was done in

1990–1991). Congress would have been in the position at that point to make an informed choice. It chose, instead, to vote under partisan pressures, with inadequate information, and thereby abdicated its constitutional duties to the president. In passing the resolution, lawmakers decided only that President Bush should decide. After the Security Council voted on November 8 that Iraq must allow inspectors into the country, the judgment on whether war would be necessary was in the hands of Bush, not Congress.

A FAILURE OF CHECKS AND BALANCES

The framers of the Constitution assumed that each branch of the government would protect its own prerogatives. Efforts by one branch to encroach upon another would be beaten back. As Madison explained in *Federalist* No. 51: "the great security against a gradual concentration of the several powers in the same department, consists in giving to those who administer each department the necessary constitutional means and personal motives to resist encroachments of the others. . . . Ambition must be made to counter ambition." To some extent, this theory has worked well. The president and the judiciary invoke a multitude of powers to protect their institutions.

Congress, on the other hand, not only fails to fight back but even volunteers in surrendering fundamental legislative powers, including the war power and the power of the purse. Members of Congress seem uncertain about the scope of their constitutional powers. Some claim that Congress can limit funds for presidential actions that were taken in the past but never for future actions. There is no constitutional support for that position. The decision to use military force against other nations is reserved to Congress, other than for defensive actions. Members may restrict a president's actions prospectively as well as retrospectively.

Some legislators suggest that a cutoff of funds would leave American soldiers stranded and without ammunition. During debate in 1995 on prohibiting funds from being used for the deployment of ground forces to Bosnia and Herzegovina, Congressman Porter Goss said: "I cannot support a complete withdrawal of funds and support for the United States troops who are already on the ground in the former Yugoslavia. These men and women are wearing the uniform of the U.S. military and obeying orders, and we cannot leave them stranded in hostile territory." Congressman George Gekas added: "I cannot vote under any circumstances to abandon our troops. Not to fund them? Unheard of. I cannot support that. Not to supply them with foods, material, ammunition, all the weapons that they require to do their mission?"[10] Cutting off funds would not have that effect. A funding prohibition would force the withdrawal of whatever troops were in place and prevent the deployment of any other troops to that region.

Theories of presidential war power that would have been shocking fifty years ago are now offered as though they were obvious and free of controversy. Instead of the two branches working in concert to create a program that has broad public support and understanding, with some hope of continuity, presidents take unilateral steps to engage the country in military operations abroad. They typically justify their actions not only on broad interpretations of the Constitution but cite "authority" granted by multinational institutions in which the United States is but one of many state actors. This pattern does not merely weaken Congress and the power of the purse. It undermines public control, the system of checks and balances, and constitutional government.

NOTES

1. See Max Farrand, ed., *The Records of the Federal Convention of 1787* (New Haven, Conn.: Yale University Press, 1937), especially vol. 1, 64–66, and vol. 2, 318–19.

2. Jonathan Eliot, ed. *The Debates in the Several State Conventions, on the Adoption of the Federal Constitution* (Washington, D.C.: 1836–1845), vol. 2, 528.

3. 91 *Cong. Rec.* 8185 (1945).

4. Richard H. Heindel et al., "The North Atlantic Treaty in the United States Senate," *American Journal of International Law* 43: 649, 650 (1949).

5. Robert H. Bork, "Comments on the Articles on the Legality of the United States Action in Cambodia," *American Journal of International Law* 65: 81 (1971).

6. *Weissman v. Metropolitan Life Ins. Co.,* 112 *F. Supp.* 420, 425 (S.D. Cal. 1953).

7. *New York Times,* June 28, 1992, 16; *New York Times,* August 14, 1992, A15.

8. Louis Fisher, *Presidential War Power* (Lawrence: University Press of Kansas, 1995), 156.

9. *Campbell v. Clinton,* 52 F.Supp.2d 34 (D.D.C. 1999), aff'd, *Campbell v. Clinton,* 203 F.3d 19 (D.C. 2000).

10. 141 *Cong. Rec.* H14820, H14822 (daily ed. December 13, 1995).

11

How National Security Advisers
See Their Role

Ivo H. Daalder and I. M. Destler

Over the past few decades, the "Assistant to the President for National Security Affairs" (as the national security adviser is formally known) has emerged as the most important foreign policy aide to the president. Whether the job is performed largely outside of public view (as by Brent Scowcroft in 1975–1977 and 1989–1993) or in a more publicly prominent manner (as was true for Henry Kissinger in 1969–1975, Zbigniew Brzezinski in 1977–1981, and Samuel Berger in 1997–2001), almost every national security adviser since McGeorge Bundy (1961–1966) ultimately emerged as a principal player in the foreign policy arena.

Yet despite the enormous power they have wielded, there has been insufficient attention to the role these advisers play in the formulation and implementation of foreign policy. Unlike the jobs of their cabinet counterparts, their position is neither rooted in law nor accountable to Congress. As the White House point person on foreign policy, the national security adviser serves at the pleasure of the president. Moreover, while the adviser heads a small (albeit growing) staff, his/her managerial duties are small compared to the huge departmental responsibilities of the secretaries of state, defense, treasury, and other principal foreign-policy makers. And though some advisers have not shunned the limelight, their public responsibilities are far more limited than those of, say, the secretary of state, who is the president's principal foreign policy spokesperson at home and abroad.

Nonetheless, the national security adviser and the NSC staff have become central foreign policy players. Indeed, over the years the NSC staff has expanded from a small group of less than fifteen policy people in the early 1960s to what is today a fully ensconced, agency-like organization of two hundred people, including about seventy-five substantive professionals. This organization has its own perspective on the myriad of national security issues confronting the government. It has become less like a staff and more like an operating agency. With its own press, legislative, communication, and speechmaking offices, the NSC conducts ongoing relations with the media, Congress, the American public, and foreign governments.

The reasons for this expansion are many. The foundation, of course, has been presidents' need for close-in foreign policy support, and advisers' success in meeting this need. Beyond this, three developments stand out. First, as can be expected of any organization that has operated for decades, the NSC has become institutionalized and even bureaucratized. The White House Situation Room, established under Kennedy, has become the focal point for crisis management. The NSC communications system, also inaugurated under Kennedy, has grown in sophistication with the advance of technology. It allows staff to monitor the overseas messages sent to and from the State Department, to have access to major intelligence material, and to communicate directly and secretly with foreign governments. Over time, these capacities, together with continuing presidential need, have built the NSC into a strong, entrenched, and legitimate presidential institution.

Second, the kinds of foreign policy issues that need to be addressed have both expanded in number and become more complex in nature. Since the end of the Cold War, national security issues have involved more dimensions, each of which has proponents somewhere in the executive branch. The traditional and long-recognized dividing lines—between foreign and domestic policy, and between the high-politics issues of war and peace and the low-politics issues of social and economic advancement—have blurred. As a result, the number and types of players concerned with each issue have grown as well—placing a premium on effective organization and integration of different interests. Of all the players in the executive branch, only the White House has the recognized power necessary to manage these disparate interests effectively. Within the White House, only the NSC has the demonstrated capacity to do so.

Third, U.S. politics no longer ends at the water's edge; it continues right on into the mainstream of foreign affairs. Aside from extraordinary events like the war against Al Qaeda in response to September 11, few issues are easily separated from domestic political turmoil—not military intervention, not diplomatic relations, and certainly not trade or economic interactions with the outside world. The necessity to provide political oversight of executive action—to ensure not only that policy is executed in the best manner possible but that the political consequences of doing so have been considered—naturally falls to the White House, and to the NSC acting as its surrogate.

Yet while the national security adviser and the NSC staff have grown in importance, their specific roles and significance remain unclear not only to the American public but even to many of the most avid followers of foreign policy in Congress, the media, and academia. To help elucidate the role of the national security adviser, two different roundtable discussions with former national security advisers were convened in recent years—one by the Brookings-Maryland project on the National Security Council on October 25, 1999 (featuring Frank Carlucci, Walt Rostow, Scowcroft, Anthony Lake for 1993–1997, and Richard Allen for 1981–1982), and the other by the Woodrow Wilson Center for International Scholars and the Baker Institute at Rice University on April 12, 2001. This second roundtable engaged six former national security advisers—Berger, Brzezinski, Carlucci, Robert McFarlane, Rostow, and Andrew Goodpaster (who was staff secretary to President Dwight Eisenhower and as such performed most of the tasks of day-to-day national security policy management carried out by national security advisers from the Kennedy administration onward).[1]

In freewheeling discussions, which ranged historically from the Eisenhower administration in the 1950s to the new Bush administration in the new century, the former advisers recounted their experiences, debated their responsibilities, and reflected on the proper role of the national security adviser under present circumstances. Three clear themes or issues emerged from the discussion, concerning respectively the adviser's role in managing the foreign policy decisionmaking process, the adviser's operational role and responsibility, and the adviser's public responsibilities, especially with respect to Congress.[2]

MANAGING THE DECISIONMAKING PROCESS

Aside from staffing the president in his personal foreign policy role—by making sure he gets the necessary information and is briefed prior to meetings, visits, and negotiations—the most important role of the national security adviser is to manage the decisionmaking process effectively. This involves three steps. First is guiding the policymaking process on major foreign and national security issues so as to ensure both that those with strong stakes in the issue are involved in the process and that all realistic policy options are fully considered—including options not favored by any agency—before these issues reach the president and his senior advisers for decision. Second is driving this process to make real choices in a timely manner. Third is overseeing the implementation of the decisions made by the president and his advisers.

Managing this process effectively is demanding in a number of ways, as became clear in the two roundtable discussions. There is, first of all, the inherent tension between the need of the national security adviser to be an effective and trustworthy "honest broker" among the different players in the decisionmaking process, and the desire of the president to have the best possible policy advice, including advice from his closest foreign policy aide. The roles are inherently in conflict. Balancing them is tricky; it is possible only if the adviser has earned the trust of the other key players. As Sandy Berger argued, "You have to be perceived by your colleagues as an honest representative of their viewpoint, or the system breaks down." Walt Rostow agreed: "The national security adviser ought to be able to state the point of view of each member the president consults, with sympathy. He may disagree with it, but if a Cabinet member ever looks at what is in the summary paper, nothing is more gratifying to a national security adviser than to have him say, 'The State Department couldn't have done any better itself.'" Zbigniew Brzezinski suggested,

> One would have to be awfully stupid to misrepresent the views of one's colleagues to the president, because you know that if the issue is important, there will be a discussion. The president will go back and discuss it, in your presence or even your absence, with his principal advisers, be they secretary of state or secretary of defense. And it would very quickly be evident that you distorted their views if you did. So you have to be absolutely precise and present as persuasively as you can the arguments that they have mustered in favor of their position.

Brent Scowcroft aptly summarized the matter in the Brookings-Maryland roundtable:

> It's always more exciting to be the adviser, but if you are not the honest broker, you don't have the confidence of the NSC. If you don't have their confidence, then the system doesn't work, because they will go around you to get to the president. . . . So in order for the system to work, you first have to establish yourself in the confidence of your colleagues to convince them you are not going to pull fast ones on them. That means when you are in there with the president alone, which you are more than anybody else, that you will represent them fairly. . . . And after you have done that, then you are free to be an adviser.

Once the national security adviser has gained the trust of his colleagues, it is also important that the president receive his unvarnished advice. While a good White House staff person would do well to follow "empirical rule number one" of the Eisenhower administration (which Goodpaster recalled as "The president is always right!"), at least in public, it is equally important to tell the president when he is wrong. As Berger maintained, "I think the national security adviser often has to be the one that says the president's wrong. I always felt it was my particular obligation to give the president the downsides of a particular step he was about to take or to simply state to him—there may be a consensus among his decision makers, but this consensus does not reflect another serious point of view that he should consider."

In short, the national security adviser must balance the role of adviser and honest broker by both earning the trust of colleagues in presenting their views fully, fairly, and faithfully to the president and giving the president his or her best advice on every issue (even—indeed, especially—if it has not been asked for), in order to ensure the president is aware of all possible points of view. Such advice, however, should be given privately, in person or by memo; in public, the national security adviser must stand with the president at all times. As Brzezinski recalls,

> While I do agree that the president's always right in public—whenever there's a group, he's right, because the national security adviser is helping him—in private, you have the obligation to tell him that he's wrong. And I did that repeatedly, and the president wanted me to. There was only one time that he finally sent me a little note saying, "Zbig, don't you know when to stop?" when I went back several times, trying to argue that this was not right.

A second balancing requirement concerns making demands on the president's time—his most precious commodity. There are many, many demands—meetings with aides, meetings with members of Congress, public ceremonies, issues other than foreign policy, etc., etc.—and only twenty-four hours in a day. A key responsibility of the national security adviser is therefore to try to minimize imposition on the president's time. Of course, many issues require his involvement and attention—but not all of them do. Deciding where and when the president should be involved is an issue that must preoccupy any national security adviser.

To minimize demands on the president's time, the adviser will often seek to forge a consensus on policy among the different players and interests. As Berger suggests, the objective is often to "try to bring the secretary of defense, the secretary of state and others to what I used to call the highest common denominator. If there was not a consensus at a fairly high level, it was better to bring the president two starkly different points of view. But some of this is a function of trying to clear the underbrush of decisions before they get to the president." Frank Carlucci recalls a similar process, in which, when he was secretary of defense, he met with his successor, Colin Powell, and the secretary of state, George Shultz, every morning at seven o'clock, without substitutes or agendas, "to lay out the day's events and see if we could reach agreement. And invariably, we reached agreement. And the number of decisions that had to go to the president was greatly reduced by that process."

Of course, while it is important to try to preserve the president's time, it is also important not to create a policy process that presents the president with faits accomplis on important policy issues. A decisionmaking process that is geared toward consensus will often lead to least, rather than highest, common-denominator policies, which invariably lack boldness or even clear direction. Equally perniciously, a consensus process can result in delay in decisionmaking in order to allow time for disagreements to be resolved—enhancing the prospect for ad hoc and reactive policymaking, and needlessly limiting the options that could logically be considered if decisions were made at an earlier stage. Finally, a consensus process increases the likelihood that mistakes will go uncorrected, as the need for maintaining bureaucratic comity outweighs the requirement to reexamine policy.

To avoid the kind of consensus-building that leads to costly inaction, it may be necessary for the national security adviser to act more forcefully than the honest-broker role implies. At the Brookings-Maryland roundtable, Anthony Lake recalled his early "mistake the first six months when I tried too much to be just an honest broker. I remember Colin Powell coming to me and saying that I needed to give my own views more push, etc. . . . [Y]ou have to drive the process, and you have to understand that only the NSC can do that." Otherwise, policymaking can stagnate.

On the other hand, when consensus is achieved rapidly and with little debate, the adviser needs to be skeptical of the outcome, to make sure all aspects of a policy have been thought through, and furthermore, to be ready to be the devil's advocate to ensure the consensus reflects the best course. As the tapes of the Cuban Missile Crisis meetings have revealed, McGeorge Bundy saw it as his role to challenge any emerging consensus, no matter whether hawkish or dovish, to ensure that all the consequences of a particular action had been considered.

One final consideration in managing the decisionmaking process concerns the kinds of issues that should fall within the NSC's coordination purview. The NSC exists for the purpose of integrating a government organized among large "stovepipes," among which there is insufficient interaction. The national security adviser will have to decide which issues will have to be coordinated among these different stovepipes, how, and at what level. Too little coordination, confined to too high a level, will likely result in the exclusion of relevant issues. Too much coordination at too low a level will invariably involve the NSC in micromanaging the policy process in ways that will soon overwhelm the capacity of the staff. For that reason, Brzezinski suggested that "coordination has to take place at the presidential level. That is to say, when the decisions are presidential-level type decisions, then NSC coordination is necessary."

Berger disagreed, insisting that among the "important functions of the National Security Council staff is to coordinate decision making, particularly at the working level, between the various agencies." Citing the case of Bosnia, Berger asserted,

> There were day-to-day decisions that needed to be made, that were not at the presidential level, but were critically important, generally made at the assistant secretary level or above. In those issues that are high priority and fast moving, it is often useful, although I think you can't generalize, for the NSC to be convening the Defense Department, the State Department and others, because the institutional tensions between State and Defense often are such that without a third party in the chair, things fall back on bureaucratic instinct.

The difference between Brzezinski and Berger on this issue was not resolved at the Wilson Center forum—and probably cannot be resolved, except on a case-by-case basis. On those issues that require presidential input or decision, NSC involvement is, of course, a must. But not all others can be left solely to the departments to resolve, for they typically have neither the incentive nor the mechanisms necessary to do so. Bureaucratic stalemate or, possibly worse, pursuit of conflicting policies that reflect departmental rather than presidential preferences can often result. Conversely, however, an NSC staff that insists on coordinating each and every issue will soon become mired in detail and incapable of concentrating on the big picture. Moreover, the adviser or an NSC staff member will often be tempted to seize control of an issue, even to the point of becoming responsible for policy implementation. That, as history tells us, can sometimes be highly effective—and also exceedingly dangerous.

HOW OPERATIONAL SHOULD THE NSC BE?

A perennial issue for every national security adviser is the question of the NSC's operational involvement in executing policy. The consensus view, especially after the Iran-Contra affair, is that the NSC performs a coordinating, oversight, and advisory function but should never become operational. That was the view expressed in 1987 by the Tower Commission, established to review the causes of that fiasco, and it has been faithfully repeated since. Yet the national security adviser and staff have repeatedly been operationally involved in the fifteen years since the Iran-Contra affair became public. Advisers have traveled on solo missions abroad. They have met with foreign diplomats and ministers on an almost daily basis. As Scowcroft recalled, "Somebody from the NSC always traveled with the secretary of state or the secretary of defense," and NSC staff members often serve as members of negotiating delegations abroad. So the question is not really whether the NSC should have an operational role but what kind and to what extent.

It is important to understand why the president might wish the national security adviser to be operationally involved. On one level, it is the result of a basic degree of confidence, comfort, and trust. Presidents know their national security advisers well and have confidence in the advisers' staffs. The same is not always true for the secretary of state and certainly not for the State Department generally, which is largely staffed by career officials. Some presidents come to power with—or develop—a distinct distrust of State (Kennedy and Nixon come to mind); others want to run foreign policy out of the White House, to secure a central personal role for themselves (Carter and Bush Sr., as well as Kennedy and Nixon). In either case, the NSC is the bureaucratic beneficiary of the president's desires. As Brzezinski puts it,

> if you have a president who comes to office intent on making foreign policy himself, on a daily basis, you have a different role than if the president comes to office, let's say, more interested in domestic affairs and more inclined to delegate foreign policy authority to his principal advisers. In the first instance, the national security adviser is the inevitable bureaucratic beneficiary of deep presidential involvement.

In addition, as Anthony Lake noted, an operational NSC role is "necessary because of the way other governments are structured. For the same reasons it's happening here, other governments more and more are revolving around presidencies, prime ministers, etc., and the international contacts between them. As Brent knows, I inherited his phone with the direct lines to our counterparts all around the world, who simply had to be engaged."

Aside from presidential intent and international governmental evolution, the normal ebb and flow of events will also tend to influence the nature and extent of the NSC's operational involvement. One major factor propelling such involvement is lack of bureaucratic responsiveness to presidential direction. As Bud McFarlane recalled in an oblique reference to Iran-Contra, there is the "frustration a president can experience as someone who is there for four years wanting to get something done, to be able to demonstrate leadership in X or Y area, and with the frustration of not seeing that the Department of State or others in his administration moving in that direction." The temptation in these situations is for the national security adviser or even the president to force the issue by having the NSC implement the policy as the president wants it implemented. It is a temptation that McFarlane warns the national security adviser to resist. It should not "lead the National Security Council or the adviser to go beyond the line and take on an operational role. You simply don't have the resources, and you don't have the mandate in law to do that. So that's a big mistake."

A further reason why the national security adviser may become operationally involved is to effect a fundamental shift in policy that, if left to the

State Department to implement, would risk being derailed in bureaucratic entanglement. This, of course, was the cited reason for the most famous and productive operational engagement by a national security assistant—Henry Kissinger's secret diplomacy with China (over opening relations), with North Vietnam (to negotiate a peace agreement), and with the Soviet Union (over arms control and détente). There also may be other occasions when it is logical for the president to send his national security adviser on a quiet diplomatic mission—both to keep the actual mission out of public view and to underscore the president's own commitment to the issue in question. Zbig Brzezinski recalled four such missions during his time in office: to normalize relations with China, to address a particular Middle East peace issue with Egypt, to reassure the Europeans over the Euromissile question, and to organize a regional response to the Soviet invasion of Afghanistan (the first of these did not prove to be very secret). Brent Scowcroft traveled twice to Beijing in the aftermath of the Tiananmen Square massacres. Tony Lake undertook two trips to Europe in connection with Bosnia and a trip to China to help repair badly frayed relations in 1996. Sandy Berger traveled to Moscow to gauge Russia's interest in an arms control deal. In each case, however, the actual trip was coordinated within the U.S. government. Unlike in Kissinger's diplomacy, carried out largely without the knowledge of Secretary of State William P. Rogers, the secretary of state was kept fully informed of these missions, and often a senior state department representative traveled with the president's adviser.

Clearly, then, the national security adviser has a unique operational role to play under certain circumstances. What makes them unique, however, is not just the issue at hand but the fact that such engagement is exceptional rather than routine.

THE PUBLIC ROLE OF THE NATIONAL SECURITY ADVISER

In recent years, the national security adviser has emerged as a prominent public spokesperson on foreign policy. Whereas Brent Scowcroft once counseled that the national security adviser "should be seen occasionally and heard even less," the reverse is increasingly the case. Now, a Sandy Berger or a Condoleezza Rice seem to be everywhere—giving speeches of major import, being quoted in newspapers and newsmagazines as a result of frequent press briefings and even more frequent media interviews, appearing on the Sunday-morning talk-show circuit.

The reason for the public emergence of the national security adviser appears to be twofold. First, the increasing politicization of foreign policy has made defense of the president's policies by the person most directly

associated with the president more important. It is not coincidental, therefore, that the three most recent national security advisers (Tony Lake, Sandy
Berger, and Condoleezza Rice) were all principal advisers to the president
during their campaigns for office. In contrast, with the exception of Zbigniew
Brzezinski and Richard Allen, prior national security advisers were not politically associated with the incoming president. The second reason for the
greater public exposure of the national security adviser in recent years is
changes in the media—especially proliferation in the number of media outlets. The need to cover all the bases requires a larger number of spokes-
people to engage—including, by extension, the national security adviser. As
Berger argues, "The pace of the news cycle is now almost continuous, and
the breadth of the media tends to pull the national security adviser out more
as part of a team of people who goes out, but always with the secretary of
state at the lead."

One of the consequences of the public emergence of the national security
adviser is the demand for increased accountability, especially on Capitol Hill,
where congressmen and senators get to ask questions of the department
heads but are unable to demand answers from the president's closest foreign
policy adviser. As former congressman Lee Hamilton put it to the panel
of former national security assistants, "I think the national security adviser
occupies a very special place. He is, if not the principal adviser, among the
two or three principal advisers to the president on foreign policy. You're
perfectly willing to go before all of the TV networks anytime they give you
a ring, if you want to go. Why should you discriminate against the Congress?"
Told by a number of the former advisers that they had always been willing
to meet with members in their offices, Hamilton continued: "But it is not the
same thing for a national security adviser to come into the private office and
meet behind closed doors with members of Congress. That's not the same
thing as going into a public body and answering questions, in my judgment.
They're two different things."

The absence of congressional accountability sometimes leads to the suggestion that the national security adviser should be confirmed—a suggestion
reviewed, and rejected, by the Tower Commission. The former advisers all
rejected that possibility. They offered a variety of reasons:

- It would prove a major diversion, because with confirmation comes the
  requirement to testify on the Hill. Brzezinski: "If you get confirmed you
  also have to testify a lot, you have to go down to the Hill a lot. The schedule demands on you are so enormous already that that would be an
  additional burden. Moreover, it would greatly complicate the issue we
  talked about earlier, namely, who speaks for foreign policy in the government besides the president? The answer should be the secretary of
  state. If you are confirmed, that would become fuzzed and confused."

- It would compromise the ability of the national security adviser to provide confidential advice to the president. Berger: "One benefit of not having confirmation is that you can say no to a congressional committee. In fact, most presidents have taken the view that under executive privilege their national security adviser, just like their chief of staff, can't be compelled to go up on the Hill."
- It would have a negative impact on the policy formation process. Carlucci: "If you make the national security adviser subject to Senate confirmation, you're going to degrade the process significantly. The president will have a very difficult time implementing a coherent foreign policy. I think the president would simply name another staff person to do what the national security adviser does and let this confirmed official run around on the Hill."
- It is unnecessary, because there is accountability in the system. Carlucci: "These are staff people to the president. And we had a case where the president was almost brought down because of the actions of National Security Council staff—Ronald Reagan. So there is an accountability system, and the president should be free to pick whomever he wants to give him advice."

The modern national security adviser has been a staple of the American foreign-policy making process for more than forty years. Although the role will evolve with each president and with the growing complexity of the world, the fundamental tasks are unlikely to change all that much—to staff the president and manage the foreign policy formulation and implementation processes. The demands and dilemmas each occupant has faced in meeting these tasks will also surely continue. It is in reflecting on how others have handled these challenges in the past that future occupants may prove able to do a job that, by any standard, has become difficult indeed.

NOTES

1. A transcript of the Wilson Center/Rice discussion is available at wwics.si.edu/ NEWS/support/nsa.pdf. The Brookings-Maryland Roundtable is available at www.brookings.edu/fp/research/projects/nsc/transcripts/19991025.htm. Also published in this latter document are interviews with Berger, McFarlane, Colin Powell (adviser to Reagan, 1987–1989) and John Poindexter (Reagan, 1985–1987).

2. The following draws on a summary of the Wilson Center roundtable prepared by Daalder, available at wwics.si.edu/NEWS/support/nsarapprpt.pdf. Unless otherwise cited, all quotations (sometimes edited for style) are drawn from the Wilson Center transcript.

12

From Deference to Activism and Back Again

Congress and the Politics of American Foreign Policy

James M. Lindsay

In 1995 Congress appeared poised to wrest control of foreign policy away from the White House. That May, Secretary of State Warren Christopher complained that the foreign aid bill then on the floor of the House waged "an extraordinary onslaught on the president's constitutional authority to manage foreign policy."[1] President William Clinton endorsed Christopher's attack, accusing members of Congress of launching "nothing less than a frontal assault on the authority of the president to conduct the foreign policy of the United States."[2] Outside of government, Anthony Lewis of the *New York Times* argued that "the Republicans who control Congress are trying to move us back toward the Articles of Confederation."[3] Even Republican officials joined the attack; Lawrence Eagleburger, secretary of state under the elder George Bush, warned that "the restrictions and demands on the President are an absolute attack on the separation of powers."[4]

Seven years later, fears that Congress had usurped presidential powers had given way to concerns that it had abdicated any foreign policy role. Many lawmakers privately questioned President George W. Bush's handling of the war on terrorism, especially his push to overthrow Saddam Hussein. But few aired their criticisms publicly. When President Bush asked Congress to give him authority to wage war on Iraq, Congress quibbled with some of the language of the draft resolution. Nonetheless, the revised bill, which the House and Senate passed overwhelmingly, amounted to a blank check that the president could cash as he saw fit. When asked why congressional Democrats had not done more to oppose a resolution so many thought unwise, Senate Majority Leader Tom Daschle (D-S.D.) replied: "The bottom line is . . . we want to move on."[5] Congress's eagerness to delegate its war power to the president drew the ire of Senator Robert Byrd (D-W.Va.), a veteran of five decades of service on Capitol Hill: "How have we gotten to this low point in the history of Congress? Are we too feeble to resist the demand of a president who is determined to bend the collective will of Congress to his will"?[6]

The contrasting balance of power in executive-legislative relations between 1995 and 2002 was dramatic. It was not, however, unprecedented. The pendulum of power on foreign policy has shifted back and forth between Congress and the president many times over the course of American history. The reason for these ebbs and flows does not lie in the Constitution. Its formal allocation of foreign policy powers, which gives important authorities to both Congress and the president, has not changed since it was drafted. Rather, the answer lies in politics. How aggressively Congress exercises its foreign policy powers turns on the critical question of whether the country sees itself as threatened or secure. Times of peace favor congressional activism. Times of war favor congressional deference. Both modes of congressional behavior have advantages—as well as create dangers.

THE CONSTITUTION AND FOREIGN POLICY

Ask most Americans who makes foreign policy in the United States and their immediate answer is the president—and to a point they are right. But even a cursory reading of the Constitution makes clear that Congress also possesses extensive powers to shape foreign policy. Article I, Section 8 assigns Congress the power to "provide for the common Defence," "To regulate Commerce with foreign Nations," "To define and punish Piracies and Felonies committed on the high Seas," "To declare War," "To raise and support Armies," "To provide and maintain a Navy," and "To make Rules for the Government and Regulation of the land and naval Forces." Article II, Section 2 specifies that the Senate must give its advice and consent to all treaties and ambassadorial appointments. Congress's more general powers to appropriate all government funds and to confirm cabinet officials provide additional means to influence foreign policy.

These powers can have great consequence. To begin with, they enable Congress—or in the case of the treaty power, the Senate—to specify the substance of American foreign policy. The most popular vehicle for doing so is the appropriations power, which while not unlimited in scope, is nonetheless quite broad. (The Supreme Court has never struck down any use of the appropriations power as an unconstitutional infringement on the president's authority to conduct foreign policy.) Dollars are policy in Washington, D.C., and by law, the president generally cannot spend money unless Congress appropriates it. Thus, by deciding to fund some ventures and not others, Congress can steer the course of U.S. defense and foreign policy. Congress can also specify the substance of foreign policy by regulating foreign commerce. One notable instance in which it used its trade power this way was a 1986 bill that placed sanctions on South Africa in order to pressure Pretoria to end its policy of apartheid. The Senate's treaty power can have similar effects. When the Senate rejected the Treaty of Versailles after World War I it blocked U.S. membership in the League of Nations and preserved the traditional U.S. policy of avoiding entangling alliances.

Congress's power to establish and direct the business of the federal bureaucracy (e.g., "to provide and maintain a Navy") also enables it influence foreign policy by changing the procedures that the executive branch must follow in making decisions. The premise underlying such procedural legislation is that changing the rules governing how the executive branch makes decisions will change the decisions it makes. In trade policy, for example, U.S. law requires the White House to consult with a wide range of consumer, industry, and labor groups whenever it is negotiating an international trade agreement. The law's sponsors calculated that including these groups in decisionmaking would make it more likely that American trade policy would reflect U.S. economic interests. Likewise, over the years Congress has directed the State Department to set up special offices to handle issues such as democracy, counterterrorism, and trafficking in persons. In each instance, the idea was that the executive branch would be more likely to address the issue in question if someone in the bureaucracy had clear responsibility for it.

The broader lesson here is that when it comes to foreign affairs, Congress and the president *both* can claim ample constitutional authority. The two branches are, in Richard Neustadt's oft-repeated formulation, "separated institutions *sharing* power."[7] The question of which branch should prevail as a matter of principle when their powers conflict has been disputed ever since Alexander Hamilton and James Madison squared off two centuries ago in their famed Pacificus-Helvidius debate. (Hamilton argued the president was free to exercise his powers as he saw fit; Madison argued the president could not exercise his authority in ways that constrained Congress's ability to exercise its powers.) While the president exercises some foreign-affairs powers that are off limits to Congress—with the power to negotiate on behalf of the United States being the most prominent—the fact that the Constitution grants Congress extensive authority in foreign policy means that most executive-legislative disputes do not raise constitutional issues.

To say that Congress can put its mark on foreign policy, however, is not the same as saying that it will try to do so. To understand why congressional activism on foreign policy varies over time, it is necessary to leave the realm of law and enter the realm of politics.

POLITICS AND FOREIGN POLICY

The reason why Congress's say in foreign policy ebbs and flows lies in an observation that the famed French commentator on American life Alexis de Tocqueville made more than 150 years ago. Surprised to find that the pre–Civil War Congress played a major role in foreign policy, he speculated that congressional activism stemmed from the country's isolation from external threat. "If the Union's existence were constantly menaced, and if its great interests were continually interwoven with those of other powerful nations, one would see the prestige of the executive growing, because of what was expected from it and of what it did."[8]

Why might perceptions of threat affect how Congress behaves? When Americans believe they face few external threats—or think that international engagement could itself produce a threat—they see less merit in deferring to the White House on foreign policy and more merit to congressional activism. Debate and disagreement are not likely to pose significant costs; after all, the country is secure. But when Americans believe the country faces an external threat, they quickly convert to the need for strong presidential leadership. Congressional dissent that was previously acceptable suddenly looks like unhelpful meddling at best and unpatriotic at worst. Members of Congress are themselves likely to feel the same shifting sentiments toward the wisdom of deferring to the president, as well as to be profoundly aware that being on the wrong side of that shift could hurt them come the next election.

Throughout American history, power over foreign policy has flowed back and forth between the two ends of Pennsylvania Avenue according to this basic dynamic. In the second half of the nineteenth century, the United States was as secure from foreign attack as at any time in American history. This was also a time when Congress so dominated foreign policy that it has been called the era of "congressional government," "congressional supremacy," and "government by Congress." When the United States entered World War I, the pendulum of power swung to the White House; Woodrow Wilson experienced few congressional challenges during his war presidency. But once the war ended, Congress—and the Senate in particular—reasserted itself. Congressional activism persisted into the 1930s and even intensified. Convinced that America would be safe only as long as it kept out of Europe's political affairs, the isolationist majority in Congress fought bitterly to prevent

President Franklin Roosevelt from doing anything that might involve the United States in the war that was brewing across the Atlantic.

Japan's bombing of Pearl Harbor punctured the isolationists' arguments and greatly expanded FDR's freedom to conduct foreign policy. He made virtually all of his major wartime decisions without reference to or input from Capitol Hill. When World War II ended, Congress began to reassert itself. Senior members of the House Foreign Affairs and Senate Foreign Relations Committees helped draft the United Nations Charter, the peace treaties for the Axis satellite states, and the NATO Treaty.

Growing concerns about the Soviet Union slowed the shift of power away from the White House. As Americans became convinced in the late 1940s that hostile communist states threatened the United States and the rest of the free world, they increasingly came to agree on two basic ideas: the United States needed to resist communist expansion, and achieving this goal demanded strong presidential leadership. Most members of Congress shared these two basic beliefs (and helped promote them); those who disagreed risked punishment at the polls. The process became self-reinforcing. As more lawmakers stepped to the sidelines on defense and foreign policy over the course of the 1950s, others saw it as increasingly futile, not to mention dangerous politically, to continue to speak out. By 1960, the "imperial presidency," the flip side of a deferential Congress, was in full bloom.[9] As one senator complained in 1965, members of Congress were responding to even the most far-reaching presidential decisions on foreign affairs by "stumbling over each other to see who can say 'yea' the quickest and loudest."[10]

The era of congressional deference to the imperial presidency came to a crashing halt with the souring of public opinion on the Vietnam War. Many Americans became convinced that communist revolutions in the Third World posed no direct threat to core U.S. security interests, just as détente persuaded many that Leonid Brezhnev's Soviet Union posed less of a threat to core U.S. security interests. With the public more willing to question administration policies, so too were members of Congress. Many more had substantive disagreements with the White House over what constituted America's vital interests and how best to protect and advance them. Moreover, lawmakers had less to fear politically by the early 1970s in challenging the White House than they had had only a few years earlier. Indeed, many calculated that challenging the president's foreign policies could actually help them at the ballot box, by enabling them to stake out positions that their constituents favored. The result was a predictable surge in congressional activism.

Members of Congress did not always succeed in putting their stamp on foreign policy in the 1970s and 1980s. Knee-jerk support of the president was gone, but elements of congressional deference persisted among senior lawmakers (who had come of age during the era of congressional deference) and moderates (who worried that defeating the president could harm the country's credibility). Presidents from Richard Nixon through the elder George Bush often prevailed on major issues because they could persuade these groups to join them with a simple argument: The administration's policy might have shortcomings, but rejecting the president's request would damage his standing abroad, perhaps embolden Moscow to act more aggressively, and ultimately harm American interests. Yet the mere fact that the post-Vietnam presidents had to make this argument showed how much had changed from the days of the imperial presidency. Presidents Carter and Reagan did not get the acquiescence from Capitol Hill that Presidents Eisenhower and Kennedy had.

THE FALL OF THE BERLIN WALL

The end of the Cold War accelerated and exacerbated the trend toward greater congressional activism that Vietnam triggered. With the Soviet Union relegated to the ash heap of history, most Americans who looked abroad saw no threat of similar magnitude on the horizon. When asked to name the most important problem facing the United States, polls in the 1990s rarely found that more than five percent of Americans named a foreign policy issue. That was a steep drop from the upward of 50 percent who had named a foreign policy issue during the height of the Cold War. Moreover, many Americans had trouble identifying *any* foreign policy issue that worried them. One 1998 poll asked people to name "two or three of the biggest foreign-policy problems facing the United States today." The most common response by far, at 21 percent, was "don't know."[11]

These public attitudes meant that members of Congress who challenged the White House on foreign policy ran almost no electoral risks. With the public not caring enough to punish them for any excesses, lawmakers went busily about challenging Bill Clinton's foreign policy. In April 1999, during the Kosovo war, the House refused to vote to support the bombing. Not to be outdone, the Senate voted down the Comprehensive Test Ban Treaty in October 1999, even though President Clinton and sixty-two senators had asked that it be withdrawn from consideration. These episodes were major departures from past practice. When members of Congress had squared off against the White House in the latter half of the Cold War on issues such as Vietnam, the MX missile, and aid to the Nicaraguan Contras, they had had vocal public support. On Kosovo and the test ban, however, few Americans were urging Congress to challenge Clinton. To the extent that they had opinions—and many did not—most Americans sided with the president.

Just as important, the once-powerful argument that members of Congress should defer to the White House on key issues lest they harm broader American interests fell on deaf ears. In 1997 the Clinton administration sought to convince Congress to give it "fast track" negotiating authority for international trade agreements. (With fast-track authority, Congress agrees to approve or reject without amendment any trade agreement the president negotiates. This simplifies trade negotiations, because other countries do not have to worry that Congress will rewrite any trade deal.) When it became clear that he lacked the votes needed to prevail, President Clinton escalated the stakes by arguing that fast-track was needed because "more than ever, our economic security is also the foundation of our national security."[12] The decision to recast a trade issue as a national security issue—a tried-and-true Cold War strategy—changed few minds, however. Recognizing defeat, Clinton asked congressional leaders to withdraw the bill from consideration, marking the first time in decades that a president had failed to persuade Congress to support a major trade initiative.

Besides encouraging members of Congress to flex their foreign policy muscles, the public's diminished interest in foreign affairs after the collapse of the Soviet Union also encouraged them to cater to groups with narrow but intense preferences on foreign policy. That is, after all, where the political credit lies in foreign policy when the broader public has turned its attention elsewhere. The result was that congressional deliberations on foreign policy increasingly became—to paraphrase the famed German military strategist Clausewitz—the continuation of domestic politics by other means. Lawmakers were more interested in how ethnic, business, and single-issue groups might help them win reelection and less in whether the programs they championed added up to a coherent foreign policy. As former representative Lee H. Hamilton (D-Ind.) put it: "Too many people place constituent interests above national interests. They don't see much difference between lobbying for highway funds and slanting foreign policy toward a particular interest group."[13]

A case in point was the House of Representative's effort in 2000 to pass a nonbinding resolution labeling the massacres of Armenians that occurred in the Ottoman Empire from 1915 to 1923 as "genocide." James Rogan (R-Calif.) sponsored the resolution. He made no claim to be a foreign policy expert—none of his committee assignments dealt with foreign policy, and he had traveled outside the United States only once in his life—but he was caught in a tight reelection race. His congressional district happened to have the highest concentration of Armenian Americans of any district in the United States. The resolution offered an easy way to build good will with constituents by promoting a cause they held dear. The Armenian Assembly of America, which routinely grades how members of Congress vote on issues affecting Armenia, had long lobbied for the resolution.

In another time, Rogan's resolution would have languished in committee. Party leaders would have allowed him to introduce the bill—enabling him to gain political credit with his constituents for "fighting the good fight"—but would have kept the bill from advancing, thereby protecting the country's broader interests. But in 2000, House Republican leaders, eager to maintain their slim majority in the face of potential Democratic inroads in the upcoming elections, embraced the bill. Speaker of the House Dennis Hastert (R-Ill.) promised Rogan that he would bring the resolution to a vote on the House floor. He personally placed the measure on the House legislative calendar. The House International Relations Committee subsequently approved it by a large margin.

As Rogan, Hastert, and other House members pushed the genocide resolution forward, they gave little thought to the consequences their symbolic gesture would have on broader U.S. interests. The result was escalating tensions with Turkey, a major American ally that among other things was letting U.S. and British fighter planes use Incirlik Air Base to patrol the skies over northern Iraq. Turkey's president expressed "grave reservations" about the resolution, repeating his country's long-standing insistence that there had been no genocide.[14] Suddenly U.S. defense companies faced the possibility that they might lose sales in Turkey, and the Pentagon the possibility that it would lose the right to fly out of Incirlik. After a barrage of phone calls from Bill Clinton, other administration officials, and senior military officers warning that the resolution would significantly harm U.S. foreign policy, Hastert agreed to put off a vote on Rogan's bill.[15]

THE DEFERENTIAL CONGRESS RETURNS

Congress's assertiveness in the first post–Cold War decade rested on the public's belief that what happened outside America's borders mattered little in their lives. September 11 punctured that illusion and ended America's decade-long "holiday from history."[16] Foreign policy suddenly became a top priority with the public. Not surprisingly, the pendulum of power swung sharply back toward the White House.

The impact of September 11 on American public opinion was dramatic. Shortly after the attacks, Gallup found that two out of every three Americans named terrorism, national security, or war as the most important problem facing the United States. Foreign policy had reached this level of political salience only twice since the advent of scientific polling—during the early stages of the Korean and Vietnam Wars. President George W. Bush's public approval ratings soared to 90 percent—a figure seen only once before, when his father waged the Gulf War. While the elder Bush's public approval ratings had quickly returned to their prewar levels, the younger Bush's remained high for months.

Many members of Congress rallied behind the president for the same principled reasons the public did. But lawmakers who might have preferred to be elsewhere in policy terms quickly decided that political reality demanded that they be there as well. Three days after the attack, all but one member of Congress voted to give the president open-ended authority to retaliate against those responsible, authorizing him "to use all necessary and appropriate force against those nations, organizations, or persons he determines planned, authorized, committed, or aided the terrorist attacks that occurred on September 11, 2001, or harbored such organizations or persons." In short, Congress effectively declared war and left it up to President Bush to decide who the enemy was.

Over the next few weeks, Congress reversed key policy stands that administration officials said interfered with the conduct of the war on terrorism. For several years conservative legislators had blocked a bipartisan plan to pay much of the outstanding U.S. dues to the United Nations. President Bush argued that this delinquency hindered his efforts to assemble a multinational coalition to prosecute the war on terrorism, so Congress appropriated the long-delayed funds without opposition. Congress did something else that had been unthinkable only a month earlier—it allowed President Bush to lift the sanctions that the United States had imposed on Pakistan to protest General Pervez Musharraf's seizure of power in 1999. When President Bush proposed increasing defense spending by thirty-eight billion dollars in 2003—a sum equal to Great Britain's entire military budget and three-quarters of China's—Congress raised few complaints. This was true even though the bulk of the spending increase went to fund defense programs that had been on the drawing boards before September 11 rather than to meet the needs of the war on terrorism.

Congress retreated from confrontations with the president on other issues as well. Senate Democrats dropped their plans to make the administration's proposals to build a missile defense and to withdraw from the 1972 Anti-Ballistic Missile (ABM) Treaty the centerpieces of foreign policy debate. Congress also voted to give President Bush what it had denied President Clinton—fast-track negotiating authority (now renamed "trade promotion" authority). When the White House set up special military commissions to try captured Taliban and Al Qaeda officials, members of Congress did not ask whether the Constitution in fact gave the president power to set up his own judicial system. Where lawmakers disagreed with the White House's foreign policy initiatives after September 11, they quickly concluded that discretion was the greater part of valor. They worried that if they challenged a popular wartime president they risked being accused of playing politics with national security. This was not an idle fear. When Senate Majority Leader Tom Daschle (D-S.D.) said in February 2002 that the Bush administration's efforts to expand the war lacked "a clear direction," Republican leaders questioned his patriotism. One went as far as to accuse him of "giving aid and comfort to our enemies"—which happens to be the legal definition of treason.[17]

Party reputations reinforced Congress's instinct to defer to the White House. Because President Bush was a Republican, challenges to his foreign policy stewardship would more likely come from congressional Democrats than congressional Republicans. But Democrats had a problem in trying to criticize a popular Republican president on foreign policy—most Americans lacked confidence in their ability to handle national security issues. Ever since the Vietnam War, Americans had given Republicans far higher marks than Democrats on defense and foreign policy. In times of peace and prosperity, like the 1990s, these perceptions did not create insurmountable obstacles for Democrats. In a wartime context, however, they left Democrats such as Daschle who offered even mild criticisms of the White House open to charges of being unpatriotic.

This political reality, perhaps more than agreement on the substance, explains why Democrats embraced President Bush's policy toward Iraq in the fall of 2002. Many congressional Democrats privately believed that President Bush's call for legislation authorizing him to wage war on Iraq was both premature and unwise.[18] At the time Congress took up the resolution, most of America's traditional allies publicly opposed the White House's policy of regime change in Iraq. Moreover, while an American victory in a second Gulf War was almost certain, it could have tremendous unintended consequences. Finally, in asking Congress to act, President Bush said repeatedly that he had not made up his mind whether to wage war against Iraq. Lawmakers understood, however, that the war power was a use-it-and-lose-it authority. Once they gave President Bush authority to wage war, he could exercise it as he saw fit, even if most members of Congress (or most Americans) thought the circumstances no longer warranted it.

But with midterm congressional elections looming, most Democratic political strategists looked at the polling data and urged their candidates to support the White House. Rallying around the president would deny Republicans the opportunity to question Democrats' patriotism. It would also get Iraq off the front pages and shift the national debate back to domestic policy, where Democratic positions were more popular with the voters. In the end, political calculations trumped. Congress did something unique in its history—it authorized a war against another country before the United States itself had been attacked and even before the president had publicly made up his mind to wage war.

CONCLUSION

The framers of the Constitution created a political system that gave Congress substantial powers to determine the course of American foreign policy. Congress's willingness to exercise those powers has ebbed and flowed over time according to the vicissitudes of politics. When Americans are at peace and believe themselves secure, congressional assertiveness grows. When Americans find themselves at war or fear great peril, congressional assertiveness gives way to congressional deference to the president.

Is there any reason to believe that America's foreign policy is better served by an assertive Congress or a deferential one? This question is easy to ask but impossible to answer. No objective standard exists for judging how to strike the proper balance between activism and deference. The temptation is always to judge Congress in light of whether one likes what the president wants to do. As one Reagan administration official commented, "I have been a 'strong president man' when in the executive branch and a 'strong Congress man' when out of the government in political opposition."[19] That answer hardly satisfies those who have different partisan preferences. What is clear is that activist and deferential congresses pose different mixes of costs and benefits. Although congressional activism usually looks unhelpful from the vantage point of the White House, it has several merits. For the same reason that an approaching test encourages students to study, the possibility that Congress might step into the fray encourages administration officials to think through their policy proposals more carefully. Members of Congress also bring different views to bear on policy debates, views that can provide a useful scrub for administration proposals. When Capitol Hill is more hawkish than the White House, congressional activism strengthens the president's hand overseas. Also, congressional debate helps to legitimate foreign policy with the public. This latter virtue should not be underestimated; the success of the United States abroad ultimately depends on the willingness of Americans to accept the sacrifices asked of them.

But if congressional activism can be helpful, it can also be harmful. At a minimum, it makes an already cumbersome decisionmaking process even more so. More people need to be consulted, and more opportunities to derail a policy are created. Such inefficiency is not inherently disastrous—after all, the maxim "he who hesitates is lost" has its counterpoint in "decide in haste, repent at leisure." It does, however, increase the burdens on the time and energy of executive-branch officials, potentially keeping them from other duties, and it can strain relations with allies who do not understand why Washington is so slow in acting. At its worst, congressional activism may render U.S. foreign policy incoherent as members of Congress push issues they do not fully understand and pursue narrow interests rather than national ones. Representative Rogan's Armenian genocide resolution, for example, greatly strained U.S. relations with Turkey. Ankara retaliated by relaxing its efforts to isolate Iraq and by sending an ambassador back to Baghdad for the first time in a decade. This helped to undermine a foreign policy objective that had widespread support in the United States, maintaining international support for the effort to isolate Saddam Hussein.

A deferential Congress avoids these problems but can easily create others. Presidents unburdened by congressional second-guessing find it easier to exploit the advantages of "decision, activity, secrecy, and dispatch" that Alexander Hamilton long ago hailed as the great virtues of the presidency.[20] But presidents and their advisers are not infallible. They can choose unwisely, and the lack of domestic checks can tempt them to overreach. It was the imperial presidency, after all, that gave America the Bay of Pigs and the Vietnam War.

It is this temptation to overreach that may be the greatest risk in American foreign policy after September 11. President Bush's dominance of the foreign policy agenda is likely to persist throughout his presidency. In domestic policy, Democrats have strong political incentives to criticize the White House; the political winds on foreign policy blow briskly in the opposite direction. A sustained period of peace could change those calculations, but that hardly seems to be in the offing. The political winds could also reverse, however, if Bush's foreign policy choices bring disaster. In that event, he would discover what President Lyndon Johnson learned more than three decades ago—the fact that members of Congress defer to the White House when his foreign policy takes off does not mean they will be deferential when it crashes.

NOTES

1. Quoted in Steven Greenhouse, "Christopher Urging Clinton to Veto a Bill to Cut Foreign Aid," *New York Times,* May 23, 1995.

2. Quoted in " 'This Legislation Is the Wrong Way,' " *Congressional Quarterly Weekly Report,* May 27, 1995, 1514.

3. Anthony Lewis, "Capitol Power Grab," *New York Times,* May 26, 1995.

4. Ibid.

5. Quoted in Frank Rich, "It's the War, Stupid," *New York Times,* October 12, 2002.

6. Robert C. Byrd, "Congress Must Resist the Rush to War," *New York Times,* October 10, 2002.

7. Richard E. Neustadt, *Presidential Power and the Modern Presidents: The Politics of Leadership from Roosevelt to Reagan* (New York: Free Press, 1990), 29.

8. Alexis de Tocqueville, *Democracy in America* (New York: Anchor Books, 1969), 126.

9. Arthur M. Schlesinger, Jr., *The Imperial Presidency* (Boston: Houghton-Mifflin, 1973).

10. Quoted in James L. Sundquist, *The Decline and Resurgence of Congress* (Washington, D.C.: Brookings Institution, 1981), 125.

11. John E. Reilly, "Americans and the World: A Survey at Century's End," *Foreign Policy* 114 (Spring 1999): 111.

12. Quoted in John M. Broder, "House Postpones Trade-Issue Vote," *New York Times,* November 8, 1997.

13. Quoted in Steven Mufson, "Local Politics Is Global as Hill Turns to Armenia," *Washington Post,* October 9, 2000.

14. Ibid.

15. Juliet Eilperin and Steven Mufson, "Hastert Withdraws 'Genocide' Resolution, Ties with Turkey Cited," *Washington Post,* October 20, 2000; and Mufson, "Local Politics Is Global."

16. Charles Krauthammer, "The Hundred Days," *Time,* December 31, 2001, 156.

17. Rep. Tom Davis (R-Va.), quoted in Helen Dewar, "Lott Calls Daschle Divisive," *Washington Post,* March 1, 2002.

18. See Elizabeth Drew, "War Games in the Senate," *New York Review of Books,* December 5, 2002, 66–68.

19. John Lehman, *Making War: The 200-Year-Old Battle between the President and Congress over How America Goes to War* (New York: Scribner, 1992), xii.

20. Alexander Hamilton, *"Federalist* No. 70," in Alexander Hamilton, James Madison, and John Jay, *The Federalist Papers,* ed. Garry Wills (New York: Bantam Books, 1982), 356.

13

Globalization and Diplomacy
The View from Foggy Bottom

Strobe Talbott

It was the early morning of Monday, October 4, 1993, and there was a new kind of trouble brewing in Moscow. Tanks had surrounded the White House, the giant parliament building on the banks of the Moscow River, where deputies of the Supreme Soviet, some of them heavily armed, were holed up in defiance of President Boris Yeltsin's order to dissolve the legislature and submit to new elections. Just hours earlier, at the urging of the insurgents inside the White House, armed mobs had attacked the Moscow mayor's office and the city's main television station.

I had spent the night camped on the couch in my office on the seventh floor of the State Department. At 3:00 A.M., I went down the corridor to the department's Operations Center, our communications hub, where we had established a round-the-clock task force to monitor the crisis that was coming to a head. Using one of the phone banks in the OpsCenter, I called Deputy Foreign Minister Georgi Mamedov, who was in his own office in the ministry's Stalin-gothic skyscraper on Smolensk Square, less than a mile from the besieged parliament. We had been in frequent touch since the showdown began 24 hours earlier.

Suddenly, in the midst of our conversation, we both fell silent. After a long moment, Mamedov asked: "Are you watching what I'm watching?" I was indeed. We both had our television sets tuned to CNN, which had begun a live broadcast of Russian commandos and armored personnel carriers moving into position to storm the White House. For the next half-hour, Mamedov and I watched transfixed, exchanging occasional impressions as the battle came to its dramatic and bloody denouement. Following a phased assault that gave those inside the White House several opportunities to surrender, government forces retook the building and arrested the leaders of the opposition.

The United States and Russia had come a long way from the era of Cold War brinkmanship over Berlin and Cuba. Now, the point of crisis was an internal power struggle in Russia, a showdown between a democratically elected leader and a reactionary legislature. Moreover, rather than being waged in secret behind the Kremlin walls, the struggle was being broadcast live to a worldwide audience of tens of millions. Here was the famous "CNN effect" at its most emblematic. Just as the network had made it possible for Mamedov and me to watch an event unfold in real time as we discussed its implications over an open phone line, so the communications revolution had contributed to the transformation of his country and of our world.

FROM BRETTON WOODS TO DENVER

By the 1980s, self-isolating dictatorships from Chile to the Soviet Union had yielded to democratic and free market ideals spread by radio, television, the fax machine, and e-mail. Since then, in addition to undermining the Berlin Wall and shredding the Iron Curtain, the powerful technological forces of the Information Age have helped to stitch together the economic, political, and cultural lives of nations, making borders more permeable to the movement of people, products, and ideas. When President Bill Clinton visited Bucharest in July [1997], his host, Emil Constantinescu, a democratic activist and reformer who had been elected president of Romania seven months before, took him into his study and proudly showed him the desktop computer that gave him access to cyberspace.

For many millions of people, globalization has meant greater freedom and prosperity. But for millions of others, the same process has brought economic disadvantage and social disruption. Striking workers in South Korea and Argentina have opposed changes that their national leaders insisted were necessary to meet the demands of the global economy. The unexpected victory of the Socialist Party in [the 1997] French legislative elections stemmed in part from voters' apprehensions about globalization. In the United States, political figures such as Ross Perot and Pat Buchanan have tapped into similar anxieties.

Not all those who are within reach of television consider themselves better off as a result—in fact, often quite the contrary. There are satellite dishes in the slums of the world's megacities, and the signals they suck in from Hollywood and Madison Avenue can trigger resentment and anger: The communications revolution has the potential to foment revolutions of a different sort.

Globalization itself is neither inherently good nor bad. Governments cannot block its effects on their citizens without also cutting them off from its opportunities and benefits. But they can shape it to their national and international advantage.

While this task is an increasingly important and explicit theme in U.S. diplomacy in the post–Cold War era, it is not new. In the economic realm, it goes back at least to the immediate aftermath of World War II and the creation of the World Bank and the International Monetary Fund at Bretton Woods. Three decades later, in 1975, the leaders of France, Italy, Japan, the United Kingdom, the United States, and West Germany took another step forward together. They met in the picturesque French farming town of Rambouillet to discuss how they could increase trade, coordinate monetary policies, and reduce their vulnerability to rising oil prices. This was the first of what became, with the addition of Canada the following year in London, the annual summit of the Group of Seven major industrialized democracies.

When the successors of those leaders met for the 22nd time in Denver [in 1997], they were joined by Boris Yeltsin—the first time that the president of the Russian Federation participated in the summit from beginning to end. Just as the cast of characters at Denver had grown since Rambouillet, so had the agenda. Transnational threats such as climate change, the spread of infectious disease, and international organized crime received almost as much attention as the economic aspects of interdependence. Patterns of energy consumption, child vaccination rates, and drug treatment programs— once thought to be almost exclusively domestic issues—had become topics of international concern and targets of concerted action.

While other nations have long paid close attention to the U.S. government's monetary and fiscal policies, there are now growing international implications to U.S. domestic actions in countless other areas. The European Union initially objected to the proposed merger between the Boeing and McDonnell Douglas corporations, arguing that it would undermine competition in the global aircraft market. Senior Mexican officials have said publicly that the new U.S. immigration law that went into effect [in 1997] violates the rights of Mexicans living in the United States. Regulatory agencies around the world often take their cue from the U.S. Food and Drug Administration in approving or banning foodstuffs and medications, with consequences for thousands of companies and millions of consumers.

By the same token, the internal policies of other nations have a growing impact on the United States. The extent to which Mexico enforces the environmental provisions of the North American Free Trade Agreement (NAFTA) will affect the quality of air and water in Arizona, California, New Mexico, and Texas. The extent to which China is prepared to protect intellectual property rights will provide, or cost, jobs for American workers. Colombia's ability and willingness to crack down on narcotics production will affect the balance of forces in the war against illegal drugs in the United States. And conversely, only if the United States can reduce its domestic demand will Colombia and other nations on the supply side of the international narcotics trade succeed in their part of the struggle.

THE IMPERATIVE FOR CHANGE

Global interdependence is affecting the way virtually all governments think about international relations and practice diplomacy. The more engaged in and affected by the process, the more they must change. For the United States, therefore, the imperative for change is especially powerful, and it is felt most acutely in the [Department of State].

The Department of State is a proud institution, and it comes by its pride honestly. But the susceptibility of an institution to reform is inversely proportional to its venerability, and the State Department is no exception. [The department is] located in a neighborhood of Washington called Foggy Bottom, a designation that has become a sometimes affectionate, sometimes sardonic nickname for the department itself, with unflattering implications for the mindset of the 13,000 people who work there and in our 249 posts abroad.

Even as the State Department strives to overcome the inertia that is built into a large organization with a long history, it must also do more—and better—with less financial support from the nation it serves. Since 1985, in real dollar terms, the international affairs budget of the United States has plummeted by 50 percent. It has also declined in relative terms. In 1984, foreign affairs spending amounted to 2.5 percent of the federal budget; [today, despite increases, it remains at] roughly 1 percent. [Since 1993], we have had to close 32 embassies and consulates around the world.... Only by leveraging our resources and being smarter in the way we marshal them can the State Department meet the challenges posed to American diplomacy by globalization and interdependence.

GOING GLOBAL

The bilateral, government-to-government approach that has traditionally been the staple of American diplomacy is often insufficient to address threats like terrorism, narcotics trafficking, and environmental degradation, which are almost always regional—and very often global—in scope. These new challenges will yield only to an internationally coordinated, long-term effort.

In response to these changing realities, at the beginning of his administration, President Clinton created the position of undersecretary of state for global affairs, which was given responsibility for several of the State Department's bureaus dealing with cross-cutting "functional" areas: the protection of the environment, the promotion of democracy and human rights, the management of population and migration issues, and law enforcement. The effect has been to elevate the attention those goals receive in the policy-making process and in diplomacy.

At the beginning of the second term, Vice President Al Gore announced a broader plan for reform and consolidation of the nation's foreign affairs agencies that is also in part a response to globalization. By integrating the Arms Control and Disarmament Agency and the U.S. Information Agency into the Department of State, and by [a . . .] partial consolidation of State and the U.S. Agency for International Development (USAID), we [are] better able to weave the core missions of these agencies into the fabric of U.S. foreign policy.

The multitude, magnitude, and complexity of transnational issues and the collaborative arrangements through which we are working to address them also require that we rethink the way we recruit and train the department's human resources. We are stepping up our efforts to hire people who already have experience in areas such as international finance, labor, environmental science, and law enforcement. We are broadening what might be called the core curriculum in the training of entry-level officers. The Foreign Service Institute, the department's center for instruction in languages, area studies, and technical skills, has introduced a survey course that covers issues like narcotics trafficking and refugee flows, as well as classes on subjects such as the expanding global market for U.S. environmental technologies.

Meanwhile, our diplomats abroad, while still giving priority to U.S. relations with individual host governments, are nurturing regional and trans-regional relationships to a greater extent than ever. Our embassies in Lima and Quito have worked with the governments of Argentina, Brazil, and Chile to resolve the border conflict between Ecuador and Peru. Our embassy in Pretoria has devoted much of its energy to working with the South African government on peace in Angola and Congo. And whatever our other differences with Beijing, we are engaged with the Chinese, together with the Japanese and South Koreans, in an ongoing effort to reduce tensions on the Korean peninsula.

NEW POLICIES, NEW PARTNERS

Globalization has also increased the need for other departments and agencies of the U.S. government to play an active role in pursuit of American

interests abroad—and for the State Department to cooperate more systematically with them. That cooperation has been particularly close on matters
of economics, defense, and law enforcement.

Economics. As trade and international investment have become more
important to the U.S. economy, the department and the U.S. government's
economic agencies have expanded and deepened their collaboration. The
agreements reached at the World Trade Organization to eliminate tariffs and
increase worldwide trade in information technology and telecommunications represent one such collaborative effort. Working with the Department
of Commerce, the Office of the U.S. Trade Representative, and the Federal Communications Commission, State Department officials at home and
abroad have played a crucial role, meeting with local representatives of U.S.
companies to refine our negotiating strategy and pressing foreign officials
in [other] countries to accept U.S. positions.

While American diplomats are helping to write the rules and build the
institutions that govern the global economy, they are also aggressively advocating the interests of U.S. businesses around the world. The department
works with the Export-Import Bank and other federal agencies to ensure
that American firms compete on a level playing field. In 1995 our embassies
and the Department of Commerce helped NYNEX [now Verizon] win a
$1.5 billion undersea fiber-optic cable project that will link countries in
Africa, Asia, and Europe and is expected to support nearly $650 million
in U.S. exports and several thousand American jobs.

Defense. There is nothing new about vans shuttling back and forth across
the Potomac between Foggy Bottom and the Pentagon. Still, the end of the
Cold War has brought a new dimension to the cooperation between the
State and Defense Departments. We are working far more closely together
to promote the institutions and habits of democracy around the world.
Through peacekeeping operations in areas that are critical to U.S. interests and through new security arrangements like the Partnership for Peace,
we are encouraging the subordination of military forces to civilian command, respect for international borders, protection of minority rights, and
free movement of people.

When the United States sent troops as part of an international coalition to
restore democracy to Haiti in 1994, the U.S. government created an innovative, unified political-military operations plan. Its purpose was to ensure that
the civilian and military aspects of the operation were implemented in concert and with equal precision. As a result, when the peacekeepers disarmed
members of the Haitian military, USAID had programs in place to help the
demobilized soldiers develop the skills they would need to reintegrate into
civilian society.

Law enforcement. The burgeoning threats of international organized
crime and narcotics trafficking require our diplomats to join forces as never

before with U.S. law enforcement authorities. Political officers have worked with Justice Department personnel stationed in key regional embassies like Moscow and Bangkok to negotiate bilateral extradition treaties, as well as agreements that help governments share information on criminal investigations. And consular officers stationed at every American diplomatic post have cooperated in person and via computer with agents from the Drug Enforcement Administration (DEA), the FBI, the Immigration and Naturalization Service, and the intelligence community to track suspected drug smugglers, terrorists, and criminals and deny them entry into the United States.

In Budapest, we . . . opened an International Law Enforcement Academy to help the new democracies of the former Soviet bloc establish the rule of law that is essential to a healthy democracy. The academy, which is funded and managed by the State Department, brings together experts from the FBI, the DEA, Customs, the Secret Service, the Internal Revenue Service, the Bureau of Alcohol, Tobacco, and Firearms, and the Department of Energy to share the latest anticrime techniques and technology with their counterparts from Central Europe, the New Independent States of the former Soviet Union, and Western Europe. . . .

Taken together, these new forms of cooperation have significantly raised the number of U.S. government personnel stationed overseas who are not employed by the traditional foreign affairs agencies. In fact, [nearly two-thirds] of those now under the authority of our ambassadors and other chiefs of mission are not State Department employees. As globalization moves forward, that number is likely to grow, as will the challenge of coordinating the American government's presence abroad.

WORKING "MULTI-MULTILATERALLY"

Paradoxically, while globalization induces international cohesion and empowers international enterprises, it also accentuates the limitations of national power. Governments are often too cumbersome to respond effectively to transnational threats—including when those threats are manifest within their own borders. Partly as a result, political authority is devolving from the top down and from the center outward, to local and regional governments, and to community organizations working at the grassroots.

Therefore, many governments, including the U.S., have sought to leverage scarce resources and improve their ability to address transnational threats by forming coalitions with "nonstate actors"—multinational corporations, nongovernmental organizations (NGOs), and international institutions like the United Nations, the World Bank, and the International Monetary Fund. These coalitions allow the United States to work not only multilaterally, but multi-multilaterally, through several organizations and institutions at the same time. In Bosnia, nine agencies and departments of the U.S. government are cooperating with more than a dozen other governments, seven international organizations, and 13 major NGOs—from the Red Cross to the International Crisis Group to the American Bar Association—to implement the Dayton Peace Accords. In the Middle East, the United States chairs the Multilateral Working Group on Water Resources, a group of 47 countries and international organizations that are working to ensure that the region's shared dependence on a scarce resource does not become a threat to political stability. The governments of Israel, Japan, Oman, South Korea, and the United States have established the Middle East Regional Desalination Center in Muscat to support research to reduce the cost of desalination.

An interagency Food Security Working Group co-chaired by the Department of State, Department of Agriculture, and USAID is looking at new ways to apply American knowledge, technology, resources, and influence to ensure that there will be adequate food to meet the demands of the [twenty-first] century. Under this group's auspices, the U.S. National Oceanic and Atmospheric Administration is leading an international initiative that brings together governments, private companies, and NGOs to begin experimental forecasting of seasonal climate patterns, so that crop planting can be adjusted to anticipated annual rainfall, thereby helping to reduce the severity of food emergencies.

The organizational chart for these kinds of collaborative efforts is a patchwork of boxes connected by overlapping and intersecting solid and dotted lines. It often falls to the State Department to coordinate the work of the other agencies of the U.S. government to make sure that their endeavors serve an overarching and coherent strategy. The department also works to integrate the American governmental effort into what other governments—and, increasingly, NGOs and others—are doing in the same areas.

THE END OF FOREIGN POLICY

In the context of the many global problems facing the United States today, and also in the context of their solutions, the very word "foreign" is becoming obsolete. From the floor of the stock exchange in Singapore to the roof of the world over Patagonia where there is a hole in the ozone layer, what happens there matters here—and vice versa. That is not only a fact of life and a useful shorthand definition of globalization itself, it is also a key selling point for those . . . , inside the government and out, who are trying to make foreign policy less foreign, and more relevant, to the American people.

In the absence of a compelling, unifying threat like the one posed by the Soviet Union during the Cold War, the need for American engagement in the world seems less obvious. Largely as a result, the interest of the American public and media in world affairs has waned markedly in the last decade.

In an effort to reverse this trend, the department [from 1995 to 1997] sponsored 40 "town meetings" at which our diplomats have discussed topics from the Middle East peace process to advancing human rights. In her first 20 weeks in office, Secretary of State Madeleine Albright traveled outside Washington 15 times to talk about foreign policy with the American people in schools, at presidential libraries, and from the deck of an aircraft carrier. She—like President Constantinescu of Romania—. . . made use of the World Wide Web, where the secretary's and the department's home pages average 1.7 million hits a month.

All this "outreach," as we call our public-education programs, is far more than special pleading for the State Department or its budget. It is a matter of making the case on the home front for American engagement and activism abroad.

. . . The United States [now] faces a number of critical decisions, each of which will be, in a larger sense, a decision about how our country will respond to the opportunities and challenges of globalization. We must persuade Congress

- that expanding the NATO alliance to include several of the new democracies of Central and Eastern Europe will enhance the stability of a region in which more than 500,000 Americans lost their lives in this century;
- that extending NAFTA to other nations in Latin America will create jobs in the United States and spur economic growth;
- that accepting binding limits on greenhouse gas emissions . . . is essential for the long-term ability of the planet to sustain its environment.

Opponents of these and other initiatives often argue that they compromise or dilute our national sovereignty. In fact, the opposite is true. Well-crafted international commitments and a comprehensive strategy of international engagement enhance rather than dilute our mastery of our own fate as a nation, which is the most pertinent definition of sovereignty. NATO, NAFTA, the Chemical Weapons Convention, the Partnership for Peace, and our participation in the United Nations—different as they are in composition and function—all have one thing in common: They help the United States to channel the forces of interdependence, bending them to the advantage of our own citizens and of other nations that share our interests and values.

When we agree to abide by common rules of the road, we gain the commitment of others to live by mutually acceptable standards in areas like labor law, intellectual property rights, environmental protection, aviation safety, and public health. In so doing, we also establish the means to measure compliance meaningfully, fairly, and enforceably.

Other nations are willing to adhere to these standards not just because they seek access to the U.S. market, or because they want to be on good terms with a major world power. They do so because they recognize that a system of equity and openness based on those standards is key to their own ability to benefit from the phenomenon of globalization. And that means working together to guide the evolution of the phenomenon itself in the direction of equitable economic development, manageable levels of population growth, sustainable use of our natural resources, and the spread and consolidation of democracy....

14

A Tale of Two Secretaries

Eliot A. Cohen

THE GREAT TRANSFORMATION

It takes remarkably little time for a Washington witticism to become a cliché. Such has been the case recently with the quip that Donald Rumsfeld may not have been a very good secretary of defense, but he is a remarkable secretary of war.

In early September 2001, the Defense Department looked to be in poor shape. Since Rumsfeld had taken over, there had been much talk of "defense transformation"—the successor term for the "revolution in military affairs," a supposedly new way of waging war—but little evidence of it. Senior military officers, excluded from early studies arranged by the new secretary, grumbled to the press that the Bush administration was treating them even worse than the Clinton administration had. This discontent may have reflected naive expectations that the Republicans would show up with genial smiles and open wallets, but the friction was real—as was the irritation of many on Capitol Hill and in the press who were put off by Rumsfeld's caustic style.

A planned $18 billion increase in the defense budget, meanwhile, most of it earmarked for personnel costs and not envisioned as part of a series of further increases, fell far short of what many felt was needed to make up for the shortfalls of the previous several years. Difficult decisions such as the cancellations of major weapon systems appeared necessary yet were not forthcoming. In the works was a Quadrennial Defense Review that spoke of shifting away from a narrowly defined set of two major contingencies as the chief planning construct for the Pentagon, but there did not seem to be much of a link between words and programs.

Then came September 11. From the moment the secretary dashed out of the burning Pentagon to rescue wounded subordinates, perceptions of his leadership reversed. In a time of war, Rumsfeld's disagreeable brusqueness appeared as refreshing honesty; his uncomfortably hard edge became the kind of resolution required of a leader; his willingness to badger his generals was not an absence of diplomacy but a firm hand on the reins. From the object of polite derision at cocktail parties, he became the hero of satirical skits on *Saturday Night Live*. For the armed forces fighting the war on terrorism, meanwhile, money was suddenly no object. Plans for [the next] defense budget increase shot to nearly $80 billion, and talk of hard choices was put off.

The jape about the two secretaries reflects a certain truth, one borne out by historical experience: the great war ministers of the past, such as Abraham Lincoln's ferocious secretary of war, Edwin Stanton, would rarely have succeeded in peacetime. But to understand defense policy as merely a function of personality would be inadequate. The pre-9/11 frustrations emerged not so much because of Rumsfeld's personal style as because of the inherent difficulties in guiding a behemoth such as the Defense Department onto a new course. And the post-9/11 amity obscures the tough questions that remain on the table: Is the Pentagon headed for fundamental change, and, if so, is that change necessary or even desirable? What lessons, if any, should its officials take away from the operations in Afghanistan? And what comes next if the war that flamed into the open on September 11 spreads and continues for years or even decades to come?

MISSION IMPOSSIBLE

Peter Drucker, the great student of management, once suggested that "any job that has defeated two or three men in succession . . . must be assumed unfit for human beings." After musing about then Secretary of Defense Robert McNamara, he concluded, "I am not yet convinced that the job of Secretary of Defense of the United States is really possible (though I admit I cannot conceive of an alternative)." Three decades later, Drucker's observation is even more apt than when it was first made, and students of the contemporary American military would do well to consider its implications rather than obsess over an individual's quirks and crotchets. The truth is that being secretary of defense is an impossible job—if one hopes to change quickly the institutions of the armed forces rather than merely preside over them.

The reasons are legion, beginning with the American system of government's reliance on political appointees. What is needed is not merely a Defense Department head but leadership four levels down (the deputy secretary, undersecretaries, assistant secretaries, and deputy assistant secretaries, along with many of their support staff—all told, a group numbering in the hundreds). This reliance is not a bad thing, but invariably, no matter what the administration, intermingled with the experienced, talented, and energetic appointees come the hacks, the political payoffs, and the incompetents.

More important, it has become increasingly difficult to staff an administration promptly. The exhaustive vetting associated with the confirmation process deters some of the best candidates available, as do compensation packages well below those available in the private sector and even universities. It frequently takes, as it has in the Bush administration, the better part of a year to staff the Pentagon, and then even the quick learners take another six months or more to learn the system, brush up on arcane jargon, and master obscure bureaucratic procedures.

For more than a year, therefore, the department is in the hands of a civilian leadership that is understaffed, overworked, and desperately behind. The natural resort of such civilians is to fall back on the bureaucracy, and the military staffers above all. From a harried political appointee's perspective, they are a godsend: masters of the details of their jobs, hard working, cheerful, bright, deferential. The disdainful phrase "captured by the bureaucracy" altogether underestimates the subtlety and power of the process that prevents new administrations from trying hard to reorient the military, let alone succeeding.

As long as the fundamental premise of military competence holds, any attempt to change the armed services by some dramatic organizational coup is doomed to fail. It is tough enough to sack failed generals, terminate programs that produce weapons that do not work, and dismantle bureaucracies responsible for battlefield disaster. A civilian leadership attempting to redirect a military that is obviously successful—and America has been winning its wars for more than a decade—is destined to have a rough time of it.

Bureaucratic norms and pressures have an almost overwhelming force. For example, even so apparently reasonable and modest a measure of the early Rumsfeld Pentagon as the creation of a senior executive council foundered. The council would have allowed the secretary of defense to exert influence through the secretaries of the different services. This move would have been useful because, under the current structure, the service secretaries have tended to defend their individual services' programs and perspectives against external attack rather than acting in coordination with their boss.

Absent such reforms, unsurprisingly, the services and existing military bureaucracy dominate Pentagon affairs—which is why the Bush administration's future defense plans, even with their dramatically increased size, basically conform to and confirm pre–Bush administration thinking. Most of the old systems scheduled for procurement did very well in the 2003 budget, including some, such as the Army's Crusader self-propelled howitzer, that had publicly been labeled as likely candidates for sacrifice on the altar of transformation. There are some new emphases—missile defense, most notably, and space-related operations—but in general the new budget is very much a Clinton plan, only far better funded.

The reasons for this inertia are obvious. Because of the sunk costs looming over decision-makers, the domestic and international trauma likely to be caused by the termination of large systems, and the sheer momentum behind long-standing programs such as the Joint Strike Fighter or the v-22 Osprey airplane, cutting major programs inevitably inflicts pain on powerful interest groups and thus requires exceptional political will.

For more than a decade, furthermore, the armed forces have suffered a procurement drought. Republicans and Democrats alike have maintained an essentially static budget, a large and reasonably well-paid force, and an extremely active military presence overseas. They have paid for that budget by skimping on purchases of new equipment, with the result that the U.S. arsenal is now filled with aging airplanes, tanks, and ships. Major replacement programs, such as a new bomber, may take a decade or more to come on-line, so even those officers who know that many of the items now being acquired are hardly cutting-edge are not willing to forgo them.

THE HIDDEN REVOLUTION

All this inertia looks like a recipe for distressing immobility, and in some ways it is. Before 9/11, more than one disappointed advocate of transformation had written off the administration's defense policy, and most of those skeptics found no reason to change their views after the release of the 2003 budget. But they may have underestimated important countervailing forces, some of which became apparent in the Afghanistan war (as indeed they had in earlier conflicts as well).

The first is sheer size. Even pre-9/11 U.S. defense planning envisioned annual expenditures of more than $310 billion—that is, roughly ten times the British defense budget, or considerably more than twice the defense spending of the rest of NATO put together. Inevitably, embedded in such a large budget will be the funds—substantial in absolute if not relative terms—for innovative projects. The Navy, for example, had reluctantly accepted financing to convert two ballistic-missile-firing submarines into a version of the arsenal ship (a submerged barge for long-range fire support) long advocated by military reformers. The Air Force put most of its weight behind big, traditional aircraft programs, but it was also willing to spend hundreds of millions of dollars developing long-range unmanned aerial vehicles (UAVs), including some that might eventually substitute for airplanes with pilots. And all the while, the boring acquisition of routers and servers, networks and data links, radios and global positioning system (GPS) receivers was laying the base for the networked war that U.S. forces ended up waging in Afghanistan.

By and large, American generals and admirals today are, as senior military officers usually have been, competent and conservative. But underneath them exists a cadre of energetic young officers whose familiarity with information technology and willingness to experiment with it represents something more radical. Increasingly, they have both operational experience and advanced technical education, and they are slowly but surely dragging the system along with them. Whatever stodginess and hierarchy may exist in the U.S. military, the truth is that the majors and lieutenant colonels, and even the sergeants operating the hardware, have a certain power to press their superiors, and they use it.

In this respect, the younger generation is powerfully reinforced by American culture. A poll of military officers will almost invariably show them committed to the revolution in military affairs, or defense transformation, or some other form of radical change—even when their practice and views (about the importance of heavy armor formations, for example) would suggest a very different array of beliefs. This is not so much hypocrisy as it is false consciousness. As Winston Churchill once noted, one should never underestimate "the enormous and unquestionably helpful part that humbug plays in the social life of great peoples." Like American pragmatism, American eagerness to change, experiment, and modernize pervades society so thoroughly that it cannot help saturating the military as well. A generalized belief in the intrinsic value of transformation can thus coexist with, and will gradually overcome, an attachment to traditional weapons and ways.

As the military has become increasingly aware of the achievements of the private sector in exploiting advanced technology, moreover, it is increasingly willing to emulate it. Once military logisticians realized that Wal-Mart and Federal Express put them to shame in efficiency, it was only a matter of time before they would, and did, figure out ways to adopt similar practices. If even a modest heating-oil distributor uses GPS data and efficient routing software to track and schedule its trucks, there is no reason why the U.S. military cannot have similar systems embedded in most vehicles deployed in the Balkans. Indeed, now it does have them, along with a completely different view of the battlefield than ever before.

It is a sociological truism that military organizations reflect the societies from which they emerge, and here at least the United States is no exception. However jerky the transmission belt, the qualities of the modern American economy—its adventurousness, spontaneity, and willingness to share information—eventually reach the American military. Just as the teenager who grew up tinkering with automobile engines helped make the motorized armies of World War II work, so do the sergeants accustomed to playing video games, surfing Web pages, and creating spreadsheets make the information-age military of today effective.

DEFENSE AFTER 9/11

All this said, the truth is that even the generous increases in defense spending . . . planned for 2003 and later will not eliminate the problems that existed before September 11. Nor will they address the new conditions in which the Pentagon operates. The fundamental problems plaguing weapons procurement and infrastructure maintenance have not been solved, as much of the new funding will go to war-related costs and increased spending on personnel. . . .

The pathologies of the military procurement system, moreover, remain intact. After the first months of the Afghan war, for example, there were reports of severe shortages in many of the precision-guided weapons used so effectively there, such as the Joint Direct Attack Munition (JDAM)—a relatively inexpensive modification for conventional bombs that enables satellite-guided precision delivery from virtually any weapons platform under all conditions. This was hardly the first time such shortages had occurred. American arsenals of precision weapons were also depleted after both the 1991 Persian Gulf War and the 1999 Kosovo campaign. The shortage in Afghanistan thus represented the third consecutive failure of the Pentagon to stockpile the right munitions or create a system for surge production of them when needed. The 2003 budget jacks up ammunition spending sharply, but the traditional bureaucratic logic of buying platforms and assuming that the weapons will follow is only slowly yielding to the imperatives of war.

The difficulty in bringing adequate spending to bear on UAVs is a good example of the Pentagon's bureaucratic rigidities, what Rumsfeld recently described as "people who come in with approaches and recommendations and suggestions and requests that reflect a mindset that is exactly the same as before September 11." The Afghan war has demonstrated the enormous value UAVs can provide by spending hour upon hour monitoring enemy positions, transmitting video and other data back to command posts and attack aircraft. It has also shown how they can be used as platforms to deliver lethal attacks. And yet the Predator UAV, one of the technological stars of Afghanistan (and Kosovo), was judged not "operationally effective or suitable" by the Pentagon's office of testing and evaluation in October 2001. This determination had less to do with the qualities of the Predator than it did with the extraordinary standards for effectiveness set by the department. It was a classic case of impossibly demanding requirements causing the Pentagon to disparage its own systems, creating pressure to defer adequate acquisition of what is good today in a perpetual quest for the extraordinary system that will do anything and everything tomorrow. In the 2003 budget, total UAV spending—including research and development as well as acquisition—comes to not much more than a billion dollars, even as the department plans to spend more than $4.5 billion buying F-22 fighters at $200 million each, and more than $3 billion to get Navy F/A-18 fighters at $70 million each.

The logic of the war, or set of wars, upon which the United States has now embarked, furthermore, will pose new challenges beyond classic military conservatism. The United States, like most imperial powers before it, will find it extraordinarily difficult to withdraw from engagements abroad. The Pentagon would dearly love to leave the former Yugoslavia to the supervision of its European allies, which together have a GDP comparable to that of the United States. Yet the political truth remains that American presence is the indispensable catalyst for NATO action, so thousands of U.S. soldiers will continue to police an uneasy peace in the hills of Bosnia and Kosovo. Rumsfeld yearns to withdraw an American infantry battalion from the Sinai desert, where its military skills rust as it presides over a decades-old peace between Egypt and Israel. Yet doing so now, as war metastasizes in the Levant, will be blocked by objections from both the State Department and the local parties.

The Air Force, meanwhile, has been wearing itself out flying combat patrol over U.S. cities, and homeland defense will not be cheap even though the National Guard will bear most of its burdens. U.S. forces have begun constructing semipermanent bases in South and Central Asia, and it is unlikely that the United States will ever revert to the minimal presence it maintained there before [late 2001]. The tempo of U.S. activity elsewhere in Asia has also picked up, with American forces engaging Muslim guerrillas in the Philippines. Other operations in Yemen and elsewhere remain a possibility, and a full-scale war with Iraq looms on the horizon. In the background, Chinese military modernization proceeds apace.

What, then, are the defense requirements of the future? They begin with the capability to project effective military power rapidly to most locations on the planet. This shift implies a bias toward systems that can either deploy very quickly, without local bases or substantial pre-positioning of supplies, or that can hover within range, hopefully below the threshold of local political visibility. Some kind of new bomber is clearly needed, whether manned or unmanned, based on older designs or not. So, too, are guided missile submarines or other versions of arsenal ships, and the kinds of ground forces that can use advanced technologies to call in decisive long-range fire, as the special forces have done in Afghanistan.

American forces are, on the whole, extremely flexible at tactics but more rigid institutionally. Although some stirrings are visible, the services have generally been unwilling to explore moving beyond old forms of organization (e.g., divisions in the Army, fixed-wing aviation in the Marine Corps, or large ships in the Navy). The coming decade, however, will generate even greater stress than the previous one. The armed forces are destined to engage in all-out conventional war and peacetime training of foreign forces, spectacular raids and humdrum military government, operational offense and tactical defense, deterrence and preemption, violent assault and patient vigilance. To handle all these tasks successfully, far broader and deeper transformation will be necessary than has occurred until now. The department's pre-9/11 battles will therefore have to be refought.

THE AGE OF SURPRISES

The common use of the term "post–Cold War era" indicates a failure by students of international affairs to characterize today's world. The Rumsfeld Pentagon, in its early presentations, always highlighted the unpredictability of the international environment, and it had a valid point: one might usefully call the past dozen years "the age of surprises." The U.S. government has been surprised by the end of the Warsaw Pact, the disintegration of the Soviet Union, the Iraqi invasion of Kuwait and the ensuing Persian Gulf War, the Asian financial crisis, the Indian and Pakistani nuclear detonations, and now the events of September 11. There is no reason to think that the age of surprises is over, and there are many reasons to think we are still at its beginning.

There are some things defense planners can know with some confidence: that the United States faces a larger and more durable threat from radical Islamists than it previously understood, and that in China it confronts a regional rival. They know that America looks out on an international order that is, for better and for worse, global and dynamic. This order's language is English and its lifeblood is the massive and instantaneous flow of information, but its economic surges and ebbs have left many societies sorely disadvantaged, elites embittered, and state structures weakened. Defense planners know above all that the United States will and must play the central role in ordering this international system, a function for which it is both uniquely suited and uniquely disabled. And they know that although the United States has an unmatched array of allies, many of them resent its dominance and willingness to act independently even though they will not pay the price or make the effort to substitute for it.

These probabilities should be reflected in defense programming—in the kinds of forces that the U.S. stations in the Pacific, for example, or the emphasis placed on recruiting and equipping special operations forces able to operate in the Arab world. But the uncertainties that lie ahead are equally significant. The pace and intensity of the current conflict will depend partly on the behavior of America's opponents. A salvo of biological agents launched at Israel from Iraq could spark a Middle Eastern war before the United States is ready for one. The shaky Pakistani regime could collapse or become embroiled in a war with India that could lead to a nuclear holocaust. Collapsing states could drag the United States into wars it has studiously avoided.

Technological breakthroughs could conceivably nullify important elements of American military strength. Terrorists could successfully use weapons of mass destruction against the United States.

The Pentagon now combines a planning device of two major theater wars with what is called "capabilities planning." Yet even the latter, a somewhat abstract statement of requirements, is not fully adequate. To meet the range of known and unknown challenges the United States faces, the military will need to cultivate two functions that it has largely neglected during the last busy decade and before: mobilization and professional education.

The increasing use of reservists and National Guard personnel for routine military operations not only puts stress on the lives of those called up for months or even a year at a time. It also runs the risk of exhausting their willingness to serve and indeed undermines the very idea of the citizen soldier. In the past, mobilization meant calling up young men for conscript service, and it is conceivable (if highly unlikely) that this could be necessary once again. More likely, however, will be the need to tap internal reservoirs of military personnel in an emergency—which is why, to take a petty example, it may not have been altogether wise to replace military sentries at major posts with cheaper contract guards. At the same time, the United States may find itself making even greater use of quasi-military contractors to do a great deal of what looks like military business—for example, flying and maintaining UAVs.

Moreover, the Pentagon will have to find better ways of creating an industrial infrastructure that can increase the production of critical munitions and platforms in short order. This change may require different procurement strategies, and perhaps even a reversion to the World War II concern for having systems that could be mass produced—a far cry from the increasingly capable, exotic, and expensive platforms of today's military. How to create a variable-sized military, which the country has not had for several decades, will be a continuing challenge.

Above all, the twenty-first-century U.S. military will require an officer corps of unprecedented versatility and intelligence. One great source of American strength in recent decades has been the excellence of its military training system. By and large, that strength remains, although it also suffered in the 1990s from underfunding and the pressure of deployment schedules that disrupted unit cohesion and the ability to hone perishable collective skills. The practices and outlook of the military toward advanced civilian and military education, however, have not kept pace with the rest of the training system. Technical degrees are generally rewarded. Advanced work in the social sciences and humanities, however, is often regarded as a ticket to be punched rather than an opportunity to grow, and younger officers are often effectively punished rather than rewarded for pursuing their intellectual ambitions. And yet never more than today has there been a need for officers who can think broadly and creatively, who can learn swiftly about unfamiliar regions of the world, and who will fall prey neither to clichés nor to comforting assumptions about societies, military organizations, or war itself....

In the future, the United States will need leaders different from those produced by the institutions of the Cold War—different, in fact, from those who dominate the senior general-officer ranks today. And it will get the officers it needs only by reconstructing its educational system, to which senior leaders so rarely pay sustained attention.

WELCOME TO THE MIDDLE AGES

Behind the need for new kinds of officers lie the changes that are taking place in war itself. The wars of the past were fought by armies organized, trained, and equipped for the kind of conflict that dominated international politics from the Peace of Westphalia in 1648 to the end of the twentieth century. This was war waged predominantly by states, for national or ideological purposes, and fought by armies that generally resembled one another.

When colonial or counterinsurgency conflict presented a different paradigm of war, states generally coped by adjusting or adapting their regular conventional forces. Some did well (the British in Malaya), some poorly (the Soviets in Afghanistan), and some turned in a mixed performance (the United States in Vietnam). Still, the dominant form of military power consisted of large forces equipped for an all-out contest of limited duration.

Today, however, war is changing, and an analogy with medieval warfare helps to show how. In the Middle Ages a variety of entities waged war—states, to be sure, but also crusading movements, religious orders, principalities, and entrepreneurs. Today, the al Qaeda terrorist network and the military contractor Brown & Root are each manifestations of the dispersal of war beyond the exclusive precincts of the state. In contrast to the modern era, moreover, when war has flowed from realpolitik, national ambition, or ideological fervor, war in the Middle Ages emerged from an even broader array of motives: state or personal ambition, religious fanaticism, or sheer banditry. And where modern armies resemble one another closely in their organization and equipment, medieval military institutions looked as different as did the individual warriors—the ponderous knights of western Europe, the highly specialized English longbow archers, or the doughty Swiss pikemen. Whereas modern warfare has tended toward well-defined beginnings and endings, finally, medieval war ebbed and flowed over decades and more, in pulses of violence, siege, and wary truce.

In one respect, however, such analogies break down. In the twenty-first century, characterized like the European Middle Ages by a universal (if problematic) high culture with a universal language, the U.S. military plays an extraordinary and inimitable role. It has become, whether Americans or others like it or not, the ultimate guarantor of international order—something quite different from what it was only a few years ago as the leader of a coalition of free states against the well-defined threats of the Cold War.

In the end, therefore, the dilemmas of U.S. defense policy today do not reflect the strengths and weaknesses of any individual, or even the institutional limitations of a giant and sometimes dysfunctional bureaucracy. They stem, rather, from America's profoundly ambivalent and only semiconscious acceptance of its unique and world-historical role. Whatever the pace at which the Pentagon adapts to that fact, it must do so, and the more swiftly and self-consciously, the better. When Rumsfeld snaps in exasperation at the "approaches and recommendations and suggestions and requests that reflect a mindset that is exactly the same as before September 11," he deserves a sympathetic hearing. The secretary of war may have gotten far better press, but the secretary of defense has the tougher job.

15

Smarter Intelligence

John Deutch and Jeffrey H. Smith

The terrorist attacks on the World Trade Center and the Pentagon understandably provoked two reactions—that this was the worst intelligence failure in recent U.S. history and that U.S. intelligence gathering and analysis must be vastly improved. Many proposals have been put forward to improve U.S. intelligence capabilities. In order to sort those that make sense from those that do not, it is important first to understand the constraints the intelligence community has inherited.

The framework for U.S. intelligence was created in a different time to deal with different problems. The National Security Act of 1947, which established the Central Intelligence Agency (CIA), envisioned the enemy to be states such as the Soviet Union and also recognized the importance of protecting citizens' rights [see box on page 223]. The result was organizations and authority based on distinctions of domestic versus foreign threats, law enforcement versus national security concerns, and peacetime versus wartime. The Federal Bureau of Investigation (FBI) was responsible for the former, and the intelligence community—comprising the CIA, the National Security Agency (NSA), the Defense Intelligence Agency (DIA), and other agencies—was responsible for the latter.

Law enforcement's focus is to collect evidence *after* a crime is committed in order to support prosecution in a court of law. The FBI is reluctant to share with other government agencies the information obtained from its informants for fear of compromising future court action. On the other hand, the CIA collects and analyzes information in order to forewarn the government *before* an act occurs. The CIA is reluctant to give the FBI information obtained from CIA agents for fear that its sources and methods for gaining that information will be revealed in court.

Clearly, the current structure is ill-suited to deal with catastrophic terrorism. Decisions on intelligence reform will revolve around this question of the proper balance between national security and law enforcement goals. Meanwhile, historical boundaries between organizations remain, stymieing the collection of timely intelligence and warnings of terrorist activity. This fragmented approach to intelligence gathering makes it quite possible that information collected by one U.S. government agency before an overt act of terrorism will not be shared and synthesized in time to avert it.

A word about intelligence "failures" is in order. By the most obvious criterion—the success of Osama bin Laden's operatives on September 11—intelligence and law enforcement failed to protect the public. But only time will tell if the information necessary to predict and stop the attacks was in government hands in advance or reasonably could have been. At some point it will be appropriate to analyze this question. For now, however, such an inquiry would only distract government agents and analysts from the critical task of identifying and preventing *future* attacks.

GIVING THE CIA THE LEAD

The FBI and CIA have been working to overcome the fragmentation of counterterrorism intelligence efforts through personnel exchanges and joint training. Yet the FBI and the intelligence community still have separate counterterrorism centers. This duplication hardly makes sense. In an era when national security must be the preeminent concern, the director of central intelligence (DCI) should manage a single National Counterterrorism Center that plans intelligence collection for all agencies and produces analysis derived from all sources of intelligence. A committee chaired by the DCI and including the national security advisor, the director of the new Office of Homeland Security, and the attorney general should set the agenda for these activities. [This article was written before the Bush administration embraced the concept of a homeland security department.—*Eds.*]

The security services of friendly nations are important sources of information for U.S. intelligence; they know their neighborhoods and have access that U.S. agencies do not. At present, the CIA, NSA, DIA, FBI, and the Drug Enforcement Administration have separate agreements with foreign counterpart organizations to obtain information. These efforts should be coordinated. The DCI's authority and responsibility to plan, monitor, and approve arrangements between all intelligence agencies and their foreign counterparts on all intelligence matters, including counterterrorism matters, should be clarified and strictly enforced.

Judging by their recent articles, some editorial writers apparently believe the collection of intelligence through technical means such as communications intercepts and imagery is not important in the fight against terrorist organizations. In fact, cooperation between human and technical intelligence, especially communications intelligence, makes both stronger. Human sources, or HUMINT, can provide access to valuable signals intelligence, which incorporates primarily voice and data communications intelligence. Communications intercepts can validate information provided by a human source. Any operation undertaken in a hostile environment is made safer if communications surveillance is possible. Currently, the NSA, which is under the authority of the secretary of defense, carries out communications intelligence, and the CIA carries out human intelligence, which is under the authority of the DCI. The secretary of defense and the DCI share authority for setting foreign collection priorities. In the case of foreign threats within the United States, the FBI has primary responsibility for setting collection priorities. Here again, the fragmentation makes no sense when considering the global terrorist threat. The new antiterrorism law took a good first step toward remedying this problem by clarifying the DCI's lead role in setting priorities for wiretaps under the Foreign Intelligence Surveillance Act (FISA) and disseminating the resulting information.

In addition, the Bush administration's current review of intelligence, under the leadership of former National Security Advisor Brent Scowcroft, should recommend greater centralization of intelligence collection and analysis under the DCI. Inevitably, strengthening the authority of the DCI will raise the question of whether this position should be separated from the position of head of the CIA. If the DCI is given budgetary, planning, and management authority over the agencies that are responsible for national-level intelligence, then the positions should be separated, just as the secretary of defense sits above the individual services.

DRAGS ON COVERT ACTION

Fragmentation also impairs covert action—activities the United States undertakes to achieve objectives without attribution. Such action has been associated with past CIA efforts to overthrow, in peacetime, political regimes considered a threat to the United States. The future purpose of covert action will be quite different: to destroy terrorist cells and facilities that may produce or store weapons of mass destruction. The distinction between CIA-sponsored covert action and military special operations will become much less relevant, if it is relevant at all. For larger paramilitary operations, a permanent planning staff under the leadership of the secretary of defense, including CIA and FBI staff members, should be put in place to strengthen counterterrorism covert action.

Current law requires both a presidential finding and reporting to Congress of all CIA covert action. No such rule governs covert military operations. In the fight against terrorists, the CIA and the military will be called to conduct joint covert operations, but the differing approval and reporting requirements of these organizations can hamper cooperation. Congress should consider streamlining the law to remove the artificial distinction.

The September 11 attacks renewed questioning about the adequacy of U.S. human intelligence capability. Use of spies is an essential aspect of combating terrorism, and the intelligence community has neither ignored human intelligence nor neglected to target terrorist groups such as Osama bin Laden's Al Qaeda organization. Indeed, there have been notable successes in penetrating terrorist groups and preventing planned terrorist acts, but because they were successes they did not come to the public's attention.

Strengthening human intelligence has been a priority of all DCIs. But human intelligence collection is not a silver bullet that can be separated from other intelligence activities and improved overnight. It takes a long time to build a team of experts who understand the language, culture, politics, society, and economic circumstances surrounding terrorist groups. Furthermore, neither bin Laden nor any other terrorist is likely to confide a full operational plan to a single individual, no matter how carefully placed as a source. Spying requires great skill and discipline, something that cannot be achieved quickly or by throwing money at it. To be sure, the morale of the operations directorate hit an unacceptable low in the early and mid-1990s. But this was not due to reduced budgets or lack of presidential support. The poor morale was due to the discovery within the CIA's ranks of Soviet spy Aldrich Ames in 1994, the revelation of CIA activity in Paris in 1995, frequent investigations by Congress and the CIA's own inspector general, and other events that indicated that professional standards had slipped badly.

HUMINT depends critically on other intelligence efforts. It is generally not decisive by itself, but must be combined with all other sources of information. A prerequisite for good human intelligence is a thorough understanding of the sources of terrorism, and much of this kind of information can be obtained from open sources such as local newspapers in the communities that spawn and protect terrorist organizations. Such analytic information is essential for planning collection strategies, successfully penetrating terrorist groups, and mounting covert operations to disrupt terrorist activities and facilities. Successful human intelligence operations rely critically on intelligence analysis to target their efforts. Thus, rather than creating a separate clandestine service, as some have proposed, the United States should support a stronger, seamless partnership between the CIA's operations and intelligence directorates.

Box 15.1 COMING FULL CIRCLE

A dramatic attack on the United States—Pearl Harbor—provided the backdrop to the last major reorganization of intelligence, which led to creation of the Central Intelligence Agency (CIA) in 1947. "I have often thought," wrote President Harry Truman in his memoirs, "that if there had been something like coordination of information in the government it would have been more difficult, if not impossible, for the Japanese to succeed in the sneak attack at Pearl Harbor."

Key administration officials agreed about the failures of wartime intelligence: "Inadequate operations have resulted in failure to anticipate intelligence needs, in failure to recognize trends, in lack of perspective, and in inadequate pooling of intelligence," wrote Bureau of the Budget Director Harold Smith in a 1945 memorandum to President Truman.

Policymakers' perceptions of intelligence also posed a problem. "There still is widespread misunderstanding of what intelligence is, how it is produced, and in what way it relates to and serves the action and policymaking people," Smith wrote in his memo to Truman. "For example, many persons whose active participation in developing an effective post-war operation is essential are still thinking narrowly in terms of spies and intrigue, in terms of current developments and the latest news, or in terms, solely, of the development of new or special sources of information."

There was no consensus on how to fix the deficiencies of wartime intelligence. The 1945 debate about what sort of intelligence operation to create focused on the question of which was the worst evil: too much centralization or too much compartmentalization. Truman complained to CIA employees in 1952 that when he took office "each Department and each organization had its own information service, and that information service was walled off from every other service." Key military officials argued for one central agency to deal with this problem. Smith, however, argued that most intelligence operations should be organized at a departmental level, and he wanted the State Department to coordinate the departments' intelligence operations.

The forces of centralization won. The 1947 National Security Act established the CIA for a peacetime world in which it was not yet clear what an intelligence agency should do and in which past intelligence failures were foremost in policymakers' minds. In 1999 the Hart-Rudman Commission called for rethinking the way the 1947 act organized intelligence in a report called "New World Coming: American Security in the 21st Century." Yet the discussion surrounding the CIA's birth makes it clear: much of the debate remains the same.

–[*Foreign Policy*]

CHANGING THE RULES

The recent terrorist attacks gave new momentum to a debate over three controversial rules governing CIA operations. The first of these governs how CIA case officers in the field may recruit agents. In 1995, the CIA established a policy requiring the Directorate of Operations headquarters to approve the recruitment of sources believed to have serious criminal or abusive human rights records. The officials apply a simple balancing test: Is the potential gain from the information obtained worth the cost that might be associated with doing business with a person who may be a murderer, rapist, or the like? Some believe this rule has constrained case officers from recruiting agents inside terrorist groups and therefore made it harder to predict and preempt terrorist acts, although senior CIA officials maintain that the rules have not reduced the quality or quantity of counterterrorism intelligence. Congress recently considered legislation directing the DCI to revoke the rule, but it ultimately enacted a "sense of the Congress" provision, as part of the new antiterrorism law, encouraging intelligence officers to "make every effort" to "establish relationships" with such individuals.

There are two reasons such rules are necessary. First and most important, case officers have been and will continue to be vulnerable when they enter arrangements with agents who do not necessarily produce valuable or accurate information and later are found to have committed atrocities against U.S. citizens or others. These case officers may be investigated by the CIA inspector general, the Department of Justice, and congressional committees. The overriding purpose of the 1995 recruiting guidelines was to keep case officers from worrying about just this possibility of prosecution. Clearance by the Directorate of Operations protected the case officer in the field. The rules did the opposite of what was feared; they gave case officers the incentive to take risks because approval from Washington meant that headquarters had to stand behind field decisions. It is a sad irony that Congress, while passing one piece of legislation that encourages case officers to take risks in recruiting agents, in another authorized the DCI to pay for personal liability insurance for case officers. Congress seems to be saying, "Go take risks, but if later we don't like the risks you took, you will be investigated. And the government will pay your legal bills." This seems an odd way to motivate case officers in the field.

The second reason for the 1995 rule governing recruiting is efficiency. The CIA should focus on recruiting agents that have access to genuinely important information and reward case officers' efforts for the quality of information collected, not just the quantity. It can be difficult to judge the appropriate balance between recruiting numbers of agents that may be valuable and recruiting a few agents that will be vital. In some cases, one can rely on the judgment of experienced station chiefs. But both prudence and experience suggest that officials at headquarters need to review these judgments.

Another contentious rule has been President Gerald Ford's 1976 executive order barring U.S. intelligence agencies from assassinating foreign political leaders. The horror of the September 11 attacks on civilians prompted many to call for a reversal of this ban to allow assassination of a terrorist leader or a political leader who supports terrorism. This move would be unwise. The United States will win the war on terrorism, but one result of this victory should not be a world in which assassination of political leaders is an acceptable norm of international law—a precedent that could be established by U.S. action.

Moreover, assassination is rarely effective in defeating motivated groups. For example, the murder of bin Laden would not necessarily remove the threat from Al Qaeda. However, the executive order does not and should not prohibit targeting individual political or military leaders, including leaders of terrorist organizations, in the process of military operations, which take place during *overt* hostilities where opposing forces and their political leadership know they are at risk.

A third change in rules concerns wiretaps on foreigners in the United States and U.S. citizens (especially those in U.S. corporations set up as front organizations) who are associated with suspected terrorist groups. In addition to clarifying the DCI's role under [the Foreign Intelligence Surveillance Act], Congress also relaxed the conditions under which courts may authorize warrants for national security wiretaps and searches. The intelligence community must have access to telecommunications and databases so it can track the movements and associations of suspected terrorists operating in the United States. Similarly, corporations such as banks and airlines will increasingly be asked or required to cooperate with authorities to trace suspected terrorists. Vigilance will be required to prevent improper spying on Americans, but it is possible to devise a system to collect large amounts of information without compromising the privacy and rights of American citizens.

UNREASONABLE EXPECTATIONS

A larger question underlying discussions of intelligence reform is, how much should Americans expect from the intelligence community? Over the past two decades, despite organizational handicaps and conflicting authorities, the intelligence community has built up a considerable counterterrorism capability that has resulted in many successes and, as is now apparent, some spectacular failures. Clearly, Congress and the executive branch are ready to grant the intelligence community greater authority to pursue the paramount mission of national security. And there are dedicated, talented men and women who will make every effort to reduce the threat of catastrophic terrorism. But while the American people can be better protected, they should be under no illusion that the intelligence community can remove all risk. Even if we destroy Al Qaeda, other terrorist groups could also mount acts of catastrophic terrorism, including attacks on our information infrastructure and the use of biological agents such as anthrax, chemical nerve agents, and perhaps even nuclear weapons.

Fortunately, there are not hundreds of such organizations but perhaps only a few dozen, which makes the intelligence task feasible. But it is unreasonable to expect 100 percent success. Thus, while intelligence is the first line of defense, other counterterrorism efforts are also important, including prevention by deterrence or interdiction, bioweapons defense, and managing the consequences of a catastrophic terrorist attack whenever and wherever it occurs.

16

Advisors, Czars, and Councils
Organizing for Homeland Security

Ivo H. Daalder and I. M. Destler

Nine days after September 11, President George W. Bush announced that the Federal government's effort to secure the American homeland against future terrorist attacks would be led by a new, White House-based Office of Homeland Security (OHS). He appointed his close friend, Pennsylvania Governor Tom Ridge, to head the office. While this step was widely welcomed, there [was] a near-consensus among Washington veterans that Ridge [lacked] the leverage necessary for the job, even as a member of the White House staff with clear and direct access to the President. "I fear that as an advisor who lacks a statutory mandate, Senate confirmation, and budget authority, he will not be as effective as we need him to be," Senator Joseph Lieberman (D., Conn.) argued. "A homeland coordinator with only advisory authority is not enough. We need a robust executive agency to carry out the core functions of homeland defense." Lieberman and others . . . accordingly introduced a number of proposals to rectify these imperfections. . . .

Almost every proposal [sought] to fix the problem by bringing widely dispersed authorities and agencies into a new central structure. But centralization alone cannot be the main answer to this formidable challenge. Currently, responsibility for preventing, protecting against, and responding to a terrorist incident is spread not only across the Executive Branch, but also across Federal, state and local authorities. Moreover, the private sector also has a critical role to play. It is simply not possible, nor is it desirable, to bring all the major homeland security functions under a single roof.

What is needed instead is leadership, coordination and mobilization of the responsible agencies and their leaders—at the Federal, state and local levels.

Note: Some footnotes have been deleted; others have been renumbered.

That is precisely the task President Bush...handed Governor Ridge. Given the number of agencies, interests and people involved, it is a task of truly mammoth proportions.... Past experiences in parallel coordinating efforts—for national security and economic policy—provide valuable lessons on how Ridge might accomplish the task.... But on their own, the structural reforms championed by many critics...will be of little help, and could even undercut Ridge's ability to influence the broad range of government activity that he can never directly control.

RE-ORGANIZATION WOULD HELP...

Prior to September 11, a succession of government commissions as well as legislators argued that terrorism constituted a real threat to U.S. security, but that the U.S. government did not give the threat the priority it deserved.[1] Consolidating homeland security functions, they argued, would give it that priority, by creating what the General Accounting Office called a "focal point."[2] In an effort to ensure that homeland security would be a White House priority most proposals sought to place the new organization within the Executive Office of the President.

Clearly, these advocates were on to something. Before terrorists turned commercial jetliners into weapons of mass destruction and killed 3,000 people on U.S. soil, homeland security was not a top priority for the U.S. government. To be sure, successive presidents had talked about the threat of terrorism. Bill Clinton frequently and often publicly worried about a germ-weapons attack by terrorists on U.S. territory. George W. Bush mentioned the threat of terrorism during his campaign, and continued to talk about it once in office (although often as an argument for developing missile defenses). Spending on counterterrorism activities also increased significantly—from $6 billion in 1998 to well over $10 billion in 2001. Finally, with the appointment of Richard Clarke in 1998—in one sense, Ridge's predecessor—as coordinator of counterterrorism, an attempt was made to pull together the myriad agencies and interests involved in preventing and responding to terrorist attacks.

Nevertheless, as of September 10, 2001—even with heightened presidential interest, increased funding and improved coordination—the terrorist threat had not moved anywhere near the top of the White House agenda. Clarke, a Clinton-era holdover, remained a senior director on the NSC staff, but reported to the national security advisor, not to the president. Terrorism was still just one concern among many. Although the various agencies all had terrorism coordinators, other concerns dominated their agendas. For the Pentagon, re-equipping the military to fight two major theater wars simultaneously remained the priority. China, not Al-Qaeda, was the rising threat, and ballistic missile attacks by rogue states, not suicide bombers, were the immediate concern. Drugs, not dangerous pathogens, were the targets of customs agents searching luggage and cargo entering the United States. Consular and immigration officers fretted about granting visas to potentially illegal immigrants rather than students-*cum*-terrorists. The FBI focused on building criminal indictments against terrorists who had committed acts of violence against U.S. interests overseas, rather than tracking non-U.S. nationals who might undertake terrorist acts on American soil. Other priorities displaced the attention and resources that should have been devoted to homeland security.

September 11 changed all that. Now, for all of these agencies, at every level, the terrorist threat stands front and center. The commissioner of the U.S. Customs Service, Robert C. Bonner, told the *New York Times* that "terrorism is our highest priority, bar none. Ninety-eight percent of my attention as commissioner of customs has been devoted to that one issue." The INS, FBI and other key agencies [were] re-organized so as to make counterterrorism their top concern. Priorities . . . shifted in agencies that [had] not been re-organized—including even the Internal Revenue Service, which has assigned some of its criminal investigators to assist in helping determine how terrorist groups are funded.

There are other reasons to consider re-organizing homeland security beyond the need to focus public attention; the key one is the fact that responsibility for homeland security really is very widely dispersed. According to the OMB, nearly seventy agencies spend money on counterterrorist activities— and that excludes the Defense and State Departments and the intelligence community.[3] One organizational chart of Federal government agencies involved in homeland security [contained] 130 separate boxes.[4] Even by more discriminating accounting standards, anywhere between forty and fifty agencies are believed to be involved in the effort—ranging from the departments of Defense, Treasury, Justice, Transportation, Health and Human Services, and Agriculture; to intelligence agencies like the Central Intelligence Agency and National Security Agency; to law enforcement agencies like the Federal Bureau of Investigation, the Secret Service, the Drug Enforcement Agency, and the Bureau of Alcohol, Tobacco, and Firearms; to agencies monitoring points of entry into the United States like the Border Control, the Coast Guard, the Customs Service and the Immigration and Naturalization Service; to agencies responsible for responding to an attack, like the Federal Emergency and Management Agency, the Centers for Disease Control and Prevention, the National Guard Bureau and the Pentagon's [newly] established Northern Command.

This diffusion of responsibility is inherent in providing homeland security because success depends on a multitude of unconnected individuals making good decisions. It is an inherently decentralized operation. A customs service agent sensed something amiss with a car traveling from Canada to the United

States in December 1999 and discovered its trunk loaded with explosive materials designed to blow up the Los Angeles International Airport. A flight instructor found it suspicious that a student was interested only in steering a commercial jetliner, not in taking off or landing, and then reported his suspicion to locally-based Federal authorities (who tried in vain to get FBI headquarters in Washington to take the matter seriously). A firefighter yelled at people coming up from the World Trade Center subway station to go back down, before himself climbing the stairs to fires burning on the 75th floor of one of the towers. A doctor re-examined the X-ray of a postal worker and diagnosed inhalation anthrax in time for an effective antibiotic treatment to be administered. A flight attendant noticed a passenger lighting a match near his feet and acted swiftly to prevent him from detonating a bomb concealed in his shoe. Ultimately, the security of the American homeland rests upon individual judgment calls by those who guard the frontlines: the border guards, immigration officers and customs agents, the doctors, nurses, firemen and police officers. Managing, coordinating, leading and mobilizing these people so that their individual decisions add up to a nation more secure, better prepared and more responsive to the terrorist threat is the organizational challenge of homeland security.

. . . BUT CENTRALIZATION WON'T WORK

The basic concept behind nearly all proposals that [were] set forth for organizing homeland security activities is centralization: the consolidation of functions now scattered across numerous agencies under one common organizational roof. As one astute commentator put it, "There is nothing that has the force of an uncompromising and powerful new entity. A Department of Homeland Security, with power and budgets and subordinate agencies, is also the only way to avoid the disconnected roots of Sept. 11. Only a department would have the ability to set changing priorities between a terrorist and non-terrorist focus, and prepare and respond accordingly."[5]

Among the earlier and more prominent proposals for centralization is that of the Hart-Rudman Commission, released in early 2001. Prophetic in its anticipation of an "end [to] the relative invulnerability of the U.S. homeland to catastrophic attack," the commission put forward "organizational realignment" as the centerpiece of its recommendation:

> The President should propose, and Congress should agree to create, a National Homeland Security Agency (NHSA) with responsibility for planning, coordinating, and integrating various U.S. government activities involved in homeland security. The Federal Emergency Management Agency (FEMA) should be a key building block in this effort. . . . The President should propose to Congress the transfer of the Customs Service, the Border Patrol, and the Coast Guard to the National Homeland Security Agency, while preserving them as distinct entities.[6]

The commission further proposed to divide managerial responsibilities within the new agency among three directorates responsible, respectively, for border security, critical infrastructure protection, and emergency preparedness and response....

As the Hart-Rudman Commission recognized, many institutions and functions that are critical to the task *cannot,* by their very nature, be included in a consolidated agency. The FBI will necessarily remain in the Justice Department (and resistant even to *its* authority). The CDC, indispensable to combating bioterrorism, should remain, albeit loosely, within the Department of Health and Human Services. Perhaps most important, the intelligence arms of domestic law enforcement and the vast and relevant resources of the CIA and the NSA cannot possibly be brought under the direct authority of ... any ... Cabinet-level homeland security official. This means that time-sensitive information requiring priority border or immigration attention will have to come from somewhere other than any conceivable homeland security agency.

The intelligence connection is part of a daunting broader reality: the need for domestically-oriented security authorities to coordinate with international policy agencies and activities under the aegis of the National Security Council. Looking in the other organizational direction, coordination also has to link downward effectively with police, health, rescue and other units under the authority of governors and mayors throughout the land.

Even for organizational units brought within a new agency, formal inclusion would not automatically guarantee effective integration. Upon his appointment, Ridge alluded to the problems of intragovernmental conflict when he declared, "The only turf we should be worried about protecting is the turf we stand on." This warning, alas, applies inside as well as outside organizational walls. The Hart-Rudman Commission sounded a cautionary note when it recommended integration with a caveat: "Transfer of the Customs Service, the Border Patrol, and Coast Guard" should be undertaken "*while preserving them as distinct entities.*" But this apt recognition of the value of each unit's internal coherence was also an acknowledgement that centralization can, and should, only go so far.

LEADERSHIP AND COORDINATION

To re-iterate, the basic organizational need of homeland security is to address activities that are highly diffused and decentralized. How to ensure that a border guard makes the right decision is more important than whether his boss is responsible directly to a central homeland security official. In the end, the real need is to have the right people in the right places with access to the right information, and who can cooperate in ways that make their individual efforts larger than the sum of the parts. This requires senior government officials working together: synchronizing their activities and sharing necessary information and developing a process that maximizes incentives for them to do so.

Forging such a process must be Ridge's central goal. He must engage and re-inforce his senior colleagues in their efforts to make their departments instruments of presidential counterterrorism policy. The attorney general, for example, is an absolutely critical player in homeland security, with oversight for the FBI, INS, and law enforcement generally. He is likely to see himself as the plausible government-wide leader in the domestic response to September 11, just as the secretary of state sees himself, not without cause, as the leader (short of the president) in U.S. foreign policy. The attorney general could very well be threatened by how the homeland security advisor plays his role—after all, successive secretaries of state waged bitter battles over foreign policy with the Henry Kissingers and Zbigniew Brzezinskis who were housed a thirty seconds' walk from the Oval Office. If Ridge appears to be mounting a broad challenge to Attorney General John Ashcroft's authority, the prospects for an effective, integrated campaign against terrorism will plunge precipitously.

The opposite scenario, a homeland security advisor who cannot assert direct authority, poses different problems. . . . Fortunately, the executive order creating Ridge's position also established the Homeland Security Council (HSC) and tasked it with "advising and assisting the president with respect to all aspects of homeland security [and] ensuring coordination of homeland security-related activities of executive departments and agencies and effective development and implementation of homeland security policies." The HSC is headed by the president, and the attorney general is prominent among its members. The homeland security advisor is simultaneously a council member and the official tasked with managing the HSC process. This offers him a vehicle for engaging senior colleagues—the attorney general above all—at a time when he has maximal presidential support and attention. He can model his approach on the successful efforts of others in parallel roles [the National Economic Council and the National Security Council]. . . .

REACHING DOWN THE ORGANIZATIONAL PYRAMID

The HSC's [Homeland Security Council] task is harder than the NSC's because its family of agencies lacks a culture of cooperation such as that which the NSC has nurtured among the intelligence and foreign policy communities since 1947. It is also different in three other important ways. Its primary impact must be at the bottom of the Federal government's organizational pyramid, not the top. Moreover, the HSC must engage state and local officials as well as Federal authorities. Finally, its effectiveness will depend on effective linkage with activities—like foreign intelligence—that will remain in the NSC, not the HSC, orbit.

National security and economic advisors mainly target presidential decisions and actions. The homeland security advisor, however, must concern himself mainly with how the system operates at ground level. The national security advisor can focus primarily on relations with a few key countries, and on top-level decisions affecting them; Ridge must concern himself with building a system that will make airplanes, food and water distribution facilities, public buildings and entire communities across the land less vulnerable to attack. National security advisors concern themselves with the top. The homeland security coordinator must look to the bottom.

It is a daunting task, but it is not his alone. The attorney general needs to guarantee that the FBI and the INS take timely preventive action or pass information on to others who can do so. The HHS secretary needs the CDC to raise the priority it gives to preparing for, detecting and countering biological weapons threats. The secretary of defense should enable the National Guard to be fully engaged in homeland security planning and action by ending the military's reliance on these units as backup for missions overseas. By firmly connecting these tasks to the president's anti-terrorism program, which he and they will craft together, the homeland security advisor can strengthen their abilities to influence those below them.

While actions by Federal agencies must be the prime HSC target, Ridge must focus also on building lines of cooperation and information-sharing with the other levels of our Federal system—and, importantly, with the private sector—much as the Clinton Administration needed to do when addressing threats to the security of the Atlanta Olympics in 1996. Ridge must lead the effort to standardize the training of first responders across the nation. Local communities, states and the Federal government need common procedures, practices and equipment to facilitate communications both to prevent attacks from occurring and to speed an effective response if one does.... If the culture of cooperation among Federal agencies is weakly established, these norms are almost completely lacking among local, state and Federal authorities. Fortunately, the experience and relationships Ridge developed as Governor of Pennsylvania should prove relevant to this task.

Ridge should also be able to draw upon two established organizations to strengthen ties across levels of government. FEMA, the agency of first resort in responding to catastrophes on the ground, has ten regional offices with multiple connections to relevant state and local authorities. The National Guard, organized and controlled by the states, has a "historic and

Constitutional mission of homeland security" (in the words of the Hart-Rudman Commission) and should "redistribute resources" to make this its primary task.[7]

Finally, Ridge and his top White House colleagues need to address the unique coordinating challenges of dealing with a transnational phenomenon like terrorism within organizations that are structured along the foreign-domestic divide....

In addressing all these challenges, what the homeland security director most needs to do is embrace and exploit his role as cross-government coordinator and mobilizer. He must conceive of himself not as a "czar" issuing orders, but as a leader working with and energizing his peers to achieve their common objective....

THE NEED FOR REFORM

...Securing the homeland against terrorism is a daunting challenge. Any new leader and organization would need simultaneously to act boldly to establish their authority and to feel their way as they learn what works and what does not. For reasons detailed above, it is best to conceive of the task *not* as one of organizational centralization and consolidation, but rather cross-governmental coordination, mobilization and leadership, with priority given to establishing collaborative, positive-sum personal relationships at senior levels.... [In 2001, shortly after this article was written, Congress and the president decided to centralize homeland security in a single cabinet-level department. This involves the largest reorganization of the government in fifty years.—*Eds.*]

NOTES

1. See, for example, *Countering the Changing Threat of International Terrorism,* Report of the National Commission on Terrorism, chaired by Ambassador L. Paul Bremer, III; *Road Map for National Security: Imperative for Change,* The Phase III Report of the U.S. Commission on National Security/21st Century, March 15, 2001, co-chaired by Senators Gary Hart and Warren B. Rudman; and *First Annual Report to the President and the Congress: I. Assessing the Threat,* Report of the Advisory Panel to Assess Domestic Response Capabilities for Terrorism Involving Weapons of Mass Destruction, December 15, 1999, *Second Annual Report to the President and the Congress: II. Toward a National Strategy for Combating Terrorism,* December 15, 2000, chaired by Gov. James S. Gilmore, III, and *Third Annual Report to the President and the Congress: III. For Ray Downey,* December 15, 2001, chaired by Gov. James S. Gilmore, III.

2. General Accounting Office, *Combating Terrorism: Selected Challenges and Related Recommendations,* GAO-01-822 (Washington: General Accounting Office, September 2001), pp. 34–43.

3. Office of Management and Budget, *Annual Report to Congress on Combating Terrorism* (August 2001).

4. As described in the *New York Times,* November 4, 2001.

5. William M. Arkin, "Protecting the United States," *Washington Post* (online version), October 7, 2001.

6. *Road Map for National Security,* pp. xiii, 13–4.

7. *Road Map for National Security,* pp. 24–5.

17

Trade Policy Making
The Changing Context

Bruce Stokes and Pat Choate

PROCESS SHAPES SUBSTANCE

The policymaking process has long shaped the ultimate substance of U.S. trade policy. What Washington determines to be America's international commercial posture has generally been a function of who has the authority to make decisions, who is in the room when those decisions are made, and how meaningful is the input of those participants in that process. The inevitable struggles that have occurred throughout U.S. history over access to and influence on this decision-making process have been both defined and driven by the awkward marriage dictated by the Constitution, which gives Congress the ultimate authority "to regulate commerce with foreign nations" and accords the president the power to negotiate treaties with foreign governments. This sharing of power and authority has, in recent years, repeatedly led to stalemates over the substance or direction of U.S. trade policy. . . .

"There have been three distinct phases in the evolution of the U.S. trade policy process," wrote trade historian Alfred Eckes . . . ,reflecting the interplay of institutions, individuals, and ideas. "First, there was a long period of congressional direction, lasting from the inauguration of the federal government in 1789 to the Great Depression of the 1930s. A second shorter period of executive leadership extended from passage of Secretary of State Cordell Hull's reciprocal trade program in 1934 to the close of the Kennedy Round [of trade negotiations under the General Agreement on Tariffs and Trade, or GATT]. And finally, since the Trade Act of 1974 established a more structured and balanced partnership (fast-track) between Congress and the Executive [branch], there have been periods of both close institutional cooperation and increased friction."[1]

Throughout this time, government actions affecting trade have been at the center of American policy deliberations. Since tariffs were to be the largest single source of revenue for the new United States, it is not surprising that the second law the first Congress enacted was the Tariff Act of 1789. For the next century and a half, tariff battles dominated congressional proceedings, because trade policy debates were in part fights over revenue. (Until 1910, tariffs accounted for about half of all federal revenues.)

Similarly, trade deliberations have historically provided a venue for battles over "trade-related" issues. Before the Civil War, for example, the antislavery movement promoted bans on the international shipment of slaves and products made by slaves to undermine the institution of slavery. And in the late nineteenth century, progressives supported the free trade cause as a means of attacking the privileged.

Throughout this long period, squabbles over trade were animated by many of the same tensions that drive the current trade policy debate. The politically well connected used their influence over tariff-setting to nurture and protect specific sectors of the economy. The disenfranchised attacked that access as undemocratic and inequitable.

For the most part, this debate took place within the halls of Congress. It was members of Congress who determined tariff levels, not the president. Interest groups seeking protection or trade liberalization made their pilgrimage to Capitol Hill, not the White House.

This constitutionally sanctioned monopoly of power was ultimately Congress's undoing. In 1930, passage of the Smoot-Hawley Tariff Act set an average duty of nearly 53 percent, the highest level in U.S. history. Other countries quickly retaliated with higher tariffs of their own and U.S. trade fell by two-thirds in just four years. Smoot-Hawley was not the primary reason for this dramatic contraction in trade (world trade had already begun to shrink), but the tariff bill came to be the scapegoat for the Great Depression and Congress got the blame.

In 1934, in an effort to reinvigorate international commerce and create American jobs, the administration of Franklin Roosevelt proposed that Congress delegate to the president the authority to make trade agreements with foreign countries and to reduce U.S. tariffs by up to 50 percent by proclamation without requiring further approval by Congress, as long as U.S. trading partners granted the United States reciprocal tariff reductions. During congressional debate on the measure, some members of Congress argued that the legislation was an unconstitutional delegation of legislative power to the executive branch. They worried that Congress was, in effect, giving advance approval to trade agreements and vesting the president with too much power to conduct tariff negotiations. In the end, Congress gave the president "tariff proclamation" authority. To preserve democratic principles in the new policymaking process, Congress, overriding State Department objections, required public hearings to be held on tariff matters. Moreover, it required publication of any intention to negotiate new trade terms, along with a list of products on which the United States was considering granting concessions. And it sought to maintain control over trade liberalization by limiting the executive branch's negotiating authority to three years, subject to review and reauthorization.

As a result, ... "Congress remained in the driver's seat. The law kept the [president] on a tight leash, forcing him to return to Congress to obtain renewed authority as well as feedback on the agreements [he] had made. The law was designed to ensure that the State Department would be responsive to the needs of specific sectors and would balance export promotion with import protection."[2] Nevertheless, the Reciprocal Trade Agreements Act of 1934 "was a profound structural shift in the balance of trade decision making that had an equally profound impact on the substantive outcome of the policy process," noted Susan C. Schwab in *Trade-Offs: Negotiating the Omnibus Trade and Competitiveness Act.*[3]

Secretary of State Cordell Hull had responsibility for administering this new trade-policymaking authority. He moved aggressively to reduce tariffs, signing thirty-two trade agreements with twenty-seven countries by 1945. But the delegation of trade authority made the executive branch, not Congress, the new focal point of constituent complaints. To shield himself, Hull relied on a small group of academics and New Deal advocates with little private-sector experience who were spread throughout the administration. The identity of these working groups of technicians, economists, diplomats, and administrators was known only to a select few in the administration. The idea was that in the face of still-powerful protectionist political forces in the nation, those advising and implementing the New Deal trade policies could operate best outside the glare of the political spotlight. Their track record is evidence of their effectiveness in implementing trade liberalization, but the closed nature of their activities and their lack of accountability to Capitol Hill only confirmed some of Congress's worst fears.

U.S. trade expanded dramatically in the post–World War II era in the wake of profound tariff cuts by the United States and its trading partners. At the same time, international commerce was also shifting from the exchange of agricultural products, raw materials, and finished goods to movements of capital, services, and technology. And, as tariffs fell, the nature of trade barriers changed. Nations used nontariff barriers, such as standards, quotas, and domestic purchase restrictions, to protect their markets from competition from foreign products and services. The adverse impact on U.S. producers and workers of these new patterns of trade and new forms of protectionism slowly became apparent.

Congress became increasingly restive about the Faustian terms of its delegation of trade responsibility to the executive branch. Since the president's tariff-cutting authority needed periodic reauthorization, Congress used such votes to slowly claw back some of its lost influence. The Trade Expansion

Act of 1962, for example, granted the executive branch its most wide-ranging negotiating authority yet. But, in return, Congress created the post of Special Representative for Trade Negotiations (now the USTR [U. S. Trade Representative]) to move trade policy-making out of the State Department, where it had often proven beyond Congress's reach, and into the White House, where it would be more politically accountable to Capitol Hill. Congress also mandated the creation of a trade policy coordination process among the various executive-branch departments, such as State, Commerce, and Agriculture, and appointed official congressional advisers to future U.S. negotiating delegations.

Then, in 1967, in a watershed event, U.S. trade negotiators returned from the Kennedy Round of multilateral trade negotiations with agreements on nontariff issues. Congress refused to implement them. Critics of the deal claimed it exceeded the executive branch's negotiating authority.

On Capitol Hill, as Aaronson recounted in her book *Taking Trade to the Streets: The Lost History of Public Efforts to Shape Globalization,* members of Congress finally confronted the changed reality: trade negotiations were no longer simply about import duties at the border.[4] Trade agreements were increasingly about industrial standards, the environment, and consumer health and safety. These issues had long been considered a congressional prerogative and were highly charged politically. For the White House, Congress's effective rejection of elements of the Kennedy Round deal was a wake-up call. Trade negotiators realized that presidential "proclamation authority" for tariff cuts would no longer suffice for more complicated trade agreements and that they would need a much broader constituency of support if future trade agreements were to stand a chance of congressional passage.

The 1974 Trade Act thus dramatically recast the balance of power between Congress and the executive branch with regard to trade and opened up the trade policymaking process to new actors. To ensure speedy and definitive action on trade matters, Congress promised to consider trade agreements on a "fast track," which would allow limited debate, no amendments, and an assured up-or-down, simple-majority vote.

This legislation did not just alter the congressional process, however; it also expanded the scope of agreements that the executive branch could negotiate. Trade negotiators were granted express authority to negotiate nontariff trade barriers, such as regulations and standards. This expansion of negotiating responsibility was necessary given the changing nature of international trade. But this delegation of authority also set the stage for much of the trade strife that divides the nation today. The agendas of trade negotiators were dramatically expanded. Public concern was aroused because, unlike tariffs, the nontariff barriers involved in such negotiations often directly affect people's lives. During the House hearings before passage of the 1974 Trade Act, these concerns were articulated by Representative Peter Frelinghuysen

(R-N.J.), who worried that negotiations on "non-tariff barriers...are so in-extricably intertwined in a web of domestic social, economic and political considerations that Congress would benefit by knowing what the executive branch has in mind before [it enters] into negotiations."[5]

To address such concerns, many of those involved in the congressional debate advocated that trade policymaking become more democratic, involving a broader cross-section of Americans, as Aaronson has chronicled. The Emergency Committee for Foreign Trade (a leading supporter of trade liberalization) suggested that "the president consider the views of the public" on nontariff barriers, since the president already had to assess public views before entering into narrower tariff negotiations. In the end, the 1974 Trade Act made trade policymaking more transparent and accountable.

Congress got a degree of consultation and oversight not included in past extensions of trade-negotiating authority. In addition, an official private-sector advisory committee system was created that included labor, industry, farming, and consumer representatives; these members were to play an integral part in trade negotiations.

Finally, in the Jackson-Vanik amendment to the 1974 Trade Act, Congress explicitly linked trade policy to the willingness of the Soviets and other communist governments to liberalize their emigration policies. By so doing, Aaronson concluded, "Congress made social results an acceptable objective for trade agreements, making it easier subsequently for groups not concerned with the economic effects of trade to influence trade policies."[6] Observed Schwab, "In exchange for delegating to the executive a generous measure of flexibility, the Congress gave itself and its constituents some assurance of ongoing input in the negotiating process."[7]

Only subsequently did it become apparent that the circle of participants was still relatively small given the growing importance of trade policy to the nation's economic health. And, without a concomitant expansion of the seats around the policymaking table, the seeds of distrust had been sown.

Conditions in the 1980s and 1990s only aggravated trade tensions among Congress, the executive branch, and those with a political and economic interest in trade, imperiling further trade liberalization. During the Reagan administration, in the face of a mounting trade deficit and amid a weak economy and high levels of unemployment, Americans' frustration with the lack of executive urgency and leadership only grew. A widespread sense was shared on Capitol Hill that the White House briefed Congress and members of its advisory committees after trade decisions were made rather than engaging them in a dialogue in advance of such actions. The perception grew that appointments to advisory committees were increasingly made on a partisan political basis.

During the Clinton administration, while Congress still worked with the White House to pass NAFTA and the implementing legislation for the results of the Uruguay Round of multilateral trade negotiations, the margin of support for trade liberalization was steadily shrinking. The administration's mishandling of efforts in 1997 and 1998 to reauthorize the president's trade-negotiating authority highlighted the gulf separating Capitol Hill and the White House on how to conduct trade policy.

Signs that the process is breaking down have been evident for some time. The Trade Act of 1974 passed by an overwhelming margin: 72 to 4 in the Senate and 323 to 36 in the House. In 1988, the Omnibus Trade and Competitiveness Act, which included fast-track legislation, passed the Senate 85 to 11 and the House 376 to 45. The margin of trade support continued to erode in 1993, when a one-year extension of fast-track passed by 76 to 16 in the Senate and 295 to 126 in the House. And the vote on NAFTA in 1994 was 61 to 38 in the Senate and 234 to 200 in the House. By 1998, support had shifted sufficiently that fast-track legislation failed in the House by a vote of 180 to 243.

This erosion of support has not been a partisan affair. The number of Republicans in the House voting against fast-track rose from 11 in 1974 to 41 in 1988, 43 in 1994, and 71 in 1998. Thirty House Republicans also voted against the African Growth and Opportunity Act and the Caribbean Basin Initiative in 2000.

Democrats moved from substantial majorities in favor of fast-track in 1974 and 1988 to substantial majorities against it in subsequent years. The Trade Act of 1974 received the support of 41 Senate Democrats, with only 3 against, and the support of 176 House Democrats, with only 25 against. By 1993, Democrats were split 38 to 10 in the Senate and 145 to 102 in the House on the vote for a one-year extension of fast-track. NAFTA legislation received 102 votes from House Democrats (with 156 against) and 27 votes from Senate Democrats (with 28 against). In 1998, House Democrats voted against fast-track by a margin of 29 to 171. And in 2000, Democrats still showed reservations about trade, with 78 in the House and 13 in the Senate voting against the Africa and Caribbean trade deals.

These votes testify to the breakdown in the delicate balance of interests in the trade policymaking process. Of course, this shifting support reflects substantive differences over trade: a rise in protectionist concerns, a decline in support for free trade and a growing value placed on traditionally non-trade issues such as labor and the environment. And these differences will certainly be difficult to resolve. But the history of trade policymaking in the United States suggests that the challenge is not to ameliorate such policy differences, which after all are rooted in differing economic and political self-interest. Rather, the lesson for policymakers is the need to constantly re-equilibrate the policymaking process to accommodate changing substantive interests in the hope that the process can continue to produce a consensus on trade policy.

THE INTERNATIONAL PROCESS

The evolution of the trade policymaking process in the United States was paralleled by the progressive articulation of trade rule-making and dispute settlement internationally. Over the years, the domestic American debate about this global regulatory process has often been driven by a concern that such policymaking lacked fundamental democratic values.

In the closing days of World War II, the governments of the United States, the United Kingdom, and the liberated countries of Europe jointly devised a global economic system based on open markets and governed by clear rules, whose purpose was to stimulate the freer flow of goods among nations and thus avoid the protectionism that was blamed for both the Great Depression and the subsequent global conflict.

The three pillars of this system were the International Monetary Fund, designed to stabilize currency markets; the World Bank, intended to provide the capital to rebuild war-torn Europe and Asia; and the International Trade Organization (ITO), which was meant to set, monitor, and adjust global trade rules. The first two organizations were duly created, but a lack of U.S. support doomed the ITO.

Since international commerce needed some framework of rules, the world's trading nations had signed GATT as an interim pact in 1947. With the failure of the ITO, GATT became the principal global forum for multilateral trade negotiations.

By design, GATT was nothing more than a contract between nations, and its enforcement depended on the goodwill of the participating countries. If a country was found in violation of its GATT commitments, it could, with impunity, refuse to comply.

Frustration with noncompliance and a desire to broaden GATT's scope led to the creation of the WTO in 1995 after the Uruguay Round of multilateral trade negotiations. The new institution's agenda goes beyond tariffs to include agriculture trade, sanitary and phytosanitary measures, rules on textile and apparel production, trade-related investment measures, rules of origin, rules on subsidies and countervailing measures, safeguards, trade in services, and global intellectual property protections.

But the WTO remains an institution of 142 sovereign states. Its rules of procedure—such as which meetings are open, which documents are public—can be changed only by an affirmative vote by two-thirds of its members. Its institutional culture still reflects the mores and values of the more select GATT, which started out with only eight members. And many of the WTO's member governments themselves are democracies in name only, with domestic political and administrative processes that are far from being transparent or participatory.

Moreover, it is the interaction of the WTO's broader mandate for international trade rule-making and its new process of dispute settlement that animates the current public debate about trade and the WTO. Those from the business community who advocate definitive dispute settlement justify their case with an appeal for due process. It is unfair, they contend, for nations to violate their international commitments with impunity. Those from labor, consumer, and environmental groups who opposed the creation of the WTO argue that an ever-wider WTO agenda intrudes on domestic regulation. In subsequent years, as the WTO has begun to make decisions about environmental standards and the like, the long-standing domestic U.S. debate about who has a legitimate role in trade decision-making has become an international debate about openness, transparency, and due process at the WTO. . . .

DOMESTIC REGULATION AND TRADE

In the 21st century, trade negotiations and international commercial agreements are less and less about tariffs, quotas, and other formal at-the-border impediments to foreign commerce, and more and more about domestic regulatory environments and how they impede or enhance international competition. The Technical Barriers to Trade provisions of the Uruguay Round Agreement, the mutual recognition agreement talks now being implemented between the European Union (EU) and the United States, and aspects of the Clinton administration's framework talks between Tokyo and Washington all reflect governments' attempts to reduce the impact on trade of domestic regulations, standards, and testing procedures. In addition, various international standards-setting bodies—such as the Codex Alimentarius Commission, which helps set global food standards, and the World Forum for the Harmonization of Vehicle Regulations—are ever more important venues for deliberations on trade facilitation.

The trade agenda is rapidly melding with the domestic regulatory agenda. Developing rules for the use of genetically modified organisms, for example, has become both a domestic environmental health concern and a trade issue. Recent transatlantic efforts to standardize headlight design had both safety and trade implications. And, in a global economy, the U.S. Food and Drug Administration (FDA) effectively set health and safety rules for the Asian, European, and Latin American pharmaceutical industries by establishing norms for the world's largest market (the United States) and for some of the world's largest drug companies (American firms).

The inclusion of regulatory issues on the trade agenda brings a whole new cast of U.S. government players into the trade policymaking process, an acronym soup that includes the EPA (Environmental Protection Agency),

OSHA (the Occupational Safety and Health Administration), and NHTSA (the National Highway Traffic Safety Administration). Each of these agencies has its own hard-fought history of establishing a level of domestic regulation, its own experience (or lack thereof) in international deliberations, and its own bureaucratic priorities. Most important, the range of issues involved—the environment, food and drug health and safety, consumer well-being—engages in the trade policymaking process a disparate new group of stakeholders: members of Congress, leaders of industry, and citizen activists.

The internationalization of the long-running debate over appropriate regulation is no less contentious than its domestic counterpart. The business community views the inclusion of domestic regulations in the international trade negotiating agenda through an entirely different lens than do consumer and environmental advocates. Corporations see common global standards as logical cost-cutting initiatives. Activists are wary that the international harmonization of health and safety rules is a prescription for lowest-common-denominator regulation. Equally important, many of the U.S. domestic regulatory agencies do not place a high priority on facilitating trade, nor do they have the budget, personnel, or congressional mandate to pursue such an agenda.

Bridging this divide will require an artful balancing between the pursuit of economic efficiency and the protection of the environment and consumer health and safety. This has long been the challenge facing domestic regulators, but now, for the first time on this scale, it is also an international task.

History suggests that the highest quality, most efficient regulation is the product of the competition of ideas. And the best competition is created by the involvement of a broad array of stakeholders. To facilitate this effort and to give its outcome public credibility, the new process of trade-related international rule-making—mutual recognition agreements, global standard-setting and regulatory harmonization, and equivalencies—must be made more accessible and accountable to the people whose lives it affects....

Failure to resolve the growing tension between trade and domestic regulatory activities will not, as some consumer and environmental activists seemingly hope, slow globalization and thus preserve high domestic standards in a pristine garden walled off from the international marketplace. A more likely scenario is that the economic rationale for international regulatory convergence will become increasingly compelling in the face of a failure to harmonize disparate domestic rules. In that commercial environment, business may simply find ways around domestic regulation or prevail upon Congress and the executive branch to force regulatory agencies to hew to international standards with insufficient regard for the level of protection those standards afford.

In the worst-case scenario, failure to act on regulatory convergence could lead to a new definition of the relationship between trade rules and domestic regulation emerging piecemeal through decisions of WTO dispute-settlement panels. Having trade experts pass judgment on health, safety, and environmental rules would prove unacceptable to domestic regulators and to citizen groups. Moreover, it would further undermine public support for the multilateral trading system. None of these outcomes is optimal.

To ensure that trade concerns do not inexorably trump domestic regulatory interests in a manner that initially harms consumer interests and eventually stokes a public backlash against globalization, some way must be found to engage regulators and trade negotiators in a proactive effort to both liberalize international commerce and upwardly harmonize domestic regulation. . . .

In the end, uniform global regulation, common product standards and equivalent testing will prove difficult at best. Differences in culture, regulatory philosophy, and experience in consumer protection preclude widespread harmonization. Different stages of development will dictate different regulatory needs. And some degree of international competition is probably healthy in developing new approaches to regulation.

Nonetheless, in a globalizing economy, some convergence of national regulation is both inevitable and potentially beneficial. There is still likely to be growing friction between the interests of those intent on facilitating trade through regulatory convergence and the interests of those intent on preserving domestic regulatory standards. In the interest of economic efficiency and consumer safety, some way must be found to minimize this friction and maximize the benefits of high standards and liberalized trade. The best way to do this is by opening up the international regulatory policymaking process to new actors.

NOTES

1. Alfred E. Eckes, "The Trade Policy Process in Historical Perspective," Council Study Group Paper, 1999.

2. Susan Aaronson, "Who Decides? Congress and the Debate over Trade Policy in 1934 and 1974," Council Study Group paper, 1999.

3. Susan C. Schwab, *Trade-Offs: Negotiating the Omnibus Trade and Competitiveness Act* (Boston, MA: Harvard Business School Press, 1994).

4. Susan Aaronson, *Taking Trade to the Streets: The Lost History of Public Efforts to Shape Globalization* (Ann Arbor, MI: University of Michigan Press, 2001).

5. Aaronson, "Who Decides?"

6. Aaronson, *Taking Trade to the Streets,* p. 60.

7. Schwab, *Trade-Offs: Negotiating the Omnibus Trade and Competitiveness Act.*

III

DECISIONMAKERS AND THEIR POLICYMAKING POSITIONS

Foreign policy choices are often made by a remarkably small number of individuals, the most conspicuous of whom is the president. As Harry S. Truman exclaimed, "I make American foreign policy."

Because of the president's power and preeminence, it is tempting to think of foreign policy as determined exclusively by presidential preferences and to personalize government by identifying a policy with its proponents. "There is properly no history, only biography," is how Ralph Waldo Emerson dramatized the view that individual leaders are the makers and movers of history. This "hero-in-history" model finds expression in the practice of attaching the names of presidents to the policies they promulgate (e.g., the Truman Doctrine, the Kennedy Round, the Bush Doctrine), as if the men were synonymous with the nation itself, and of routinely attributing foreign policy successes and failures to the administrations in which they occur.

The conviction that the individual who holds office makes a difference is one of the major premises underlying the electoral process. Thus, each new administration seeks to distinguish itself from its predecessor and to highlight policy departures as it seeks to convey the impression that it has engineered a new (and better) order. The media's tendency to label presidential actions "new" abets those efforts. Hence leadership and policy are portrayed as synonymous, and changes in policy and policy direction are often perceived as the results of the predispositions of leaders themselves.

Clearly leaders' individual attributes exert a potentially powerful influence on American foreign policy, and no account of policy sources would be complete without a discussion of them. Still, many scholars question the accuracy of this popular model. They argue that the hero-in-history, or idiosyncratic, model is misleading and simplistic, that it ascribes too much influence to the individuals responsible for the conduct of American foreign policy and implicitly assumes that this influence is the same for all leaders in all circumstances.

That individuals make a difference is unassailable, but it is more useful to ask (1) under what circumstances the idiosyncratic qualities of leaders exert their greatest impact; (2) what types of institutional structures and management strategies different leaders are likely to follow; and (3) what policy variations are most likely to result from different types of leaders. These questions force us to examine how individual characteristics find expression in foreign policy outcomes and how the policymaking roles that leaders occupy may circumscribe their individual influence.

When we consider the mediating impact of policymakers' roles, we draw attention to the fact that many different people, widely dispersed throughout the government, contribute to the making of American foreign policy. In Part II we examined some of the departments and agencies of government involved in the process. Here, in Part III, the concern is with decisionmakers and how the roles created by the government's foreign policy–related organizational structures influence the behavior of the policymakers occupying these roles and, ultimately, American foreign policy itself. As a rival hypothesis to the hero-in-history image of political leadership, "role theory" posits that the positions and the processes, rather than the characteristics of the people who decide, influence the behavior and choices of those responsible for making and executing the nation's foreign policy. Furthermore, in this view, changes in policy presumably result from changes in role conceptions rather than from changes in the individuals who occupy these roles.

Role theory also leads us to other perspectives on how policymakers make foreign policy choices. Considerable evidence drawn from foreign policy case studies points toward the pressures for conformity among those responsible for choosing among competing foreign policy alternatives, pressures that may lead to less than optimal choices. Furthermore, the principal actors in the foreign affairs government often compete with one another as they consider competing policy alternatives, with their respective bargaining positions dictated by organizational preferences rather than national interests. In particular, the "bureaucratic politics" model of decisionmaking stresses the importance of the roles individuals occupy in large-scale organizations and the struggles that occur among their constituent units. Proponents of the model claim it captures the essence of the highly politicized foreign policy decisionmaking process more accurately than does the model of rational behavior, which assumes that the government operates as a single, unitary actor. That popular decisionmaking model maintains that policymakers— notably the president and his principal advisers—devise strategies and implement plans to realize goals "rationally"—that is, in terms of calculations about national interests based upon the relative costs and benefits associated with alternative goals and means.

Graham Allison's book *Essence of Decision,* a study of the 1962 Cuban Missile Crisis, is the best-known effort to articulate and apply the bureaucratic politics model as an alternative to the rational actor model. Allison developed two alternative strands of the bureaucratic politics model. One, which he calls the *organizational process* paradigm, reflects the constraints that organizational procedures and routines place on decisionmakers' choices. The other, which he calls *governmental politics,* draws attention to the "pulling and hauling" that occurs among the key bureaucratic participants in the decision process.[1]

How, from the perspective of organizational processes, do large-scale bureaucracies affect policymaking? One way is by devising *standard operating procedures* for coping with policy problems when they arise. For example, when the George W. Bush administration began talking about options for dealing with weapons of mass destruction in mid-2002, the absence of large forces-in-being in situ constrained its choice of military options. Over the next several months the administration began deploying large military forces to the Middle East as a possible prelude to a war with Iraq. Ground forces were moved into Kuwait and surrounding countries; naval forces were dispatched to the Persian Gulf, the Indian Ocean, and the Mediterranean Sea; and reserve forces at home were mobilized to replace and supplement those sent abroad. The deployments' purpose was to maximize the military options available to the administration even as it pursued diplomatic strategies. Still, it is reasonable to assume that the deployments themselves and planning for various military options followed previously rehearsed routines, much as they had more than a decade earlier as a prelude to the Persian Gulf War. The organizational routines of the various units deployed arguably shaped what was possible and what was not (could missiles placed near Islamic mosques be destroyed from the air without also destroying the mosques?), thus constraining the menu of choice available not only to military leaders but also to the president and his civilian advisers.

Governmental politics, the second strand in the bureaucratic politics model as articulated by Allison, draws attention to the way individuals act in organizational settings. Not surprisingly, and as role theory predicts, the many participants in the deliberations that lead to foreign policy choices often define issues and favor policy alternatives that reflect their organizational affiliations. "Where you stand depends on where you sit" is a favorite aphorism reflecting these bureaucratic (role) imperatives. Furthermore, because the players in the game of governmental politics are responsible for protecting the nation's security, they are "obliged to fight for what they are convinced is right." The consequence is that "different groups pulling in different directions produce a result, or better a resultant—a mixture of conflicting preferences and unequal power of various individuals—distinct from what any person or group intended."[2]

Sometimes, however, these bureaucratic differences can lead to policy conflict and stalemates, as witnessed by the Bush administration during the summer of 2002 when options about possible actions toward Iraq were considered. While some within the administration favored quick action to remove Saddam Hussein because of his development and use of weapons of mass destruction, others, including Secretary of State Colin Powell and his deputy, Richard Armitage, contended that that approach had "risks and complexities" that needed more review.[3] Opinion was also reportedly divided within the Department of Defense, with civilian officials more favorable to military action than military officers. Furthermore, members of Congress and officials in the earlier George H. W. Bush administration also argued against rapid escalation to military action. Policy development was thus stalled for a time, and the administration pursued resolutions in the UN Security Council and Congress to garner more support for more vigorous action against Saddam Hussein.

The example is consistent with the logic of the bureaucratic politics model, suggesting that sometimes the explanation for why states make the choices they do lies not in their behavior vis-à-vis one another but rather in the disputes within their own governments. Furthermore, rather than presupposing the existence of a unitary actor, as the rational model does, the bureaucratic politics model suggests that "it is necessary to identify the games and players, to display the coalitions, bargains, and compromises, and to convey some feel for the confusion" in the policymaking process.[4]

In virtually every situation in which the United States has contemplated the use of force in recent years—in the Persian Gulf, Somalia, Bosnia, Rwanda, Haiti, Kosovo, and Iraq—policymakers and critics alike have worried about the specter of Vietnam and the "lessons" it taught. In part this is because the protracted series of decisions that took the United States into Vietnam— and eventually out of it, on unsatisfactory terms after years of fighting and the loss of tens of thousands of lives—is fertile ground for probing how American foreign policy is made and implemented.

Part III of this book begins with an account, informed by role theory and bureaucratic politics, of how the United States became involved in and conducted the prolonged war in Southeast Asia. "How Could Vietnam Happen?" asks James C. Thomson, Jr., almost rhetorically. The failure in Vietnam, Thomson contends, was the failure of America's policymaking process, not of its leadership. Vietnam shows that some of the most catastrophic of America's foreign policy initiatives have been the result not of evil or stupid people but of misdirected behaviors encouraged by the nature of the policymaking system and the roles and bureaucratic processes embedded in the way the government's foreign policy system is organized. Thomson's argument, however disturbing, provides insight into the milieu of decisionmaking and identifies many syndromes crucial to understanding how the roles created by the decisionmaking setting influence the kinds of decisions that leaders make and that bureaucracies are asked to implement.

In "Law in Order: Reconstructing U.S. National Security," William Wechsler also discusses how alternate roles of differing agencies within the government affect the actions that are taken (or not taken) to protect national security. In particular, he laments the fact that the law enforcement agencies within the government could be important tools of foreign policy, especially in the current fight against terrorism, but are not. These agencies have failed to assume this role for two crucial reasons: they have refused "to see themselves as components of U.S. foreign policy," and "there are structural impediments to effective coordination" between them and the formal national security agencies. Furthermore, these two kinds of agencies have tended to draw a "bright line" between their respective responsibilities, with the law enforcement agencies focused on the domestic criminal threats and the national security agencies focused on international security threats. Such distinctions no longer hold, if they ever did, Wechsler argues, and they must be erased if U.S. security is going to be ensured.

Further, Wechsler contends that "international crime in *all* of its various forms [threatens] U.S. national security interests" and thus should be addressed in a unified way by governmental agencies. The threats are both direct and indirect. Direct threats, such as those posed by Al-Qaeda and smugglers of arms and people, are familiar; indirect threats, such as crime networks that corrupt governmental leaders abroad, impair a country's economic development through drug trafficking, and create regional instability by financing civil wars, are equally pernicious for American security interests. For both kinds of threats, there has been a failure of communication and coordination between law enforcement and national security agencies, which by law and tradition have long viewed their roles differently.

While Wechsler acknowledges that effective leadership can assist in promoting greater coordination and cooperation, structural changes and the redirection of some agencies are also necessary. Wechsler outlines four principles to guide those processes: *consolidation of functions* into three major agencies, *coordination of activities* among them, *centralization of accountability,* and *creation of new posts* within the Justice Department and across the new agencies to focus on international and national security issues. Whether the newly created Department of Homeland Security is able through these or analogous changes to meet the law enforcement and security needs that Wechsler sees as lacking remains to be seen.

The next chapter, "Roles, Politics, and the Survival of the V-22 Osprey," by Christopher M. Jones, draws explicitly on Allison's work but he extends the model to show how bureaucratic organizations' roles and interests and those of other policy actors predict their policy stands. The case examined is that of the V-22 Osprey, an innovative tilt-rotor transport plane that the Marine Corps wanted to replace its helicopters. The Osprey survived during the period of 1989 to 1992 despite "two separate crashes, the falsification of maintenance records, and unfavorable reports concerning [its] safety and reliability." Its survival is explained by "a diverse but durable group of political actors" who worked to save it, despite having "different reasons based upon their distinct organizational roles and interests."

Four principal players were involved in the decision. Support came from members of Congress, the Marine Corps, and the plane's contractors. The principal opposition came from the Office of the Secretary of Defense (OSD) within the Pentagon, whose civilian staff are the principal advisers to the secretary of defense, and the secretary himself.

The Program Analysis and Evaluation office within the OSD had long been opposed to the V-22 on cost grounds, and its opposition was enhanced when Dick Cheney became secretary of defense. Indeed, Cheney actually announced the cancellation of the plane in April 1989, but he was unable to make that decision stick because of the other actors involved. Cheney's opposition focused on the plane's high cost and his belief that the transport mission of the plane "could be accomplished by less expensive helicopters." To support its position, the OSD regularly proposed alternatives to the Osprey in its annual budget messages to Congress, tried to "transfer, defer, or rescind V-22 appropriations," and even "refused to spend money Congress had appropriated." OSD used other tactics as well to undermine the V-22 program, but all of them failed. Ultimately the Bush administration "dropped its opposition and indicated that it would not stand in the way of spending $1.5 billion on the program."

The OSD and the Bush administration lost this bureaucratic battle because of the sustained support that the V-22 received from the other players. Congress, as noted, was a supporter of the plane. Its support "was not unanimous," Jones acknowledges, but "it was pervasive, encompassing conservative Republicans as well as liberal Democrats." Key states (e.g., Texas and Pennsylvania) with lots of jobs and votes at stake were involved in the production of the Osprey, for example, but that was only part of the reason. Members of Congress were also able to muster numerous arguments to support the program. Their arguments ranged from the cutting-edge technology that the plane represented to its flexible and multiple uses, from warfighting to drug interdiction, and to its safety, speed, and range. While policy arguments were important in the battle between the executive and legislative branches, Jones also points out that interbranch conflict was evident, with Congress seeking to protect its "power of the purse" and its right to legislate in the military area.

The two other actors involved also aided these congressional arguments. The position of the Marine Corps, the leading proponent of the Osprey within the executive branch, was based largely on its "role and interests." The Marines Corps saw this new transport plane as an important way to meet its organizational mission. Even after the Bush administration announced its opposition to the Osprey, the marines were still able to undertake "a vigorous, behind-the-scenes campaign on Capitol Hill" on behalf of the aircraft.

By contrast, the contractors for the Osprey, Bell Helicopter Textron and Boeing, were "active and aggressive proponents." These manufacturers took several actions to widen support for the plane, expanding its domestic appeal by subcontracting out production components and engaging in public relations measures to gain greater support. The manufacturers, of course, were motivated by economic benefits, which distinguished them from the Marine Corps or members of Congress, but the three groups' shared interests were enough to ensure the survival of the Osprey—despite the opposition of the executive branch and the Pentagon leadership.

As noted above, "where you stand depends on where you sit" is a central maxim of the bureaucratic politics model. The aphorism purports to explain why participants in the deliberations that lead to foreign policy choices often define issues and favor policy alternatives that reflect their organizational affiliations. Jones shows that it applies to organizations inside and outside of government. Does it also apply to individuals, including those at the highest levels of government? Steve Smith concludes that is does, in his "Policy Preferences and Bureaucratic Position: The Case of the American Hostage Rescue Mission." As the title suggests, Smith examines the process that led the Carter administration to the fateful decision to attempt a covert, paramilitary rescue of American diplomats held hostage by Iran beginning in late 1979. Like Vietnam, this is a tale of policy shortcomings—of policy failure. How did it happen?

Smith does not attempt a complete answer to this question, but he does show that the key participants in the decision process

> acted in accordance with what the bureaucratic politics approach would suggest: namely, that the National Security Adviser, the Secretary of Defense, the Chairman of the Joint Chiefs of Staff and Director of the CIA would support military action . . . ; the Secretary of State, and in his absence his deputy, would oppose it; those individuals who were bureaucratically tied to the president (the vice president, the press secretary and the political adviser) would be fundamentally concerned with what was best for the Carter presidency; and President Carter, although clearly more than just another bureaucratic actor, would act in a way that reflected bureaucratically derived as well as personal influences.

Smith's analysis is compelling not only as a study of an important episode in American foreign policy but also as an illustration of the logic of the bureaucratic politics model. It is important also because it shows the pitfalls as well as promises of the perspective and why we must examine not only policymaking roles but also policymakers themselves. Smith's conclusions are important in this respect: "Role, in and of itself, cannot explain the positions adopted by individuals.... Yet role occupiers do become predisposed to think in certain, bureaucratic ways, and for a variety of psychological reasons they tend to adopt mind-sets compatible with those of their closest colleagues. In addition, individuals are often chosen for a specific post because they have certain kinds of world-views." In the final analysis, then, to understand the impact of decisionmakers and their policymaking positions on American foreign policy, we must understand both.

James Goldgeier, in his "NATO Expansion: The Anatomy of a Decision," supports the argument about the crucial importance of individuals in molding policy and illustrates the limitation on bureaucracies in shaping it. On the basis of extensive interviews with officials knowledgeable or involved in the initial NATO expansion decision during the Clinton administration, Goldgeier demonstrates that the bureaucracies, and the individuals in those bureaucracies, can shape debate over an issue and can "pull" and "haul" to promote different positions, but they cannot determine policy. Instead, the issue of whether NATO membership would formally expand or whether the Partnership for Peace option would continue ultimately depended on President Clinton. Not until Clinton made a series of speeches in Brussels, Prague, and Warsaw were bureaucratic differences settled. As Clinton stated, "The question is no longer whether NATO will take on new members but when and how."

The NATO case illustrates the importance of individuals in other ways. For example, Anthony Lake, the national security adviser at the time, and other foreign policy principals were able to move Clinton to make statements that seemingly committed the United States to NATO expansion. They in turn used his remarks as the basis for establishing a working group that set forth an "action plan," thus demonstrating the influence that individuals are sometimes able to exercise in the face of bureaucratic resistance. Particularly interesting is how Richard Holbrooke, assistant secretary of state for European affairs, became the "enforcer" of the NATO expansion decision within the interagency process. Invoking the president's wishes with the argument "either you are on the president's program or you are not," he was able to crystallize the president's key role in the policy choice.

The mind-sets, perceptions of reality, and the information that policymakers possess also affect the nature of the policy choices they pursue. In "Sources of Humanitarian Intervention: Beliefs, Information, and Advocacy in U.S. Decisions on Somalia and Bosnia," Jon Western argues that the initial decisions of the administration of George H. W. Bush in these cases were primarily functions of the belief systems among key policymakers and of their ability to use information and advocacy to shape those policy decisions. Yet Western's case study also demonstrates how information and advocacy can change the direction of American policy, as the Bush administration did in late 1992 toward Somalia.

Prior to its 1992 policy shift, Western argues, the Bush administration's polices toward Bosnia and Somalia were a function of the pervasive perception among key officials (the president, his key aides, and especially the Joint Chiefs of Staff) that the events in those two countries did not affect U.S. national interests and that American interventions "could only lead to a Vietnam-style quagmire." This perception of the "selective engagers" stood in contrast to the views of the "liberal humanitarians," who sought to intervene to prevent human tragedies, massive killings, and wholesale starvation then occurring in Bosnia and Somalia. In addition, the perceptions of the key policymakers dominated the policy process, because the administration controlled much of the information and more of the policy advocacy machinery. As Western notes, "the U.S. media . . . had little expertise in the Balkans," and "there was no galvanizing force that either linked disparate humanitarian organizations or mobilized the press corps." In short, the selective engagers had a clear edge over the liberal humanitarians in the policy process.

By the summer of 1992, however, perceptions began to change as both the media and liberal humanitarians "gradually developed and dedicated more resources for their own information collection efforts to challenge the Administration's framing of the respective conflicts." Most notable were a report by the U.S. ambassador to Kenya about his visit to a refugee camp on the Somali-Kenyan border, and a fact-finding visit by two U.S. senators to Somalia. At about the same time, reports surfaced about radical Serb nationalist and paramilitary forces "committing horrific atrocities" and about Serb-run concentration camps in Bosnia. These and other revelations began to challenge seriously the thinking of the selective engagers within the Bush administration, as did the challenge from presidential candidate Bill Clinton, who argued for more robust American actions in Bosnia.

Later that year, the Bush administration began to modify its position. Although President Bush "ordered his team to contest the liberal humanitarian view that U.S. intervention could quickly break the siege of Sarajevo with little cost to American lives," he ordered the air force to provide assistance in transporting relief to Somalia and agreed to American funding for Pakistani peacekeepers in that county. Western argues that this shift occurred due to increased political pressure on the administration regarding its policies in Somalia and Bosnia.

The change in policy direction continued even as selective engagers and liberal humanitarians continued their propaganda campaigns. After his victory in early November, Clinton visited Washington for various briefings, contributing to what Western calls the "cumulative pressure" on the selective engagers to change course. Within days, the Joint Chiefs of Staff reversed their opposition to intervention in Somalia. President Bush followed suit a few days later. Western attributes the policy reversal to the "mobilized political opposition" and its ability "to challenge the administration's framing of the crisis."

The last two chapters in this book look beyond the bureaucratic politics approach and the role of individuals in bureaucratic organizations. Both focus instead on the role of individual cognition (or worldviews) in shaping behavior and, ultimately, foreign policy. Although roles and bureaucratic context do matter, prior experiences and personality predispositions are crucial in determining policymakers' decision styles and policy choices, as the two chapters demonstrate.

In his "The Changing Leadership of George W. Bush: A Pre- and Post–9/11 Comparison," noted presidential scholar Fred I. Greenstein discusses how the leadership style of the president compares in these two periods. As he explains, Bush has grown in office, and "even many of his critics grant that he has become strikingly more presidential." The president not only experienced approval ratings that skyrocketed from 51 percent to more than 80 but demonstrated an "impressive increase in political competence."

In what ways did Bush change between these two periods? Greenstein begins by profiling the background experiences that shaped the president prior to his taking office. George W. Bush was born in Connecticut but grew up in Texas and, unlike his father, "has the brashness and the directness of a typical Texan." Those qualities would remain with him during his presidency. Similarly, although he was a mediocre student, he used his academic experiences to hone "his social skills and popularity," traits that would assist in his political career. In addition, as Greenstein notes, Bush's work on his father's various political campaigns and on the Senate campaigns of others aided development of his own political skills, as did his co-ownership of the Texas Ranger baseball team, where he was able to "[demonstrate] that he could manage a complex organization." All of these activities assisted in propelling Bush to the Texas governorship and remain important personal characteristics that he brought to the White House.

Greenstein assesses six leadership qualities—Bush's emotional intelligence, cognitive style, political skill, policy vision, organizational capacity, and effectiveness as a public communicator—before and after 9/11. He finds that Bush's emotional intelligence, political skills, policy vision, and organizational capacity were less affected by 9/11 than were his cognitive style and effectiveness as a public communicator.

In these latter two areas, however, Bush was more fully affected by September 11. From the outset of his campaign for the presidency and from his first days in office, Bush was criticized because his cognitive style failed to exhibit "intellectual curiosity" or to be "drawn to the play of ideas." Greenstein points out that though Bush has "ample intelligence," the president has adopted the "corporate model of political leadership," a model in which he relies heavily on his aides for policy assistance and direction. While that basic approach continued after 9/11, Greenstein reports that Bush has been more "thoughtful" and "focused" since the events of that day. But the area where Bush "has been the most dramatically transformed" is as a public communicator. In his early days as president, for example, Bush was often "awkward and unpolished" in addressing the public, but since 9/11, "Bush has made himself a public presence." His immediate actions after the tragedy, visits to the World Trade Center and the Pentagon, and his attendance at the memorial service at the National Cathedral, illustrated this transformation, but he has continued since to exhibit this quality.

Analyses of presidents' personalities and the role their backgrounds play in policy decisions are often less dramatic than those of Bush's transformation following 9/11. Yet analyses of presidential style rooted in personality and background factors demonstrate their impact across a range of phenomena. Political scientist Alexander George, for example, describes three different approaches presidents have evolved for mobilizing information, expertise, and analytical resources for effective policymaking: the "formalistic," "competitive," and "collegial" models. What approach a president chooses and how it operates in practice will be shaped by the president's personality—by his cognitive style, his sense of efficacy and competence, and his general orientation to political conflict.[5]

Thomas Preston and Margaret G. Hermann build on these ideas in the concluding chapter of this book. "Presidential Leadership Style and the Foreign Policy Advisory Process" draws on a wide range of theory and evidence from psychology as well as political science to show how presidents' individual characteristics shape their choice of foreign policy advisers, the presidential advisory process, and, ultimately, American foreign policy. Importantly, Preston and Hermann include in their analysis the contexts in which presidents must decide. Like Greenstein, for example, they demonstrate how the terrorist attacks on the United States transformed George W. Bush's approach to the management of foreign policy, as he became more focused and engaged with his own advisory system. But they add a cautionary note. Arguing that Bush sees the world in black-or-white, "you are either with us or against us" terms, they warn that "Bush will have a problem if the current foreign policy equation . . . becomes more nuanced and complex[;] . . . Bush is likely to have far greater difficulty adapting to a changing, more complicated environment than he had in his earlier shift."

Preston and Hermann's prognoses about Bush are drawn from their broader analysis of the factors that shape presidents' leadership styles: their need for control and involvement in the policy process, their need for information and sensitivity to the political context, and their prior policy experience and expertise. These, in turn, will "shape the way presidents structure and manage their advisory systems." Based on variations in leadership styles, Preston and Hermann propose an eightfold typology of presidential advisory systems, encapsulating the kinds of relations we should expect to find between different presidents and their advisers. They then apply their ideas to the advisory systems Presidents Bill Clinton and George W. Bush devised. They hypothesize that Clinton would develop an advisory system that would reflect a low need for control and involvement but a high need for information and sensitivity to the context. Clinton would thus prefer advisers who "were more politically inclined as well as those who were more expert on a particular topic." Bush, they hypothesize, would develop an advisory system that would reflect a low need for control and involvement and low need for information and political sensitivity. This approach, much like that of Ronald Reagan, would produce advisers who were delegated a considerable amount of authority and responsibility and would be quite influential with the president on decisions. In both instances they conclude that the presidents' actual behavior conforms to expectations. Thus, they show, first, that "differences in leadership style are related to differences in the way the executive branch of government works," and, second, that "how presidents try to deal with institutional constraints is often shaped by who they are." In this sense, George W. Bush is very much like his predecessors.

NOTES

1. See Graham T. Allison, *Essence of Decision: Explaining the Cuban Missile Crisis* (Boston: Little, Brown, 1971), and Graham T. Allison and Philip Zelikow, *Essence of Decision: Explaining the Cuban Missile Crisis,* 2nd ed. (New York: Longman, 1999).

2. Allison, *Essence of Decision,* 145.

3. Todd S. Purdom and Patrick E. Tyler, "Top Republicans Break with Bush on Iraq Strategy," *New York Times,* August 16, 2002.

4. Allison, *Essence of Decision,* 146.

5. Alexander L. George, *Presidential Decisionmaking in Foreign Policy: The Effective Use of Information and Advice* (Boulder, Colo.: Westview Press, 1980).

18

How Could Vietnam Happen?

An Autopsy

James C. Thomson, Jr.

As a case study in the making of foreign policy, the Vietnam War will fascinate historians and social scientists for many decades to come. One question that will certainly be asked: How did men of superior ability, sound training, and high ideals—American policymakers of the 1960s—create such a costly and divisive policy?

As one who watched the decisionmaking process in Washington from 1961 to 1966 under Presidents Kennedy and Johnson, I can suggest a preliminary answer. I can do so by briefly listing some of the factors that seemed to me to shape our Vietnam policy during my years as an East Asia specialist at the State Department and the White House. I shall deal largely with Washington as I saw or sensed it, and not with Saigon, where I . . . spent but a scant three days, in the entourage of the vice president, or with other decision centers, the capitals of interested parties. Nor will I deal with other important parts of the record: Vietnam's history prior to 1961, for instance, or the overall course of America's relations with Vietnam.

Yet a first and central ingredient in these years of Vietnam decisions does involve history. The ingredient was *the legacy of the 1950s*—by which I mean the so-called "loss of China," the Korean War, and the Far East policy of Secretary of State Dulles.

This legacy had an institutional by-product for the Kennedy administration: In 1961 the U.S. government's East Asian establishment was undoubtedly the most rigid and doctrinaire of Washington's regional divisions in foreign affairs. This was especially true at the Department of State, where the incoming administration found the Bureau of Far Eastern Affairs the hardest nut to crack. It was a bureau that had been purged of its best China expertise, and of farsighted, dispassionate men, as a result of McCarthyism. Its members were generally committed to one policy line: the close containment and isolation of mainland China, the harassment of "neutralist" nations which sought to avoid alignment with either Washington or Peking, and the maintenance of a network of alliances with anticommunist client states on China's periphery.

Another aspect of the legacy was the special vulnerability and sensitivity of the new Democratic administration on Far East policy issues. The memory of the McCarthy era was still very sharp, and Kennedy's margin of victory was too thin. The 1960 Offshore Islands TV debate between Kennedy and Nixon had shown the president-elect the perils of "fresh thinking." The administration was inherently leery of moving too fast on Asia. As a result, the Far East Bureau (now the Bureau of East Asian and Pacific Affairs) was the last one to be overhauled. Not until Averell Harriman was brought in as assistant secretary in December 1961 were significant personnel changes attempted, and it took Harriman several months to make a deep imprint on the bureau because of his necessary preoccupation with the Laos settlement. Once he did so, there was virtually no effort to bring back the purged or exiled East Asia experts.

There were other important by-products of this "legacy of the fifties."

The new administration inherited and somewhat shared a *general perception of China-on-the-march*—a sense of China's vastness, its numbers, its belligerence; a revived sense, perhaps, of the Golden Horde. This was a perception fed by Chinese intervention in the Korean War (an intervention actually based on appallingly bad communications and mutual miscalculation on the part of Washington and Peking, but the careful unraveling of the tragedy, which scholars have accomplished, had not yet become part of conventional wisdom).

The new administration inherited and briefly accepted *a monolithic conception of the communist bloc*. Despite much earlier predictions and reports by outside analysts, policymakers did not begin to accept the reality and possible finality of the Sino-Soviet split until the first weeks of 1962. The inevitably corrosive impact of competing nationalisms on communism was largely ignored.

The new administration inherited and to some extent shared *the "domino theory" about Asia*. This theory resulted from profound ignorance of Asian history and hence ignorance of the radical differences among Asian nations and societies. It resulted from a blindness to the power and resilience of Asian nationalisms. (It may also have resulted from a subconscious sense that, since "all Asians look alike," all Asian nations will act alike.) As a theory, the domino fallacy was not merely inaccurate but also insulting to Asian nations. . . .

Finally, the legacy of the fifties was apparently compounded by an un-easy sense of a worldwide communist challenge to the new administration after the Bay of Pigs fiasco. A first manifestation was the president's trau-matic Vienna meeting with Khrushchev in June 1961; then came the Berlin crisis of the summer. All this created an atmosphere in which President Kennedy undoubtedly felt under special pressure to show his nation's met-tle in Vietnam—if the Vietnamese, unlike the people of Laos, were willing to fight.

In general, the legacy of the fifties shaped such early moves of the new ad-ministration as the decisions to maintain a high-visibility SEATO (by sending the secretary of state himself instead of some underling to its first meeting in 1961), to back away from diplomatic recognition of Mongolia in the summer of 1961, and, most important, to expand U.S. military assistance to South Vietnam that winter on the basis of the much more tentative Eisenhower commitment. It should be added that the increased commitment to Vietnam was also fueled by a new breed of military strategists and academic social scientists (some of whom had entered the new administration) who had developed theories of counterguerrilla warfare and were eager to see them put to the test. To some, "counterinsurgency" seemed a new panacea for coping with the world's instability.

So much for the legacy and the history. Any new administration inherits both complicated problems and simplistic views of the world. But surely among the policymakers of the Kennedy and Johnson administrations there were men who would warn of the dangers of an open-ended commitment to the Vietnam quagmire?

This raises a central question, at the heart of the policy process: Where were the experts, the doubters, and the dissenters? Were they there at all, and if so, what happened to them?

The answer is complex but instructive.

In the first place, the American government was sorely *lacking in real Vietnam or Indochina expertise.* Originally treated as an adjunct of Em-bassy Paris, our Saigon embassy and the Vietnam Desk at State were largely staffed from 1954 onward by French-speaking Foreign Service personnel of narrowly European experience. Such diplomats were even more closely restricted than the normal embassy officer—by cast of mind as well as language—to contacts with Vietnam's French-speaking urban elites. For in-stance, Foreign Service linguists in Portugal are able to speak with the peas-antry if they get out of Lisbon and choose to do so; not so the French speakers of Embassy Saigon.

In addition, the *shadow of the "loss of China"* distorted Vietnam reporting. Career officers in the department, and especially those in the field, had not forgotten the fate of their World War II colleagues who wrote in frankness from China and were later pilloried by Senate committees for critical comments on the Chinese Nationalists. Candid reporting on the strengths of the Viet Cong and the weaknesses of the Diem government was inhibited by the memory. It was also inhibited by some higher officials, notably Ambassador Nolting in Saigon, who refused to sign off on such cables.

In due course, to be sure, some Vietnam talent was discovered or developed. But a recurrent and increasingly important factor in the decisionmaking process was the *banishment of real expertise.* Here the underlying cause was the "closed politics" of policymaking as issues become hot: The more sensitive the issue, and the higher it rises in the bureaucracy, the more completely the experts are excluded while the harassed senior generalists take over (that is, the secretaries, under secretaries, and presidential assistants). The frantic skimming of briefing papers in the back seats of limousines is no substitute for the presence of specialists; furthermore, in times of crisis such papers are deemed "too sensitive" even for review by the specialists. Another underlying cause of this banishment, as Vietnam became more critical, was the replacement of the experts, who were generally and increasingly pessimistic, by men described as "can-do guys," loyal and energetic fixers unsoured by expertise. In early 1965, when I confided my growing policy doubts to an older colleague on the NSC staff, he assured me that the smartest thing both of us could do was to "steer clear of the whole Vietnam mess"; the gentleman in question had the misfortune to be a "can-do guy," however, and [was subsequently] highly placed in Vietnam, under orders to solve the mess.

Despite the banishment of the experts, internal doubters and dissenters did indeed appear and persist. Yet as I watched the process, such men were effectively neutralized by a subtle dynamic: *the domestication of dissenters.* Such "domestication" arose out of a twofold clubbish need: on the one hand, the dissenter's desire to stay aboard; and on the other hand, the nondissenter's conscience. Simply stated, dissent, when recognized, was made to feel at home. On the lowest possible scale of importance, I must confess my own considerable sense of dignity and acceptance (both vital) when my senior White House employer would refer to me as his "favorite dove." Far more significant was the case of the former under secretary of state George Ball. Once Mr. Ball began to express doubts, he was warmly institutionalized: He was encouraged to become the in-house devil's advocate on Vietnam. The upshot was inevitable: The process of escalation allowed for periodic requests to Mr. Ball to speak his piece; Ball felt good, I assume (he had fought for righteousness); the others felt good (they had given a full hearing to the dovish option); and there was minimal unpleasantness. The club remained intact; and it is of course possible that matters would have gotten worse faster if Mr. Ball had kept silent, or left before his final departure in the fall of 1966. There was also, of course, the case of the last institutionalized doubter, Bill Moyers. The president is said to have greeted his arrival at meetings with an affectionate, "Well, here comes Mr. Stop-the-Bombing. . . ." Here again the dynamics of domesticated dissent sustained the relationship for a while.

A related point—and crucial, I suppose, to government at all times—was *the "effectiveness" trap,* the trap that keeps men from speaking out, as clearly or as often as they might, within the government. And it is the trap that keeps men from resigning in protest and airing their dissent outside the government. The most important asset that a man brings to bureau-cratic life is his "effectiveness," a mysterious combination of training, style, and connections. The most ominous complaint that can be whispered of a bureaucrat is "I'm afraid Charlie's beginning to lose his effectiveness." To preserve your effectiveness, you must decide where and when to fight the mainstream of policy; the opportunities range from pillow talk with your wife, to private drinks with your friends, to meetings with the secretary of state or the president. The inclination to remain silent or to acquiesce in the presence of the great men—to live to fight another day, to give on this issue so that you can be "effective" on later issues—is overwhelming. Nor is it the tendency of youth alone; some of our most senior officials, men of wealth and fame, whose place in history is secure, have remained silent lest their connection with power be terminated. As for the disinclination to resign in protest: While not necessarily a Washington or even American specialty, it seems more true of a government in which ministers have no parliamen-tary back-bench to which to retreat. In the absence of such a refuge, it is easy to rationalize the decision to stay aboard. By doing so, one may be able to prevent a few bad things from happening and perhaps even make a few good things happen. To exit is to lose even those marginal chances for "effectiveness."

Another factor must be noted: As the Vietnam controversy escalated at home, there developed *a preoccupation with Vietnam public relations as opposed to Vietnam policymaking.* And here, ironically, internal doubters and dissenters were heavily employed. For such men, by virtue of their own doubts, were often deemed best able to "massage" the doubting in-telligentsia. My senior East Asia colleague at the White House, a brilliant and humane doubter who had dealt with Indochina since 1954, spent three-quarters of his working days on Vietnam public relations: drafting presiden-tial responses to letters from important critics, writing conciliatory language for presidential speeches, and meeting quite interminably with delegations of outraged Quakers, clergymen, academics, and housewives. His regular callers were the late A. J. Muste and Norman Thomas; mine were members of the Women's Strike for Peace. Our orders from above: Keep them off the backs of busy policymakers (who usually happened to be nondoubters). In-cidentally, my most discouraging assignment in the realm of public relations was the preparation of a White House pamphlet entitled *Why Vietnam,* in September 1965; in a gesture toward my conscience, I fought—and lost—a battle to have the title followed by a question mark.

Through a variety of procedures, both institutional and personal, doubt, dissent, and expertise were effectively neutralized in the making of policy. But what can be said of the men "in charge"? It is patently absurd to suggest that they produced such tragedy by intention and calculation. But it is neither absurd nor difficult to discern certain forces at work that caused decent and honorable men to do great harm.

Here I would stress the paramount role of *executive fatigue.* No factor seems to me more crucial and underrated in the making of foreign policy. The physical and emotional toll of executive responsibility in State, the Pentagon, the White House, and other executive agencies is enormous; that toll is of course compounded by extended service. Many . . . Vietnam policymakers [had] been on the job for from four to seven years. Complaints may be few, and physical health may remain unimpaired, though emotional health is far harder to gauge. But what is most seriously eroded in the deadening process of fatigue is freshness of thought, imagination, a sense of possibility, a sense of priorities and perspective—those rare assets of a new administration in its first year or two of office. The tired policymaker becomes a prisoner of his own narrowed view of the world and his own clichéd rhetoric. He becomes irritable and defensive—short on sleep, short on family ties, short on patience. Such men make bad policy and then compound it. They have neither the time nor the temperament for new ideas or preventive diplomacy.

Below the level of the fatigued executives in the making of Vietnam policy was a widespread phenomenon: *the curator mentality* in the Department of State. By this I mean the collective inertia produced by the bureaucrat's view of his job. At State, the average "desk officer" inherits from his predecessor our policy toward Country X; he regards it as his function to keep that policy intact—under glass, untampered with, and dusted—so that he may pass it on in two to four years to his successor. And such curatorial service generally merits promotion within the system. (Maintain the status quo, and you will stay out of trouble.) In some circumstances, the inertia bred by such an outlook can act as a brake against rash innovation. But on many issues, this inertia sustains the momentum of bad policy and unwise commitments—momentum that might otherwise have been resisted within the ranks. Clearly, Vietnam [was] such an issue.

To fatigue and inertia must be added the factor of internal confusion. Even among the "architects" of our Vietnam commitment, there [was] persistent *confusion as to what type of war we were fighting* and, as a direct consequence, *confusion as to how to end that war.* (The "credibility gap" [was], in part, a reflection of such internal confusion.) Was it, for instance, a civil war, in which case counterinsurgency might suffice? Or was it a war of international aggression? (This might invoke SEATO or UN commitment.) Who was the aggressor—and the "real enemy"? The Viet Cong? Hanoi? Peking? Moscow? International communism? Or maybe "Asian communism"? Differing enemies dictated differing strategies and tactics. And confused throughout, in like fashion, was the question of American objectives; your objectives depended on whom you were fighting and why. I shall not forget my assignment from an assistant secretary of state in March 1964: to draft a speech for Secretary McNamara which would, inter alia, once and for all dispose of the canard that the Vietnam conflict was a civil war. "But in some ways, of course," I mused, "it *is* a civil war." "Don't play word games with me!" snapped the assistant secretary.

Similar confusion beset the concept of "negotiations"—anathema to much of official Washington from 1961 to 1965. Not until April 1965 did "unconditional discussions" become respectable, via a presidential speech; even then the secretary of state stressed privately to newsmen that nothing had changed, since "discussions" were by no means the same as "negotiations." Months later that issue was resolved. But it took even longer to obtain a fragile internal agreement that negotiations might include the Viet Cong as something other than an appendage to Hanoi's delegation. Given such confusion as to the whos and whys of our Vietnam commitment, it is not surprising, as Theodore Draper has written, that policymakers [found] it so difficult to agree on how to end the war.

Of course, one force—a constant in the vortex of commitment—was that of *wishful thinking.* I partook of it myself at many times. I did so especially during Washington's struggle with Diem in the autumn of 1963 when some of us at State believed that for once, in dealing with a difficult client state, the U.S. government could use the leverage of our economic and military assistance to make good things happen, instead of being led around by the nose by [foreign dictators]. If we could prove that point, I thought, and move into a new day, with or without Diem, then Vietnam was well worth the effort. Later came the wishful thinking of the air-strike planners in the late autumn of 1964; there were those who actually thought that after six weeks of air strikes, the North Vietnamese would come crawling to us to ask for peace talks. And what, someone asked in one of the meetings of the time, if they don't? The answer was that we would bomb for another four weeks, and that would do the trick. And a few weeks later came one instance of wishful thinking that was symptomatic of good men misled: In January 1965, I encountered one of the very highest figures in the administration at a dinner, drew him aside, and told him of my worries about the air-strike option. He told me that I really shouldn't worry; it was his conviction that before any such plans could be put into effect, a neutralist government would come to power in Saigon that would politely invite us out. And finally, there was the recurrent wishful thinking that sustained many of us through the trying months of 1965–1966 after the air strikes had begun: that surely, somehow, one way or another, we would "be in a conference in six months," and the escalatory spiral would be suspended. The basis of our hope: "It simply can't go on."

As a further influence on policymakers I would cite the factor of *bureaucratic detachment*. By this I mean what at best might be termed the professional callousness of the surgeon (and indeed, medical lingo—the "surgical strike" for instance—seemed to crop up in the euphemisms of the times). In Washington the semantics of the military muted the reality of war for the civilian policymakers. In quiet, air-conditioned, thick-carpeted rooms, such terms as "systematic pressure," "armed reconnaissance," "targets of opportunity," and even "body count" seemed to breed a sort of games-theory detachment. Most memorable to me was a moment in the late 1964 target planning when the question under discussion was how heavy our bombing should be, and how extensive our strafing, at some midpoint in the projected pattern of systematic pressure. An assistant secretary of state resolved the point in the following words: "It seems to me that our orchestration should be mainly violins, but with periodic touches of brass." Perhaps the biggest shock of my return to Cambridge, Massachusetts, was the realization that the young men, the flesh and blood I taught and saw on these university streets, were potentially some of the numbers on the charts of those faraway planners. In a curious sense, Cambridge [was] closer to this war than Washington.

There is an unprovable factor that relates to bureaucratic detachment: the ingredient of *cryptoracism*. I do not mean to imply any conscious contempt for Asian loss of life on the part of Washington officials. But I do mean to imply that bureaucratic detachment may well be compounded by a traditional Western sense that there are so many Asians, after all; that Asians have a fatalism about life and a disregard for its loss; that they are cruel and barbaric to their own people; and that they are very different from us (and all look alike?). And I *do* mean to imply that the upshot of such subliminal views is a subliminal question of whether Asians, and particularly Asian peasants, and most particularly Asian communists, are really people—like you and me. To put the matter another way: Would we have pursued quite such policies—and quite such military tactics—if the Vietnamese were white?

It is impossible to write of Vietnam decisionmaking without writing about language. Throughout the conflict, words [were] of paramount importance. I refer here to the impact of *rhetorical escalation* and to the *problem of oversell*. In an important sense, Vietnam [became] of crucial significance to us *because we . . . said that it [was] of crucial significance.* (The issue obviously relates to the public relations preoccupation described earlier.)

The key here is domestic politics: the need to sell the American people, press, and Congress on support for an unpopular and costly war in which the objectives themselves [were] in flux. To sell means to persuade, and to persuade means rhetoric. As the difficulties and costs . . . mounted, so [did] the definition of the stakes. This is not to say that rhetorical escalation is an orderly process; executive prose is the product of many writers, and some concepts—North Vietnamese infiltration, America's "national honor," Red China as the chief enemy—. . . entered the rhetoric only gradually and even sporadically. But there [was] an upward spiral nonetheless. And once you have *said* that the American Experiment itself stands or falls on the Vietnam outcome, you have thereby created a national stake far beyond any earlier stakes.

Crucial throughout the process of Vietnam decisionmaking was a conviction among many policymakers: that Vietnam posed a *fundamental test of America's national will.* Time and again I was told by men reared in the tradition of Henry L. Stimson that all we needed was the will, and we would then prevail. Implicit in such a view, it seemed to me, was a curious assumption that Asians lacked will, or at least that in a contest between Asian and Anglo-Saxon wills, the non-Asians must prevail. A corollary to the persistent belief in will was a *fascination with power* and an awe in the face of the power America possessed as no nation or civilization ever before. Those who doubted our role in Vietnam were said to shrink from the burdens of power, the obligations of power, the uses of power, the responsibility of power. By implication, such men were soft-headed and effete.

Finally, no discussion of the factors and forces at work on Vietnam policymakers can ignore the central fact of *human ego investment.* Men who have participated in a decision develop a stake in that decision. As they participate in further, related decisions, their stake increases. It might have been possible to dissuade a man of strong self-confidence at an early stage of the ladder of decision; but it is infinitely harder at later stages since a change of mind there usually involves implicit or explicit repudiation of a chain of previous decisions.

To put it bluntly: At the heart of the Vietnam calamity [was] a group of able, dedicated men who [were] regularly and repeatedly wrong—and whose standing with their contemporaries, and more important, with history, depended, as they [saw] it, on being proven right. These [were] not men who [could] be asked to extricate themselves from error.

The various ingredients I have cited in the making of Vietnam policy . . . created a variety of results, most of them fairly obvious. Here are some that seem to me most central:

Throughout the conflict, there [was] *persistent and repeated miscalculation* by virtually all the actors, in high echelons and low, whether dove, hawk, or something else. To cite one simple example among many: In late

1964 and early 1965, some peace-seeking planners at State who strongly opposed the projected bombing of the North urged that, instead, American ground forces be sent to South Vietnam; this would, they said, increase our bargaining leverage against the North—our "chips"—and would give us something to negotiate about (the withdrawal of our forces) at an early peace conference. Simultaneously, the air-strike option was urged by many in the military who were dead set against American participation in "another land war in Asia"; they were joined by other civilian peace-seekers who wanted to bomb Hanoi into early negotiations. By late 1965, we had ended up with the worst of all worlds: ineffective and costly air strikes against the North, spiraling ground forces in the South, and no negotiations in sight.

Throughout the conflict as well, there [was] *a steady give-in to pressures for a military solution* and only minimal and sporadic efforts at a diplomatic and political solution. In part this resulted from the confusion (earlier cited) among the civilians—confusion regarding objectives and strategy. And in part this resulted from the self-enlarging nature of military investment. Once air strikes and particularly ground forces were introduced, our investment itself had transformed the original stakes. More air power was needed to protect the ground forces; and then more ground forces to protect the ground forces. And needless to say, the military mind develops its own momentum in the absence of clear guidelines from the civilians. Once asked to save South Vietnam, rather than to "advise" it, the American military could not but press for escalation. In addition, sad to report, assorted military constituencies, once involved in Vietnam, . . . had a series of cases to prove: for instance, the utility not only of air power (the Air Force) but of supercarrier-based air power (the Navy). Also, Vietnam policy . . . suffered from one ironic by-product of Secretary McNamara's establishment of civilian control at the Pentagon: In the face of such control, interservice rivalry [gave] way to a united front among the military—reflected in the new but recurrent phenomenon of JCS unanimity. In conjunction with traditional congressional allies (mostly Southern senators and representatives) such a united front would pose a formidable problem for any president.

Throughout the conflict, there [were] *missed opportunities, large and small, to disengage ourselves from Vietnam on increasingly unpleasant but still acceptable terms.* Of the many moments from 1961 onward, I shall cite only one, the last and most important opportunity that was lost: In the summer of 1964 the president instructed his chief advisers to prepare for him as wide a range of Vietnam options as possible for postelection consideration and decision. He explicitly asked that all options be laid out. What happened next was, in effect, Lyndon Johnson's slow-motion Bay of Pigs. For the advisers so effectively converged on one single option—juxtaposed against two other, phony options (in effect, blowing up the world, or scuttle-and-run)—that the president was confronted with unanimity for bombing the North from all his trusted counselors. Had he been more confident in foreign affairs, had he been deeply informed on Vietnam and Southeast Asia, and had he raised some hard questions that unanimity had submerged, this president could have used the largest electoral mandate in history to deescalate in Vietnam, in the clear expectation that at the worst a neutralist government would come to power in Saigon and politely invite us out. . . .

In the course of these years, another result of Vietnam decisionmaking [was] *the abuse and distortion of history.* Vietnamese, Southeast Asian, and Far Eastern history [was] rewritten by our policymakers, and their spokesmen, to conform with the alleged necessity of our presence in Vietnam. Highly dubious analogies from our experience elsewhere—the "Munich" sellout and "containment" from Europe, the Malayan insurgency and the Korean War from Asia—[were] imported in order to justify our actions. And [later] events [were] fitted to the Procrustean bed of Vietnam. Most notably, the change of power in Indonesia in 1965–1966 has been ascribed to our Vietnam presence; and virtually all progress in the Pacific region— the rise of regionalism, new forms of cooperation, and mounting growth rates—has been similarly explained. The Indonesian allegation is undoubtedly false (I tried to prove it, during six months of careful investigation at the White House, and had to confess failure); the regional allegation is patently unprovable in either direction (except, of course, for the clear fact that the economies of both Japan and Korea . . . profited enormously from our Vietnam-related procurement in these countries; but that is a costly and highly dubious form of foreign aid).

There is a final result of Vietnam policy I would cite that holds potential danger for the future of American foreign policy: *the rise of a new breed of American ideologues who saw Vietnam as the ultimate test of their doctrine.* I have in mind those men in Washington who have given a new life to the missionary impulse in American foreign relations: who believe that this nation, in this era, has received a threefold endowment that can transform the world. As they see it, that endowment is composed of, first, our unsurpassed miliary might; second, our clear technological supremacy; and third, our allegedly invincible benevolence (our "altruism," our affluence, our lack of territorial aspirations). Together, it is argued, this threefold endowment provides us with the opportunity and the obligation to ease the nations of the earth toward modernization and stability: toward a full-fledged *Pax Americana Technocratica.* In reaching toward this goal, Vietnam [was] viewed as the last and crucial test. Once we . . . succeeded there, the road ahead [was seen to be] clear. . . .

Long before I went into government, I was told a story about Henry L. Stimson that seemed to me pertinent during the years that I watched the Vietnam tragedy unfold—and participated in that tragedy. It seems to me more pertinent than ever. . . .

In his waning years Stimson was asked by an anxious questioner, "Mr. Secretary, how on earth can we ever bring peace to the world?" Stimson is said to have answered: "You begin by bringing to Washington a small handful of able men who believe that the achievement of peace is possible.

"You work them to the bone until they no longer believe that it is possible.

"And then you throw them out—and bring in a new bunch who believe that it is possible."

19

Law in Order

Reconstructing U.S. National Security

William Wechsler

Few tools of U.S. foreign policy are as vitally important *and* as consistently overlooked as law enforcement. Terrorism, organized crime, drug trafficking, arms smuggling, sanctions busting and foreign corruption are serious challenges confronting American policymakers, and law enforcement has an important—sometimes central—role in combating each of these threats. That role suffers, however, from two fatal flaws. First, differences in bureaucratic culture and viewpoints between the law enforcement and national security communities make coordination difficult. Law enforcement agencies generally refuse to see themselves as components of U.S. foreign policy. Nor does the traditional foreign policy establishment adequately appreciate the distinct culture, capabilities and constraints that characterize U.S. law enforcement agencies. Second, there are structural impediments to effective coordination, both among the various law enforcement agencies and between such bodies and the traditional national security agencies. Federal law enforcement agencies, themselves riven by turf battles, lack proper civilian oversight and are organizationally ill-suited for integration into the wider foreign policy community.

Previous administrations have tried, but failed, to solve these problems. Too many important actors prefer things as they are, most significantly the various Federal law enforcement agencies themselves. In the past, the need to fix the systematic inefficiencies bedeviling Federal law enforcement seemed less pressing. But the world has changed, and U.S. law enforcement must change with it. Just as war is too important to be left to the generals,

Note: Some footnotes have been deleted; others have been renumbered.

law enforcement reform is too important to be left to FBI directors and Customs commissioners.

INTERNATIONAL CRIME: A THREAT TO U.S. NATIONAL SECURITY

For most of American history, there has been a bright line on the Federal level between national security threats on the one hand and criminal threats on the other. The former were international, the latter domestic. The international side was the purview of the military and intelligence agencies; the domestic side that of the law enforcement agencies. This separation was primarily intended to prevent military encroachments on civilian authorities and civil liberties. The fear of militarism in American civil society remains deeply embedded in the national consciousness and has long been incorporated into American governance. U.S. government actions are still defined by the Posse Comitatus Act, passed in 1878 to prohibit the military from performing certain domestic police functions.

In recent decades this bright line has blurred. Traditional crimes in the United States have increasingly been found to have links to criminal networks overseas. Narcotics trafficking, most obviously, cannot possibly be combated by domestic law enforcement operations alone. A bipartisan consensus also has emerged that the threat from foreign narcotics trafficking is not just a law enforcement concern but a matter of national security as well. Thus in 1987 did President Reagan overrule his Secretary of Defense and instruct the military to go abroad to help fight the war on drugs.

As technology advanced and borders became increasingly porous after the Cold War, it became increasingly evident that international crime in *all* of its various forms threatened U.S. national security interests. Sometimes the threats were direct. Terrorists groups like Al-Qaeda, no longer as dependent on state sponsorship, began targeting Americans at home and abroad. They also engaged in a host of criminal activities apart from terrorism, from arms trafficking to people smuggling to securities fraud. Vast networks of criminals based in Russia, Nigeria, Latin America, East Asia and elsewhere went global, infiltrating the United States as one of the world's most lucrative targets. Hackers halfway around the world broke into U.S. computer systems, including sensitive systems belonging to the military and intelligence agencies.

International crime also poses indirect threats to U.S. national security. Criminal syndicates have corrupted government officials, undermined democratic governance, and hindered economic development in many countries. This has been well documented in post-communist states like Russia, developing countries like Nigeria, post-conflict societies like Bosnia and countries of particular concern to the United States like Mexico. In Colombia, groups engaged in drug trafficking, terrorist activity and other serious crimes even challenge the government itself for control over territory and the population, just as typical communist insurgencies did a few decades ago.

Criminal syndicates have also helped to undermine regional stability. In Sierra Leone, for instance, the illegal smuggling of "conflict" diamonds helped finance a brutal civil war. Elsewhere in Africa and around the world, arms trafficking by organized criminal networks has stoked regional conflicts that might otherwise have died down. Criminal syndicates have been instrumental in violating U.S. and international sanctions regimes in such places as Iraq and Serbia. Russian criminal organizations are reportedly involved in smuggling materials for weapons of mass destruction—chemical, biological and nuclear. In other places, such as in Albania, criminal organizations have driven regime change, as when the collapse of a pyramid scheme precipitated anarchy and flooded next-door Kosovo with small weapons. Financial crimes such as money laundering and counterfeiting have the potential to undermine national banking systems and thereby to destabalize the global financial system. Economic crimes such as piracy—both physical and intellectual—affect U.S. companies' competitiveness in foreign markets.

WHAT WE HAVE HERE IS A FAILURE TO COMMUNICATE

Given these considerable stakes, all appropriate foreign policy tools should be employed to combat criminal threats to U.S. security interests, and those tools should be employed in a coordinated process according to a comprehensive strategy. Unfortunately, this commonsense view is far too uncommon in Federal law enforcement agencies today.

As to the direct threats to this country—terrorism, drug trafficking and international organized crime—nobody denies that Federal law enforcement has a critical and even a predominant role to play. But other tools of U.S. foreign policy also need to be deployed to combat international crime, including bilateral diplomacy, cooperation in multilateral forums, financial sanctions, and in some cases covert operations and overt military campaigns. In these cases, obviously, law enforcement activities must be integrated into the overall strategies, even in those instances when law enforcement has the lead. Sometimes this works well. When it comes to the rendition of terrorists from abroad, for instance, U.S. law enforcement agencies have developed excellent working relationships with the military and intelligence agencies. But law enforcement officials who are accustomed to the considerable freedom of action and limited civilian oversight that domestic operations afford often chafe when confronted with the need to coordinate with others when operating abroad.

Americans are proud that nobody in the United States, not even the president, is above the law. This principle is drilled into the consciousness of every law enforcement officer. Since the abuses of Federal law enforcement by the Nixon Administration, Federal agents have taken refuge in the axiom that criminal trails should be followed to their conclusion by non-political technical experts, no matter what the wider consequences may be. Law enforcement officers remain suspicious that requests for "coordination" with other government agencies, even on matters of foreign policy, are subterfuges for political interference. Even worse from the point of view of many Federal law enforcement agents is the argument that law enforcement objectives—putting individual criminals behind bars—should sometimes be subordinate to other objectives, such as disrupting a terrorist network, winning a military campaign, or "merely" maintaining positive bilateral relations with certain other countries. Some law enforcement agencies have become especially adept at using the media and the Congress to draw attention to allegations of "political interference" in such cases.

This viewpoint is extremely short-sighted. First, the isolation of law enforcement agencies from other agencies and from the interagency process harms the effectiveness of law enforcement operations themselves. U.S. diplomacy is too often unable to assist law enforcement efforts because ambassadors are not informed about specific cases or are not asked to secure cooperation from foreign governments. Yet such diplomatic efforts can be extremely valuable, not least because many foreign governments are more comfortable speaking with U.S. diplomatic (or intelligence) agencies than with U.S. law enforcement agencies. Diplomats sometimes possess additional leverage to use on behalf of the national interest, as well.

One example: for years U.S. law enforcement strained hard and usually failed to trace criminal money trails overseas to countries with strict bank secrecy laws. Then, in 2000, a multilateral diplomatic initiative to "name and shame" certain money laundering havens successfully coerced several countries to change their laws and adopt stronger international anti-money laundering standards.[1] Now, U.S. law enforcement can track money in ways it never could before. [Recently] Liechtenstein and the Bahamas—two countries "named and shamed"—have provided important information to the United States about elements of Al-Qaeda's financial network. It is inconceivable that the United States would have had access to this same information [a few] years ago, before diplomacy was brought to bear on this problem.

Second, the lack of coordination with law enforcement agencies can harm U.S. foreign policy. Sometimes U.S. foreign law enforcement operations anger foreign heads of government when they are kept out of the loop. Not that foreign governments should be allowed to halt or hinder U.S. investigations; their anger and irritation is often a price we must pay to enforce U.S. laws. But law enforcement objectives can often be achieved without harming bilateral diplomatic relations—if only law enforcement personnel would stop intentionally hiding their activities from the State Department and the National Security Council.

Information as well as activities relevant to U.S. national security that come from law enforcement sources also often go unshared with the national security community. There are complicated, painstaking and heavily-scrutinized methods for disseminating intelligence information to law enforcement agencies, always scrubbed so it can be used in court without revealing intelligence sources and methods. But there are no similar procedures for information gathered by law enforcement agencies to routinely make its way into intelligence agencies and thereby into the wider national security community. It is up to law enforcement officials themselves to decide when information they have is relevant to national security, but such decisions often require expertise that law enforcement officials, through no fault of their own, do not possess. Nonetheless, for many years during the Clinton Administration, the Justice Department and the associated law enforcement agencies refused to agree to a basic memorandum of understanding to establish even first principles as to how information should be shared.

The problems that have arisen from this state of affairs are not merely hypothetical. Former CIA Director James Woolsey has publicly complained that he was unable to obtain terrorist-related information once the Justice Department decided to bring the 1993 World Trade Center bombing case to court. In another situation during the Clinton Administration, the FBI discovered that the wife of the former Russian delegate to the International Monetary Fund might have been involved in illegally moving $7 billion in Russian money of unknown origin through the Bank of New York. Not until this case was reported in the *New York Times* did the Justice Department and the FBI think to brief the National Security Advisor or the Secretary of State on the matter. More recently, when on February 11 [2002] the FBI announced a terror alert concerning a 23-year-old Yemeni named Fawaz Yahya Al-Rabeei and his cell, it did not even bother to inform the U.S. embassy in Sanaa, or to share with it obviously relevant information that led the FBI to declare the alert.

Third, law enforcement objectives often differ from wider U.S. objectives, and that is natural. The FBI's job is to arrest criminals in such a way that a court case against them will result in a conviction that can stand the test of an appeal. But law enforcement goals should not be presumed pre-eminent by definition. Even when U.S. laws have clearly been broken, other objectives may be more important to the nation. One such case is President Bush's wise decision to treat Al-Qaeda primarily as a military adversary rather than a law enforcement concern. Another example: During the Clinton Administration, the Justice Department repeatedly objected to the use of economic sanctions against foreign drug cartels as proposed by the national security agencies, preferring that efforts be restricted to building cases in U.S. courts. This view was held by the law enforcement agencies despite the success of President Clinton's 1995 order, under the International Emergency Economic Powers Act, to disrupt the Cali cartel's financial network. Not until 1999 were additional sanctions imposed, and then only after the Congress, frustrated by the lack of similar actions against other cartels, passed the Foreign Drug Kingpin Designation Act.

PROBLEMS OF THE INDIRECT

When it comes to direct threats to the United States from international crime, U.S. law enforcement agencies generally object to the involvement of national security agencies, believing that the latter may curtail or otherwise interfere with their operations. But this dynamic is reversed when it comes to indirect threats. In these cases, law enforcement agencies generally refuse to become substantially involved, notwithstanding pleas from the State Department. The reason is that many in U.S. law enforcement simply do not care if foreign countries and their governments are being harmed by international crime, unless there is a clear connection to a case that can be brought to trial in U.S. courts. As they see it, it is not their job to worry about damage to U.S. national security interests or regional stability abroad. That is also why law enforcement agencies give low priority to foreign law enforcement training and technical assistance efforts, administration of justice development programs, post-conflict governance initiatives, and the civilian policing components of UN peacekeeping operations. This reluctance has even carried over with respect to places such as the Balkans and Haiti, where conditions had previously deteriorated to the point that U.S. military forces had to be called into action. State Department officials are therefore left more or less on their own to deal with international arms trafficking, sanctions busting, alien smuggling, trafficking in women, corruption and all the rest of the dark side of globalization.

The costs of this abnegation are huge. The transformation of Russia into a functioning, market democracy was one of the primary objectives of U.S. foreign policy in the 1990s. Yet U.S. law enforcement took no serious interest in combating Russian organized crime, unless it set foot on U.S. soil. Moreover, Russian organized crime gained strength and influence in Hungary, a new NATO member and an important ally for U.S. efforts in the Balkans. This was of great concern to Hungary's President and had been identified as one of the primary threats to Hungary's economic and political development by the U.S. ambassador. Yet the FBI refused for years to assign even one agent to the U.S. embassy in Budapest, much less actively assist the

Hungarian National Police in combating Russian organized crime. It took a meeting between President Clinton and the Hungarian President, and then a personal request from the National Security Advisor to the FBI Director, before even this small step could be taken.

The traditional national security agencies also share blame for the lack of integration of the law enforcement agencies into U.S. foreign policy. Most foreign policy experts know little and care less about the capabilities and limitations of U.S. law enforcement. As a result, unfair expectations are sometimes set or improper requests are made. International law enforcement issues are too often a secondary concern of the foreign policy establishment, and sometimes they are ignored entirely. Particularly when foreign governments themselves are implicated in crimes, U.S. diplomats can be reflexively unwilling to press issues that might result in a deterioration of bilateral relations. The State Department's Bureau of International Narcotics and Law Enforcement Affairs, despite relatively strong leadership in recent years, is still considered a bureaucratic backwater. It only rarely attracts the most capable civil servants and foreign service officers, and has historically been marginalized by the leadership of the department.

STRUCTURAL IMPEDIMENTS

Some of these problems might be solved by changes in leadership, but structural changes will be necessary as well. In 1995, President Clinton issued Presidential Decision Directive 42 which, for the first time, defined international crime as a national security threat. An NSC-chaired interagency working group was established to coordinate the government's efforts to combat this threat. And in 1998 President Clinton released the first-ever International Crime Control Strategy, describing the goals and objectives of this new effort.

It paid off. Achievements include the aforementioned "naming and shaming" of money laundering havens, a series of multilateral treaties negotiated by the State Department on subjects such as small arms trafficking, a series of bilateral Mutual Legal Assistance Treaties negotiated by the Justice Department, greater efforts to combat trafficking in women, and the financial sanctions on the Cali drug cartel (the first time this tool was used against a non-state actor). There were also some successes in the wars on drugs and terrorism, and new initiatives to protect critical infrastructures from information warfare and cyber crime. But overall, despite President Clinton's personal interest and strong pushes from the National Security Council and the State Department, the effort left too much undone. Part of the problem flowed from the differing viewpoints and failures of coordination between law enforcement agencies and national security agencies, but other difficulties stemmed from structural flaws in the law enforcement community. These flaws deserve special attention, and remediation.

The very structure of the Justice Department illustrates the low priority assigned to curtailing international crime. Its international training, technical assistance, counter-intelligence and criminal programs are spread out over several different offices and report to a multitude of different Justice Department officials. Most regrettably, a single assistant attorney general oversees both international and domestic criminal investigations. One person who held that post during the Clinton Administration told me he had not spent even ten minutes thinking about international crime before he took the job. While the State Department, Pentagon and CIA are all organized geographically, no one in the Justice Department is responsible for what the department and its subordinate agencies are doing with regard to, say, Russia.

Even if there were such a position, the Justice Department would *still* suffer from its institutional inability to oversee its subordinate law enforcement agencies. During the Clinton Administration FBI Director Louis Freeh was rarely if ever held accountable by Attorney General Janet Reno. In keeping with the legacy of J. Edgar Hoover, Freeh functioned without effective civilian oversight, a pattern that was replicated down the chain of authority. The law enforcement agencies that fall under the Treasury Department's jurisdiction, too, operate more or less independently from the civilians to whom they are allegedly accountable. This became evident in 1997 when Ray Kelly, then the Under Secretary of the Treasury for Enforcement, took what seemed to be a demotion to become the Commissioner of the U.S. Customs Service—one of many law enforcement agencies that he *already supposedly oversaw*. The move only made sense upon recognition that Customs operates with little effective civilian oversight.

Even if the problem of civilian oversight were somehow fixed, the massive problems stemming from the sheer number of Federal law enforcement agencies would still exist, as would the lack of coordination among them, the lack of cooperation with state and local authorities, and the vast operational inefficiencies that result. In 1991 the General Accounting Office identified an astonishing 148 different Federal agencies with some law enforcement functions. On far too many issues jurisdictional confusion hampers investigations. The various law enforcement agencies are notoriously turf-conscious, regularly refusing to share information with each other, always focused on securing "credit" for convictions.

The mission statements of many law enforcement agencies reflect this focus; to an outsider (and even to many insiders) they seem oddly centered on ensuring institutional primacy with regard to specific crimes, particularly ones where legal jurisdictions are unclear. "Interagency" offices and task forces are established to great fanfare and then become ineffective because key law enforcement agencies refuse to join or to genuinely participate, fearing "subordination" to others. Databases are therefore rarely combined between agencies and equipment is often not interoperable. Basic data on the number and types of crimes are often incomplete and are tracked according to differing methodologies in different agencies. Standardized procedures do not even exist across the law enforcement community in such areas as recruitment, selection and training; surveillance; rules of engagement; forensic laboratory management and classification and use of forensic data. In the course of virtually every high-profile case, state and local law enforcement officials complain that Federal law enforcement agencies refuse to share information, making it harder for them to function.

These are not new insights. Every decade or so an outside group of experts examines the structure of Federal law enforcement, and they all come to virtually the same conclusion: it's a dysfunctional mess. Sadly, these conclusions have all been ignored. In 1996, for instance, after the public outcry over law enforcement actions in Waco and Ruby Ridge, the Congress asked Judge William H. Webster, a former director of both the FBI and the CIA, to chair a commission to examine the state of Federal law enforcement. Its admirable final report was published four years later and, alas, promptly shelved. This was a shame. The Webster report is as comprehensive a review of the structure of Federal law enforcement as has ever been written, and includes a number of far-reaching recommendations. It is still not too late to adopt some of them.[2]

TIME FOR CHANGE

The Webster report's overall conclusion was that "the current organization of Federal law enforcement needs to be changed." While that call went unheeded during the final year of the Clinton Administration, the Bush Administration can and should take up the challenge now, and if it does it has good reason to expect success. That is because a rare confluence of events has pushed Federal law enforcement to a crisis.

First, a string of high profile debacles have recently embarrassed the FBI, puncturing its public image and finally allowing criticisms to be voiced in public. Consecutive episodes such as the Robert Hanssen spy case, the botched investigation of Wen Ho Lee, the media leaks attacking Richard Jewell, the cover-up of deficiencies in its crime lab, its improper withholding of documents in the Timothy McVeigh case, and the intelligence and operational failures in the domestic war on terrorism have finally put many in Congress in the mood to ask some hard questions.

Second, there is a growing consensus that simply ponying up more resources will not solve the problem. After all, the Clinton Administration tripled the FBI's counter-terrorism budget and the number of its agents, and the FBI still failed utterly to detect the events of September 11 being planned on American soil. Nor had it any knowledge that Al-Qaeda was planning to attack Los Angeles International Airport during the millennium celebrations, something that came to light only after a terrorist was caught with explosives by an alert Customs agent at the Canadian border.

And third, now that the United States is at war with terrorism, questions about law enforcement reform have taken on a new urgency. The continuing investigation into Al-Qaeda's operations in the United States makes clear how much was missed and has highlighted the need for various law enforcement agencies to better share information concerning suspected terrorists. On September 11, as the public has now learned, the FBI had no computer system to centralize its intelligence and share it with other agencies.

Attorney General John Ashcroft and FBI Director Robert Mueller have already taken initial steps that show cognizance of the need for structural change. Mueller has overhauled the bureau's top management to place more emphasis on counter-terrorism and cyber crime. Ashcroft has rightly taken control of the terrorism investigation from the Southern District of New York, begun to separate the service and enforcement functions of the Immigration and Naturalization Service, and, at long last, given the Justice Department's inspector general jurisdiction over allegations of FBI misconduct—a fundamental step if the FBI is to be accountable to civilian oversight.

President Bush should now take the next step and call for a comprehensive review of law enforcement, with the intention of producing lasting, systemic reform. Politically, such an effort is more likely to succeed if sponsored by a Republican administration, because the GOP has stronger traditional ties to law enforcement than the Democrats. President Bush will also benefit from the absence of the adversarial relationship that existed between some law enforcement agency heads and the Clinton White House, in part due to the several investigations of the President.

A NEW VISION FOR LAW ENFORCEMENT

Before the administration sets forth to fix this problem, it would do well to recognize that the structural deficiencies facing Federal law enforcement are not without precedent. The reform of the U.S. military after World War II, which led ultimately to the Goldwater-Nichols Act in 1986, is a salutary model for study. This is not the place to review what has already been widely analyzed and well appreciated, except to stress three principal lessons. The first and most important lesson to be drawn is that the incrementalist approach does not work; the entrenched interests that oppose reform can be overcome only when leaders at the highest levels of the Executive and Legislative Branches work in a bipartisan spirit to seek comprehensive changes. The second lesson is that unification is the goal, "jointness" is the means, and clear lines of authority are the prerequisite. And the third lesson is that it is possible to ensure professionalism and even independence among career officers while still guaranteeing effective civilian oversight and wider integration into the foreign policymaking process.

So, then, what would a reformed Federal law enforcement community look like? There are four necessary components of reform: *consolidation* of proliferating law enforcement agencies; *coordination* among the remaining agencies; *centralization* of both civilian and agency accountability; and *integration* into the wider foreign policy community.... [At this point the author makes several recommendations that would relate to a consolidated homeland security organization. The Department of Homeland Security was approved shortly after this article was written.—*Eds.*]

NOTES

1. See my "Follow the Money," *Foreign Affairs* (July/August 2001).

2. *Law Enforcement in a New Century and a Changing World: Improving the Administration of Federal Law Enforcement,* Report of the Commission on the Advancement of Federal Law Enforcement, January 2000.

20

Roles, Politics, and the Survival of the V-22 Osprey

Christopher M. Jones

The early years of the twenty-first century have been a difficult period for the V-22 Osprey, a tilt-rotor transport plane designated to replace the Marine Corps's aging helicopter fleet. The deaths of twenty-three marines in two separate crashes, the falsification of maintenance records, and unfavorable reports concerning the V-22's safety and reliability have focused new attention on arguably the most controversial weapons system of the last two decades. These developments have prompted intense media coverage, a review by an independent panel of experts, and yet another series of design modifications, reminding observers that the program has absorbed more than ten billion dollars of federal funding without producing a single plane for regular military duty (see Bolkcom 2001). A final decision on full-scale production has been postponed indefinitely as the V-22 undergoes a new series of expensive operational tests. This setback has provided an opportunity for longtime critics to reopen the debate on the wisdom of building 458 aircraft at a cost of $38.1 billion (Bolkcom 2001, 1). The marines plan to procure 360 Ospreys to transport troops, while the navy and air force will employ the remainder for search and rescue, special warfare, logistics support, and special operations.

The events of 2000 and 2001 have placed the V-22's future in jeopardy. Yet these difficulties hardly represent the first time the plane has encountered trouble. Over the course of its two-decade development period, it has demonstrated a remarkable capacity to endure serious challenges. During the 1990s the program experienced intense political opposition, the crashes of two prototypes, a fire in another model, the resignation of the chief test pilot, and the deaths of seven crewmembers. In addition, the Osprey's per unit cost rose steadily as the program fell years behind schedule and the original plan to procure 913 aircraft was cut in half. However, these problems and more recent setbacks have not led to the plane's demise. A diverse but durable group of political actors has ensured its survival as a viable weapons procurement program. The cohesiveness of this coalition can be attributed to a common policy goal that the participants strongly support for different reasons based on their distinct organizational roles and interests.

To understand the members, motivations, and effectiveness of this political alliance, one need only look to the period when the V-22 faced and ultimately survived its greatest challenge—four years of intense opposition from the Office of the Secretary Defense (OSD). The program was initiated during President Ronald Reagan's defense buildup; while the Clinton administration devoted less funding to the project through a low-rate production commitment than V-22 supporters preferred, it honored a 1992 campaign pledge to build the plane. The Bush administration (1989–1992), however, tried repeatedly to cancel the Osprey. Each year, money to develop the aircraft was removed from the president's proposed defense budget. Each year, the Congress, Marine Corps, and the primary contractors, Boeing Company and Bell Helicopter Textron, fought jointly and effectively to restore it. Clearly congressional budget authority was critical to the coalition's success. But given the intensity of executive branch opposition, which included a refusal to spend appropriations, V-22 proponents on Capitol Hill would have had difficulty sustaining the program without the steady commitment of the marines and the political skill of the manufacturers.

Drawing upon interviews, congressional testimony, private documents, and other available material, this analysis carefully reconstructs the decision to develop the V-22 Osprey from 1989 through 1992. In doing so it seeks to provide a clear basis for understanding the actors and interests that have protected the program in the past and will work to ensure its survival for the foreseeable future. Further, it employs the bureaucratic politics literature to argue that organizational mission provides a compelling explanation of the participants' policy preferences and the politics that shaped a significant national security decision with long-term fiscal and military implications. Last, the case suggests that the key assumptions of the bureaucratic politics literature, which have long been used to explain the behavior of the executive branch, can be applied to legislative and societal actors. The finding lends support to scholars who have advocated the need to broaden and refine the bureaucratic politics frameworks developed thirty years ago.

THEORETICAL BACKGROUND

Of the theories available for understanding defense policy behavior, the bureaucratic politics paradigm (Allison and Halperin 1972) provides a compelling explanation of the four-year battle over the V-22 Osprey. Since the actors and interests supporting the program have not changed since the 1989–1992 period, it also provides insight into the forces that will attempt to safeguard the plane as it confronts a new series of challenges. The framework views the actions of government as political resultants. The resultants emerge from a defense policy process, characteristic of a game, where multiple players holding different conceptions of the national interest struggle, compete, and bargain over the substance and conduct of policy. The policy positions taken by the decisionmakers are determined largely by their own organizational roles and interests. The final outcome either represents a compromise between the actors or reflects outright the policy preferences of the actors who won the political game. The presence and effective use of bargaining advantages, including the formal authority to control the decisionmaking process or *action-channel* ("a regularized means of taking government action on a specific kind of issue" [Allison and Zelikow 1999, 300]), are critical to determining which actors prevail.

Allison and Zelikow (1999, 255–324) give the most recent statement of the bureaucratic politics approach. For the purposes of this study, however, Allison and Halperin's earlier work offers a distinct advantage. They argue it is appropriate to treat organizations as well as individuals as single policy actors (1972, 47). In these instances, an organization's mission (like a decisionmaker's bureaucratic position or job title) becomes a strong predictor of its policy stand on a particular issue. The "organizations as unitary actors" assumption is particularly useful in the case under study, because the documentary record reveals that the participants' behavior within the V-22 policy process was remarkably consistent over time.

Before proceeding further, some theoretical points are in order. For example, this study diverts from most applications of the bureaucratic politics approach by focusing on a decisionmaking process that extends beyond the executive branch to include other actors, such as Congress and private companies. While proponents of the approach do not highlight legislative and societal actors within their theoretical statements or case studies, nothing within their work precludes the involvement of such participants. In fact, they recognize this possibility by referring to such actors as *ad hoc players* (e.g., Allison and Halperin 1972, 47; Allison and Zelikow 1999, 296).

In addition, the bureaucratic politics explanation offered by this study should not be interpreted as a statement that other theories, especially those commonly used to understand weapons procurement decisions, are inapplicable to the V-22 episode. For instance, an iron triangle or structural policymaking pattern between congressional, bureaucratic, and private sector actors is distinguishable in the case under study. However, an explanation based solely on the cooperative politics of the iron triangle model would not capture the executive-legislative or interbranch conflict, which also shaped the V-22 decision. Further, it would not draw proper attention to the Office of the Secretary of Defense's (OSD) involvement and role-based behavior.

A bureaucratic politics explanation also does *not* preclude the presence of rational behavior. Actors are rational in an instrumental sense if they can form preferences and select the most preferred outcome when confronted with multiple options (see Zagare 1990, 239–43). This conception of rationality has two implications. On one hand, it allows decisionmakers to be purposeful or goal-directed without being pure utility-maximizers. Thus, it is rational for actors to prefer one policy alternative to another based on their bureaucratic roles and interests. On the other hand, the assumption that individuals or organizations arrive at policy preferences through instrumental rationality does not prevent the final decision or action from being politically determined. We can assume, for instance, a two-step process. Actors will initially and independently prefer a particular policy option based on their specific organizational roles. Then, the policy stands of the various actors within the decisionmaking process will be aggregated politically through such means as bargaining, coalition building, logrolling, and compromise. This perspective would account for the politics within the V-22 case as well as participants' statements, such as "our behavior within the budget process was rationally driven" (O'Keefe 1997).

After a brief background section, the remainder of this study illustrates the presence of role-based behavior and, therefore, the utility of bureaucratic politics paradigm in explaining the case of the V-22 Osprey during 1989–1992. It demonstrates how the four central actors' policy positions and supporting arguments were directly related to their distinct roles and interests. Each player's organizational mission predisposed it to have a different conception of the national interest and, therefore, a different reason for supporting or opposing the development of the V-22. The case further illustrates how specific actors, bargaining advantages, and political interactions were critical in shaping the final policy outcome.

CONTEXT OF THE DECISION

In April 1989, shortly after the first flight of an Osprey prototype, Secretary of Defense Richard Cheney announced the cancellation of the V-22 program. His decision was not a complete surprise. Serious discussions about postponing or eliminating major weapons programs started within the Bush transition team. The incoming administration's search for budget savings was driven by the reality that the massive defense spending of the Reagan era could not continue. After all, the Soviet threat was waning; the federal budget deficit was soaring; the president-elect had pledged "no new taxes"; and the Congress was eager to reduce overall defense spending. It was within this environment that the new administration scrutinized several expensive weapons programs, including the V-22.

Once President George H. W. Bush took office, the pressure to make significant defense cuts intensified. In April 1989, the Republican president and leaders of the Democratic-controlled Congress convened a budget summit in an effort to meet a legally mandated deficit-reduction target. The subsequent bipartisan agreement led to a ten-billion-dollar reduction in the fiscal year (FY) 1990 defense budget, which was $4 billion deeper than Cheney's original proposal. As a result, the FY 1990 defense budget fell from President Reagan's request of $305.6 billion to $295.6 billion. Secretary Cheney decided to address this decline by ordering the navy "to absorb almost half of the $10 billion" with the major casualty being naval aviation. As part of the Department of the Navy, the marines were impacted in the worst possible way when the V-22 was placed at the top of the hit list.

Executive branch opposition to the Osprey, while more widespread in the Bush administration, was not a new phenomenon. In fact, critics emerged shortly after the navy launched the program in 1982. The most consistent opposition came from Program Analysis and Evaluation (PA&E), which was the office within OSD responsible for monitoring the design and cost of weapons. Given its role and relative success throughout the 1970s, PA&E was unpopular with the service departments. Yet this disdain was negligible, because the watchdog office enjoyed the backing of consecutive secretaries of defense.

To the delight of the military services, PA&E's importance came to an abrupt end when the Reagan administration took control of the Pentagon in 1981. Seeing PA&E as an obstacle to the administration's massive defense buildup, including his plan for a six-hundred-ship navy, Secretary of Defense Caspar Weinberger "muted its role, downgrading the office head's title from assistant secretary to office director. Moreover, his controversial decentralization of the Pentagon seriously reduced the influence of PA&E as well as other central offices" (Griffiths 1986, 84). Thus when the head of PA&E, David S. C. Chu, argued that modified CH-53E and UH-60 helicopters could perform the same multiservice mission as the Osprey at half the cost, he was ignored.

However, PA&E and its quest to eliminate the V-22 program were given new life when Mr. Cheney became secretary of defense in March 1989. He assumed the post belatedly after the first nominee, Senator John Tower (R-Tex.), failed to win Senate confirmation in early March. Mr. Tower, who was from one of the two states where the Osprey was being built, was a major supporter of the plane. Faced with a new position and confronted with the challenge of having to reduce the FY 1990 budget by ten billion dollars, Mr. Cheney turned to PA&E for assistance. David Chu, who had served in the Congressional Budget Office when Mr. Cheney was a representative from Wyoming, happily obliged. It was an opportunity for PA&E to regain its influence and strike back at the services, which in its view were spending far too much money on the wrong types of weapons.

Mr. Chu had opposed the V-22 since 1983, when it was awarded a preliminary design contract. Thus it came as little surprise that the plane was one of the first weapons systems he advised Cheney to cut. Specifically, Chu and his colleagues "recommended the marines substitute a 950 mix of CH-53E and UH-60 [helicopters] for 552 V-22s" (Flanagan 1990, 42). The Marine Corps, however, was quick to point out that Chu's plan was more expensive. So Chu responded by changing his proposal to 650 helicopters. This adjustment brought the cost below the V-22 package, but "these numbers were inadequate to lift the Marines and tonnage required" (AW&ST Staff Report 1989). After a number of confrontations with the Marine Corps over costs and military requirements, Chu softened his position and "recommended a one-year slip in the program" (Flanagan 1990, 42). However, Chu's willingness to delay a final decision on the Osprey came too late. Constrained by the budget summit agreement and Bush's preferred weapons projects (e.g., B-2 bomber and Strategic Defense Initiative), Mr. Cheney saw no alternative. He acted on Chu's earlier advice and cancelled the V-22.

THE OFFICE OF THE SECRETARY OF DEFENSE

From 1989 through 1992, OSD was the most vigorous opponent of the Osprey. Its policy stand and corresponding arguments in favor of eliminating the plane were related to its organizational role. The traditional mission of the Defense Department is to ensure the defense and security of the United States and its allies. As the secretary of defense's principal staff unit for exercising civilian authority over the Pentagon, OSD must ensure defense policy reflects presidential priorities and corresponds to available fiscal resources. A key element of OSD's officially prescribed role is to "provide oversight to assure the effective allocation and efficient management of resources consistent with [administration] approved plans and programs" (U.S. Department of Defense 2001). Since OSD may choose to forego certain military capabilities to save or redirect money, it has the potential to clash with the armed services.

To promote its policy stand against the Osprey, OSD drew on a number of bargaining advantages. For instance, OSD had the power to initiate the annual defense budget process, compelling Congress to react to its cancellation of the Osprey each year. OSD was also aided by a wealth of expertise generated from its own bureaus, the military services, and other executive departments. In addition, Secretary Cheney had the support of the president on this issue until August 1992, when the Bush administration abruptly dropped its opposition to the program. Further, given OSD's opposition to the program and the lines of authority within the Pentagon, the marines were prevented from lobbying publicly on behalf of the plane (discussed below). Of course, the budget authority of the Congress overshadowed these assets.

Within the budget process, OSD's central reason for opposing the plane was its high cost relative to helicopters. As Cheney stated in 1991: "Cost is the driving issue, and the V-22 is too costly.... At these budget levels...we can afford to deploy operational systems embodying only those technologies that offer the greatest combat capability payoff per dollar invested. The V-22 is not such a system" (U.S. Congress, House Armed Services Committee, hereafter USHASC 1991a, 104). In April 1989, Cheney also told Congress: "[We cannot] justify spending the amount of money...proposed...when we are just getting ready to move into procurement of the V-22 to perform a very narrow mission I think can be performed...by using helicopters" (Cooper 1991, 3). This statement captures three points OSD would reiterate throughout the four-year period. First, the V-22's primary mission, ship-to-shore transport, could be accomplished by less expensive helicopters. Second, while the Osprey possessed greater speed and range than helicopters, it would not add much to the Marine Corps's capacity to fight. For instance, Cheney argued the marines would rarely, if ever, be asked to conduct operations like the 1980 Iranian hostage rescue mission, which proponents of the plane said the V-22 was well suited to perform. Third, with the army's decision to leave the program in 1987, the V-22 would not be the multiservice, multimission aircraft it was intended to be.

Given who was to use the Osprey and what it was to be used for, OSD believed the program was not cost effective. At no time did the civilian leadership of the Pentagon dispute the marines' contention that their helicopters needed to be replaced. Similarly there was no criticism of the Osprey's capabilities or the tilt-rotor concept. Instead OSD consistently approached the development of the V-22 from the perspective of affordability. Sean O'Keefe, the Pentagon's comptroller, best captured OSD's policy stand in 1991: "The V-22 may appear to be superior to existing helicopters.... But our goal is to find ways of performing our most critical mission acceptably, at a funding level that does not draw excessively from our many other critical military missions" (USHASC 1991b, 146).

In addition to arguments, OSD sought to advance its policy position through a number of actions. For instance, it continually proposed modified or redesigned helicopters as a prudent alternative to the Osprey. Each year the Bush administration submitted a defense budget to Congress that included a request for helicopters rather than the V-22. In addition, Deputy Secretary of Defense Donald J. Atwood challenged congressional budget authority in December 1989 by ordering the Department of Navy to terminate the V-22's production contracts. In his memorandum, Mr. Atwood indicated that it was not in the "public fiscal interest" to spend advanced procurement funds when OSD had no intention of moving beyond the Osprey's research and development phase. Further, Secretary Cheney made several unsuccessful attempts during the four-year period to transfer, defer, or rescind V-22 appropriations. Moreover, OSD obstructed a Cost Operational Effectiveness Analysis (COEA) of V-22 alternatives commissioned by the Congress and conducted by the Institute for Defense Analyses (IDA)—an organization funded by the Defense Department but technically independent. Defying the language of the previous year's appropriations act, OSD failed to submit the study with its FY 1991 budget proposal in February 1990. It also ignored subsequent requests to send the document to Capitol Hill. When the IDA study was finally released in June and revealed that in the long run the Osprey was the most cost effective and capable option for satisfying the marines' need and the navy's search-and-rescue mission, OSD immediately challenged its findings. Secretary Cheney told Congress: "[T]he investment cost to procure [the V-22] remains too high. In the current era of declining defense budgets, we must give up certain capabilities" (Cooper 1991, 6).

Last, OSD refused to spend money Congress had appropriated for the V-22. Angered by this pattern of defiance and the need to issue annual orders to release funds, members of Congress, including some with no interest in the Osprey, declared in 1992 that the Pentagon was illegally impounding $790 million. Some lawmakers went so far as "to intimate that they might go to court to challenge the right of Cheney . . . to override a line item in an appropriations act" (Forman 1994). After all, Congress had inserted special language in the FY 1992 Appropriations Act to ensure the money was spent. OSD argued its actions were motivated not by defiance but by an inability to implement another portion of the same appropriations act. The law called for the "development, manufacture, and operational test of three production representative V-22 aircraft" by December 31, 1996. OSD maintained that limited funds, time constraints, and engineering problems precluded this goal (USHASC 1992b, 3, 6).

The U.S. Comptroller General's subsequent ruling that OSD had violated the law by impounding Osprey funding led Secretary Cheney to offer a compromise. On July 2, 1992, he told Congress he would release $1.5 billion to build six production representative aircraft *if* he were allowed to use some of the money to explore other options. The alternatives included updated models of existing helicopters, a new medium-lift helicopter, and a modified, less costly version of the V-22. Cheney also asked that the requirement to produce three production representative Ospreys by December 1996 be relaxed. Knowing the contractors were not ready to manufacture the planes, Congress agreed.

This good faith, however, quickly dissipated. In late July 1992, the Pentagon took three actions that appeared to contradict Cheney's earlier commitment. First, it ordered the marines to reexamine their medium-lift requirement and suggested performance standards could be lowered. Second, the Defense Department's Joint Requirements Oversight Council (JROC) decided the medium-lift replacement no longer had to meet the speed and long-range requirements necessary for special operations and search-and-rescue missions. Third, JROC rejected a Marine Corps statement of operational requirements corresponding to the V-22's capabilities. Instead, it retained a statement of requirements that could be met by existing helicopters. The Osprey's congressional allies were outraged. They charged that OSD's actions amounted to nothing more than an attempt to remove the V-22 from the medium-lift replacement competition (Morrocco 1992, 25). In a special hearing on the matter in August 1992, OSD countered its latest efforts were not "duplicitous," but were simply aimed at finding the most capable and affordable replacement for the marines' aging helicopters (USHASC 1992b, 3, 21).

The controversy continued after the hearing, but soon became irrelevant. In late August 1992, the Bush administration dropped its opposition to the V-22 and indicated it would not stand in the way of spending $1.5 billion on the program. Even though the policy reversal coincided with a similar announcement related to the army's M-1 tank and a decision to sell nine million dollars' worth of fighter jets to Taiwan and Saudi Arabia, the administration denied there was any connection to the upcoming presidential election. Instead it took the position that the Osprey now complemented the emerging post–Cold War military strategy of projecting force in "hot spots." Political calculations, however, were salient. The Bush administration recognized it lacked the political support and constitutional authority to win the battle over the Osprey. Congress was intent on funding the program. Thus as the presidential election approached, the White House considered its public backing of the plane, including a visible contract announcement, a prudent political tactic. Texas and Pennsylvania were not only the sites of the two V-22 plants, but large electoral states.

THE CONGRESS

From 1989 through 1992, the Congress was a firm proponent of the Osprey. Support for the plane within the House and Senate was not unanimous, but is was pervasive, encompassing conservative Republicans as well as liberal Democrats. Two letters sent to President Bush regarding the V-22, one from 218 representatives and another signed by forty senators, were indications of the program's broad bipartisan support. This strong backing was the product of role-based behavior on the part of lawmakers who approached the issue from either a political or policy perspective.

On one hand, representatives and senators are politicians who want to be reelected to their offices. In order to attain this goal, they seek to secure benefits for their constituents. Thus, it is no surprise that some V-22 supporters were attracted to the program for what it offered their districts and states. Since the Osprey was being built in Texas and Pennsylvania, the senators and large congressional delegations from those states were firmly behind the program. Surely, Representatives Pete Geren (D-Tex.) and Curt Weldon (R-Pa.), who each had a V-22 plant in their district, backed the program for the jobs it would create and sustain. In August 1992, the primary contractors estimated a production rate of three or four Ospreys a month would employ between two and three thousand people at each of the two production facilities (Ferguson 1992). Further, there is reason to believe members of Congress from other states also sought to protect or expand local employment. The Engineering and Manufacturing Development (EMD) phase, for instance, involved an estimated 1,800 to two thousand subcontractors (Harrison 1994). As of October 1994, nearly $353 million in subcontracts had been distributed to businesses in forty-two states and 258 congressional districts. Twenty-five states had purchase orders or letter contracts in excess of $500,000. Bell and Boeing calculated that there were ten thousand jobs tied to subcontracts (Bell-Boeing 1994a, 1994b; Arnold 1994).

On the other hand, members of Congress are policymakers, who must defend their policy positions on a daily basis. Through legislative experience, committee service, and consultations with staff, they develop a capacity to evaluate public policy and communicate it effectively to their constituents. In the case of the V-22, many lawmakers simply determined there were valid policy reasons for favoring the program. Some backed the plane because they were proponents of a strong national defense or traditional supporters of the Marine Corps. Others found compelling, nonmilitary justifications for developing the aircraft (discussed below). Relatedly, many legislators were not beneficiaries of major subcontract awards or the roughly fifteen thousand estimated V-22-related jobs. Yet they still chose to back the project.

Congressional arguments on behalf of the Osprey embraced a far broader range of substantive issues than OSD's financial rationale or the marines' military perspective. Depending on the particular senator or representative, these diverse policy concerns enabled lawmakers to mask parochial concerns, counter OSD opposition, persuade undecided colleagues, and justify the program to constituents. Moreover, the range of possible policy reasons for building the V-22 explains why congressional support was so extensive and sustainable.

In some instances, legislators advocated the V-22 on the same issue OSD used to oppose it. That is, they challenged the Pentagon's contention that the Osprey (when compared to helicopter alternatives) was too expensive to develop and procure. For instance, Rep. Curt Weldon (R-Pa.) stated in May 1989: "The Navy and Marine Corps presented data to the Secretary [of Defense] showing him that in fact over the 20-year life cycle the V-22 was the most cost-effective solution" (USHASC 1989, 282). However, it was more common for lawmakers to discuss how the Osprey's cutting-edge technology was capable of enhancing military performance, revolutionizing civilian aviation, and improving the country's trade balance.

Members of Congress employed a number of militarily oriented arguments related to the plane's tilt-rotor technology. First, both the age of existing helicopters and the fact that they were based on 1940s technology were referenced. Second, lawmakers argued the plane's speed, range, and operational flexibility complemented the military challenges of the post–Cold War era, including the need to project U.S. military power in the developing world. Third, congressional supporters reinforced the marines' view of the program. Rep. James Bilbray (D-N.Y.) commented: "I have never met a Marine yet from the pilot that is a second lieutenant . . . to some of the top people in the Marine Corps that did not whisper in my ear . . . the V-22 . . . is the plane we want" (USHASC 1992a, 203). Last, the Osprey was advocated on the basis of safety, with an emphasis on how aging helicopters were plagued by maintenance problems and a restricted set of training maneuvers.

Another set of congressional arguments encompassed problems beyond the Marine Corps's medium-lift need. For instance, some senators and representatives claimed the Osprey would aid national security and law enforcement agencies with drug interdiction. Other legislators were convinced a government funded, tilt-rotor program would spawn civilian models that would revolutionize domestic air travel. On one hand, "with its ability to lift off from downtown helipads, they argue[d] the new plane could relieve the growing traffic jams at municipal airports" and better protect the environment (Waller 1989). On the other hand, lawmakers, such as Senator Ted Stevens (R-Alaska), a powerful member of the Senate Appropriations Committee, argued the V-22's speed and range would make rural and remote areas of the country more accessible. The Osprey, therefore, was championed as a national asset, capable of relieving two transportation problems without the construction of new runways or airports.

Besides improving civil aviation, congressional arguments focused on the relationship between tilt-rotor technology and the nation's economic well being. For example, civilian spin-offs of the V-22 were seen as a way to boost the domestic economy by keeping the U.S. aerospace industry competitive in the international marketplace. Members of Congress also made it clear if the United States did not develop and produce tilt-rotor aircraft, then other countries would. Rep. Curt Weldon (R-Pa.) stated: "The Japanese and Europeans want to take this away from us, because they see the tilt-rotor as the next generation of commercial aviation. We are not going to let that happen" (ABC News 1993; also see USHASC 1990, 102). This was a particularly strong argument, because both a Japanese conglomerate and a consortium of European firms had designed tilt-rotor aircraft. Lawmakers, therefore, argued that thousands of actual and potential American jobs would be sacrificed if the Osprey and a subsequent civilian program were not pursued. This issue even won over "deficit hawks," such as Rep. John Kasich (R-Ohio) and Senator Warren Rudman (R-N.H).

Congressional support for the V-22 was not confined to policy arguments. It also included actions. For instance, lawmakers made it clear that they were fully committed to production. Rep. James Bilbray (D-N.Y.) told Deputy Secretary of Defense Atwood in April 1992: "[Y]ou can go back to the Marines or to the Navy and [tell them to] come up with an alternative, but you are going to come back to this subcommittee and find out [it] is going to continue with the V-22" (USHASC 1992a, 202). Also, members of Congress openly and repeatedly questioned whether OSD really had a legitimate alternative to the Osprey. Many believed its search for "other options" was simply a delay. Further, legislators countered OSD opposition by frequently reprising the findings of the *Pentagon's* IDA study, which indicated the V-22 was the most cost-effective option for replacing Marine Corps helicopters. Last, Congress was not receptive to OSD's annual refusal to spend appropriations earmarked for the V-22. In April 1991, Rep. Marilyn Lloyd (D-Tenn.) remarked: "The Department's actions, in my judgement, amount to an unconstitutional attempt to exercise a line-item veto. This is not acceptable" (USHASC 1991b, 220). Lloyd's anger was not unique. Lawmakers, including those with no interest in the V-22 program, supported two actions. Beginning in 1990, special language was inserted into each appropriations act to ensure V-22 funds were obligated without delay. Then in 1992, the House Armed Services Committee decided that for every month appropriations went unspent the Pentagon comptroller's budget would be reduced by five percent.

Thus the battle surrounding the Osprey had two dimensions. On one hand, Congress and OSD were engaged in a policy dispute over the future of the program. At the center of this controversy was the issue of whether the plane's assets outweighed the high cost of development and procurement. On the other hand, there was an interbranch conflict over the Pentagon's disregard for the legislative power of the purse. This second dimension served to solidify and broaden support for the V-22 on Capitol Hill. In the end, Congress won the programmatic and constitutional conflicts because it possessed two valuable bargaining advantages. First, it had the formal authority to control the budget authorization and appropriation process and, therefore, the ultimate fate of the V-22. Second, legislative backing would not have remained as cohesive and well organized without the Marine Corps's unwavering commitment to the program and the political skill of the contractors. This assistance was critical given the president's wishes, OSD's ardent opposition, and the reality that congressional support for the plane was strong but not unanimous.

THE MARINE CORPS

Over the four-year period, the marines were the strongest proponents of the V-22 within the executive branch. Like the other actors in the case, their policy stand was related to their role and interests. In fact, the Osprey was actually a means for improving the performance of the Marine Corps's organizational mission. As an amphibious, expeditionary, "national force in readiness," the marines are called upon to move rapidly to faraway places to perform a variety of military duties. Moreover, the regional and nontraditional security threats of the post–Cold War world will require a more mobile and flexible military posture, including an active Marine Corps.

For decades, helicopters were critical to fulfilling the marines' demanding responsibilities. By the late 1960s, however, it was determined that time and new combat circumstances would increasingly render existing helicopters obsolete. Consequently, "the Marine Corps first defined a requirement for a replacement helicopter in 1968" (Forman 1994, 2). Of course, this need was not met immediately. Nearly two decades passed before the V-22 program was approved in 1982 and a full-scale development contract was awarded in 1986. This delay made the marines truly eager, if not desperate, for the plane. Limited speed, noise, maintenance problems, and an inability to transport the necessary tonnage or conduct evasive maneuvers plagued their aging helicopter fleet. Moreover, the marines were drawn to the Osprey's impressive capabilities, which include the capacity to carry twenty-four fully equipped combat troops internally or up to fifteen thousand pounds of cargo externally, at a speed of more than 250 knots over a distance of two hundred nautical miles. With less personnel and cargo, the Osprey's ferrying range extends to 2,100 nautical miles, enabling it to fly independently to military bases, aircraft carriers, and "hot spots" throughout the world (Dady 1998).

Consequently, just months before Cheney cancelled the Osprey in 1989, Marine Corps General A. M. Gray told Congress: "[The V-22] is the most important advance in military aviation since the helicopter. . . . It is my number one aviation priority" (Scharfen 1990, 180). Shortly thereafter, the marines offered to forgo procurement of the M-1 tank to save the Osprey. The proposal, which was rejected, illustrated the organization's acute aviation needs. It also demonstrated a strong desire to acquire a weapons system that would enhance its mission as well as distinguish it from the army at a time when the armed services were competing for post–Cold War duties. Thus the V-22 was not merely critical to the Marine Corps's standing as an over-the-horizon strike force but essential to its very existence.

Secretary Cheney's rejection of the marines' offer marked a transition in their behavior. Throughout the Reagan years and during the first few months of the Bush administration, the Marine Corps pushed strongly and openly for the Osprey. But when it became clear Cheney was determined to cancel the program, the marines employed a quieter approach. The marines were likely told by the Pentagon's leadership that they were not to make statements or take actions in public that contradicted OSD's position. During authorization hearings, members of Congress referred to "the gag order" and "the subtle pressures" on the Marine Corps (USHASC 1992a, 126–28; USHASC 1992b, 13). Also, the marines feared a public campaign on behalf of the V-22 would anger Cheney and affect how they fared in the interservice conflict over post–Cold War roles and missions. Given the level of congressional support, however, the marines were confident they could refrain from public lobbying and the program would still survive.

A number of bargaining advantages reinforced the marines' conviction that Congress would promote its policy preference. As part of the Department of the Navy, for instance, the marines have a congressional liaison staff that is far larger than the OSD contingent. There is also a strong tradition of support for the organization among senators and representatives who were once active-duty marines. In terms of the V-22 case, two of the most notable members of this formidable group were Senator John Glenn (D-Ohio), an influential member of the Senate Armed Services Committee, and Rep. Jack Murtha (D-Pa.), chairman of the subcommittee on defense and appropriations. Further, there is a general perception on Capitol Hill that the Marines Corps is "conservative, realistic, and above all, honest in defining its needs" (Forman 1994, 7–8). Last, the Congress considers the marines to be the underdog of the four services, because its needs are often overridden by the budget priorities of the army, navy, and air force. Consequently, when marines ask for the same budget item over an extended period, the request is usually honored.

These factors, however, did not preclude the Marine Corps from playing an important role in the case. There is evidence to suggest the organization engaged in a vigorous, behind-the-scenes campaign on Capitol Hill. More important, the marines demonstrated a clear commitment to the program through candid congressional testimony. Consistent with their organizational mission, they employed a number of militarily oriented arguments related to combat realities and the V-22's impressive speed, range, and operational flexibility. Even though this backing came in the form of answers to questions, it was critical in maintaining widespread legislative support. In fact, lawmakers often countered OSD opposition by referencing the statements of the Marine Corps leaders (discussed above).

For most of the four-year period, the Pentagon had one official position on the Osprey. According to OSD, the V-22 was unaffordable, and therefore, subject to cancellation. The marines, cognizant of the lines of authority within the Defense Department and perhaps fearing retaliation by Secretary Cheney, publicly supported this policy stand by avoiding unsolicited statements or action on behalf of the program. When testifying before Congress and maneuvering behind the scenes, however, the marines made it clear there was a serious need to replace the service's aging helicopter fleet and the V-22 was the most capable option. Thus the official Pentagon position was accompanied by an unofficial Marine Corps stand in favor of the plane.

THE CONTRACTORS

With the exception of a few zealots in Congress, the most active and aggressive proponents of the V-22 Osprey were its manufacturers—Bell Helicopter Textron and Boeing Company. Like the other actors in the case, their policy stand and corresponding behavior were consistent with their roles. Bell and Boeing, as economic actors, saw the plane as a way to guarantee profits and employment in an era of shrinking defense budgets. In addition to the economic benefits associated with military procurement, the contractors soon discovered there was considerable interest, both at home and abroad, in the civilian application of tilt-rotor technology. The V-22 program, therefore, held the potential to generate long-term business for both companies. Not surprisingly, this commercial stake compelled the Bell-Boeing Team to take a number of actions to protect and promote the Osprey.

One sign of the contractors' political acumen was their effort to control development and production costs. For example, in an effort to keep the V-22 program on schedule, the Bell-Boeing Team began full-scale development without a contract and with its own funds in 1985. The contractors also invested in the initial production tooling for the Osprey. This expenditure simultaneously reduced the government's up-front costs and demonstrated the companies' long-term commitment to the project. In addition, a fixed-priced development contract was signed in May 1986 by the two companies and the Department of the Navy (the contracting service for the Marine Corps). In the pact, Bell-Boeing agreed to absorb all costs over the ceiling price of $1.825 billion. This arrangement transferred the financial risk of development to the contractors. Furthermore, when the Osprey enters full production, Bell and Boeing (which were cooperative development partners) will each have the ability to manufacture the entire plane. This capacity will ensure the government receives a more cost-effective V-22, because the two contractors will compete for production lots. Last, the Bell-Boeing Team improved its manufacturing and assembly techniques to make production more efficient and affordable.

Besides these efforts to control costs, the contractors widened the plane's domestic constituency. Among the strongest actions Bell-Boeing took was the distribution of subcontracts to nearly two thousand companies. Two hundred of these companies were major or first tier subcontractors. Examples include Grumman Aerospace (tail section), Lockheed Martin (flight control system), and IBM (avionics). Thus, the number of states with an economic interest in the Osprey grew from two (Pennsylvania and Texas) to over forty. Once part of the large Bell-Boeing Team, V-22 suppliers were encouraged to make their congressional representatives aware of the program's impact on local employment (Uchitelle 1992; Arnold 1994). Yet the subcontractors were only one part of the constituency Bell-Boeing strategists built. For instance, labor unions were involved. Organizations, such as the United Auto Workers and AFL-CIO, lobbied Congress, because thousands of their members had jobs related to the Osprey program. Another significant patron of the V-22 was the Federal Aviation Administration (FAA). In 1985, the contractors realized if the Osprey was to be billed as a civilian asset, then FAA backing was critical (Forman 1994, 10–11). Two years later, Bell-Boeing convinced the FAA to cosponsor a civil tilt-rotor study and to participate in the Osprey's test-flight program. FAA endorsement activated other interested parties, such as the California Department of Transportation and the Port Authority of New York and New Jersey. Last, the contractors were instrumental in establishing the Tilt-rotor Technology Coalition—a collection of contractors, subcontractors, members of Congress, retired Marines, and private sector groups—that became a unified lobbying force.

The final means the contractors employed to promote the Osprey were public relations activities. For example, Bell-Boeing began a guest pilot program for members of Congress, the marines, and the private sector. The goal was to create an affinity for the plane among members of the policy community (Forman 1994, 9–10). In addition, the contractors launched a congressional awareness program that included events, such as "Tilt-rotor Appreciation Day" and the landing of a demonstrator aircraft on Capitol Hill. The *Osprey Fax* newsletter, full-page advertisements in newspapers and magazines, and television commercials during the Sunday morning talk shows were also aimed at building legislative and public support. Last, Bell-Boeing kept information about the Osprey freely available. This flow of information enabled the contractors to attract support, counter criticism and misinformation, and demonstrate to the media and public that the V-22 was worthy of finite defense dollars.

Like the other actors involved in the V-22 case, the contractors employed arguments to support their policy stand. In fact, they used every conceivable justification for continuing the program. It was actions rather than arguments, however, that made the Bell-Boeing Team such an invaluable member of the Osprey coalition. Through its political skill, Bell-Boeing was able to make the V-22 appealing to a diverse group of actors and interests. Instead of simply promoting the Osprey as a badly needed weapons system, it was packaged as a national asset, which would complement post–Cold War military strategy, create jobs, remedy domestic transportation problems, and become an attractive export.

CONCLUSION

Consistent with the central assumptions of the bureaucratic politics paradigm, the decision to fund the development of the V-22 Osprey from 1989 through 1992 emerged from a policy process pervaded by role-based politics. The major actors within this decisionmaking environment, the Office of the Secretary of Defense, Congress, Marine Corps, and contractors, held policy positions on the plane that were directly related to their organizational missions. These distinct roles caused the actors to have different interests and, therefore, disparate reasons for supporting or opposing the V-22 program. Conflict arose between the executive and legislative branches, because OSD and the Congress had competing interests as well as diametrically opposed policy goals. The disagreement grew wider and more intense when OSD challenged congressional budget authority by refusing to spend V-22 appropriations.

Despite four years of ardent opposition by OSD, Congress won the programmatic and constitutional battles related to the Osprey. As noted, its success was largely the result of two bargaining advantages. First, Congress had enough formal authority through its "power of the purse" to control the "action-channel" or budget process and, therefore, the ultimate fate of the Osprey. Second, a committed Marine Corps and a politically skillful team of contractors backed Congress. These actors ensured congressional support remained broad, cohesive, and well organized. In essence, it was the strength of this tripartite coalition that overrode OSD's policy stand and saved a program with potentially long-term military, fiscal, and economic implications.

This case study extends to the present, because the coalition of actors and interests that protected the plane in the Bush administration (1989–1992) has not disappeared. In fact, there is good reason to believe this political alliance is stronger today, because it has more at stake. Congress has invested billions of dollars; the contractors and subcontractors have thousands of jobs deeply tied to building the Osprey and designing civilian spin-off models; and Marine helicopters have aged to a point where they are near the end of their life cycle with no ready replacement except the V-22. Moreover, the plane is well suited for the post–Cold War security environment. These actors, therefore, have a strong interest in ensuring the program's survival. Even if the aircraft's rising cost and most recent problems finally lead to its demise, one would still have to marvel at its capacity to survive for two decades without entering into full production. The Osprey's longevity is testimony to its supporters' effectiveness and the difficulty of stopping a weapons project once it is under development.

Finally, a note about theory is in order. The case clearly shows that actors can be rational, in an instrumental sense, and still behave politically. Moreover, the applicability of the theory's key assumptions to legislative and nongovernmental actors suggests the importance of devoting attention to the development of a political decisionmaking approach that recognizes the true diversity of players, interests, and processes capable of shaping defense and foreign policy. One possibility is a "governmental politics paradigm" encompassing multiple analytical models. On one level, the models might share a common set of assumptions capturing the general characteristics of governmental politics: fragmented power, multiple actors, instrumental rationality, role-based policy stands, different interests, and politically generated outcomes. On another level, each model could be distinguished by a specific type of governmental politics defined by particular actors, forms of politics, action-channels, and other procedural characteristics. These assumptions might vary with the salience of the issue or the locus of decisionmaking. For instance, there might be different models to explain defense and foreign policy made by (1) the president and senior-level advisors, (2) bureaucracies, (3) the executive and legislative branches, and (4) executive, legislative, and private sector actors. With further refinement, such a framework would build upon the valuable work of Allison and Halperin while addressing the legitimate concerns of their critics.

REFERENCES

ABC News. 1993. "Your Money, Your Choice." *World News Tonight*. Aired March 3.

Allison, G., and M. Halperin. 1972. "Bureaucratic Politics: A Paradigm and Some Policy Implications." *World Politics* 24: 40–80.

Allison, G., and P. Zelikow. 1999. *Essence of Decision: Explaining the Cuban Missile Crisis*. New York: Longman.

Arnold, T. 1994. Manager, Tiltrotor Communications, Bell Helicopter Textron. *Telephone interview and follow-up correspondence*. November 21.

AW&ST Staff Report. 1989. "Naval Aviation Modernization Hit Hard by Pentagon Cuts." *Aviation Week & Space Technology*. April 24.

Bell-Boeing. 1994a. Status of V-22 Subcontracts (Including EMD and Uprated Drive System). *Internal memorandum and attachments*. October 12. Distributed to author.

———. 1994b. U.S. Map, V-22 EMD Supplier Dollars. *Internal memorandum*. Bell Helicopter Textron, Inc. October 12.

Bolkcom, Christopher. 2001. *CRS Issue Brief for Congress: V-22 Osprey Tilt-Rotor Aircraft*. November 5 (Congressional Research Service). Washington, D.C.

Cooper, B. 1991. *CRS Issue Brief for Congress: V-22 Tilt-Rotor Aircraft (Weapons Fact)*. February 25 (Congressional Research Service). Washington, D.C.

Dady, G. 1998. V-22 Public Affairs Office, U.S. Department of Navy. *Telephone interview and follow-up correspondence.* December 7.

Ferguson, D. W. 1992. V-22 Production Employment. *Internal memorandum.* Bell Helicopter Textron. August 25. Distributed to author.

Flanagan, R. 1990. "The V-22 is Slipping Away." U.S. Naval Institute *Proceedings* 116: 39–43.

Forman, B. 1994. "The V-22 Tiltrotor Osprey: The Program That Wouldn't Die." Paper distributed to author by Bell-Boeing Team.

Griffiths, D. 1986. "Weinberger Puts Muzzle on Pentagon Watchdog." *Business Week.* September 5.

Harrison, M. 1994. *Internal memorandum.* Boeing Space Group, Helicopter Division. 12 December. Distributed to author.

Morrocco, J. 1992. "Pentagon Narrows V-22 Mission, Reaffirms Medium-Lift." *Aviation Week & Space Technology.* July 27.

O'Keefe S. 1997. Former Secretary of the Navy and Department of Defense Comptroller. *Telephone interview.* January 13.

Scharfen, J. 1990. "U.S. Marine Corps in 1989." U.S. Naval Institute *Proceedings* 116: 178–89.

Uchitelle, L. 1992. "An Odd Aircraft's Tenacity Shows Difficulty of Cutting Arms Budget." *New York Times.* November 2.

U.S. Congress, House Armed Services Committee. 1989. Navy Program Review. *Hearings on National Defense Authorization Act for Fiscal Year 1990–H.R. 2461 and Previously Authorized Programs.* 101st Congress, 1st Session, May 11. Washington, D.C.

———. 1990. Department of the Navy and U.S. Marine Corps FY 1991 RTD&E Budget Request. *Hearings on National Defense Authorization Act for Fiscal Year 1991–H.R. 4753 and Oversight of Previously Authorized Programs.* 101st Congress, 2nd Session, March 7. Washington, D.C.

———. 1991a. Fiscal Years 1992–1993 National Defense Authorization Request. *Hearings on National Defense Authorization Act for Fiscal Years 1992 and 1993–H.R. 2100 and Oversight of Previously Authorized Programs.* 102nd Congress, 1st Session, February 7. Washington, D.C.

———. 1991b. V-22 Osprey Program Review. *Hearings on National Defense Authorization Act for Fiscal Years 1992 and 1993–H.R. 2100 Oversight of Previously Approved Programs.* 102nd Congress, 1st Session, April 11. Washington, D.C.

———. 1992a. Procurement and Military Nuclear Systems Subcommittee Hearings. *Hearings on National Defense Authorization Act for Fiscal Year 1993–H.R. 5006 and Oversight of Previously Authorized Programs.* 102nd Congress, 2nd Session, April 28. Washington, D.C.

———. 1992b. *The Status of the V-22 Tiltrotor Aircraft Program.* 102nd Congress, 2nd Session, August 5. Washington, D.C.

U.S. Department of Defense. 2001. *Office of the Secretary of Defense Mission Statement.* February 5. Electronic version obtained via http://www.defenselink.mil/osd.

Waller, D. 1989. "Will the Osprey Ever Fly?" *Newsweek.* July 24.

Zagare, F. 1990. "Rationality and Deterrence." *World Politics* 42: 238–60.

21

Policy Preferences and Bureaucratic Position

The Case of the American Hostage Rescue Mission

Steve Smith

Within two days of the seizure by student revolutionaries of the American embassy in Tehran on 4 November 1979, planning began on a possible rescue mission. Initial estimates of the probability of success were "zero," given the severe logistical problems involved in getting to the embassy in Iran and back out of the country without losing a large number of the hostages as casualties. Nevertheless, as negotiations dragged on with very little promise of success, and as the 1980 American presidential election campaign approached, the decision was made to undertake a very bold rescue mission. Photographs of the charred remains of the burnt-out helicopters in the Dasht-e-Kavir desert provide the most vivid image of the failure of that mission.

The decisions about the mission were taken at three meetings on 22 March, 11 April, and 15 April 1980 by a very small group of people (on average, there were nine participants). Since 1980, the hostage rescue mission has received considerable coverage in the press and in the memoirs of the participants in that decisionmaking process. As such, it is an excellent case study for one of the most widely cited but rarely tested theories of foreign policy behavior: the bureaucratic politics approach.

Note: Some notes have been deleted; others have been renumbered.

THE THEORETICAL BACKGROUND

The dominant theories of why states act as they do derive from the basic assumption of rationality. Most theories of foreign policy are based on the premise that states act in a more or less monolithic way: Foreign policy is, accordingly, behavior that is goal-directed and intentional. Of course, many practitioners and academics quickly move away from the monolith assumption, but they can rarely command the kind of detailed information that would enable them to assess precisely what the factions are and how the balance of views lies in any decisionmaking group. It is, therefore, very common to talk of states as entities and to analyze "their" foreign policies according to some notion of a linkage between the means "they" choose and the ends these must be directed toward. Since practitioners and academics do not literally "know" why State X undertook Action Y, it becomes necessary to impute intentions to the behavior of states. The rationality linkage makes this task much easier; hence the popularity of the idea of the national interest, which incorporates very clear and powerful views on what the ends of governments are in international society and, therefore, on how the behavior can be linked to intentions. The most important attack on this viewpoint has been the "bureaucratic politics approach," most extensively outlined by Graham Allison in his *Essence of Decision.*[1] According to this approach, foreign policy is the result of pulling and hauling between the various components of the decisionmaking process. Foreign policy may, therefore, be better explained as the outcome of bureaucratic bargaining than as a conscious choice by a decisionmaking group. As Allison puts it, the outcome of the decisionmaking process is not really a result but "a resultant—a mixture of conflicting preferences and unequal power of various individuals—distinct from what any person or group intended."[2] The critical point is that these conflicting preferences are determined, above all, by bureaucratic position. Foreign policy, according to this perspective, is therefore to be explained by analyzing the bureaucratic battleground of policymaking, rather than imputing to something called the state a set of motives and interests. On the bureaucratic battleground, the preferences of the participants are governed by the aphorism . . . "where you stand depends on where you sit."[3] . . .

The decision of the United States government to attempt a rescue of the 53 American hostages held in Iran offers an excellent opportunity . . . to test . . . Allison's claims about bureaucratic position and policy preference. . . .

The planning process for the rescue mission began on 6 November 1979, just two days after the hostages were seized in Tehran. During the winter and spring the planning continued, focusing on the composition and training of the rescue force, on the precise location of the hostages and the nature and location of their captors, and on the enormously complex logistical problems involved in mounting the mission. These preparations continued in secret alongside an equally complex process of negotiation for the release of the hostages with the various elements of the Iranian government (including a secret contact in Paris). Bargaining was also under way with the United States's allies, in an attempt to persuade them to impose sanctions on Iran. As noted above, there were three key meetings at which the rescue plan was discussed (on 22 March, 11 and 15 April 1980), although the actual decision to proceed, taken on 11 April and confirmed on 15 April, was in many ways only the formal ratification of what had by then become the dominant mode of thinking among President Carter's most senior advisors. There were two schools of thought in the initial reaction to the seizure of the hostages: first, that the United States should impose economic sanctions on Iran; second, that it should make use of international public opinion and international law to force the Iranian government to release the hostages. As these measures appeared less and less likely to succeed, the U.S. government became involved in attempts to persuade its allies to join in economic sanctions—a move that succeeded just two days before the rescue mission.

President Carter's initial reaction to the seizure was to stress the importance of putting the lives of the hostages first. He declared on 7 December 1979, "I am not going to take any military action that would cause bloodshed or cause the unstable captors of our hostages to attack or punish them." Yet leaks from the White House indicated that military plans were being considered. By late March 1980, President Carter and his advisers were becoming convinced that negotiations were not going to be successful, a view confirmed by the secret source in the Iranian government. At a meeting held on 22 March at Camp David, the president agreed to a reconnaissance flight into Iran to find an initial landing site for the rescue force (Desert One). The plan called for eight RH-53 helicopters from the aircraft carrier *Nimitz* to fly nearly 600 miles, at a very low altitude and with radio blackout, from the Arabian Sea to Desert One. There, they would meet the rescue force of 97 men (code named "Delta Force") who would have arrived from Egypt via Oman on four C-130 transport aircraft. The helicopters would refuel from the C-130s and then take Delta Force to a second location (Desert Two) some 50 miles southeast of Tehran, where Central Intelligence Agency (CIA) agents would meet them and hide the rescue force at a "mountain hideout." Delta Force would remain hidden during the day before being picked up by CIA operatives early the next night and driven to a location known as "the warehouse" just inside Tehran. From there they would attack the embassy and the Foreign Ministry where three of the hostages were held, rescue the hostages, and take them to a nearby soccer stadium, where the helicopters would meet them and transfer them to a further airstrip at Monzariyeh, to be taken to Egypt by the C-130s. The planning process had meant that very definite deadlines had emerged: By 1 May there would only be 16 minutes of darkness more than required for the mission; by 10 May, the temperature would be so high that it would seriously hamper helicopter performance. 1 May appeared to be the latest feasible date for the mission, and by late March the planners were recommending 24 April for the mission (primarily because a very low level of moonlight was expected that night). But the rescue mission failed. It never got beyond Desert One. Of the eight helicopters assigned to the mission, one got lost in a duststorm and returned to the *Nimitz* and two suffered mechanical breakdowns. This left only five helicopters in working order at Desert One, whereas the plan had called for six to move on to Desert Two. The mission was subsequently aborted, and, in the process of maneuvering to vacate Desert One, one of the helicopters hit a C-130, causing the deaths of eight men.

It is critical, in any discussion of the applicability of the bureaucratic politics approach, to focus on the actual decisions that led to this mission and to review the positions adopted by the participants. . . . We know that the three meetings of 22 March, 11 and 15 April were the decisive ones, and we know who took part and what they said. The key meeting in terms of the actual decision was on 11 April, when the "go-ahead" was given. The meeting on 22 March was important because at it President Carter gave permission for aircraft to verify the site for Desert One. The meeting of 15 April was important because Cyrus Vance, the secretary of state, presented his reservations about the decision. As Zbigniew Brzezinski, President Carter's national security adviser, pointed out: "In a way, the decision [on 11 April] had been foreshadowed by the discussion initiated at the March 22 briefing at Camp David. From that date on, the rescue mission became the obvious option if negotiations failed—and on that point there was almost unanimous consent within the top echelons of the Administration."[4] A virtually identical set of people were present at those meetings. On 22 March, there attended President Carter, Walter Mondale (the vice president) Cyrus Vance (the secretary of state), Harold Brown (the secretary of defense), David Jones (the chairman of the Joint Chiefs of Staff), Stansfield Turner (the director of the CIA), Zbigniew Brzezinski (the national security adviser), Jody Powell (the press secretary), and David Aaron (the deputy national security adviser). On 11 April, the same participants convened, except that Warren Christopher, the deputy secretary of state, replaced Cyrus Vance, and Carter's aide Hamilton Jordan replaced Aaron. The final meeting on 15 April was attended by the same people who attended on 11 April, except that Vance replaced Christopher.

In order to outline the positions adopted by the participants in this decisionmaking group, the participants can be divided into four subgroups: President Carter, "hawks," "doves," and "presidential supporters." (These terms are only intended as analytical shorthand.) . . . Although there is a risk of fitting evidence to a preconception, the conclusion . . . is that these groups acted in accordance with what the bureaucratic politics approach would suggest: namely, that the national security adviser, the secretary of defense, the chairman of the Joint Chiefs of Staff, and the director of the CIA would support military action . . . ; the secretary of state, and in his absence his deputy, would oppose it; those individuals who were bureaucratically tied to the president (the vice president, the press secretary, and the political adviser) would be fundamentally concerned with what was best for the Carter presidency; and President Carter, although clearly more than just another bureaucratic actor, would act in a way that reflected bureaucratically derived as well as personal influences.

PRESIDENT CARTER

The key to understanding President Carter's position lies in the interaction between his desire to avoid the blatant use of American military power and the great pressure on him to satisfy his public and "do something." From the earliest days of the crisis, he was attacked in the press and by the Republican party for failing to act decisively. 1980 was, of course, a presidential election year, the president's public opinion rating was poor, and he was being challenged strongly for the Democratic party's nomination. His promise not to campaign for the election so long as the hostages were in Iran made his situation worse. He was advised by his campaign staff that decisive action was needed (especially after the fiasco of the morning of the Wisconsin primary, on 1 April, when the president announced that the hostages were about to be released). That inaccurate assessment was seen by many as a reflection of his lack of control over events; it was also portrayed as manipulating the issue for his own political ends.

Another factor which added to the president's frustration was the desire to make the allies go ahead with sanctions against Iran. It later turned out that the allies' belief that the U.S. administration was planning military action was their main incentive to join in the sanctions, in the hope of forestalling it. But the critical moment came when the president felt that the only alternative to military action was to wait until, possibly, the end of the year for the release of the hostages by negotiation. That was the impression he gained in the early days of April: Information coming out of Tehran indicated that the release of the hostages would be delayed for months by the parliamentary elections due to be held in Iran on 16 May. Indeed, by the time the rescue mission was undertaken, the favorite estimate of how long the new government in Iran would take to negotiate was five or six months. So, as a result of fear that the hostages might be held until the end of 1980, President Carter determined on a change in policy: "We could no longer afford to depend on diplomacy. I decided to act."[5] In fact, the president threatened military action on 12 and 17 April, unless the allies undertook economic sanctions. This action (which, he said, had not been decided on yet) would involve the interruption of trade with Iran. (This was widely interpreted as meaning a naval blockade or the mining of Iranian harbors.) Of course, this was a deliberate smokescreen: Accordingly, when on 23 April the European countries agreed to the imposition of sanctions on Iran, the White House let it be known that this would delay any military action until the summer!

Yet the desire of the president for drastic action is only part of the story. It is evident that he was also extremely concerned to limit the size of the operation, in order to avoid unnecessary loss of life. At the briefing with the mission commander, Colonel Beckwith, on 16 April, Carter said: "It will be easy and tempting for your men to become engaged in gunfire with others and to try and settle some scores for our nation. That will interfere with your objective of getting our people out safely. In the eyes of the world, it is important that the scope of this mission be seen as simply removing our people." William Safire has argued that the reason why the mission was unsuccessful was precisely because Carter wanted the rescue to be a humanitarian rather than a combat mission and stipulated only a small force with very limited backup.[6] Hence, in explaining President Carter's position on the rescue mission, two factors seem dominant: a personal concern to ensure that the mission was not to be seen as a punitive military action and a role-governed perception that American national honor was at stake....

Carter's actions were, of course, a response to a number of factors. The bureaucratic politics approach draws our attention to certain of these: specifically, his desire for reelection and his perception of his responsibility as the individual charged with protecting American national honor. Clearly, Carter's personality was an important factor..., but the bureaucratic politics approach seems much more useful in identifying the kinds of considerations that would be important to Carter than concentrating on notions of what would be most rational for the American nation. This is not to imply that bureaucratic factors are the only important ones in explaining what Carter did, but it is to claim that a bureaucratic perspective paints a far more accurate picture of what caused Carter to act as he did than any of the rival theories of foreign-policy making.

THE HAWKS

The leading political proponents of military action throughout the crisis were Brzezinski and Brown. Drew Middleton wrote, "For months, a hard-nosed Pentagon view had held that the seizure of the hostages itself was an act of war and that the United States was, therefore, justified in adopting a military response."[7] Indeed, just two days after the hostages were taken, Brzezinski, Brown, and Jones began discussing the possibilities of a rescue mission. Their discussions led to the conclusion that an immediate mission was impossible, but Brzezinski felt that "one needed such a contingency scheme in the event...that some of the hostages either were put on trial and then sentenced to death or were murdered.... Accordingly, in such circumstances, we would have to undertake a rescue mission out of a moral as well as a political obligation, both to keep faith with our people imprisoned in Iran and to safeguard American national honor." In fact, Brzezinski felt a rescue mission was not enough: "It would [be] better if the United States were to engage in a generalized retaliatory strike, which could be publicly described as a punitive action and which would be accompanied by the rescue attempt. If the rescue succeeded, that would be all to the good; if it failed, the U.S. government could announce that it had executed a punitive mission against Iran."[8] This punitive action, he thought, could take the form of a military blockade along with airstrikes. In the earliest days of the crisis, Brzezinski, Turner, Jones, and Brown began to meet regularly in private and discuss military options; Brzezinski alone took (handwritten) notes. It was this group which directed the planning for the mission (which used military and CIA personnel) and gave the eventual plan its most detailed review. Similarly, it was Brzezinski who pressed for the reconnaissance flight into Iran, agreed on 22 March, and the same group of four who proposed the rescue plan at the 11 April meeting, led by Brown and Jones. But it is clear from the available evidence that Brzezinski was the political force behind military action.

As early as February, Brzezinski felt increasing pressure from the public and from Congress for direct action to be taken against Iran. Brzezinski thought there were three choices: to continue negotiations, to undertake a large military operation, or to mount a small rescue mission. What swung him away from his earlier first choice, a punitive military operation, was the consideration that, after the Soviet intervention in Afghanistan in December 1979, any military action might give the Soviet Union additional opportunities for influence in the Persian Gulf and Indian Ocean: "It now seemed to me more important to forge an anti-Soviet Islamic coalition. It was in this context that the rescue mission started to look more attractive to me."[9] As negotiations failed, Brzezinski sent a memorandum to Carter on 10 April in which he argued that a choice must be made between a punitive military action or a rescue mission. Given his fears about the spread of Soviet influence, Brzezinski recommended the latter option, concluding, "We have to think beyond the fate of the 50 Americans and consider the deleterious effects of a protracted stalemate, growing public frustration, and international humiliation of the U.S."[10] At both the 11 April and 15 April meetings, Brzezinski spoke forcefully in favor of the mission.

Brown and Jones were the main advocates of the actual rescue plan.... These two men presented the plan to the 11 April meeting and conducted the detailed private briefing with Carter on 16 April; it was Harold

Brown who gave the detailed account, and defense, of the mission to the press after its failure. It was also Brown who spoke against the Christopher/ Vance position at the 11 April and 15 April meetings. Finally, both Brown and Brzezinski spoke very strongly in justification of the mission after its failure, stating that it had been morally right and politically justified. Brzezinski was said to be "downright cocky about it [the mission] in private and insisting that military action might be necessary in the future."[11] He also warned America's opponents: "Do not scoff at America's power. Do not scoff at American reach."[12]

Turner, the director of the CIA, was also very much in favor of the mission, so much so that it appears that he did not voice the very serious doubts about the mission which had been expressed in a report by a special CIA review group, prepared for him on 16 March 1980. According to this report, the rescue plan would probably result in the loss of 60 percent of the hostages during the mission: "The estimate of a loss rate of 60 percent for the AmEmbassy hostages represents the best estimate." The report also estimated that the mission was as likely to prove a complete failure as a complete success. Yet it was exactly at this time that the review of the plan was undertaken by Brzezinski's small group. To quote Brzezinski again: "A very comprehensive review of the rescue plan undertaken by Brown, Jones, and me in mid-March led me to the conclusion that the rescue mission had a reasonably good chance of success though there probably would be some casualties. *There was no certain way of estimating how large they might be* [emphasis added]."[13] Turner was involved in the detailed briefings of the president; at the meeting of 11 April he even said, "The conditions inside and around the compound are good." The evidence does not suggest that he made his agency's doubts public at any of these meetings, either in the small group or in the group of nine.

To sum up: The positions adopted by those classified here as "hawks" could have been predicted in advance. What is striking about the evidence is the consistency with which these four men—Brown, Brzezinski, Jones, and Turner—proposed policies that reflected their position in the bureaucratic network. . . . To the extent that the bureaucratic politics approach explains the policies adopted by these individuals, it illustrates the weaknesses of rationality-based theories of U.S. foreign policy.

PRESIDENTIAL SUPPORTERS

The next group to consider are those who do not fit into the traditional "hawks–doves" characterization of U.S. government. These are individuals whose primary loyalty is to the president and who would therefore be expected to adopt positions that promised to bolster the president's domestic standing. Unlike those groups discussed so far, the first concern of this group is not the nature of U.S. relations with other states, but, rather, the domestic position of the president. Mondale, Powell, and Jordan seem to have been neither "hawks" nor "doves" in their views of the Iranian action; rather, their policy proposals show that their concern was first and foremost with the effect of the crisis on the Carter presidency. This can be seen very clearly in Jordan's memoirs,[14] which reveal both a loyalty to Carter and an evaluation of the rescue mission in terms of how it helped Carter out of a domestic political problem. "I knew our hard-line approach would not bring the hostages home any sooner, but I hoped that maybe it would buy us a little more time and patience from the public." The rescue mission was "the best of a lousy set of options." Throughout his memoirs, at every juncture of the mission's planning, failure, and consequences, Jordan's position is consistently one in which he advocates what he believed would benefit the president. This determined his reaction to Vance's objections (Vance was failing to support the president when he needed it, thereby putting Carter in an uncomfortable position), to the failure of the mission (Congress's reaction would be to concentrate on the lack of consultation, and it might accuse Carter of violating the War Powers Resolution), and to Vance's resignation and his replacement by Ed Muskie (the former created a problem for Carter, the latter was a vote of confidence in Carter's political future).

The evidence also unambiguously supports the contention that Mondale and Powell were motivated above all by an awareness of the president's domestic standing and their perceptions of how it might be improved. Brzezinski notes that Powell, Mondale, and Jordan "were feeling increasingly frustrated and concerned about rising public pressures for more direct action against Iran."[15] All of them seemed to think that direct action was needed to stem this public pressure, *especially* after the Wisconsin primary announcement on 1 April. As Powell put it on 1 April: "We are about to have an enormous credibility problem. The combination of not campaigning and that early-morning announcement has made skeptics out of even our friends in the press." Salinger argues that Carter's "campaign for reelection registered the frustrations of the American public. While his political fortunes had risen after the taking of the hostages, he was beginning to slip in the polls and had lost a key primary in New York to Senator Kennedy. Jimmy Carter was now in the midst of a fight for his political life, and it looked as if he was losing. A military operation that freed the hostages would dramatically alter the odds."[16] The position of the "presidential supporters" was summed up in Mondale's contribution to the 11 April meeting, when he said, "The rescue offered us the best way out of a situation which was becoming intolerably humiliating."

The "presidential supporters," then, proposed policies which reflected their own bureaucratic position. Mondale, Powell, and Jordan had no vast bureaucratic interests to represent, nor was their chief concern the relationship between U.S. foreign policy and other states. Each of them owed their influence to their position vis-à-vis President Carter (as, of course, did Brzezinski), and their concern was to act so as to aid his presidency, above all his domestic political fortunes. In contemporary press reports, it was these three men who voiced concern about the president's relations with Congress and his chances of reelection. This was in contrast to both the "hawks" and the "doves" who were far more concerned with Carter's relations with Iran, the Soviet Union, and U.S. allies. As in the case of the "hawks," the policy preferences of the "presidential supporters" seem to have been predominantly determined by their bureaucratic role.

THE DOVES

The evidence that bureaucratic role determines policy stance is strongest of all in the case of the "doves": Cyrus Vance, the secretary of state, and Warren Christopher, the deputy secretary of state. Not only did the two men take virtually identical stands on the subject of the rescue mission, but, as will be discussed below, Christopher did not know what Vance's position was when he attended the 11 April meeting.

From the earliest days of the crisis Vance had advised against the use of military force. At the meeting on 22 March, Vance agreed that a reconnaissance flight should go ahead in case a rescue mission should prove necessary (in the case of a threat to the hostages' lives), but argued against

> the use of any military force, including a blockade or mining, as long as the hostages were unharmed and in no imminent danger. In addition to risking the lives of the hostages, I believed military action could jeopardize our interests in the Persian Gulf.... Our only realistic course was to keep up the pressure on Iran while we waited for Khomeini to determine that...the hostages were of no further value. As painful as it would be, our national interests and the need to protect the lives of our fellow Americans dictated that we continued to exercise restraint.

After this meeting, Vance felt there was no indication that a decision on the use of military force was imminent, and on 10 April he left for a long weekend's rest in Florida.

But on the very next day the meeting was held that made the decision to go ahead with the rescue mission. Jody Powell explained to the press later that Cyrus Vance was on a well-earned vacation and that "Vance was not called back because it would have attracted too much attention when the operation had to remain secret." There is no evidence as to why the meeting was called in his absence, but it is clear that Vance did not know that the mission was being so seriously considered and that everyone else involved knew that Vance would disagree. Tom Wicker argues that Vance was deliberately shunted aside from the critical meeting in order to weaken his (and the State Department's) ability to prevent the mission from proceeding.[17] All the Carter, Brzezinski, and Jordan memoirs say is that Vance was on "a brief and much needed vacation" (Carter), "on vacation" (Brzezinski), and "in Florida on a long overdue vacation" (Jordan). In many ways the exclusion of Vance can be interpreted as a symptom of what Irving Janis calls "groupthink"; other symptoms can also be determined in this case study of the phenomenon, which refers to the tendency for groups to maintain amiability and cohesiveness at the cost of critical thinking about decisions.[18]

The president opened the meeting of 11 April by saying that he was seriously considering undertaking a rescue mission, and he invited Brown and Jones to brief those present on the planned mission. At this point, Jordan turned to Christopher and said: "What do you think?" "I'm not sure. Does Cy know about this?" "The contingency rescue plan? Of course." "No, no— does he realize how far along the President is in his thinking about this?" "I don't know. . . . I assume they've talked about it." When the briefing finished, Christopher was first to speak. He outlined a number of alternatives to a rescue mission: a return to the U.N. for more discussions, the blacklisting of Iranian ships and aircraft, the possibility of getting European support for sanctions against Iran. Brown immediately dismissed these as "not impressive," and he was supported by Brzezinski, Jones, Turner, Powell, and Jordan, all of whom wanted to go ahead. Christopher was alone in his opposition to the plan. He declined to take up a formal position on the rescue mission since he had not been told about it in advance by Vance; he therefore felt that Vance had either accepted the plan or had felt that the State Department could not really prevent its going ahead. . . . His impression was reinforced when Carter informed the meeting that Vance "prior to leaving for his vacation in Florida, had told the President that he opposed any military action but if a choice had to be made between a rescue and a wider blockade, he preferred the rescue." Christopher knew that Vance had opposed the use of military force, but it is logical to assume that he felt all he could do was to offer nonbelligerent alternatives (they were, after all, State Department people being held hostage) to any use of military force, but remain silent on the actual mission; particularly as it had been strongly suggested that Vance had *already* agreed to it. In support of this conclusion, it is interesting to note that Christopher did not contact Vance on holiday to tell him what had happened. . . .

Vance's reaction to the news was "that he was dismayed and mortified."[19] Vance writes: "Stunned and angry that such a momentous decision had been made in my absence, I went to see the President."[20] At this meeting Vance listed his objections to the mission, and Carter offered him the opportunity

to present his views to the group which had made the original decision
in the meeting to be held on 15 April. Vance's statement at that meeting
focused on issues almost entirely dictated by his bureaucratic position. He
said, first, that to undertake the mission when the United States had been
trying to get the Europeans to support sanctions on the explicit promise that
this would rule out military action would look like deliberate deception;
second, the hostages, who were State Department employees, were in no
immediate physical danger; third, there were apparently moves in Iran to
form a functioning government with which the United States could negotiate;
fourth, that even if it succeeded, the mission might simply lead to the taking
of more American (or allied) hostages by the Iranians; fifth, it might force
the Iranians into the arms of the Soviet Union; and, finally, there would
almost certainly be heavy casualties (he cited the figure of 15 out of the
53 hostages and 30 out of the rescue force as a likely death toll).

After Vance's comments, Brown turned to him and asked him when he
expected the hostages to be released; Vance replied that he did not know.
No one supported Vance: His objections were met by "a deafening silence."
Although Vance said later that, after the meeting, a number of participants
told him that he had indeed raised serious objections, no one mentioned
them at the time—an example of "groupthink"? Carter noted that Vance "was
alone in his opposition to the rescue mission among all my advisers, and he
knew it."[21] In their memoirs, Carter and Brzezinski put Vance's subsequent
resignation down to tiredness: "He looked worn out, his temper would
flare up, his eyes were puffy, and he projected unhappiness. . . . Cy seemed
to be burned out and determined to quit" (Brzezinski); "Vance has been
extremely despondent lately . . . for the third or fourth time, he indicated
that he might resign . . . but after he goes through a phase of uncertainty and
disapproval, then he joins in with adequate support for me" (Carter). Even
worries expressed by Vance about the details of the plan at the 16 April
briefing were dismissed on the grounds that they reflected his opposition
to the raid in principle. On 21 April, Vance offered his resignation to Carter;
it was accepted, with the agreement that it would not be made public until
after the rescue mission, whatever the outcome. Vance duly resigned on
28 April. The press reports about his resignation suggested that opposition
to the mission was only the last incident in a long line and that Vance's
resignation stemmed from his battle with Brzezinski over the direction of
U.S. foreign policy. As a White House aide said, it had been "clear for some
time that Mr. Vance was no longer part of the foreign policy mainstream in
the Carter administration."

That Vance and Christopher opposed the rescue mission is not, in itself,
proof of the applicability of the bureaucratic politics approach. What is critical is that their opposition was generated *not* simply from their personal
views, but more as a result of their bureaucratic position (although there

is a problem in weighting these). These factors warrant this conclusion. First, Christopher, without knowing Vance's position on the rescue mission, and having been told (erroneously) that Vance supported it, still outlined alternatives. In fact, his opposition to the mission was on the same grounds as Vance's, even though he was led to believe that his superior had given the go-ahead. Second, Vance's statement at the 15 April meeting very clearly reflected State Department concerns. The response of Brown and Brzezinski did not address the problems Vance had outlined (for example, the position of the allies), but stressed issues such as national honor and security. These are role-governed policy prescriptions. Third, Vance was not opposed to a rescue mission as such, but only to one at a time when negotiation was still possible; his objection did not simply reflect a personal attitude toward violence. . . .

CONCLUSION

In the three key meetings that led to the decision to undertake the hostage rescue mission, the evidence presented here suggests that the participants adopted positions that reflected their location in the bureaucratic structure. The influence of bureaucratic structure makes it possible to explain the change in policy that occurred between the 22 March meeting and that of 11 April. In each case, the same group proposed a rescue mission, and the same group (Vance on 22 March, Christopher on 11 April) opposed it. The change came about because the "presidential supporters" and President Carter himself felt that the situation had altered significantly. While this alteration was due in part to external events (the breakdown of negotiations), the evidence . . . suggests that an even stronger reason was the extent of domestic criticism of Carter's inaction (especially after the Wisconsin primary fiasco). The "presidential supporters" felt it was "time to act." For similar reasons, Cyrus Vance's inability to change the rescue decision at the 15 April meeting is also explicable from a bureaucratic political standpoint. In the event, of course, his doubts were only too clearly vindicated. What this case study shows, therefore, is the limitations of an attempt to explain foreign policy decisionmaking as if the state were monolithic and as if "it" had interests. Such an approach makes policymaking appear rational, and this is a major reason for the popularity of such a perspective; but the case of the hostage rescue mission amply demonstrates the limitations of such conceptions of rationality, in that the key decisions are more powerfully explained by the bureaucratic politics perspective.

However, this conclusion requires some qualification since it raises fundamental problems about the precise claims advanced by proponents of the bureaucratic politics approach. . . . The question that must be addressed is whether bureaucratic position alone leads to the adoption of certain policy positions. As it stands, the bureaucratic politics approach is rather mechanical and static; it commits one to the rather simplistic notion that individuals will propose policy alternatives because of their bureaucratic position. Two problems emerge when this is applied to a case study such as this one. The first is that the bureaucratic politics approach lacks a causal mechanism; it cannot simply be true that occupying a role in a bureaucratic structure leads the occupant to hold certain views. The second relates to the wider issue of belief systems, in that certain individuals are "hawkish" irrespective of their precise position in a bureaucracy. The latter problem is most clearly illustrated by the case of Brzezinski, since it is arguable that whatever position he had occupied in Carter's administration, he would have adopted roughly similar views. Together, these problems force us to focus on one issue, namely, the exact meaning of the notion of role in the context of the bureaucratic politics approach.

This issue had been dealt with . . . in the work of Alexander George and of Glenn Snyder and Paul Diesing.[22] George is concerned with the ways in which U.S. decisionmakers use (and abuse) information and advice in the policy process. He examines in some depth the ways in which individuals and bureaucracies will select information to assist their rather parochial goals. In other words, through his study of the use of information, George arrives at precisely the same kind of concern that this study has led to, namely, the relationship between individuals and their policy advocacy. More salient, in their comprehensive survey of crisis decisionmaking, Snyder and Diesing discuss the psychological makeup of those groups of individuals named in their study (as in this) "hawks" and "doves." They believe that "hard and soft attitudes are more a function of personality than of governmental roles," and they offer a very useful summary of what the worldviews of hard- and soft-liners are. As such, the works of George and of Snyder and Diesing are the best available discussions of the impact of role on belief and of belief on information processing. . . .

While it is clear that it is simplistic to assume that bureaucratic position *per se* causes policy preference, it is equally clear that bureaucratic position has some impact. Role, in and of itself, cannot explain the positions adopted by individuals; after all, the very notion of role implies a certain latitude over how to play the role. Further, a role does not involve a single goal, and there is therefore significant room for maneuver and judgment in trading off various goals against each other. Thus, for example, it is not a sufficient explanation of Vance's position just to say that he was secretary of state. There was a complex interplay between his role, his personality, the decision under consideration, and other personal and bureaucratic goals. Yet role occupiers do become predisposed to think in certain bureaucratic ways, and for a variety of psychological reasons they tend to adopt mind-sets compatible with those of their closest colleagues. In addition, individuals are often chosen for a specific post *because* they have certain kinds of worldviews. So for reasons of selection, training, and the need to get on with colleagues, it is not surprising that individuals in certain jobs have certain worldviews.... Thus, while it is clearly the case that Brzezinski was a hawk, it is neither accurate to say that this was because he was national security adviser (since this would not in and of itself cause hawkishness), nor to say that his views were simply personal (since it is surely the case that, had he been secretary of state, he would have had to argue for courses of action other than those he did argue for—given the State Department's concern with getting the allies to agree on sanctions).

This case study therefore leaves us with some critical questions unanswered. On the one hand, the empirical findings are important in that they illustrate the weaknesses of the rational actor approach as an explanation of foreign policy behavior. States are not monoliths, and we might impute very misleading intentions to them if we assume that decisions are rational in this anthropomorphic way. The evidence indicates that the bureaucratic politics approach is very useful in explaining the decision to make an attempt to rescue the hostages. The linkage between the policy preferences of those individuals who made the decision and their bureaucratic position is a more powerful explanation of that decision than any of the alternatives. But... the bureaucratic politics approach overemphasizes certain factors and underemphasizes others. On the other hand, the theoretical implications of this case study force us to consider the issue of the sources of the beliefs of decisionmakers. The "hawks–doves" dichotomy is brought out very strongly in this case study; and yet the bureaucratic politics approach as it stands is not capable of supporting a convincing mechanism for linking position and worldview.... What is needed is to link the concept of individual rationality with the structural influence of bureaucratic position.... This [chapter], therefore, points both to the utility of the bureaucratic politics approach and to its theoretical weaknesses. The very fact that bureaucratic position was so important in determining policy preference over the decision to attempt to rescue the hostages makes the clarification of the nature of bureaucratic role all the more important....

NOTES

1. Graham Allison, *Essence of Decision* (Boston: Little, Brown, 1971).
2. Allison, *Essence of Decision,* p. 145.
3. See Allison, *Essence of Decision,* p. 176.
4. Zbigniew Brzezinski, *Power and Principle* (London: Weidenfeld & Nicolson, 1983), p. 493.
5. Jimmy Carter, *Keeping Faith* (London: Collins, 1982), p. 506.

6. W. Safire, *International Herald Tribune,* 29 April 1980, p. 5.

7. Drew Middleton, "Going the Military Route," *New York Times Magazine,* 17 May 1981, p. 103.

8. Brzezinski, *Power and Principle,* pp. 487–488.

9. Brzezinski, *Power and Principle,* p. 489.

10. Brzezinski, *Power and Principle,* p. 492.

11. *The Times,* 1 May 1980, p. 16.

12. *International Herald Tribune,* 28 April 1980, p. 1.

13. Brzezinski, *Power and Principle,* pp. 489–490.

14. Hamilton Jordan, *Crisis: The Last Year of the Carter Presidency* (New York: G. P. Putnam's Sons, 1982), pp. 248–289.

15. Brzezinski, *Power and Principle,* p. 490.

16. Pierre Salinger, *America Held Hostage* (New York: Doubleday, 1981), p. 235. See also *Newsweek,* 5 May 1980, pp. 24–26, for a discussion of the domestic context.

17. Tom Wicker, "A Tale of Two Silences," *New York Times,* 4 May 1980, p. E23.

18. See Irving Janis, *Groupthink,* 2nd ed. (Boston: Houghton Mifflin, 1982).

19. Brzezinski, *Power and Principle,* p. 493.

20. Cyrus Vance, *Hard Choices* (New York: Simon & Schuster, 1983), p. 409.

21. Carter, *Keeping Faith,* p. 513.

22. Alexander George, *Presidential Decision-Making in Foreign Policy: The Effective Use of Information and Advice* (Boulder, Colo.: Westview, 1980); and Glenn Snyder and Paul Diesing, *Conflict Among Nations* (Princeton, N.J.: Princeton University Press, 1977).

22

NATO Expansion
The Anatomy of a Decision

James M. Goldgeier

In deciding to enlarge the North Atlantic Treaty Organization (NATO) Bill Clinton's administration followed through on one of its most significant foreign policy initiatives and the most important political-military decision for the United States since the collapse of the Soviet Union. The policy... involved a difficult tradeoff for the administration between wanting to ensure that political and economic reform succeeds in Central and Eastern Europe and not wanting to antagonize Russia, which has received billions of dollars to assist its transition to a democratic, market-oriented Western partner. Skeptics of the NATO expansion policy within the government also worried about its costs, its effect on the cohesiveness of the Atlantic Alliance, and the wisdom of extending security guarantees to new countries. How did President Clinton, often criticized for a lack of attention to foreign policy and for vacillation on important issues, come to make a decision with far-reaching consequences for all of Europe at a time when NATO faced no military threat and in the context of diminishing resources for foreign policy?

This article analyzes the process the U.S. government followed that led to this major foreign policy initiative. I have based my findings largely on interviews I conducted in 1997 with several dozen current and former U.S. government officials, from desk officers deep inside the State and Defense Departments all the way up to President Clinton's foreign policy advisers. The interviews reveal that the administration decided to expand NATO despite widespread bureaucratic opposition, because a few key people wanted it to happen, the most important being the president and his national security adviser, Anthony Lake. Other senior officials—particularly those in

Note: Some notes have been deleted; others have been renumbered.

the State Department—became important supporters and implementers of NATO expansion, but Lake's intervention proved critical early in the process. Keenly interested in pushing NATO's expansion as part of the administration's strategy of enlarging the community of democracies, Lake encouraged the president to make statements supporting expansion and then used those statements to direct the National Security Council (NSC) staff to develop a plan and a timetable for putting these ideas into action. The president, once convinced that this policy was the right thing to do, led the alliance on this mission into the territory of the former Warsaw Pact and sought to make NATO's traditional adversary part of the process through his personal relationship with Russian president Boris Yeltsin.

Rather than being a story of a single decision, this policy initiative came about through a series of decisions and presidential statements made during three key phases of the process in 1993 and 1994. During the summer and fall of 1993, the need to prepare for Clinton's January 1994 summit meetings in Brussels pushed the bureaucracy into action. The product of this bureaucratic activity was the October 1993 proposal to develop the Partnership for Peace (PFP), which would increase military ties between NATO and its former adversaries. In the second phase, which culminated in his January 1994 trip to Europe, Clinton first signaled U.S. seriousness about NATO expansion by saying the question was no longer "whether" but "when." The final phase discussed here encompasses the period from April to October 1994, when key supporters of NATO expansion attempted to turn this presidential rhetoric into reality. At the end of this period, the newly installed assistant secretary of state for European affairs, Richard Holbrooke, bludgeoned the bureaucracy into understanding that expansion was presidential policy, and an idea that had been bandied about for a year and a half finally started to become reality.

PHASE ONE: BUREAUCRATIC DEBATE AND ENDORSEMENT OF THE PFP

In the first few months of his administration, President Clinton had not given much thought to the issue of NATO's future. Then in late April 1993, at the opening of the Holocaust Museum in Washington, he met one-on-one with a series of Central and Eastern European leaders, including the highly regarded leaders of Poland and the Czech Republic, Lech Walesa and Vaclav Havel. These two, having struggled so long to throw off the Soviet yoke, carried a moral authority matched by few others around the world. Each leader delivered the same message to Clinton: Their top priority was NATO membership. After the meetings, Clinton told Lake how impressed he had been with the vehemence with which these leaders spoke, and Lake says Clinton was inclined to think positively toward expansion from that moment.

At the June 1993 meeting of the North Atlantic Council (NAC) foreign ministers in Athens, Greece, U.S. Secretary of State Warren Christopher said enlarging NATO's membership was "not now on the agenda." But Christopher understood that NATO needed to assess its future, and with White House endorsement, he pushed his fellow foreign ministers to announce that their heads of state would meet six months later, in January 1994.[1] This announcement set in motion a process back in Washington to discuss the contentious issue of expansion. At the White House, Lake wrote in the margins of Christopher's statement, "why not now?," and his senior director for European affairs, Jenonne Walker, convened an interagency working group (IWG) to prepare for the January 1994 meeting in Brussels and to recommend what the president should do there. The working group involved representatives from the NSC staff, the State Department, and the Pentagon. According to several participants, Walker informed the group at the start that both the president and Lake were interested in pursuing expansion.

On September 21, 1993, nine months into the Clinton administration, Lake gave his first major foreign policy speech, in which he developed ideas on promoting democracy and market economies that Clinton had enunciated during his campaign. Clinton had stressed the theme that democracies do not go to war with one another and thus that U.S. foreign policy strategy should focus on promoting democracy. Lake had helped to develop this approach, which leading campaign officials saw as a foreign policy initiative behind which different wings of the Democratic party could rally. In the 1993 speech, Lake argued that "the successor to a doctrine of containment must be a strategy of enlargement—enlargement of the world's free community of market democracies." And he added, "At the NATO summit that the president has called for this January, we will seek to update NATO, so that there continues behind the enlargement of market democracies an essential collective security."[2]

Although Lake tried rhetorically to push the process along, the bureaucracy greatly resisted expanding the alliance. Officials at the Pentagon unanimously favored the Partnership for Peace proposal developing largely through the efforts of General John Shalikashvili and his staff, first from Shalikashvili's perch as Supreme Allied Commander in Europe and then as chairman of the Joint Chiefs of Staff. PFP proponents sought to foster increased ties to all the former Warsaw Pact states as well as to the traditional European neutrals, and to ensure that NATO did not have to differentiate among its former adversaries or "draw new lines" in Europe. Every state that accepted its general principles could join the PFP, and the countries themselves could decide their level of participation. Many officials viewed the partnership as a means of strengthening and making operational the North

Atlantic Cooperation Council (NACC), which had been NATO's first formal outreach effort to the East, undertaken in 1991. From the Pentagon's standpoint, it did not make sense to talk about expansion until after NATO had established the type of military-to-military relationships that would enable new countries to integrate effectively into the alliance. Several participants in the IWG say that Pentagon representatives made clear that both Secretary of Defense Les Aspin and General Shalikashvili opposed expansion and, in particular, feared diluting the effectiveness of NATO. . . .

In addition to concern about NATO's future military effectiveness, the bureaucracy also feared that expansion would antagonize Russia and bolster nationalists and Communists there. Many State Department debates at this time focused on this fear, and views on expansion there were more divided than those in the Pentagon. In September, Yeltsin had written a letter to Clinton and other NATO heads of state backtracking on positive remarks he had made in Warsaw on Polish membership in NATO and suggesting that if NATO expanded, Russia should be on the same fast track as the Central Europeans. Then, in early October, Yeltsin's troops fired on his opposition in Parliament, and it appeared to many that the political situation in Russia was deteriorating.

During this period a small group at the State Department—including Lynn Davis, the under secretary for arms control and international security affairs, Thomas Donilon, the chief of staff, and Stephen Flanagan, a member of the Policy Planning Staff—advocated a fast-track approach to expansion. This group argued that in January 1994, NATO should lay out criteria, put forward a clear timetable, and perhaps even offer "associate membership" to a first set of countries. At a series of lunches with Secretary Christopher, organized to present him with the pros and cons of expansion, these individuals pressed him to move the process forward as quickly as possible, saying, as one participant [recalled], that NATO should "strike while the iron is hot." . . . Flanagan, Donilon, and Davis worried that without the prospect of membership in a key Western institution, Central and Eastern Europe would lose the momentum for reform. NATO and the European Union (EU) were the premier institutions in Europe, and the EU, absorbed in the internal problems associated with the Maastricht Treaty, would clearly postpone its own expansion. These officials wanted to encourage states such as Poland and Hungary to continue on the path of reform—to adopt civilian control of the military, to build a free polity and economy, and to settle border disputes—by providing the carrot of NATO membership if they succeeded.

This pro-expansion group also drew on compelling arguments from two other government officials. Charles Gati, a specialist on Eastern Europe serving on the Policy Planning Staff, had written a memo in September 1993 arguing that the new democracies were fragile, that the ex-Communists were likely to gain power in Poland, and that if NATO helped Poland succeed in carrying out reforms, it would have a huge impact on the rest of the region. Donilon took this memo straight to Christopher, who found the reasoning impressive. When the ex-Communists did win parliamentary elections in Poland weeks later, Gati's words carried even greater weight.

The other argument came from Dennis Ross, the special Middle East co-ordinator for the Clinton administration, who had been director of policy planning under Secretary of State James A. Baker III. Given his involvement in the German unification process and the development of the NACC, Ross attended two of the Christopher lunches on NATO. During one, he reminded the group that critics had believed that NATO could not successfully bring in a united Germany in 1990, but it did, and without damaging U.S.-Soviet relations. He suggested that NATO involve Russia in the expansion process rather than confront its former enemy. Ross argued that the previous administration's experience with German unification offered good reason to believe that the current administration could overcome problems with Russia.

Inside the State Department's regional bureaus dealing with Europe and with the New Independent States (NIS), however, bureaucrats expressed tremendous opposition to a fast-track approach and in a number of cases to any idea of expansion. Many who worked on NATO issues feared problems of managing the alliance if Clinton pushed ahead with this contentious issue. Those who worked on Russia issues thought expansion would undermine reform efforts there.

In these State Department debates, the most important proponent of a much more cautious and gradualist approach to expansion was Strobe Talbott, then ambassador-at-large for the NIS. Talbott proved important for two reasons: As a longtime friend, he had direct access to Clinton, and as a former journalist, he could write quickly, clearly, and persuasively. Christopher asked Talbott and Nicholas Burns—the senior director for Russian, Ukrainian, and Eurasian Affairs at the NSC—to comment on the fast-track approach. He and Burns argued to both Christopher and Lake that Russia would not understand a quick expansion, which would impair the U.S.-Russia relationship and, given the domestic turmoil in Russia in late September and early October, might push Russia over the edge.

One Saturday in mid-October, when Talbott was out of town, Lynn Davis forcefully argued to Christopher at a NATO discussion lunch that NACC and the PFP were simply not enough. When Talbott returned that afternoon and learned about the thrust of the meeting, he quickly wrote a paper reiterating the importance of a gradual approach to expansion. The next day, he delivered a memo to Christopher, stating, "Laying down criteria could be quite provocative, and badly timed with what is going on in Russia." Instead, he suggested, "Take the one new idea that seems to be universally accepted,

PFP, and make that the centerpiece of our NATO position." Talbott argued that the administration should not put forward any criteria on NATO membership that would automatically exclude Russia and Ukraine, and that the administration could never manage the relationship if it did not offer Russia the prospect of joining the alliance at a future date. He firmly believed that Clinton should mention neither dates nor names in Brussels.[3]

By Monday morning, October 18, Christopher had decided to support the gradual rather than fast-track approach, which meant that any agreement among leading officials would place the policy emphasis on the PFP. Among Clinton's top foreign-policy advisers, Lake sought to push ahead with expansion, Aspin and Shalikashvili sought to delay consideration of expansion and instead supported the PFP, and Christopher fell somewhere in between, open to gradual expansion but concerned about Russia's reaction. At the White House later that day, Clinton endorsed the consensus of his principal foreign policy advisers that, at the January summit, the alliance should formally present the PFP, and he should announce NATO's intention eventually to expand. This decision reflected the consensus that had emerged from the bargaining within agencies and in the IWG, which had easily agreed on the PFP, but which could not agree on issues such as criteria, a timetable, or "associate membership" status. In the end, the IWG agreed on what its principals in turn could accept: to put forward the PFP and to say something general about NATO's eventual expansion.

The consensus emerged because, as with many decisions, opponents and proponents of expansion had different interpretations of what they had decided, and this ambiguity created support for the decision throughout the bureaucracy. Vociferous opponents of NATO expansion believed the administration's principals had decided to promote the PFP while postponing a decision on enlargement. Those in the middle, who could live with expansion but did not want to do anything concrete in 1994, also saw the October decision as consistent with their preferences. Finally, the decision that Clinton should comment on expansion pleased proponents of near-term enlargement, as they believed such a treatment would help to move the process along on a faster track.

The October 18 meeting would be the last of its kind on NATO expansion for another year. Given the meeting's ambiguous outcome—the foreign policy principals had not given the president a timetable to endorse—confusion reigned concerning the policy's direction. For the moment, the decision to develop the PFP was the Clinton administration's NATO outreach policy.

Yet from the moment the participants went their separate ways observers could tell they interpreted the decision differently. Secretary of State Christopher's entourage, on its way to Budapest to brief the Central Europeans (and then on to Moscow to explain the policy to Yeltsin), said the

January summit would send the signal that NATO's door would open at some future date (and apparently even State Department officials on Christopher's plane disagreed about how to present the decision). The senior official conducting the airborne press briefing stated, "We believe that the summit should formally open the door to NATO expansion as an evolutionary process."[4] Meanwhile, Secretary of Defense Aspin and his advisers, attending the NATO defense ministers' meeting in Travamünde, Germany, to gain alliance endorsement of the PFP, emphasized that NATO would not enlarge soon. According to one report, Lake called Aspin in a pique saying the secretary of defense had veered from the script.[5]

PHASE TWO: THE PRESIDENT SPEAKS

After mid-October, administration officials knew the president would say something about NATO enlargement on his trip to Europe in January. But no one was sure how much he would say and how specific he would be. After all, the bureaucratic wrangling had produced a decision that the president should emphasize the PFP while delivering a vague statement that NATO could eventually take in new members. The first official statement prior to the summit came from Secretary Christopher at the plenary session of the Conference on Security and Cooperation in Europe (CSCE) in Rome on November 30. Noting that the United States was proposing a Partnership for Peace, he also stated, "At the same time, we propose to open the door to an evolutionary expansion of NATO's membership."[6] Two days later, at the NAC ministerial in Brussels, he said, "The Partnership is an important step in its own right. But it can also be a key step toward NATO membership."[7]

Meanwhile, prominent figures from previous administrations pressured Clinton to be more forthcoming on expansion at the summit. Former secretary of state Henry Kissinger complained in an op-ed piece that the PFP "would dilute what is left of the Atlantic Alliance into a vague multilateralism," and he called for movement to bring Poland, Hungary, and the Czech Republic into some form of "qualified membership." Former national security adviser Zbigniew Brzezinski urged NATO members to sign a formal treaty of alliance with Russia and to lay out a more explicit path to full NATO membership for the leading Central European candidates. Former secretary of state James Baker also made the case for a "clear road map" with "clear benchmarks" for the prospective members.[8]

During this time, Brzezinski had been meeting with Lake to share ideas about his two-track approach to expansion, and he also invited Lake to his home to meet a number of Central and Eastern European leaders. Since the debate at the White House focused more on "whether" than concretely "how," these meetings with Brzezinski helped Lake to clarify his own thinking and emphasized to him the importance of keeping the process moving forward. Significantly, Brzezinski argued that Russia would be more likely to develop as a stable, democratic presence in Europe if the West removed all temptations to reassert imperial control and precluded Russia's ability to intimidate its former satellites.

In late December, Lake's staff members, who were in general opposed to moving expansion onto the near-term agenda, presented him with the draft briefing memoranda for the different stops on the president's upcoming trip to Europe. Several of his staffers say he threw a fit on seeing the initial work, because the memos emphasized the Partnership for Peace. According to Nicholas Burns, Lake wanted a presidential statement in January that would leave no doubt about the policy's direction.

But high-level opposition to any push toward expansion continued to color the agenda. The Pentagon appeared unanimously to share the view that the policy should be sequential; countries would participate in the PFP for a number of years and then the alliance might start addressing the issue of expansion. General Shalikashvili, at a White House press briefing on January 4, emphasized the value of the Partnership for Peace as a way of ensuring that the alliance create no new divisions in Europe, and he suggested postponing discussions of membership to a future date....

But, he added, in words that Clinton would make much more significant a week later, "It is useful to remember that we are talking so much less today about whether extension of the alliance [should take place], but so much more about how and when." Pentagon officials, however, had a much different view of what "when" meant than did proponents of expansion at the NSC and State, believing the PFP should operate for several years before the alliance began thinking about expansion.

Prior to the summit, even Clinton still seemed unsure of how far he wanted to go. The strong showing of nationalists and Communists in the December 1993 Russian parliamentary elections had sent shockwaves through the administration. On January 4, Clinton said in an exchange with reporters at the White House,

> I'm not against expanding NATO. I just think that if you look at the consensus of the NATO members at this time, there's not a consensus to expand NATO at this time and we don't want to give the impression that we're creating another dividing line in Europe after we've worked for decades to get rid of the one that existed before.[9]

This was hardly the signal the Central Europeans had hoped to receive.

Just prior to his trip, Clinton sent Polish-born General Shalikashvili, Czech-born U.S. ambassador to the UN Madeleine Albright, and Hungarian-born State Department adviser Charles Gati to Central Europe to explain the administration's policy and to quell criticisms stemming from this region prior to the summit. Albright argued forcefully to the Central European leaders that the Partnership for Peace would provide the best vehicle for these countries to gain future NATO membership, and she reiterated that it was not a question of whether, but when.

In Brussels, Clinton said that the PFP "sets in motion a process that leads to the enlargement of NATO." According to Donilon, Lake wanted the president to make a more forceful statement in Prague to give a clear impetus to expansion. Sitting around a table in Prague prior to Clinton's remarks, Lake, Donilon, and presidential speechwriter Robert Boorstin wrote the statement that Clinton agreed to deliver. Echoing what Albright had told the Central Europeans, the president said, "While the Partnership is not NATO membership, neither is it a permanent holding room. It changes the entire NATO dialogue so that now the question is no longer whether NATO will take on new members but when and how."[10]

To proponents such as Lake, this statement was a clear victory, and it laid the basis for moving the process along. He wanted the alliance to address the "when" as soon as possible. For expansion skeptics, to whom "when" meant after the PFP had created a new military environment in Europe, the president's words meant nothing specific and reflected, they believed, the outcome of the October 18 decision; they concluded that although the president had stated that expansion was theoretically possible, the administration would not undertake any actual effort to expand the alliance anytime soon. Their failure to recognize the importance of the president's remarks—at least as Lake and other expansion proponents interpreted them—would lead to their surprise later in the year that the process had been moving forward.

Administration critics would later suggest that Clinton supported expansion purely for political purposes, to woo voters of Polish, Czech, and Hungarian descent. Numerous foreign policy officials in the administration, who deny that domestic political considerations came up in their meetings on expansion, hotly disputed this claim. Lake says that although everyone knew the political context of the NATO enlargement debate, he never had "an explicit discussion" with the president about the domestic political implications of expansion. Domestic politics probably played a more complicated role in this policy decision than a simple attempt to court ethnic votes in key midwestern and northeastern states. First, for several political reasons, Clinton needed to demonstrate U.S. leadership. His administration's policy in Bosnia was failing miserably, and this failure overshadowed every other foreign policy issue at the time. Second, even if ethnic pressures did not drive the decision, Clinton would have alienated these vocal and powerful domestic constituencies had he decided against expanding NATO; Republicans thus would have gained another issue to use in congressional elections later that year. If domestic politics did not drive the decision, they gave it more resonance for the White House, and both parties certainly used the policy for political purposes: Clinton's speeches in places like Cleveland and Detroit in 1995–96 provide clear evidence of the perceived value of NATO expansion to those communities, and the Republicans included NATO expansion as a plank in their Contract with America during the 1994 congressional campaign.

The bureaucratic decision-making process had not advanced much between October 1993 and the president's trip to Europe in January 1994. But regardless of where the bureaucratic consensus remained, Clinton had opened the door for expansion with his forceful remarks in Brussels and Prague. This is turn gave Lake the impetus he needed, and because of his proximity and access to the president, for the moment he could move the process along without having to gain the backing of the rest of the bureaucracy.

PHASE THREE: FROM RHETORIC
TO REALITY

For several months after Clinton's pronouncements in January, neither his advisers nor the bureaucracy paid much attention to NATO expansion, largely because of the crises in Bosnia that winter and because of the attention they paid to getting the PFP up and running. In early spring, the NATO expansion process began moving forward again, at Lake's instigation. In April, Lake held a meeting with his deputy, Samuel R. "Sandy" Berger, and one of his staffers, Daniel Fried, a specialist on Central and Eastern Europe, to discuss how to follow up on the president's January remarks and to prepare for the president's trip to Warsaw that July. Lake asked for an action plan on enlargement, and when Fried reminded him of the bureaucracy's continued strong opposition, Lake replied that the president wanted to move forward and Lake therefore needed an action plan to make it happen.

To write the policy paper, Fried brought in two old colleagues: Burns at NSC and Alexander Vershbow, then in the European bureau of the State Department but soon to become the NSC's senior director for European affairs.... Despite his NSC portfolio on Russian affairs, Burns was not opposed to NATO expansion, which pleased Fried; Burns in turn appreciated that Fried accepted a gradual approach and understood that the strategy had to include a place for Russia. Unlike the authors of many policy papers that need approval, or clearance, from key actors at each of the relevant agencies, this troika worked alone, thus sidestepping the need for bureaucratic bargaining. Before the president's Warsaw trip, Lake invited Talbott and State Department Policy Planning director James Steinberg to the White House to discuss the draft paper with Fried and Burns. Talbott sought assurances that the proposed process would be gradual, consistent with the policy he had pushed the previous October.

Many people believe Talbott opposed enlargement during this time, especially because most of the Russia specialists outside government vehemently opposed expanding NATO. Talbott clearly opposed making any immediate moves and emphasized that the process must be gradual and include rather than isolate Russia. But many of Talbott's colleagues say that once he became deputy secretary of state in February 1994 and more regularly considered the broader European landscape and the needs of the Central and Eastern Europeans, he warmed to expansion. . . . Talbott encouraged Christopher to bring Richard Holbrooke back from his post as ambassador to Germany to be assistant secretary of state for European affairs in summer 1994, both to fix the Bosnia policy and to work on NATO expansion. By the following year, Talbott had become one of the most articulate Clinton administration spokespersons in favor of the NATO expansion policy.

By summer, the NSC and State Department positions had converged. Thinking in more gradual terms than Lake had been pushing earlier in the year, the troika's views now coincided with the consensus that had developed in the State Department. The efforts to begin figuring out a way to develop a timetable for both the expansion track and the NATO-Russia track led to a major push in summer and fall 1994 to get an expansion policy on firmer footing.

In Warsaw in July, Clinton spoke more forcefully on the issue than many in the bureaucracy would have preferred, just as he had done in Brussels and Prague earlier in the year. In an exchange with reporters after his meeting with Lech Walesa, he said, "I have always stated my support for the idea that NATO will expand. . . . And now what we have to do is to get the NATO partners together and to discuss what the next steps should be."[11] By emphasizing the need to meet with U.S. allies, the president gave a green light to those who wanted a concrete plan.

Two months later, addressing a conference in Berlin, Vice President Al Gore proved even more outspoken, saying,

> Everyone realizes that a military alliance, when faced with a fundamental change in the threat for which it was founded, either must define a convincing new rationale or become decrepit. Everyone knows that economic and political organizations tailored for a divided continent must now adapt to new circumstances—including acceptance of new members—or be exposed as mere bastions of privilege.[12]

Holbrooke apparently had major input on this speech and one staffer for the Joint Chiefs [said] the vice president's remarks gave the military its first inkling that the administration's NATO policy had changed since January.

Senior military representatives objected to the draft text of Gore's remarks, but to no avail.

Despite his inclination toward expanding the alliance, Clinton understood concerns about Russia's reaction. After all, Clinton's foreign policy had centered in part on U.S. assistance for the Yeltsin government's reform program, and he did not want to undercut Yeltsin before the 1996 Russian presidential election. In late September, Yeltsin came to Washington, and Clinton had a chance to tell him face to face that NATO was potentially open to all of Europe's new democracies, including Russia, and that it would not expand in a way that threatened Russia's interests. At a White House luncheon, Clinton told Yeltsin that he had discussed NATO expansion with key allied leaders, and he made sure Yeltsin understood that NATO would not announce the new members until after the Russian and U.S. 1996 presidential elections. At the same time, Clinton wanted to ensure that any advances in the process that might take place in the meantime—during the NATO ministerials—would not surprise the Russian president.

With Holbrooke coming back to the State Department and with Vershbow and Fried both now special assistants to the president at the NSC, expansion proponents had gained more power within the bureaucracy than they had during the previous autumn. Lake successfully circumvented bureaucratic opposition to get Clinton to make forceful statements that expansion would occur. His troika had continued to update its action plan throughout the summer and fall, and by October 1994 its strategy paper proposed the timeline that the alliance eventually followed: a series of studies and consultations designed to lead to a membership invitation to the first group and a NATO-Russia accord in 1997. But concerns about the military dimension of expansion still existed in the Pentagon, without whose efforts to address the nuts and bolts of expanding the military alliance the decision could not have moved from theory to practice.

For their next task, proponents had to convince skeptics within the administration that the president was serious. . . . For NATO expansion, the enforcer would be Holbrooke, the newly installed assistant secretary of state, whom Christopher had brought back to the department at the urging of Talbott, Donilon, and Under Secretary for Political Affairs Peter Tarnoff.

Holbrooke held his first interagency meeting on NATO expansion at the State Department in late September, almost immediately after taking office. He wanted to make clear that he would set up and run the mechanism to expand NATO, because the president wanted it to happen. Holbrooke knew that most Pentagon officials preferred concentrating on making the PFP work rather than moving ahead with expansion, and he wanted to make sure everyone understood that he was taking charge. His opportunity came at this meeting when the senior representative from the Joint Chiefs of Staff (JCS), three-star General Wesley Clark, questioned Holbrooke's plans to move forward on the "when" and "how" questions of expansion. To the Pentagon's way of thinking, no one had yet made a decision that would warrant this action. Holbrooke shocked those in attendance by declaring, "That sounds like insubordination to me. Either you are on the president's program or you are not."[13]

According to participants, Deputy Assistant Secretary of Defense Joseph Kruzel, one of the key figures in developing the PFP program, argued that the issue had been debated in October 1993 and the decision at that time, the last formal meeting on the subject at the highest levels, was *not* to enlarge. Other Pentagon officials in attendance argued that only the "principals" could make this decision, and thus another meeting needed to be held at the highest level. Holbrooke responded that those taking this view had not been listening to what the president had been saying. The skeptics simply could not believe that Holbrooke was resting his whole case on remarks Clinton had made in Brussels, Prague, and Warsaw. Former defense secretary William Perry still refers to Holbrooke as having "presumed" at that point that the administration had decided to enlarge NATO, whereas Clinton had made no formal decision to that effect.

After this dramatic outburst, Holbrooke asked Clark to set up a meeting to brief this interagency group on what they would need to do to implement the policy. Through this request, Holbrooke enabled the Joint Chiefs of Staff to voice their concerns but also forced them to begin acting on the issue. At the Pentagon two weeks later, a team with representatives from both the Office of the Secretary of Defense (OSD) and the JCS presented to the interagency group the full range of military requirements each country would need to meet to join NATO. The JCS briefer pointed, for example, to the 1,200 Atlantic Alliance standardization agreements the former Warsaw Pact armed forces would have to address to become compatible with NATO. Holbrooke, now playing "good cop," responded by saying that this briefing was exactly what the group needed, and he invited them to work with him to make the process a smooth one. This briefing would, in fact, serve as the basis both for the briefing to the NAC later in the fall and for the NATO study conducted the following year.

Because Pentagon officials did not believe the administration had ever made a formal decision, Perry . . . called Clinton and asked for a meeting of the foreign policy team to clarify the president's intentions. At the meeting, Perry presented his arguments for holding back and giving the PFP another year before deciding on enlargement. He wanted time to move forward on the NATO–Russia track and to convince Moscow that NATO did not threaten Russia's interests, before the alliance moved ahead on the expansion track. Instead, the president endorsed the two-track plan that Lake and his staff, as well as the State Department, now pushed—the plan that ultimately led to the May 1997 signing of the NATO–Russia Founding Act and the July 1997

NATO summit in Madrid inviting Poland, Hungary, and the Czech Republic to begin talks on accession to full NATO membership.

THE AMBIGUITY OF THE DECISION

Like so many decision-making processes, the NATO expansion process was not at all clearcut. The best evidence of its ambiguities comes from asking participants a simple question: "When did you believe that the decision to expand NATO had been made?" Their answers demonstrate that what you see depends on where you stand; attitudes toward the decision affected individuals' views of what was happening. Most supporters, including Lake, cite the period between the October 1993 meeting of the principals and Clinton's trip to Europe in January 1994. The answers of opponents, on the other hand, generally range over the second half of 1994, depending on when they finally realized the president was serious. One State Department official who opposed expansion said that when he objected to language circulating in an interagency memo on the issue in August 1994, a colleague told him it was the same language the president had used in Warsaw the previous month. At that point, he says, he understood that the policy had moved from theory to reality. Others, such as Perry, did not start to believe that expansion was on the table until after the Holbrooke interagency meeting in September 1994. In support of this last interpretation, Brzezinski pointed out at the time that until Clinton *answered* the questions "when" and "how," rather than simply *asking* them, the United States had no decisive plan for Europe.[14]

These interpretations vary so widely because the president and his top advisers did not make a formal decision about a timetable or process for expansion until long after Clinton had started saying NATO would enlarge. The when, who, how, and even why came only over time and not always through a formal decision-making process. In January 1994, when the president first said that he expected the alliance to take in new members, no consensus existed among his top advisers on the difficult questions of "when" and "how." Clinton's advisers could as reasonably believe that his remarks amounted to no more than a vague statement that NATO might someday expand as they could believe that the president wanted to begin moving forward *now.* Whereas proponents of expansion took his statements as a signal to begin planning how to put theory into practice, the president did not make an explicit decision in the presence of his top foreign policy advisers until nearly a year later, and some opponents therefore choose to believe that the course was not set until that meeting.

Readers may find it unsatisfying that I have not uncovered either *the* moment of decision or the president's ulterior motive. Truthfully, however, most policies—even those as significant as this one—develop in a more ambiguous fashion. This process was hardly unique to the Clinton administration. White House meetings often result in participants, as well as those they inform, having conflicting understandings of what the administration has decided. Policy entrepreneurs use presidential statements to push forward an issue that remains highly contentious in the bureaucracy. Each step alone seems trivial. But cumulatively, they can result in momentous policies.

As for motive, Walesa and Havel may well have made a huge impression on a president open to emotional appeals. Still, given that Clinton cared so much about the fate of Russian reform, Walesa's appeal to bring Poland and other Central European nations into the West could hardly have been sufficient. Rather, Clinton's motive was probably more complex, and he probably had only a vague idea of when he himself made the formal commitment to expand NATO. For Clinton, the appeal by the Central Europeans to erase the line drawn for them in 1945, the need to demonstrate U.S. leadership at a time when others questioned that leadership, the domestic political consequences of the choice, and his own Wilsonian orientation toward spreading liberalism combined by the second half of 1994—if not earlier—to produce a presidential preference favoring expansion.... Once Clinton spoke out in favor of NATO expansion in January 1994, expansion supporters within the administration had what they needed to begin to turn rhetoric into reality.

NOTES

1. For information on Secretary Christopher's intervention at the June 1993 NAC meeting, see *U.S. Department of State Dispatch* 4, no. 25, p. 3.

2. Anthony Lake, "From Containment to Enlargement," *Vital Speeches of the Day* 60 (October 15, 1993), pp. 13–19.

3. For quotations from the Talbott memo, see Michael Dobbs, "Wider Alliance Would Increase U.S. Commitments," *Washington Post,* July 5, 1995, pp. A1, 16; Michael R. Gordon, "U.S. Opposes Move to Rapidly Expand NATO Membership," *New York Times,* January 2, 1994, pp. A1, 7.

4. The official is quoted in Elaine Sciolino, "U.S. to Offer Plan on a Role in NATO for Ex-Soviet Bloc," *New York Times,* October 21, 1993, pp. A1, 9.

5. Elaine Sciolino, "3 Players Seek a Director for Foreign Policy Story," *New York Times,* November 8, 1993, pp. A1, 12; Stephen Kinzer, "NATO Favors U.S. Plan for Ties with the East, but Timing is Vague," *New York Times,* October 22, 1993, pp. A1, 8.

6. *U.S. Department of State Dispatch,* December 13, 1993.

7. Ibid.

8. See Henry Kissinger, "Not This Partnership," *Washington Post,* November 24, 1993, p. A17; Zbigniew Brzezinski, "A Bigger—and Safer—Europe," *New York Times,* December 1, 1993, p. A23; and James A. Baker III, "Expanding to the East: A New NATO," *Los Angeles Times,* December 5, 1993, p. M2.

9. Remarks by the president in a photo op with Netherlands prime minister Ruud Lubbers, January 4, 1994, *Public Papers* (1994), pp. 5–6.

10. On the Brussels statement of January 10, 1994, see *U.S. Department of State Dispatch Supplement,* January 1994, pp. 3-4; for the Prague remarks, see Clinton, *Public Papers* Book I (1994), p. 40.

11. For his exchange with reporters in Warsaw after meeting with Walesa on July 6, 1994, see Clinton, *Public Papers* (1994), p. 1206.

12. *U.S. Department of State Dispatch,* September 12, 1994, pp. 597–598.

13. Quoted in Dobbs, "Wider Alliance." Confirmed by author interviews with numerous officials who attended the meeting.

14. Zbigniew Brzezinski, "A Plan for Europe," *Foreign Affairs* 74 (January/February 1995), pp. 27–28.

23

Sources of Humanitarian Intervention

Beliefs, Information, and Advocacy in U.S. Decisions on Somalia and Bosnia

Jon Western

On November 21, 1992, General Colin Powell's chief deputy on the Joint Chiefs of Staff, Admiral David Jeremiah, stunned a National Security Council Deputies Committee meeting on Somalia by announcing, "If you think U.S. forces are needed, we can do the job."[1] Four days later President George H. W. Bush decided U.S. forces were needed. On December 9, 1992, 1,300 marines landed in Mogadishu, and within weeks more than twenty-five thousand U.S. soldiers were on the ground in Somalia.

Prior to the November 21 deputies meeting, virtually no one in or out of the administration expected that President Bush or his top political and military advisers would support a major U.S. humanitarian mission to Somalia.[2] For more than a year, the Bush administration, and General Powell and the Joint Chiefs of Staff in particular, had steadfastly opposed calls for humanitarian military interventions in Somalia, Liberia, Bosnia, and elsewhere.[3] None of these conflicts was relevant to U.S. vital interests.[4] They were simply humanitarian tragedies.

With respect to Somalia, senior Bush administration and military officials had argued repeatedly throughout most of 1992 that the deeply rooted inter-clan conflicts that permeated Somalia would make any military intervention extraordinarily risky. The basic position of the Joint Chiefs of Staff and the senior White House staff was that military force would not be able to protect itself or the distribution of humanitarian relief, because the nature of the conflict made it virtually impossible to distinguish friend from enemy or civilian from combatant. In short, the administration argued, roaming armed bandits fueled by ancient hatreds and intermingled with the civilian population was a recipe for disaster.

Yet after nearly a year of extensive opposition to the use of American military force in Somalia, in November 1992 President Bush, with the firm support of all of his key advisers—including General Powell—decided to launch a massive U.S. military intervention in Somalia. Why did the Joint Chiefs of Staff reverse its estimates from that of July 1992, that Somalia was a "bottomless pit," to its November proclamation that "we can do the job?" Nothing in that period changed the political, military, or logistical factors on the ground. The crisis had long before reached a critical humanitarian mass. What explains the sudden change of heart within the Bush administration on Somalia?

This chapter details the factors that led to the decision to intervene in Somalia. It reveals a circuitous path by which the Bush administration adamantly opposed intervention for more than a year and then abruptly shifted its position following the election of Bill Clinton in November 1992. It is a case study on the influence of domestic politics, competing elite beliefs, information advantages, and advocacy strategies on military intervention, with the major chasm coming between "selective engagers" in the Bush administration—those who argued that U.S. military intervention should be reserved for those isolated cases when U.S. vital strategic interests were directly threatened, not strictly humanitarian considerations—and "liberal humanitarianists"—those who supported military intervention to provide humanitarian relief to aggrieved populations and to stop or prevent atrocities perpetrated against civilians. Ultimately, the decision to intervene in Somalia became intertwined with the humanitarian tragedy of Bosnia and the presidential election of 1992.

SELECTIVE ENGAGERS AND NO VITAL INTERESTS

In 1990 and 1991 civil wars erupted in Somalia and in Yugoslavia. While neither war captured much U.S. public or elite attention, by the end of 1992 both conflicts had become the focal point of American foreign policy. But in 1990 and 1991, U.S. policy toward Somalia and the former Yugoslavia, respectively, reflected the prevailing views among President Bush and his core advisers—almost all of whom could be classified as selective engagers—that with the end of the Cold War, both the horn of Africa and the Balkans had dramatically diminished in strategic importance to the United States. For selective engagers, the dissolution of Yugoslavia was of concern to the extent that unleashed ancient ethnic hatreds might create regional instability. The prudent choice in Yugoslavia—despite the profound transitions occurring throughout the rest of Eastern and Central Europe—was to support some form of centralized authority and to press for gradual change. From 1990 until the outbreak of war in Croatia in 1991 and Bosnia in March 1992, the administration devoted its diplomatic energies to strategies to forestall the collapse of the Yugoslav federation. Once violence erupted, the policy shifted from prevention to containment.

In Somalia, U.S. policy was similarly focused. During the Cold War, the United States contributed vast sums to Somali leader Siad Barre in an effort to stabilize the Horn of Africa in the face of the Soviet-backed regime of Mengistu Haile Mariam in Ethiopia. With the erosion of Soviet influence and competition, U.S. contributions to Barre were no longer seen as imperative to U.S. geostrategic interests. Without the financial backing of the United States to prop up Barre's corrupt regime, Somalia quickly disintegrated into interethnic civil conflict. Because the 1991–1992 crisis posed little threat to U.S. political or economic interests and did not constitute a threat to regional or international stability, the Bush administration's position throughout much of 1991 and most of 1992 was that the crisis was an internal Somali problem. The Somali leaders needed to resolve the crisis themselves.

INITIAL INFORMATION AND PROPAGANDA ADVANTAGES

Bosnia

Prior to the war in Bosnia, few Americans or foreign policy elites focused on Bosnia. To the extent that attention was paid to the crisis during the initial months of violence, the widely accepted view was that presented by selective engagers in the Bush administration. The administration criticized the Serb leadership in Belgrade for the violence and worked diplomatically to isolate Slobodan Milosevic's regime, but it nonetheless firmly believed and publicly emphasized the view that the conflict was the inevitable consequence of intractable and primordial hatreds that had been unleashed with the collapse of the tight communist control. On numerous occasions, President Bush and his advisers equated the Bosnian crisis as rooted in ethnic animosities that went back hundreds of years. Based on this analysis of the conflict, the administration argued publicly that the prudent policy was to refrain from involvement in a situation that could only lead to a Vietnam-style quagmire for the United States. Consequently, most Americans came to perceive Bosnia as the tragic but inevitable resurrection of ancient hatreds. The public supported the administration's limited policy to contain the conflict from spreading to areas that were of geostrategic interest to the

United States—in particular to Kosovo, Macedonia, Albania, Greece, Turkey, or Bulgaria.

Initially, no one was in a position to challenge critically the administration's paradigmatic framing of the conflict. In the spring of 1992, no clear precedent had been set for post–Cold War humanitarian interventions, and because Yugoslavia had been a relatively advanced economic and political society during the Cold War, very few nongovernmental humanitarian organizations had any presence or experience there. Furthermore, because only a few members of Congress had much interest in or understanding of events in Yugoslavia, most deferred to the administration's resources and expertise on the conflict. As a result, those who might have opposed the administration's analysis—such as a few liberal humanitarianists in Congress who did have some regional interest—lacked a strong organizational and political base on which to mobilize public and political opposition to the Bush administration's policies on Bosnia.

For its part, the U.S. media covering Eastern and Central Europe also had little expertise in the Balkans. Few of the major news organizations had experienced correspondents on the ground. When the war in Croatia broke out in June 1991, journalists scrambled to cover the story. As early as the fall of 1991, American reporters and administration officials began warning that although the violence in Croatia was terrible, conditions in the more ethnically diverse Bosnia would be much worse. Consequently, when violence erupted in Bosnia in March 1992, there was widespread acceptance, at least initially, among journalists that the conflict there was simply a further manifestation of the unchecked nationalist hatreds that had been widely predicted.

In addition, many journalists and editors wanted to ensure "objective" and "balanced" reporting, which meant that stories often identified and reported atrocities as though all sides were equally culpable. All of this produced predictable pressures and influences on the reporting during the first several months of the war in Bosnia, reporting that portrayed the violence as tragic but ultimately endorsed the administration's line that the conflict was caused by age-old ethnic hatreds and was one in which all sides were equally culpable.

Further aiding the Bush administration's policies were the support and informational advantages of Joint Chiefs of Staff chairman General Colin Powell and his senior advisers. Powell and his advisers strongly believed that foreign military intervention in limited conflicts would inevitably degenerate into a Vietnam-type quagmire. The Joint Chiefs stressed the inherent military dilemmas associated with any type of U.S. force deployment in Bosnia. For example, during a discussion in June on whether to use U.S. military aircraft in support of an emergency humanitarian airlift to Sarajevo, senior planners told members of Congress that even such a limited operation would require the presence of more than fifty thousand U.S. ground troops to secure a perimeter of thirty miles around the airport. Brent Scowcroft, who had been national security adviser during these deliberations, acknowledged that the Joint Chiefs "probably inflated the estimates of what it would take to accomplish some of these limited objectives, but once you have the Joint Chiefs making their estimates, it's pretty hard for armchair strategists to challenge them and say they are wrong."[5]

Consequently, throughout the first four months of the conflict in Bosnia the American public largely accepted the administration's view that the conflict was fueled by ancient hatreds about which the United States could do little. Little information emanated from the scene of the conflict to contradict that judgment, and in the face of a proliferation of "objective" reporting from Bosnia, there was very little discernable tendency within American public opinion toward a more forceful U.S. response to the crisis.

Somalia

Meanwhile, the collapse of nearly all state structures in Somalia and intense fighting between rival factions—led respectively by General Mohamed Farah Aideed and Ali Mahdi Mohamed—in the wake of Siad Barre's flight from Mogadishu in January 1991 left much of the country's civilian population under severe threat of malnutrition and starvation. Amid increasing security concerns, the United Nations withdrew its relief operations in mid-1991, leaving only a few nongovernmental organizations (NGOs) to deal with the escalating humanitarian crisis. By January 1992, the International Committee of the Red Cross was estimating that almost half of the country's six million people faced severe nutritional needs, with many liable to die of starvation without some form of immediate assistance.[6] Three hundred thousand had already died of malnutrition; more than three thousand people were starving to death daily.[7]

As with the former Yugoslavia, selective engagers in the Bush administration did not see any tangible U.S. interests at stake in Somalia. The administration deferred to the United Nations for a response to the crisis. But even here, selective engagers were focused on their own perceptions of U.S. interests and remained wary of supporting new military initiatives through the United Nations. During UN Security Council debates in April 1992, the Bush administration opposed initiatives to create an armed UN security force, fearing that new peacekeeping missions would further bloat an already inefficient UN bureaucracy and inevitably necessitate greater U.S. military involvement.

For liberal humanitarianists, Somalia was significant but only one of many regional conflicts that had humanitarian concerns. Wars in Afghanistan, Angola, Chad, Liberia, Mozambique, southern Sudan, Sri Lanka, the former

Yugoslavia, and elsewhere were all producing humanitarian challenges that diverted concentrated liberal attention and resources from Somalia. The few NGOs working in Somalia issued reports beginning in the fall of 1991 citing catastrophic conditions, and efforts were made by UN Secretary-General Boutros Boutros-Ghali to mediate a settlement between the warring factions. But neither the UN mediation efforts nor the ad hoc reports from humanitarian organizations attracted attention. No galvanizing force either linked disparate humanitarian organizations or mobilized the press corps. Consequently, even though the famine intensified dramatically in the fall of 1991 and early 1992, Somalia emerged in the public discourse very slowly in 1992, and there was very little discussion on the crisis within the elite foreign policy community.

By June 1992, nearly 4.5 million were on the brink of starvation in Somalia, and nearly a hundred thousand people were dead in Bosnia, with another million displaced from their homes; still there was no concerted pressure on the selective engagers within the Bush administration to alter their policies on either Somalia or Bosnia. The administration strongly believed that even though both crises were tragic, each was rooted in intractable causes and each ultimately fell outside of U.S. interests. Furthermore, military commanders in the Joint Chiefs who opposed U.S. participation in limited wars remained convinced that military options in both Somalia and Bosnia were wholly untenable.

THE EROSION OF INITIAL
INFORMATION ADVANTAGES

The Bush administration's position in Somalia and Bosnia, however, began to come under pressure in the summer of 1992. Throughout the summer, both the media and liberal humanitarianists gradually developed and dedicated more resources for information-collection efforts to challenge the administration's framing of the two conflicts.

In Somalia, in late June, the U.S. ambassador to Kenya, Smith Hempstone, Jr., traveled to refugee camps on the Somali-Kenyan border for the first time. He reported his trip in a cable entitled "A Day in Hell," which presented a vivid report of the humanitarian suffering. The cable resonated with many liberal humanitarianists in the State Department who believed that the Bush administration needed to do more in Somalia, and it was immediately leaked to the press. Meanwhile, liberal humanitarianists in Congress, led by Senators Nancy Kassebaum (R-Kans.) and Paul Simon (D- Ill.), conducted fact-finding missions to Somalia in June and July, and reported horrific conditions. They returned and urged their colleagues to support sending an armed UN security mission to Somalia. As other international aid organizations also began to weigh in heavily on the political debate in Washington, Boutros-Ghali again stressed that a million Somali children were at immediate risk and that more than four million people needed food assistance urgently.

All of this political pressure began to find a response at the White House. In late July, President Bush encouraged his staff to examine additional diplomatic efforts to enhance the UN efforts in Somalia. However, if the president was beginning to feel some political pressure to take action, his concern was limited to finding ways in which the United States could assist the United Nations in dealing with the problem. The United States supported a Security Council resolution passed on July 26 authorizing an emergency airlift to provide relief to southern Somalia, but according to Brent Scowcroft, "there was no discussion of using U.S. force for any purpose at this point."[8]

At the staff level, this constraint led to a bureaucratic deadlock. Some liberal humanitarianists sought to put forward military options for provision of relief, whereas selective engagers remained opposed to the use of force, calling Somalia a "bottomless pit."[9] This opposition frustrated the liberal humanitarianists. James Bishop, who was then acting assistant secretary of state for human rights and humanitarian affairs, recalls:

> I went to one interagency meeting and there was this brigadier general from the Joint Staff. We came up with this option to use helicopter gunships to support relief delivery. This general sat there and said we couldn't use helicopters in such a dusty environment. Hell, we had just fought a massive war in the Persian Gulf desert with lots of helicopters. I was evacuated from Mogadishu in January 1991 in a Marine Corp helicopter that operated just fine. But that was their attitude. They didn't want anything to do with it and they were prepared to lie to keep them out of it. At every meeting, no matter the proposal, the Joint Chiefs opposed it.[10]

By early August, according to Herman Cohen, then the assistant secretary of state for African affairs, "We were [being] told to be forward leaning, but the president paid even less attention to us."[11]

Bosnia: Impact of Camp Disclosure

Meanwhile, throughout July and early August, liberal humanitarianists greatly intensified their pressure on the Bush administration to intervene in Bosnia. At the time, the administration's control of the public message on Bosnia began to be challenged as independent reports from Bosnia started to contradict its statements. Instead of suggesting that the conflict was the spontaneous actions of neighbor killing neighbor, journalists reported on the activities of small bands of radical Serb nationalists and paramilitaries accused of committing horrific atrocities in highly organized campaigns.

This view of a highly coordinated and systematic campaign of violence was reinforced in early August by the disclosure of Serb-controlled concentration-style camps in Bosnia. The images were haunting and, for many, conclusive proof that the U.S. administration was deliberately distorting the events in Bosnia, especially given the administration's initial attempts to downplay the reports on the camps.

The pressure on the selective engagers in the wake of the camp disclosures in early August was particularly intense. Between August 2 and August 14, forty-eight news stories on Bosnia, totaling 151 minutes and thirty seconds, were broadcast on the three major network evening news programs.[12] The stories challenged Bush's policies and gave significant attention to the views and criticisms of Bush's political rival, Bill Clinton. Several stories contrasted Clinton's visible outrage at the concentration camps with Bush's tempered reaction.[13] On August 9, *ABC World News Tonight* ran a profile distinguishing Clinton and Bush's approaches to Bosnia, extensively quoting Clinton on the need for strong, decisive U.S. leadership.

Liberal humanitarianists in Congress also escalated pressure on the president. On August 14, the Senate Foreign Relations Committee released a scathing report on ethnic cleansing, presenting the Serb campaign as a deliberate and highly coordinated, politically driven campaign of violence—not the result of spontaneous, bottom-up hatreds.

Amid this escalation in political pressure surrounding the disclosure of the camps in Bosnia, Bush urgently assembled his national security team on August 8 at his vacation home in Kennebunkport, Maine, to discuss the matter. Although there is no evidence that public opinion had shifted toward greater support for direct U.S. involvement in Bosnia, the 1992 Republican Presidential Convention was only two weeks away, and the mobilized political opposition to Bush's handling of the crisis struck a nervous chord among Bush's political advisers. Bush, who had taken tremendous pride in his foreign policy accomplishments—overseeing the fall of the Berlin Wall, the reunification of Germany, the Persian Gulf War, and the dissolution of the Soviet Union—was now being publicly castigated by highly respected foreign policy commentators. This was a particularly sensitive issue among Bush's senior political advisers—James Baker, Dennis Ross, Margaret Tutwiler, and Robert Zoellick—all of whom had moved from the State Department to the White House on August 1 to take charge of Bush's failing reelection bid.

In particular, selective engagers in Bush's political camp feared that liberal humanitarianists and hard-line interventionists in the bureaucracy were altering the public conception of Bosnia and making the administration look callous in the face of an egregious humanitarian crisis. Several liberal humanitarianists and hard-line commentators and members of Congress suggested that intervention could be done without fear of U.S. forces becoming embroiled in a Vietnam-style situation. They focused their attention on Serb aggression and on Milosevic as the primary culprit for the violence. Their prescription was that if the United States removed Milosevic or directed a targeted military strike against him and his radical supporters, the violence in Bosnia would quickly dissipate.

Despite the intensity of the political pressure, selective engagers at the White House and within the military remained convinced that Bosnia would be a quagmire. After meeting his advisers on August 8, Bush reiterated his caution: "We are not going to get bogged down in some guerrilla warfare."[14] He also ordered his team to contest the liberal humanitarian view that U.S. intervention could quickly break the siege of Sarajevo at little cost in American lives. Scowcroft recalls his reaction to the domestic criticism unleashed at the time: "I was very suspicious that people who had never supported the use of force for our national interests were now screaming for us to use force in Yugoslavia. . . . I disagreed with the humanitarianists who deliberately downplayed the intractability of the conflict, who demonized Milosevic and saw this simply as a war of aggression. Milosevic was a factor, but to that extent there were also national hatreds there, that couldn't be ignored."[15]

Over the next several days, selective engagers in the Bush camp and within the Joint Chiefs intensified their public campaign to sell their beliefs about the potential dangers associated with direct U.S. involvement in the conflict. On August 11, Lieutenant General Barry McCaffrey, a principal deputy to General Powell, publicly discussed the Joint Chiefs' views with *ABC World News Tonight,* saying emphatically that despite the tragedy, "there is no military solution." Earlier that day, senior military planners told a congressional hearing that between 60,000 and 120,000 ground troops would be needed to break the siege of Sarajevo and ensure uninterrupted relief.[16] Other commanders suggested that a field army of at least four hundred thousand troops would be needed to implement a cease-fire.

Somalia: Airlift Is Supported

In the midst of the public furor over the camp disclosure in Bosnia, President Bush announced an abrupt shift on his Somalia policy and ordered U.S. Air Force C-130s to assist in providing relief to famine victims in Somalia. The president also reversed his opposition to funding the deployment of five hundred Pakistani peacekeepers to Somalia; in fact, he announced that the Pentagon would provide transportation for the five-hundred-man team and its equipment.

Conventional arguments suggest that the media compelled the president to act in Somalia—that vivid images of starving and emaciated children in

Somalia provoked a sense of moral outrage within the American populace. However, among the three major U.S. television networks, Somalia was mentioned in only fifteen news stories in all of 1992 prior to Bush's decision to begin the airlift, and nearly half of these "showed only fleeting glimpses of Somalia's plight" as part of other stories.[17]

The evidence suggests that Bush's policy shift on Somalia in fact came in response to both the increasing pressure to do something in Somalia and also in response to the political backlash on Bosnia that occurred on the eve of the Republican Convention. Scowcroft recalls, "It [the Bosnian camp issue] probably did have a significant influence on us. We did not want to portray the administration as wholly flint-hearted realpolitik, and an airlift in Somalia was a lot cheaper [than intervention in Bosnia] to demonstrate that we had a heart."[18]

FURTHER MOBILIZATION OF INTERVENTIONISTS

On Bosnia, the selective engagers in the administration continued their public strategy to downplay the magnitude of the violence and to characterize the conflict as one of ancient blood feuds. Acting Secretary of State Lawrence Eagleburger proclaimed, "It is difficult to explain, but this war is not rational. There is no rationality at all about ethnic conflict. It is gut; it is hatred; it's not for any common set of values or purposes; it just goes on. And that kind of warfare is most difficult to bring to a halt."[19] Later in a television interview he argued, "I'm not prepared to accept arguments that there must be something between the kind of involvement of Vietnam and doing nothing, that the *New York Times* and the *Washington Post* keep blabbing about, that there must be some form in the middle. That's again, what got us into Vietnam—do a little bit, and it doesn't work. What do you do next?"[20]

By September, liberal humanitarianists began a concerted effort to identify the likely effect of the upcoming winter on the civilian population in Bosnia. As part of the effort, they detailed estimates of civilian casualties that displaced populations would face in the impending winter months. Andrew Natsios, the assistant administrator for food and humanitarian assistance for the Agency for International Development, warned Eagleburger in a letter that "immediate and massive action must be taken now to avert a tragedy by the onset of the winter season."[21] A week later, a secret Central Intelligence Agency analysis estimate that as many as 250,000 Bosnian Muslims might die from starvation and exposure was leaked to the press even before it was briefed to the National Security Council (NSC).[22] NGOs began working with professional staff members of the Senate Intelligence Committee to increase congressional oversight of the intelligence community's collection and analysis of war crimes and atrocities and to report as to whether Serb actions constituted genocide under the 1948 UN Convention on the Prevention and Punishment of the Crime of Genocide.[23]

As liberal humanitarian and hard-line interventionist voices began to permeate Washington's political debate, serious concern emerged among the Joint Chiefs of Staff that the intense political and public debate over intervention was leading toward direct U.S. involvement in Bosnia.[24] In response, General Powell embarked on an unprecedented public campaign to keep U.S. troops out of Bosnia. On September 27, Powell invited Michael Gordon of the *New York Times* to his office for an extensive interview. Gordon describes Powell as at times angry during the interview and that he had "assailed the proponents of limited military intervention to protect the Bosnians." Powell argued that "as soon as they tell me it is limited, it means they do not care whether you achieve a result or not. As soon as they tell me 'surgical,' I head for the bunker." He further complained about the civilians calling for military action in Bosnia:

These are the same folks who have stuck us into problems before that we have lived to regret. I have some memories of us being put into situations like that which did not turn out quite the way that the people who put us in thought, i.e., Lebanon, if you want a more recent real experience, where a bunch of Marines were put in there as a symbol, as a sign. Except those poor young folks did not know exactly what their mission was. They did not know really what they were doing there. It was very confusing. Two hundred and forty-one of them died as a result.[25]

Two days later, the *New York Times* published a scathing editorial directed at General Powell, "At Least Slow the Slaughter." It strongly criticized Powell and his reluctance to intervene in Bosnia:

The war in Bosnia is not a fair fight and it is not war. It is slaughter.

When Americans spend more than $280 billion a year for defense, surely they ought to be getting more for their money than no-can-do. It is the prerogative of civilian leaders confronting this historic nightmare to ask the military for a range of options more sophisticated than off or on, stay out completely or go in all the way to total victory.

With that in hand, President Bush could tell General Powell what President Lincoln once told General McClellan: "If you don't want to use the Army, I should like to borrow it for a while."[26]

By all accounts, Powell was livid. In his memoirs, he recalls that he "erupted" in anger. He then dashed off a scathing rebuttal in which he argued that the conflict is "especially complex" and has "deep ethnic and religious roots that go back a thousand years."[27]

In sum, all of these various pressures put Powell and his advisers on the defensive. The State Department was initiating new policy initiatives that, while stopping short of outright U.S. intervention, were seen by the military command staff as the initial steps to a much greater U.S. involvement. Liberal humanitarianists in Congress were demanding more. In addition, the media was openly questioning Powell's leadership. This was the cumulative pressure on Powell and the Bush administration in early November when Bill Clinton, who had campaigned on an activist policy in Bosnia, won the 1992 presidential election.

Throughout much of September, October, and early November, Somalia again fell off the radar screen. After an initial wave of news broadcasts and printed reports on Somalia following the decision to begin the airlift, the media moved to other international stories. Within the NSC also Somalia quickly disappeared. Those within the NSC who worked on Africa turned their focus toward the negotiations in South Africa leading up to free elections and to the brutal civil wars in Angola and Mozambique—both cases that were deemed more important to overall U.S. geostrategic interests than was Somalia.

This indifference to the situation in Somalia was felt within the bureaucracy and the interagency task force that had been established to monitor the airlift. The U.S. air relief was dropping food into Baidoa, and feeding centers had been established, but those most in need were not able to get to the supplies. On November 6, the Office of Food and Disaster Assistance reported that more than 25 percent of Somali children under the age of five had already died. Despite these conditions, there was very little bureaucratic movement on additional remedies to the crisis.

THE PRESIDENTIAL ELECTION

When on November 8 Bill Clinton won the presidential election, the general belief within the Washington foreign policy elite community was that the new team would shift markedly toward a liberal humanitarian foreign policy agenda.

There was wide speculation that Clinton would take quick action on Bosnia, lifting the arms embargo and possibly using U.S. air power to strike Serb targets. Sensing the power shift, within days of the election liberal humanitarianist staffers at the State Department circulated a new initiative to lift the arms embargo against Bosnia. By November 16, every relevant bureau in the State Department had signed on to the policy proposal. Furthermore, momentum quickly grew for dramatically expanding UN peacekeeping forces in Bosnia and dedicating NATO air assets to support the peacekeepers; the UN Security Council agreed to the measure on November 16.

Somalia: Pressure Builds Again

In early November, dozens of international relief groups and representatives from the UN High Commission on Refugees again urged the international community to step up its efforts to mitigate the famine. InterAction, a coalition of 160 U.S.-based nongovernmental relief organizations, issued public and private appeals to President Bush detailing the extensive problems that relief groups were facing in Somalia without any security from roaming bandits. InterAction requested that the United States increase its support for the UN to provide security for relief operations. Furthermore, the UN secretary-general reiterated his criticism that the Bush administration—with all of its public focus on the Bosnian war in Europe—was ignoring the more acute plight of millions of black Africans in Somalia.

In response to this pressure, a wide range of policy options was discussed at a series of interagency meetings during the first three weeks of November. The question of military intervention was not open for discussion, because of continued and absolute opposition from the military. Instead, the interagency group outlined a series of recommendations short of U.S. military participation and forwarded them to a Deputies Committee meeting of the NSC on November 20.

Clinton's First Trip to Washington

On November 19, two weeks after the election, President-elect Bill Clinton arrived in Washington for separate briefings from President Bush and General Powell. Although both meetings were designed to be thorough discussions of U.S. national security priorities (i.e., U.S. relations with Russia and China, and the future of the NATO alliance, including NATO expansion), in both meetings Clinton pressed Bush and Powell extensively about Bosnia. On this subject, the meeting with Powell was especially tense. Even before the meeting, Powell and his colleagues in the Joint Chiefs had been highly concerned that Clinton might propel the United States into Bosnia on an ambiguous, feel-good mission. According to Powell's account, Clinton started their meeting by asking, "Wasn't there some way, he wanted to know, that we could influence the situation [in Bosnia] through air power, something not too punitive?" Powell lamented later: "There it was again, the ever-popular solution from the skies, with a good humanist twist; let's not hurt anybody." Powell says he didn't want to sound too negative on the first meeting and that he told the president-elect that he would have his staff "give the matter more thought."[28]

Cumulative Pressure

By now, liberal humanitarianists had mobilized extensive public and internal political pressure on the administration on both Somalia and Bosnia.

At the White House, Scowcroft recalls that the president, coming off of his postelection blues, was personally affected by the reports and by the pressure he was receiving on Somalia from groups like InterAction. Bush began asking his advisers whether anything could be done on Somalia. At the same time, the Joint Chiefs were increasingly anxious that the new president might escalate U.S. military involvement in Bosnia. They were especially embittered—as is strikingly evident in Powell's discussion with Clinton—by liberal humanitarianist claims that intervention in support of humanitarian missions, and in Bosnia in particular, could be done on the cheap.

This cumulative pressure ultimately catapulted a policy reversal by the Joint Chiefs—again, not on Bosnia but on Somalia. The day after Powell's meeting with Clinton, the Deputies Committee met to discuss the situation in Somalia. Three options were put on the table: increasing U.S. financial and material support for the current UN peacekeeping forces in Somalia; coordinating a broader UN effort in which the United States would provide logistical support but no ground troops; and initiating a U.S.-led multinational military intervention to Somalia. According to John Hirsch and former ambassador to Somalia Robert Oakley's account, however, the only consensus at the November 20 meeting was that the third option "was not a serious option."[29] In fact, the option of military intervention was not even raised for discussion.

The next day, however, Admiral Jeremiah returned and, as we have seen, stunned the deputies meeting by announcing that if force was desired in Somalia, the military could do the job. Admiral Jeremiah recalls that by then, the frustration within the Joint Chiefs had reached a critical mass:

> There was a lot of pressure on us to do something. . . . [W]e had [had] weeks of hand wringing and futzing around [by the civilian policymakers] trying to figure out the right thing to do. Nobody wants to send troops . . . [where groups] . . . have been fighting for hundreds of years.
>
> When I said it, I was frustrated because we were taking all of the heat on Somalia and Bosnia. Everyone wanted us to volunteer—to go into Bosnia and to go into Somalia—but nobody was making decisions about what they wanted to do.
>
> During the November 21 deputies meeting, I presented our [i.e., the Joint Chiefs'] view that—*if you decide*—this is what it will take to do the job. Were our figures overkill? Probably. But we weren't going to go in with a weak force. We said just give us the resources and let's get on with it already.[30]

Scowcroft recalls that he too was startled by the Joint Chiefs' abrupt shift: "I know that the military had long felt that [Somalia would be a quagmire because the combatants would be virtually indistinguishable from the civilians]. I was struck, and I still am, with the alacrity with which Colin Powell changed gears."[31]

The President's Decision

On November 25, after receiving briefings on the famine and the military situation, the president told his advisers that he wanted to deploy U.S. forces to Somalia. The president's decision was directly linked to the cumulative pressures of the public criticism on both Somalia and Bosnia. It was also tied to the fact that the Joint Chiefs were prepared to support the action, that military commanders now believed they could effectively mitigate the famine. In addition, according to Scowcroft, by this time, Bush had become more sensitive to his presidential legacy, which had become jeopardized by the exhaustive liberal criticism of the administration's apparent callousness to humanitarian crises. Somalia seemed like a good contribution to that legacy.

For their part, the Joint Chiefs' abrupt shift on Somalia also reflected the cumulative pressure and criticism from liberals on them for their reluctance to use force in support of the crisis in Bosnia. Powell's support for intervention in Somalia was explicitly based on the condition that U.S. forces would not be called into a similar effort in Bosnia.

CONCLUSION

The cases of Somalia and Bosnia in 1992 have several idiosyncrasies that make generalizations difficult. But one implication from these cases is that a starting point for future research on why the United States intervenes in some humanitarian crises and not others is to examine competing normative beliefs and the politics of intervention. After Bosnia, Haiti, Kosovo, northern Iraq, Rwanda, Sierra Leone, Somalia, Sudan, and elsewhere, in the past decade American foreign policy elites have expressed differing normative beliefs about when and where the United States should intervene. These competing beliefs appear to rotate around the selective-engager and liberal-humanitarian axis. The cases presented here suggest that these beliefs not only exist but are significant contributors to our understanding of why the United States intervenes.

This suggests in turn that humanitarian impulses have increasingly become part of the political discourse within American foreign policy and probably cannot be ignored or rejected outright. Indeed, those who seek to establish some universal grand strategy restricting the use of force to only those situations where American vital interests are directly threatened may well find themselves under intense and persistent pressure that will detract attention from other foreign policy initiatives and ultimately could lead to some form of intervention under less than desirable or optimal terms.

In addition to competing beliefs, the intervention decision on Somalia also reveals that advocacy, information, and advocacy resources can also influence American foreign policy outcomes. Initially, President Bush and his advisers faced little opposition to their policies on Somalia and Bosnia. They captured significant information advantages on both Somalia and Bosnia, with little or no liberal humanitarian or media presence on the ground in either; selective engagers effectively portrayed the conflict as one fueled by ancient tribal hatreds about which the United States could do little.

The shifts in the Bush administration's policy on Somalia—first in August 1992 and then again in November 1992—came only in the face of mobilized political opposition. The critical variables behind these policy shifts stem from the shift in information and propaganda advantages once competing elites and the media developed and dedicated resources to the conflict areas to challenge the administration's framing of the crisis. Given the vast increases in global telecommunications technologies, future administrations are likely to find it difficult to develop and sustain information advantages.

NOTES

1. Quoted in John L. Hirsch and Robert B. Oakley, *Somalia and Operation Restore Hope: Reflections on Peacemaking and Peacekeeping* (Washington, D.C.: U.S. Institute of Peace, 1995), 43.

2. In fact, the option of U.S. military deployment was not even on the agenda for discussion for the November 21 meeting, according to several participants. Author interview with Admiral David Jeremiah, Oakton, Virginia, April 29, 1999; telephone interview with Andrew Natsios, who was then the president's special representative on Somalia, Boston, Massachussets, March 29, 1999; interview with Herman Cohen, who was then assistant secretary of state for African affairs, Arlington, Virginia, March 30, 1999; interview with James Woods, who was then deputy assistant secretary of defense for Africa and international security policy, Arlington, Virginia, March 30, 1999; and interview with Walter Kansteiner, who was the staff member responsible for Africa on the National Security Council, Washington, D.C., March 29, 1999.

3. Interviews with Kansteiner, Cohen, Natsios, and with James Bishop, who was then acting assistant secretary of state for human rights and humanitarian affairs, Washington, D.C., March 29, 1999.

4. U.S. Department of State *Dispatch* Supplement (DSDS), September 1992, 14; interview with Walter Kansteiner.

5. Interview with Brent Scowcroft, Washington, D.C., April 29, 1999.

6. Cited in Walter Clarke, *Somalia: Background Information for Operation Restore Hope, 1992–1993* (Carlisle Barracks, Pa.: U.S. Army War College, December 1992).

7. Mohamed Sahoun, *Somalia: The Missed Opportunities* (Washington, D.C.: U.S. Institute of Peace, 1994), 16.

8. Interview with Scowcroft.

9. Quoted from Don Oberdorfer, "The Path to Intervention: A Massive Tragedy We Could Do Something About," *Washington Post,* December 6, 1992, A1.

10. Interview with James Bishop, Washington, D.C., March 29, 1999.

11. Interview with Herman Cohen, Arlington, Virginia, March 30, 1999.

12. Data Source: Network Evening News Abstracts, Television News Archives, August 2–14, 1992, Vanderbilt University, at tvnews.vanderbilt.edu/eveningnews. html.

13. See, for example, *ABC World News Tonight,* August 8, 9, and 10, 1992; *NBC Nightly News,* August 7, 8, and 10, 1992; and *CBS Evening News,* August 8 and 9, 1992, all from Network Evening News Abstracts, Television News Archives, Vanderbilt University, tvnews.vanderbilt.edu/eveningnews.html.

14. Quoted in Jim Hoagland, "August Guns: How Sarajevo Will Reshape U.S. Strategy," *Washington Post,* August 9, 1992, C1.

15. Interview with Scowcroft.

16. Quoted in Michael Gordon, "Conflict in the Balkans: 60,000 Needed for Bosnia, A U.S. General Estimates," *New York Times,* August 12, 1992, 8.

17. Warren P. Strobel, *Late-Breaking Foreign Policy: The News Media's Influence on Peace Operations* (Washington, D.C.: U.S. Institute of Peace, 1997), 131–37.

18. Interview with Scowcroft.

19. Quoted in U.S. Department of State *Dispatch* Supplement (DSDS), September 1992, 14.

20. Ibid.

21. Quoted in Michael Gordon, "Winter May Kill 100,000 in Bosnia, the CIA Warns," *New York Times,* September 30, 1992, 13.

22. Ibid.

23. Interview with William Hill, director, Office of East European Analysis, Bureau of Intelligence and Research, U.S. Department of State, Washington, D.C., March 22, 1999.

24. Interview with Admiral David Jeremiah, Oakton, Virginia, April 29, 1999.

25. Quoted in Michael Gordon, "Powell Delivers a Resounding No on Using Limited Force in Bosnia," *New York Times,* September 28, 1999, 1.

26. "At Least Slow the Slaughter," *New York Times,* October 4, 1992, 16.

27. Colin Powell, "Why Generals Get Nervous," *New York Times,* October 8, 1992, 35.

28. Colin Powell, *My American Journey: An Autobiography* (New York: Random House, 1995), 562.

29. Hirsch and Oakley, *Somalia and Operation Restore Hope,* 43.

30. Interview with Jeremiah.

31. Interview with Scowcroft.

24

The Changing Leadership of George W. Bush

A Pre- and Post–9/11 Comparison

Fred I. Greenstein

The American presidency is said to be an office in which some incumbents grow and others swell. If ever a president has fallen in the first of these categories, it is George W. Bush. Before the suicide bombings of September 11, 2001, even a number of Bush's strong supporters were not persuaded that he was fully up to his responsibilities. Since then, even many of his critics grant that he has become strikingly more presidential. A Gallup poll completed a day before the bombing of the World Trade Towers and the Pentagon found that only 51 percent of the public expressed approval of his presidential performance. Three days after the attacks, Gallup fielded the first of an extended run of polls in which Bush registered approval levels in excess of 85 percent.

Bush has not only played well with the public. It is widely viewed in the political community that there has been an impressive increase in his political competence, a perception that extends beyond the United States. Five weeks after the terror attacks, a front-page column in the influential *Frankfurter Allgemeine* likened George W. Bush to Harry S. Truman. Noting that the unassuming Truman had risen to the challenge of the cold war presidency, the writer declared that Bush had grown "before our eyes," becoming "more profound and more sure-footed."[1]

In what follows, I present my own comparison of the pre- and post-9/11 political leadership style of George W. Bush. . . . My remarks fall under the six

Note: Some footnotes have been deleted; others have been renumbered.

headings I employ . . . to identify presidential leadership qualities: emotional intelligence, cognitive style, political skill, policy vision, organizational capacity, and effectiveness as a public communicator.

I introduce my comparison with a review of Bush's background, political emergence, and prepresidential political performance.

FORMATIVE YEARS

George W. Bush was born on July 6, 1946, in New Haven, Connecticut, where his war hero father was a Yale undergraduate. In contrast to George H. W. Bush, whose claim to be a Texan was belied by his Eastern accent and diffident manner, George W. Bush is very much a product of the Lone Star State. Whereas the senior Bush attended a private day school in the wealthy New York suburb of Greenwich, Connecticut, the younger Bush went to public school in the West Texas town of Midland, where oil was the dominant economic force and the ambience was that of tract houses, little league baseball, and easy informality. Acknowledging the difference between his Connecticut-bred father and himself, Bush has commented that while his father was mild-mannered and avoided confrontation, he has the brashness and directness of a typical Texan.[2]

In 1953, the Bush family was devastated by the death of George's three-year-old sister from leukemia. The seven-year-old George, who had no idea that his sister was gravely ill, was stunned when he was taken out of school and told that Robin had died. His mother sank into a depression. His father was at a career stage in which he was frequently away from home on business, and he sought to be his mother's consoler. He did so by playing the clown, developing the bantering manner that is one of his adult hallmarks.

Bush attended the Midland public schools for all but one of his elementary school years. He then followed in his father's footsteps and attended two intellectually rarified schools in the Northeast: Phillips Academy in Andover, Massachusetts, and Yale University. He had unhappy experiences at both. At Andover, he wrote a composition about the wrenching experience of learning of his sister's death but used an inappropriate word to refer to the tears he shed. He was deeply hurt when the instructor ignored the content of the paper and berated him for the way it was written. At Yale, he was offended when the college chaplain commented that his father had been beaten by "a better man" in his 1964 run for the Senate. The ironic effect of Bush's exposure to Andover and Yale was to alienate him from what he came to think of as the "intellectual snobs" who set the tone of these institutions.

While Bush was a lackluster student in prep school and college, he stood out for his social skills and popularity. At Andover, he became the football team's head cheerleader and "high commissioner" of a tongue-in-cheek stickball league. At Yale, he won ready admission to a fraternity that was legendary for its parties and beer consumption after revealing that he could name all of the fifty-odd fellow applicants. (None of the others could name more than a half-dozen.) He went on to become the fraternity's president and to win admission to Yale's most exclusive secret society, returning to Texas with friendships that served him well when he went into politics.

Bush's freshman year at Yale saw the beginning of the Johnson administration's military intervention in Vietnam. By his senior year, the campus was wracked with antiwar protest. The political ferment of the 1960s largely passed Bush by, but he was far from indifferent to politics. In 1964, the eighteen-year-old Bush took part in his father's race for the Senate, delighting in the hoopla of campaign politics. By his mid-thirties, he had worked on the campaigns of two other senatorial aspirants and participated in two more of his father's campaigns: his second run for the Senate in 1970 and his 1980 quest for the Republican presidential nomination.

EARLY ADULTHOOD

After Yale, Bush spent two years on active duty in the Texas Air National Guard and went on to Harvard Business School, graduating in 1974 with an MBA. He then returned to Midland, first holding an entry-level position in the oil industry and then forming an oil exploration company with funds raised through family connections. In 1978, the congressman in the district that included Midland announced that he was retiring, and Bush entered the race to succeed him. He won the Republican nomination but lost the general election to a conservative Democrat, who portrayed him as a carpetbagger from the Northeast and a representative of his party's moderate wing. Still, he received 47 percent of the vote in a traditionally Democratic congressional district and learned a lesson he took to heart when he reentered electoral politics—that of not being outflanked from the Right.

There is another theme in Bush's early adulthood. For much of the two decades after he finished college, he was conspicuous as the underachieving son of a superachieving father. He drank to excess and had a devil-may-care lifestyle that was marked by periodic alcohol-related scrapes. Gradually, his life came together. In 1977, he married the levelheaded librarian Laura Welch. In 1981, he became a father. During the next several years, he experienced a religious awakening and began a regimen of regular Bible reading. Then, on the morning of his fortieth birthday, after waking up with a fierce hangover, he abruptly swore off alcohol, anchoring his resolve in his Christian faith.

POLITICAL ASCENT

Oil prices declined sharply in the 1980s, and Bush's oil exploration company went deeply in the red. Because of favorable provisions in the tax code, he was able to sell it for $2.2 million to a firm specializing in takeovers. The sale coincided with the initial stage of his father's efforts to become the 1988 Republican presidential nominee. Bush moved his family to Washington and became codirector with the veteran political consultant Lee Atwater of his father's campaign staff. Bush's account of the part he played in the campaign provides insight into his managerial philosophy:

> I was a loyalty enforcer and a listening ear. When someone wanted to talk to the candidate but couldn't, I was a good substitute; people felt that if they said something to me, it would probably get to my dad. It did only if I believed it as important for him to know. A candidate needs to focus on the big picture, his message and agenda, and let others worry about most of the details.[3]

After his father's election, Bush returned to Texas, where a promising business opportunity came his way. He was asked to organize an investment group to buy the Texas Rangers, a second-tier major league baseball team that had come on the market. Bush was an ideal fund-raiser. He had never struck it rich in the oil business, but he had been successful in raising capital, and it did not hurt that his father was president of the United States. He assembled a consortium of investors that purchased the team, which named him its managing general partner. With new leadership and greater resources, the team prospered, hiring star players, and finally making its way to the play-offs. Bush proved to be an excellent front man. He became a popular speaker at meetings of Texas business, civic, and athletic groups and was regularly seen on television, rooting for the team from the sidelines. Before long, he was a state celebrity.

Baseball was Bush's political springboard. It publicized him, demonstrated that he could manage a complex organization, and gave him financial independence. After his father was defeated for reelection in 1992, Bush felt free to resume his own political career. The next year, he entered the running to become the 1994 Republican opponent of Ann Richards, the state's feisty, popular, Democratic governor. Assembling a highly professional campaign staff, he raised an impressive war chest and handily won his party's nomination.

His next hurdle was the outspoken Richards, who had famously declared at the 1988 Democratic convention that the senior George Bush was born "with a silver foot in his mouth." Richards derided the younger Bush, calling him "shrub." Rather than replying in kind, Bush ran an issue-driven campaign. Taking as a warning his father's failure to enunciate a clear policy vision during his time as president, Bush ran on a small number of explicitly stated issues that already had a degree of support in the Democratically controlled legislature: greater local control of education, welfare reform, stiffer penalties for juvenile offenders, and limitations on the right to litigate against businesses. He campaigned vigorously, staying on message and ignoring Richard's provocations and went on to win with 53 percent of the two-party vote. Bush conducted his governorship in a whir of interpersonal activity. Even before the election results were in, he forged a personal and political bond with the legislature's most influential Democrat. On taking office, he formally proposed the program with which he had campaigned. By the end of the first legislative session, he had advanced that program in more than one hundred meetings with lawmakers of both parties. All four of his signature measures were enacted. Although he had gone along with a number of compromises in their provisions, Bush declared victory and went on to run for a second term in 1998. He was reelected with a record 69 percent of the vote. Drawing solidly from such traditionally Democratic groups as women and minorities, he became an instant front-runner for the 2000 Republican presidential nomination.

TO THE WHITE HOUSE

As the 2000 presidential primary season approached, the leading figures in the GOP yearned for a candidate who would not lead the party to defeat a third time. Because of his front-runner status, Bush managed to raise more that $90 million in campaign funds. He suffered a stinging blow in the season-opening New Hampshire primary, when he was defeated by Arizona Senator John McCain, but he rebounded, clinching the nomination in March with victories in California, New York, and seven other states. Vice President Al Gore locked in the Democratic nomination the same week, and the candidates settled in for the longest presidential campaign in American history.

Gore was widely held to have the advantage in the general election. He represented an incumbent administration in time of prosperity, was a formidable debater, and had far more governmental experience than Bush. But the economy began to sag, depriving Gore of the prosperity issue; Bush held his own in the presidential debates; and the vice president ran an unimpressive campaign. As he had in Texas, Bush ran on a small number of highly explicit issues, calling for lower taxes; educational, health, and social security reform; and a ballistic missile defense system. As the campaign moved to its conclusion, the polls showed the candidates to be neck and neck. What ensued was one of the closest election outcomes in the nation's history. Gore led in the popular vote by a half of 1 percent, and the electoral vote was so evenly divided that the outcome hinged on Florida, where Gore and Bush were in a dead heat and there were a host of controversies about the mechanics of the voting. The thirty-six-day impasse over the Florida vote count that followed was ended with a ruling by the United States Supreme Court, which made Bush the winner.

THE BUSH STYLE, PRE- AND POST-9/11

Emotional Intelligence

It is not necessary that a chief executive be a paragon of mental health, but the nation may be at risk if he (and someday she) lacks the ability to control his emotions and turn them to productive use. This ability, which has come to be referred to as "emotional intelligence," is—or should be—a threshold requirement for the custodian of the most potentially lethal military arsenal in human experience.[4]

By the standard of emotional intelligence, George W. Bush would have been a poor presidential prospect in his years of excessive drinking and drift. It would not be surprising if someone with such life experiences proved to be an emotional tinder box, but Bush's business and political careers have been largely free of emotional excesses. He bore up well in the seemingly endless presidential campaign that brought him to the White House, rebounding after his defeat in New Hampshire, and he weathered the lengthy post–Election Day stalemate with seeming equanimity. Bush did face a minor national security crisis in April 2001, when an American surveillance plane was forced down on China's Hainan Island and China interned its crew. After a blustery initial statement, he was cool, measured, and patient. Still, it was by no means evident before September 11 how he might respond to a national security crisis of major proportions.

Bush's performance since September 11, 2001, is reassuring from the standpoint of his emotional intelligence. In the chaotic first day of the episode, he came across to some observers as being less than fully confident. But from then on, he radiated a sense of self-assurance and calm determination. It is instructive to contrast Bush's actions with those of Richard Nixon in the 1970 events that led to the killing of four student protestors at Kent State University. In April of that year, Nixon concluded that it was necessary for the United States to attack a concentration of communist troops that were using Cambodia as a sanctuary. Ignoring advice to inform the public of the action as a routine Pentagon statement, Nixon chose to announce it in a confrontational address and went on to refer to student protestors as "bums." By the end of the week, the nation's campuses were wracked with antiwar protests, Washington was under siege by demonstrators, and the moribund peace movement had been reinvigorated.

Cognitive Style

Late-night television comedians notwithstanding, George W. Bush has ample native intelligence. However, he has not been marked by intellectual curiosity or drawn to the play of ideas. Moreover, he is the nation's first MBA chief executive, and he lets it be known that he favors a corporate model of political leadership in which he avoids immersing himself in detail and relies on subordinates to structure his options. As governor of Texas, Bush was sweeping in his acts of delegation. A study of his Texas schedule found, for example, that when he was delivering a lengthy report on a tragedy in which a number of Texas A&M students were killed in a faultily constructed bonfire, he read neither it nor its executive summary, leaving it to his aides to highlight a few paragraphs of the report's conclusions. Even in the sensitive realm of capital punishment, Bush relied heavily on the recommendations of his aides, reducing the time he spent on reviews of death sentences from thirty to fifteen minutes in the course of his governorship.

When Bush went on to Washington, it remained to be seen whether he could remain as remote from specifics as he had in Austin. There were a number of instances during the pre-9/11 period of his presidency when it seemed evident that he needed to dig deeper into policy content than had been his wont. A notable example was his response on April 26 to an interviewer's question about whether it is American policy to defend the island republic of Taiwan against an invasion from mainland China. Bush remarked that the United States would do "whatever it takes" to help Taiwan, but it quickly became evident that he had not meant to signal a departure from the longtime policy of maintaining ambiguity about how the United States would respond to such a contingency.

Bush has exhibited a far firmer grasp of policy specifics after than before September 11. Particularly striking was his masterful review of his administration's policies at his first full-scale East Room press conference, a month to the day following the acts of terror. The impression that he is now delving more deeply into the problems of the day has been strongly confirmed by the legwork on Capitol Hill of Steven Thomma, the Washington correspondent of the Knight Ridder newspaper chain, who quotes a number of members of Congress who found Bush to be disengaged before September 11 and now find him to be thoughtful and focused. As one of them put it, "He's as smart as he wants to be."

Political Skill

The congenitally gregarious George W. Bush resembles his fellow Texan Lyndon Johnson in his aptitude for personal politics and his readiness to seek support on both sides of the aisle. In his December 2000 speech to the

Texas legislature immediately following Al Gore's concession, Bush stressed that he intended to apply the bipartisan methods he had used in Texas in the nation's capital. He had chosen to deliver the speech in the chamber of the Texas House of Representatives, he explained, "because it has been home to bipartisan cooperation," adding that "the spirit of cooperation we have seen in this hall is what is needed in Washington, D.C."

In the first several weeks after his inauguration, Bush spent so much time courting Democrats that the press characterized his efforts as a "charm offensive." But he went on to focus almost exclusively on mobilizing his party's narrow congressional majority to advance one of the issues on which he had campaigned—his proposal for a $1.6 trillion tax cut. He did so until it became clear that he would have to compromise, at which point he settled for a smaller reduction and declared victory. By the time the political community had engaged in the ritual of assessing the first hundred days of the Bush presidency, the prevailing view was that he is an exceptionally able politician. Still, it was too early to tell what his skill and that of his highly experienced associates would enable him to accomplish given the close balance of forces in the policy-making community. It also remained to be seen whether his gestures toward the Democrats were just that or whether he would be capable of engaging in genuine bipartisan policy making.

In the aftermath of September 11, Bush employed the same face-to-face political skills that marked the earlier months of his presidency, reinforcing his bonds with members of the policy-making community, including key Democrats. Two examples of the latter are noteworthy: on September 20, on the way out of the House chamber following his much-praised address to a joint session of Congress, Bush strode up to Senate Majority Leader Tom Daschle and embraced him. On November 20, Bush presided over the naming of the Justice Department building for Robert Kennedy, doing so in the presence of some fifty members of the Kennedy family. The success of year-long negotiations that led to passage in December 2001 of a much-modified version of Bush's education bill made it clear that he in fact was willing and able to bring about bipartisan policy outcomes. As Senator Kennedy, who had been one of the bill's negotiators, put it, "President Bush was there every step of the way."

Policy Vision

In contrast to Bill Clinton, who was fascinated with the intricacies of public policy, George W. Bush evinces little interest in policies in and of themselves. When Bush's fellow participants in his father's 1988 election campaign socialized with him, they found that he liked to talk about baseball, not issues. Yet unlike his father, Bush does have the "vision thing," adopting policy positions to preempt his opponents as well as because of their appeal to him. Having seen his father fail to amass a record on which to win reelection,

Bush's practice is to campaign and govern on the basis of a clear-cut set of goals. He did this in Texas, and he has done it in his presidency, but he also has been unsentimental about jettisoning portions of his programs if it becomes evident that they are not attainable.

Bush continued to show a clear sense of direction in the aftermath of September 11, but his primary focus shifted to combating terror. He was explicit, but not unrealistic, in stating his administration's war aims, both abroad and on the home front. Meanwhile, he put much of what remained unenacted in his domestic program on hold with one important exception—the aforementioned education bill, a landmark measure that increases school spending by many billions of dollars and targets the expenditures to poorly performing schools and their students.

Organizational Capacity

It speaks well for Bush's organizational capacity that he surrounded himself with a cadre of able loyalists who served him in Texas for the better part of a decade and followed him to Washington. Further evidence of his aptitude for team leadership is to be found in the personnel choices he made during and after the presidential campaign. He has staffed his White House and cabinet with an impressive array of seasoned public servants. Especially notable were his selection of the strategically gifted Washington insider Dick Cheney as his running mate and his appointment of Secretary of State Colin Powell, Secretary of Defense Donald Rumsfeld, and National Security Adviser Condoleezza Rice, who constitute one of the most experienced national security teams in the history of the presidency.

Bush's choice of his national security team has been more than vindicated by the rapid overthrow of the Taliban regime in Afghanistan. That team of what once had been deprecated as "retreads" is impressive in that it reflects a healthy diversity of viewpoints but has not evinced the scarcely concealed bureaucratic conflict that afflicted many earlier national security teams. It is too early to be tell how Bush's domestic team will shake down. Its most controversial member by far is Attorney General John Ashcroft, whom Bush may be employing as a lightning rod, much as President Eisenhower left it to Secretary of State John Foster Dulles and Chief of Staff Sherman Adams to promulgate policies that clashed with his own image as an ecumenical head of state.

Effectiveness As a Public Communicator

In a manner that is reminiscent of the early Harry S. Truman, George W. Bush began his presidency with an unassertive, less-than-fluent approach to public communication. He did not address the public as often as many of his predecessors had, and his public presentations were awkward and unpolished. He also met with the press infrequently and took a minimalist approach to his responsibilities as the nation's symbolic leader. Thus, he did not seize upon an outbreak of racial disturbances in Cincinnati, Ohio, to address the nation, and he failed to take part in the welcome for the air force personnel who had been interned on Hainan Island. The result, as columnist David Broder commented, was that Bush's political persona lacked "clear definition."

Since September 11, George W. Bush has made himself a public presence. Public communication is the realm in which he has been most dramatically transformed. Bush's brief address to the nation on the evening of September 11 was strong in content but brief and flat in delivery. In the days and weeks that followed, he became strikingly more articulate and assertive. During the three days following the suicide bombings, he made strong presentations at the sites of the World Trade Center and Pentagon disaster and delivered a moving set of remarks at the memorial service for the tragedy's victims in the National Cathedral. He went on in later weeks to give forceful addresses to a joint session of Congress and the United Nations General Assembly and to field the questions of journalists in rich detail at his October 11 press conference. He has even begun to preside over Bill Clinton–style town halls.

CODA

As these remarks were written, the unexpectedly eventful Bush presidency was less than a year old. There remained the lesson of the first President Bush, who in the immediate aftermath of the Gulf War achieved the highest public approval rating in the history of the Gallup poll, a record the younger Bush has now exceeded. A year after the Gulf War, the focus of public attention shifted from military victory to economic malaise and George H. W. Bush was defeated for reelection. How will the second Bush presidency fare? We can only watch and wait.

NOTES

1. Leo Weiland, "Bush's New Image," *Frankfurter Allegemeine* (English-language ed.), October 20, 2001.

2. George W. Bush, *A Charge to Keep: My Journey to the White House* (New York: HarperCollins, 1999), 182.

3. Bush, *A Charge to Keep*, 180.

4. "Emotional intelligence" is as much a term of art as of science. It was popularized by the science writer Daniel Goleman in *Emotional Intelligence* (New York: Bantam, 1995), and it provides a convenient catchall for summarizing the many specific ways in which emotional flaws can impede the performance of one's responsibilities.

25

Presidential Leadership Style and the Foreign Policy Advisory Process

Thomas Preston and Margaret G. Hermann

As the world becomes more complex and interconnected and its issues less well defined, presidents face an increasing dilemma in the making of foreign policy: More parts of the government have become involved in the foreign-policy making process and have a stake in the administrations' decisions. As a result, presidents routinely find themselves confronted with an ever increasing number of agencies, institutions, and people who are trying to influence what the United States does in the international arena. Presidents must work to maintain control over their administrations' foreign policy as this myriad of other actors seeks to define the foreign policy agenda, generate alternative plans, and shape the implementation of decisions. To improve their capacity to coordinate foreign policy, presidents have been forced over time to increase greatly the size of the White House staff and develop more elaborate advisory systems both to gather information and assist in maintaining control over policy. As a result, the modern presidency evolved into a complex organization requiring staffing and managing.

The presidency can be managed in a variety of ways. Presidents usually rely on styles and practices that have served them well before and with which they are comfortable. Indeed, because presidents participate in the selection of members of their advisory systems and set into place the norms that govern the advisory process, what presidents are like often influences what their advisers are like and how their organizations tackle foreign policy issues. "Leadership in the modern presidency is not carried out by the president alone, but rather by presidents with their associates. It depends ... on both the president's strengths and weaknesses and on the quality of the aides' support" (Greenstein 1988, 352). The kinds of people presidents choose or allow to be chosen as well as how they configure these people have implications for not only how the advisory system itself will function but how successful each president will ultimately be in the struggle for control over the conduct of American foreign policy.

In this chapter we explore how presidents' leadership styles influence the ways in which they structure their advisory systems. The framework we use builds on previous studies of how presidents have organized their relations with their advisers. To illustrate the framework we examine how Presidents Bill Clinton and George W. Bush organized and used their advisers in foreign-policy making.

CHARACTERISTICS OF PRESIDENTIAL LEADERSHIP STYLES

A review of the literature on presidential leadership styles highlights three characteristics that appear to influence how presidents structure and use their White House advisory systems: (1) need for control and involvement in the policy process; (2) general need for information and sensitivity to the political context; and (3) prior policy experience or expertise in a particular policy domain (see Preston 2001). In what follows, we will argue that these characteristics interact to shape the way presidents structure and manage their advisory systems.

Need for Control and Involvement

Presidents who perceive themselves as controlling what happens generally want to make the final decisions—that is, to have their preferences prevail. Such presidents view themselves as the ultimate authorities, whose positions cannot be reversed. These presidents are likely to organize authority into a hierarchical system with themselves at the apex of a formal chain of command. Information processing, problem definition, and option generation occur at lower levels of the chain of command and percolate up to the president. The advisory system is organized into a formal and rather inflexible hierarchy. In effect, there is a correct way to do things; the pattern of authority is well defined. If, on the other hand, the president's belief that what happens can be controlled is more moderate, or even low, the president is less likely to use a formal hierarchical pattern of authority and often is more comfortable when decisions are made through consensus or concurrence. Who participates in decisionmaking and how structured the process is become determined largely by the situation and problem the president faces. There is a looseness and informality to the pattern of authority that facilitates the president's building of consensus. The president is still on top but has deliberately chosen to involve others directly in decisionmaking and to use more informal channels of authority because there is no need to be in charge of everything that occurs.

Generally presidents who are intent on controlling their environments seek to mitigate conflict among their advisers and to achieve their goals by putting in place a structure that they can manipulate and in which they have the most authority (see, e.g., Johnson 1974; Hess 1988). They want people around them who are loyal, interested in their goals, and willing to help them implement these goals. Such presidents would like to clone advisers who share their raison d'être so that their worldview permeates the executive branch of government. Presidents who are not so intent on control often are willing to tolerate conflict among advisers because it stimulates debate and dialogue in the advisory organization, enhancing the opportunities for a range of points of view and options to be raised and discussed. Advisers who represent the "best and the brightest" and some diversity are preferable to having an advisory system of only "those like us." It is possible to tolerate "equals" and to encourage them to have areas of expertise that build on and broaden the president's.

The need for power is a personality characteristic whose impact upon style has been extensively studied in the leadership literature (see, e.g., Winter 1973; McClelland 1975; House 1990). One would expect presidents with progressively higher psychological needs for power to be increasingly dominant and assertive in their leadership styles in office and to assert greater control over subordinates and policy decisions. Indeed, studies have repeatedly shown that high-power leaders exhibit more controlling, domineering behavior toward subordinates and are more associated with the suppression of open decisionmaking and discussion within groups than are leaders low in power needs (see, e.g., Winter 1973; Fodor and Smith 1982; Preston 2001). Further, across recent U.S. presidents, those with high power needs have been shown to prefer formal, hierarchical advisory system structures designed to enhance their own personal control over the policy process. These leaders tended to centralize decisionmaking within tight inner circles of trusted advisers and to insist upon direct personal involvement and control over policy formulation and decisions. They were found to possess assertive interpersonal styles in which they would actively challenge or seek to influence the positions taken by their advisers. Further, these leaders were also more likely to override or ignore the conflicting or opposing policy views of subordinates. In contrast, low-power leaders preferred less hierarchical advisory structures and required less personal control over the policy process. As a result, the input of subordinates played a greater role in policymaking (Preston 2001).

Need for Information and Sensitivity to Context

A second important facet of presidential leadership style is the president's general need for information and sensitivity to the political context in which foreign policy decisions are made. How important does the president perceive it is to take into account and respond to the domestic and international constraints on what the United States can do in its foreign policy at any point in time? In other words, are constraints to be respected and worked with or to be challenged and worked around? (See, e.g., Burke and Greenstein 1991; Hermann and Kegley 1995.) Presidents seek different kinds of information from the political environment depending on their answers to these questions.

Presidents willing to challenge perceived constraints often have an idea (cause, ideology, strategy) that they want to further, and they search for information that is supportive or consonant with what they want to do. Advocacy and persuasion are collectively the "name of the game." These presidents evince less sensitivity to the nuance and complexity in their political environments, focusing primarily on distilling the arguments needed to line up a majority on the problem at hand. They are likely to rely upon analogies and stereotypical images of their opponents during policy deliberations and to be quite decisive, since they know what they want. Those who are prone to respect and react to perceived political constraints are interested in information that shows the range of opinion on how to solve a problem and what constituencies hold which opinions—there is a desire to know both consonant and dissonant information to facilitate locating oneself in the political terrain. Being the hub of the communication wheel is important to such presidents, as is having advisers who have access to a broad array of constituencies. These presidents have been found to be highly sensitive to their political environments, desiring an extensive search for information, considerable discussion about future policy contingencies, and policy debate before arriving at a decision.

Further, as George (1980) observed in examining the foreign-policy making of American presidents, those who were less sensitive or responsive to the political context tended to come to office with agendas that framed how situations were perceived and interpreted. They were intent on finding that information in the environment that supported their definitions of the situation or their positions and overlooked evidence that was disconfirmatory. Their attention was focused on persuading others of their position. Indeed, such presidents use their time to build a case and lobby others to their side. They are advocates who seek in advisers people who are also convinced of particular points of view and able to line up the "votes" or constituencies that are needed to ensure success. These presidents are interested in meeting a situation head-on, in achieving quick resolution of problems, in being decisive, and in advancing their agendas in the process. Their emphasis is on mobilization, implementation, and effective problem solving.

Presidents who are more responsive to the context are more empathetic to their surroundings and intent on ascertaining how relevant constituents are viewing events and on seeking their support. They perceive that politics involves bargaining, trade-offs, and compromise. They view flexibility, political timing, and consensus building as important leadership tools. Such presidents both define the problem and identify a position by checking what important others are advocating and doing. They consider the range of alternative scenarios that are possible in the current context, often "running ideas up the flagpole to see who salutes them." Feedback is critical in helping these presidents modify their behavior to fit the situation. Their focus is on the development of networks, collegial interactions, and the empowerment of others. Relationships are important to these presidents, as is mapping the terrain of support and opposition on any issue. That which is doable and feasible at the moment is what is tried.

The individual trait of complexity has long been linked to how attentive or sensitive leaders are to information from (or nuances within) their surrounding political or policy environments, and to the extent to which they require (or need) information when making decisions (see, e.g., Schroder et al. 1967; Nydegger 1975; Ziller et al. 1977). Indeed, the more sensitive leaders are to information from the decision environment, the more receptive they are to the views of colleagues or constituents, the views of outside actors, and the value of alternative viewpoints and discrepant information. In contrast, leaders with a low sensitivity to contextual information will be less receptive to feedback from the outside environment, will operate from a previously established and strongly held set of beliefs, will selectively perceive and process incoming information in order to support or bolster this prior framework, and will be unreceptive or closed-minded toward alternative viewpoints and discrepant information. Low-complexity individuals also tend to show symptoms of dogmatism, view and judge issues in black-and-white terms, ignore information threatening to their closed belief systems, and have limited ability to adjust their beliefs to new information.

Across modern American presidents, Preston (2001) found those high in complexity preferred more open advisory and information-processing systems than did those low in complexity—no doubt reflecting differing cognitive needs for both information and differentiation in the policy environment. Further, high-complexity presidents tended to be far more sensitive than others to the external policy context, as well as to the existence of multiple policy dimensions or perspectives on issues. During policy deliberations, they engaged in broad information-search routines emphasizing the presentation of alternative viewpoints, discrepant information, and multiple policy options by advisers. Such leaders focused substantial discussion within their advisory groups upon future policy contingencies and the likely views or reactions of other policy actors in the environment. They were also less likely to employ simplistic analogies, black-and-white problem representations, or stereotypical images of their opponents during policy deliberations.

However, complex leaders also had less decisive, more deliberative (and time-consuming) decisionmaking styles in office—a finding consistent with the heavy emphasis placed by such leaders upon extensive policy debate and information search within their advisory groups.

Less complex presidents—with their lower cognitive need for extensive information search or examination of multiple policy perspectives—tended to be far less sensitive to both information and the external policy environment. This reduced sensitivity to information and to context manifested itself in limited information search and in limited emphasis upon the presentation by advisers of alternative viewpoints, discrepant information, and multiple policy options. Such leaders were more likely to rely upon simplistic analogies, black-and-white problem representations, or stereotypical images of their opponents during their policy deliberations. Further, given their limited interest in extensive policy debate or broad information search, low-complexity presidents were found to have very decisive and less deliberative decisionmaking styles.

Prior Policy Experience and Expertise

Presidents are far more likely to participate in the foreign-policy making process if they are interested in foreign policy and have had experience with foreign policy (see, e.g., Barber 1972; George 1980). Indeed, prior policy experience has been shown to have an effect on presidential style, the nature of advisory interactions, and how forcefully presidents assert their own positions on policy issues (Preston 2001). Such is the case because presidents' sense of efficacy in the foreign policy arena is likely to be enhanced when they are either interested or believe they have experience in foreign-policy making (George 1980). The job is both more satisfying and easier with interest or experience, and there is a tendency to focus on foreign policy when the president can choose what to attend to. With personal engagement in the process comes a desire to be part of what is happening, to be on top of any problem solving that centers around foreign policy. Without this sense of efficacy and comfort, presidents are likely to delegate the authority for foreign policy to others.

Past experience provides leaders with a sense of what actions will be effective or ineffective in specific policy situations, as well as which cues from the environment should be attended to and which are irrelevant. Leaders with prior policy experience are more likely to insist upon personal involvement or control over policymaking than are those low in experience. Also, leaders with substantive expertise in a given policy area are far less dependent upon the views of their advisers and, because of their own substantive knowledge, rely less frequently on simplistic stereotypes or analogies to understand policy situations. In other words, prior policy experience or

Table 25.1.   Typology of Possible Presidential Advisory Systems Based on the Presidents' Leadership Styles

| | | | *Prior Experience or Expertise in Policy Domain* | |
			High	*Low*
High *Need to Control Or Be Involved* 	*Sensitivity to Context*	*High*	**Director-Navigator** (Eisenhower and Kennedy foreign policy style)	**Magistrate-Observer** (Carter foreign policy style)
		Low	**Director-Sentinel** (Johnson domestic policy style)	**Magistrate-Maverick** (Truman and Johnson foreign policy style)
Low	*Sensitivity to Context*	*High*	**Administrator-Navigator** (Clinton domestic policy style and George Bush Sr. foreign policy style)	**Delegator-Observer** (Clinton foreign policy style and George Bush Sr. domestic policy style)
		Low	**Administrator-Sentinel** (Ronald Reagan domestic policy style)	**Delegator-Maverick** (George W. Bush and Ronald Reagan foreign policy style)

expertise influences how much learning must be accomplished on the job, the repertoire of behaviors presidents have at their fingertips, and their confidence in their own judgments when interacting with experts (see, e.g., Khong 1992; Preston 2001).

A TYPOLOGY OF PRESIDENT-ADVISER RELATIONS

The three presidential leadership style variables create an eightfold typology of possible advisory systems. This typology is presented in table 25.1. The placement of presidents in its cells is based upon their measured scores on these three style variables, using a leader evaluation and assessment-at-a-distance technique (Hermann 1999; Preston 2001). Presidents' scores indicate the extent to which they feel a need to control or influence what happens or the actions of those around them; their ability to differentiate among people and objects in their environment (are things categorized into black/white, either/or categories, as opposed to being viewed as more contextualized and nuanced?); measured sensitivity to the political context; and their previous experience or expertise in a particular policy domain. Each cell of the typology indicates a kind of relationship between the president and his advisers based on the president's leadership style. The terms in the cells give an overall impression of the way in which a president's leadership style can shape the advisory system. The terms describe the role that a president with each set of characteristics is likely to play in the policymaking process and, in turn, the kinds of advisers such a president will choose and how they will be organized (see Preston 2001). Being categorized as "high" on a leadership style variable in table 25.1 means that the president's score on that variable was higher than the mean of the nine presidents included in the figure; being categorized as "low" indicates that the president's score was lower than the mean.

It is important for us to note, however, that under certain circumstances presidents can move between the cells in table 25.1. One such situation involves presidents who are normally less engaged by foreign policy problems due to a lack of prior experience or expertise. They can be forced by events—for example, an international crisis, a persistent international problem, a summit meeting, a speech before an international body, a request from another country's leadership—to be more actively involved in the foreign-policy making process. On such occasions, these presidents will temporarily exhibit the style of their more involved, experienced counterparts.

For example, George W. Bush was forced by the events of September 11 to focus upon foreign policy and the "War on Terrorism," nearly to the exclusion of all else. His normal lack of interest in foreign affairs and desire to delegate the formulation and implementation of foreign policy to others, which had been the dominant pattern within his advisory system before the terrorist attacks, was forced to give way to his current, more active and involved pattern. Though Bush still lacks the substantive knowledge needed to avoid dependence upon his expert policy advisers, who continue to be delegated the "nuts and bolts" aspects of policy formulation and implementation, his style now mimics far more closely that of a more involved or experienced president due to his now active, personal engagement in the policy process. In such circumstances, Bush's low complexity and sensitivity to context actually facilitates such engagement. As one who sees the world in simple, black-and-white terms of right and wrong, Bush's comfort level with a conflict in which "you are either with us or against us" will be high enough to allow a far more forceful level of participation in policy debates than would normally be expected. Bush will have a problem if the current foreign policy equation, which has been framed in quite simple terms, becomes more nuanced and complex—for instance, with a war with Iraq and its likely aftermath. Less contextually sensitive, low-complexity leaders tend toward rigidity and dogmatism, especially when a strongly held belief system (or policy) comes under threat. In such a situation, Bush is likely to have far greater difficulty adapting to a changing, more complicated environment than he had in his earlier shift to a more simplified one.

Similarly, Lyndon Johnson, as the Vietnam War heated up, had to focus (against his wishes) more of his attention away from his Great Society program and onto the war effort. As a consequence, he became more actively engaged and directive in both the way he set up his advisory system and the people he chose to participate. Otherwise, Johnson preferred to play the *Magistrate* (or arbiter) in foreign-policy making with his advisers, deciding from among the options presented to him by his experts (Preston 2001).

Another situation in which leaders may move between cells involves those, like Ronald Reagan, who are generally seen to lack policy expertise or interest in a particular policy domain but for whom certain policy issues matter a great deal for ideological reasons. This is especially noticeable for less sensitive or complex leaders who tend to be more ideologically driven. In both his governorship of California and the presidency, Reagan took charge—setting up programs and priorities—in areas of interest to him and delegated authority in areas that were of little interest to him. In foreign policy, issues related to the East-West conflict and Cold War were important to Reagan; he wanted to have, and took, control over policymaking that was focused on these issues (Cannon 1982). With these few notable exceptions, Reagan's style on most foreign policy matters was to be uninvolved and to delegate policymaking authority to his subordinates.

Table 25.2 elaborates on the terms in the cells in table 25.1 to describe the kinds of advisory systems we can expect around presidents with the different leadership styles. These descriptions synthesize the research on presidents with that on organizations, groups, and political leadership in general (see, e.g., Burns 1978; 't Hart, Stern, and Sundelius 1997; Preston and 't Hart 1999). The information in table 25.2 suggests that presidents' advisory systems are more hierarchical and formal the higher the president's need for control and involvement. There is more centralization of authority in the president. Advisers' input to problem definition, option generation, and planning is more valued the more sensitive the president is to the political context, while there is more emphasis on advisers who share the concerns, vision, and ideology of presidents who are less sensitive to the political context. The advisory systems are more open to outside influences the more sensitive and responsive the president is to contextual information. As the prior policy experience or substantive expertise increases, so does a president's willingness to be actively engaged in the process, to trust their own policy judgment, and to

Table 25.2. The Proposed Influence of Presidential Leadership Style on the Selection and Organization of Advisers.

			Prior Experience or Expertise in Policy Domain	
Need to Control Or Be Involved			High	Low
High	Sensitivity to Context	High	Interested in planning and anticipating problems. Advisers used as sounding board. Time spent considering options and consequences. Coherence in policy is valued. Advisers represent important constituencies.	Seek doable solution that will sell politically. Advisers seen as part of team. Advisers propose and delineate problems and options. Compromise is valued. Seek experts as advisers. Policy by discussion.
		Low	Interested in framing policy agenda. Interested in focusing on important decisions. Loyalty is important. Procedures well-defined and highly structured. Disagreements allowed on means but not ends.	Interested in evaluating not generating options. Select advisers with similar policy concerns. Decision shaped by shared vision. Advisers viewed as implementers and advocates of policy.
Low	Sensitivity to Context	High	Interested in noncontroversial policy. Advisers' input is valued. Sharing of accountability. Seek advisers whom they know. Interested in reactions inside and outside advisory system. Consensus valued.	Advisers have leeway to decide policy. Seek advisers with skills that match position. Seek advisers who are interested in acting independently.
		Low	Interested in shaping option. Seek advisers with similar vision. Discussion focuses on how to coordinate policy. Groupthink is possible. Advisers provide psychological support.	Interested in overseeing policy. Seek advisers who can act on own within particular framework. One or two advisers play gatekeeper role for information and access.

perceive accurately the nature and characteristics of constraints in the policy environment.

THE BILL CLINTON AND GEORGE W. BUSH ADVISORY SYSTEMS

Using the classifications of the last two American presidents—Bill Clinton and George W. Bush—based on their leadership styles and our expectations about what their advisory systems should look like, do we find support for our typology in writings about their presidencies? In exploring the Clinton administration, we will rely on assessments of his advisory system by those who served with him, journalists, and scholars of the presidency (see, e.g., Drew 1994; Rockman 1996; Maraniss 1995; Stephanopoulos 1999; Reich 1997). For the Bush presidency we will use a similarly diverse set of materials (see, e.g., Bruni 2002; Mitchell 2000; Ivins and Dubose 2000). How do these authors view the ways Clinton and Bush fashioned their advisory organizations?

Clinton and His Advisers

Our assessment of Bill Clinton's leadership style suggests that he would tend to exhibit a *Delegator's* preferences for control and involvement in the policy process, coupled with an *Observer's* high needs for information and sensitivity to the contextual environment (see table 25.1). Literature on Clinton and his foreign policy advisory system lends support to our classification of him. Clinton entered the White House with an extremely limited foreign affairs background. Devoting himself to his true policy interests, Clinton developed tremendous expertise in domestic policy and the art of political campaigning (Maraniss 1995). A virtuoso in domestic politics, Clinton was noticeably out of his element when dealing with foreign affairs:

> Clinton on domestic policy is a sort of controlled volcano, ad-libbing furiously, tearing off ideas. Clinton on foreign policy is far less confident. When he speaks to congressional leaders on the telephone he writes his own script; when he calls foreign leaders he sets up a speakerphone so aides can listen in and, if necessary, quietly pass him notes. The president rarely departs from the prepared text of foreign policy speeches, which often makes them sound wooden (Elliott and Cohn 1994, 28).

Generally, Clinton saw foreign policy as a "distraction" from his domestic agenda and sought to delegate its formulation to others whenever possible (Elliott and Cohn 1994, 28). As a result, Secretary of State Warren Christopher and NSC Adviser Anthony Lake's joint role was to "not let foreign policy get in the President's way as he focused on domestic policy" (Drew 1994, 28). Clinton tended to rely heavily on subordinates with the expertise he lacked when making decisions. Indeed, reminiscent of Truman's reliance upon Marshall and Acheson, Clinton consistently delegated—whether on Bosnia, Russia, North Korea, or Kosovo—to his expert subordinates the general formulation and implementation of foreign policy (Gordon and Sciolino 1998; Sciolino and Purdum 1995; Sigal 1998).

A hallmark of the Clinton White House, in both foreign and domestic policy, was the president's informal, nonhierarchical advisory structure and collegial style of leadership (Drew 1994). In fact, this loose, free-ranging management style mimicked that used by Clinton during his years as governor of Arkansas (Maraniss 1995). Unfortunately, though this open advisory system allowed an immense range of feedback to reach the White House, the nearly complete lack of coordination and structure often resulted in information overload and a painfully slow decision process (Reich 1997; Stephanopoulos 1999). Indeed, some associates have described Clinton's decisionmaking method as "a postponement process" (Drew 1994, 232). Clinton populated his advisory system with advisers who would not necessarily agree with one another. For example, in his cabinet appointments, there were both strong left-of-center leanings (Donna Shalala, Henry Cisneros, Robert Reich) and strong moderate leanings (Lloyd Bentsen, Janet Reno, William Cohen), ensuring that Clinton would get conflicting views from his advisers (Renshon 1996, 260–61). Clinton was uncomfortable with unanimity of opinion from advisers and liked to hear contradictory things from his staff (Woodward 1994, 258).

Perhaps Clinton's greatest individual strengths were his ability to see multiple perspectives and the "shades of gray" on issues, his probing curiosity, his unrelenting search for ever more information or advice on problems, and his amazing sensitivity to the political environment and the needs of his constituents. However, as was true of his high-complexity predecessors (Eisenhower, Kennedy, Carter, Bush Sr.), Clinton's complexity of mind led to criticism for indecisiveness, tentative decisionmaking, and "waffling" on the issues (Drew 1994; Woodward 1994; Preston 2001).

For Clinton, policy was made by discussion. "He needs time to talk, to bring people together" (Drew 1994, 56). By his very nature he "wants to get as much information as possible. . . . He wants the satisfaction of knowing that he has reached out to advisers, to groups of people, to friends" (Harris 1997, A8). "Clinton is Mr. Wiggling Antenna, who tries to read every face in the room and smooth down any hard edges . . . that are an obstacle to accommodation" (Wiebe cited in Harris 1997, A8). Clinton also was intent on coming up with policy that was doable, or politically feasible. "He is a consummate politician" (Burton cited in Harris 1997, A8) who understood and reveled in the horse trading, cajolery, logrolling, and persuasiveness that are pivotal in achieving workable compromises. Thus, he often tested ideas to see who reacted how; he was interested as well in exploring "a variety of perspectives" (Rockman 1996, 352) and keeping a "balance around the table" (Drew 1994, 69).

This preference often meant that Clinton wanted the advice of those who were more politically inclined as well as those who were more expert on a particular topic. Thus the Clinton advisory system automatically made foreign policy look more domestic in orientation, given the president's own interests and those of the large majority of his advisers. At the same time, however, those who observed Clinton from both within his inner circle and outside of it note that he was not rigidly ideological or partisan but willing to consider alternative viewpoints in his quest for addressing policy problems and achieving policy goals (Maraniss 1995; Stephanopoulos 1999; Reich 1997). As Woodward (1994,14–15) observed, Clinton is an experimental person, always reaching out for new ideas and people, not a "bare-fanged partisan."

George W. Bush and His Advisers

President Bush, who scores low in power, complexity, and prior foreign policy experience, would fit the *Delegator-Maverick* style (the same style as Ronald Reagan). Even more than Clinton, Bush would be expected not to require active personal involvement in policymaking tasks, to heavily delegate policy formulation and implementation tasks to subordinates, and to be almost entirely dependent upon the expertise or policy judgments of his senior specialist advisers when making decisions. Unlike Clinton, however, Bush's low complexity and lack of policy expertise results in an information-processing style that does not require a great deal of information or advice when making decisions. Instead, one would expect a very rapid, decisive decisionmaking style, driven by black-and-white reasoning, rigid adherence to existing ideological beliefs, extensive use of simple stereotypes and analogies, and advice from people who share his general idiosyncratic views of the world. Bush would not be expected to monitor his political environment for diverse information or feedback on policy or political issues but instead to proceed from the basis of his own ideological or political belief system.

The early evidence of Bush's style in office supports this designation. He is an individual who tends to be less personally engaged or involved in the formulation and making of policy, preferring to delegate these tasks to subordinates, but who nevertheless greatly enjoys "being" president (Milbank 2000; Kahn 2000). Bush's own advisers concede that he is not by nature a "hands-on" president (Berke 2001) but one who prefers to delegate substantially to subordinates (Milbank 2000). The White House transition illustrates Bush's delegative pattern well; Vice President Dick Cheney was essentially given organizational leeway to select personnel and structure the incoming administration (Milbank 2000; Bruni 2002). Bush's own style favors a "flat hierarchy and gives authority to a wide range of underlings," but Cheney's style has moderated this, due to his own preference for "a more tightly controlled inner circle" and his own role in shaping existing White House structures (Milbank 2000; Bruni 2002). As a result, Bush's advisory system is structured more hierarchically (due to Cheney's influence) than might be expected for a leader with low power needs, but it functions in the gathering of information and advice as would be expected given the president's style. In this sense, it will likely bear a resemblance to the advisory systems of Ronald Reagan and Lyndon Johnson with respect to how it functions.

One consequence of Bush's extremely delegative nature is to enhance the potential for bureaucratic conflict over policy among subordinates (see Preston and 't Hart 1999). Bureaucratic infighting and conflicts over the shape of Bush's foreign policy have been quite visible over the past two years, pitting administration hard-liners like Defense Secretary Donald Rumsfeld and Vice President Cheney against the more moderate Secretary of State Colin Powell (see Sipress 2002; Zakaria 2002). For example, Powell's efforts to pursue mediation to break the deadlock between the Israelis and the Palestinians were repeatedly undercut and blocked by Bush's more influential hard-line advisers (Sipress 2001). As a result of this infighting, Bush's foreign policy in the Middle East and elsewhere has been inconsistent, at times incoherent (Duffy 2002; Sanger 2002). Similar conflicts have occurred between Powell, Rumsfeld, and Cheney over policy toward Iraq, North Korea, the United Nations, and over continued U.S. commitments to international agreements. Further, Bush's own personal dislike for conflict and controversy, as well as his own lack of substantive policy knowledge, makes it difficult for him to end these adviser conflicts (Ivins and Dubose 2000; Bruni 2002). Instead, Bush seeks the comfort zone provided by those advisers (principally Rumsfeld and Cheney) who share his own ideological beliefs, and he usually is more influenced by their advice. This often results in a rather closed information-gathering advisory system, where his more hard-line inner circle excludes the participation of Powell or external actors who differ with them over policy.

Bush also has a tendency to see the world in stark, undifferentiated terms, a pattern that is complicated by his often reported lack of attention to the details of policy (Mitchell 2000; Bruni 2002). For example, Bush's categorization of Iraq, Iran, and North Korea as an "axis of evil" served to simplify three quite distinct regions and policy situations into a more easily understood, black-and-white frame for policymaking. After the events of 9/11, Bush's simple "moral clarity" about the world seemed to resonate with a changed political climate in America in which good and evil seemed easily delineated. Stating that "either you are with us or you are with the terrorists" and that

Osama bin Laden would be brought back "dead or alive," or that the new struggle was between good versus evil, civilization versus anarchy, that it was a "crusade" that America was now embarked upon—all resonated with the American public, if not always with foreign publics (Duffy 2002). Unlike earlier in his administration, where his less nuanced views of the world were seen as a liability and indicator of unreadiness to govern, now Bush found support in his belief that "My job isn't to try to nuance. My job is to tell people what I think" (Duffy 2002). Further, as would be expected under such circumstances, since 9/11 Bush has been more focused and engaged in policy matters; aides note that he is a "better listener at meetings than he was before" the terrorist attacks (Berke 2001). However, Bush continues to be uncomfortable in "unscripted" situations (Ivins and Dubose 2000; Bruni 2002), and although more engaged than before 9/11 on foreign policy matters, his increased involvement is primarily centered on the conduct of the "War on Terror" (not on foreign policy more generally), and he remains highly dependent upon a like-minded inner circle of advisers for policy guidance. Yet as another Texan (who shared Bush's lack of prior policy experience, less complex worldview, and dependence upon a similarly tight-knit inner circle of advisers) discovered to his cost, if the expert advice upon which one is so dependent is good, one will be successful. But if it is faulty, a highly structured, closed advisory system lacks the "checks and balances" found in a more open, less restrictive system, where policy differences are debated more openly and alternative viewpoints encouraged.

CONCLUSION

As one scholar (Hess 1988) has observed, presidents' styles, work habits, how they like to receive information, the people they prefer around them, and the way they make up their minds are all key to how the White House is organized. "In the end, an American president is responsible for organizing his own White House and his own administration" (Rockman 1996, 353). What the president is like shapes the nature of that advisory system. In this chapter, we have focused on how the president's leadership style influences the nature of the foreign policy advisory system. We have presented a typology of advisory systems that is derived from information about presidents' need to control, their sensitivity or responsiveness to the political context, and their prior experience and interest in foreign policy issues. An examination of the Bush and Clinton foreign policy advisory systems has lent some support to the typology—at least, to the ways in which these two presidents were classified. These illustrations suggest that differences in leadership style are related to differences in the way the executive branch of government works. Unfortunately, "obeisance to the view that presidents can do little [because they are institutionally constrained] has limited attention to the relationship between personality, management style, and presidential performance during the last fifteen years" (Campbell 1996, 57). This chapter indicates the importance of reversing this trend. After all, as we have shown, how presidents try to deal with institutional constraints is often shaped by who they are.

REFERENCES

Barber, James D. 1972. *The Presidential Character: Predicting Performance in the White House.* Englewood Cliffs: Prentice-Hall.

Berke, Richard L. 2001. "Jokes Remain, but Many Say Bush Is Showing Signs of War's Burden." *New York Times,* December 9, B7.

Bruni, Frank. 2002. *Ambling into History: The Unlikely Odyssey of George W. Bush.* New York: HarperCollins.

Burke, John P., and Fred I. Greenstein. 1991. *How Presidents Test Reality: Decisions on Vietnam, 1954 and 1965.* New York: Russell Sage Foundation.

Burns, James MacGregor. 1978. *Leadership.* New York: Harper and Row.

Campbell, Colin. 1996. "Management in a Sandbox: Why the Clinton White House Failed to Cope with Gridlock." In *The Clinton Presidency: First Appraisals,* edited by Colin Campbell and Bert A. Rockman. Chatham, N.J.: Chatham House.

Cannon, Lou. 1982. *Reagan.* New York: G. P. Putnam's Sons.

Drew, Elizabeth. 1994. *On the Edge: The Clinton Presidency.* New York: Touchstone.

Duffy, Michael. 2002. "Trapped by His Own Instincts." *Time,* May 6, 24–29.

Elliott, Michael, and Bob Cohn. 1994. "A Head for Diplomacy? Clinton: One year In, He's Still Struggling to Get His Mind around Foreign Policy." *Newsweek,* March 28, 28–29.

Fodor, Eugene M. and T. Smith. 1982. "The Power Motive as an Influence on Group Decision Making." *Journal of Personality and Social Psychology* 42: 178–85.

George, Alexander L. 1980. *Presidential Decisionmaking in Foreign Policy: The Effective Use of Information and Advice.* Boulder, Colo.: Westview Press.

Gordon, Michael R., and Elaine Sciolino. 1998. "Fingerprints on Iraqi Accord Belong to Albright." *New York Times,* February 25, A1 and A10.

Greenstein, Fred I. 1988. "Nine Presidents: In Search of a Modern Presidency." In *Leadership in the Modern Presidency,* edited by Fred I. Greenstein. Cambridge, Mass.: Harvard University Press.

't Hart, Paul, Eric K. Stern, and Bengt Sundelius, eds. 1997. *Beyond Groupthink: Political Group Dynamics and Foreign Policymaking.* Ann Arbor: University of Michigan Press.

Harris, John F. 1997. "Winning a Second Term; Waiting for a Second Wind." *Washington Post National Weekly Edition,* January 20, A8.

Hermann, Margaret G., and Charles W. Kegley, Jr. 1995. "Rethinking Democracy and International Peace: Perspectives from Political Psychology." *International Studies Quarterly* 39: 511–33.

Hermann, Margaret G. 1999. *Assessing Leadership Style: A Trait Analysis.* Columbus, Ohio: Social Science Automation, Inc.

Hess, Stephen. 1988. *Organizing the Presidency.* Washington, D.C.: Brookings Institution.

House, Robert J. 1990. "Power and Personality in Complex Organizations." In *Personality and Organizational Influence,* edited by Barry M. Staw and L. L. Cummings. Greenwich, Conn.: JAI Press.

Ivins, Molly, and Lou Dubose. 2000. *Shrub: The Short but Happy Political Life of George W. Bush.* New York: Vintage Books.

Johnson, Richard T. 1974. *Managing the White House: An Intimate Study of the Presidency.* New York: Harper and Row.

Kahn, Joseph. 2000. "Bush Filling Cabinet with Team of Power-Seasoned Executives." *New York Times,* December 31, A1.

Khong, Yuen F. 1992. *Analogies at War: Korea, Munich, Dien Bien Phu, and the Vietnam Decisions of 1965.* Princeton, N.J.: Princeton University Press.

Maraniss, David. 1995. *First in His Class: A Biography of Bill Clinton.* New York: Simon and Schuster.

McClelland, David C. 1975. *Power: The Inner Experience.* New York: Irvington.

Milbank, Dana. 2000. "The Chairman and the CEO: In Incoming Corporate White House, Bush Is Seen Running Board, Cheney Effecting Policy." *Washington Post,* December 24, A01.

Mitchell, Elizabeth. 2000. *W: Revenge of the Bush Dynasty.* New York: Hyperion.

Nydegger, Rudy V. 1975. "Information Processing Complexity and Leadership Status." *Journal of Experimental Social Psychology* 11: 317–28.

Preston, Thomas, and 't Hart, Paul. 1999. "Understanding and Evaluating Bureaucratic Politics: The Nexus between Political Leaders and Advisory Systems." *Political Psychology* 20, no. 1 (March): 49–98.

Preston, Thomas. 2001. *The President and His Inner Circle: Leadership Style and the Advisory Process in Foreign Affairs.* New York: Columbia University Press.

Reich, Robert B. 1997. *Locked in the Cabinet.* New York: Alfred A. Knopf.

Renshon, Stanley A. 1996. *High Hopes: The Clinton Presidency and the Politics of Ambition.* New York: New York University Press.

Rockman, Bert A. 1996. "Leadership Style and the Clinton Presidency." In *The Clinton Presidency: First Appraisals,* edited by Colin Campbell and Bert A. Rockman. Chatham, NJ: Chatham House.

Sanger, David E. 2002. "War Was Easy. The Rest of the World Is a Mess." *New York Times,* April 21, sec. 4, 1 and 4.

Schroder, H., M. Driver, and S. Streufert. 1967. *Human Information Processing.* New York: Holt, Rinehart, and Winston.

Sciolino, Elaine, and Todd S. Purdum. 1995. "Gore Is No Typical Vice President in the Shadows: He Carves Out a Niche as Trouble-Shooter and Close Adviser." *New York Times,* February 19, A1 and A16.

Sigal, Leon. 1998. *Disarming Strangers: Nuclear Diplomacy with North Korea.* Princeton, N.J. Princeton University Press.

Sipress, Alan. 2001. "Policy Divide Thwarts Powell in Mideast Effort: Defense Department's Influence Frustrates State Department." *Washington Post,* April 26, A1.

Stephanopoulos, George. 1999. *All Too Human: A Political Education*. Boston: Little, Brown.

Winter, David G. 1973. *The Power Motive*. New York: Free Press.

Woodward, Bob. 1994. *The Agenda: Inside the Clinton White House*. New York: Simon and Schuster.

Zakaria, Fareed. 2002. "Colin Powell's Humiliation: Bush Should Clearly Support His Secretary of State—Otherwise He Should Get a New One." *Newsweek*, April 29, 28.

Ziller, R. C., W. F. Stone, R. M. Jackson, and N. J. Terbovic. 1977. "Self-Other Orientations and Political Behavior." In *A Psychological Examination of Political Leaders*, edited by M. G. Hermann, 337–53. New York: Free Press.

Index

Note: Page references to figures or tables have been set in *italic type*.

About the Editors and Contributors

EDITORS

Eugene R. Wittkopf received his doctorate from Syracuse University. He is currently R. Downs Poindexter Endowed Professor of Political Science at Louisiana State University. He has also held appointments at the University of Florida and the University of North Carolina at Chapel Hill. Wittkopf is author of *Faces of Internationalism: Public Opinion and American Foreign Policy* (1990); coauthor, with Charles W. Kegley Jr., of *World Politics: Trend and Transformation* (9th ed., 2004) and, with Charles W. Kegley, Jr., and James M. Scott, of *American Foreign Policy: Pattern and Process* (6th ed., 2003); and coeditor, with Christopher M. Jones, of *The Future of American Foreign Policy*. He has also published extensively in the professional journal literature. In 1997 he was named the LSU Distinguished Research Master of Arts, Humanities, and Social Sciences, and in 2002 he received the Distinguished Scholar Award of the Foreign Policy Analysis Section of the International Studies Association.

James M. McCormick is professor and chair of the department of political science at Iowa State University. He has also held positions at the University of New Mexico, Ohio University, the University of Toledo, and Texas A & M University. He received his Ph.D. from Michigan State University and served as an American Political Science Association Congressional Fellow in 1986–1987. McCormick is the author of *American Foreign Policy and Process* (3rd ed., 1998) and editor of *A Reader in American Foreign Policy* (1986). He has also published numerous articles and chapters on foreign policy and international politics in such journals as *World Politics, American Political Science Review, American Journal of Political Science, The Journal of Politics,* and *Legislative Studies Quarterly.* He was recipient of the Iowa State University Foundation Award for Outstanding Research at Mid-Career in 1990, a Fulbright Senior Award to New Zealand in 1993, and the Fulbright-SyCip Distinguished Lecturer Award to the Philippines in 2003.

CONTRIBUTORS

Philip Brenner is professor of international relations at American University.

Pat Choate is director of the Manufacturing Policy Project and vice chair of the board of directors of the Congressional Economic Leadership Institute.

Eliot A. Cohen is professor of strategic studies at the Paul H. Nitze School of Advanced International Studies, The Johns Hopkins University.

Ivo H. Daalder is a senior fellow in foreign policy studies at the Brookings Institution.

I. M. Destler is a professor in the University of Maryland's School of Public Affairs.

John Deutch is a former director of central intelligence and currently institute professor of chemistry at the Massachusetts Institute of Technology.

Peter D. Feaver is associate professor of political science at Duke University.

Louis Fisher is senior specialist in separation of powers at the Congressional Research Service of the Library of Congress.

James Goldgeier is associate professor of political science and international affairs at The George Washington University.

Fred I. Greenstein is professor emeritus of politics at Princeton University.

Patrick J. Haney is associate professor of political science at Miami University (Ohio).

Margaret G. Hermann is Gerald B. and Daphna Cramer Professor of Global Affairs in the Department of Political Science and the Maxwell School of Citizenship and Public Affairs, Syracuse University.

Stanley Hoffmann is Paul and Catherine Buttenwieser University Professor at Harvard University.

Samuel P. Huntington is the Albert J. Weatherhead III University Professor at Harvard University.

Christopher M. Jones is associate professor and assistant chair and director of undergraduate studies in the Department of Political Science at Northern Illinois University.

Richard H. Kohn is professor of history and chair of the Curriculum in Peace, War, and Defense at the University of North Carolina at Chapel Hill.

James M. Lindsay is a senior fellow in foreign policy studies at the Brookings Institution.

Michael Medved hosts a nationally syndicated radio talk show focusing on politics and popular culture.

Shoon Kathleen Murray is associate professor in the School of International Service at American University.

Michael Nelson is professor of political science at Rhodes College.

Miroslav Nincic is professor of political science at the University of California at Davis.

Joseph S. Nye is Don K. Price Professor of Public Policy and dean of the Kennedy School of Government at Harvard University.

Thomas Preston is associate professor of international relations at Washington State University.

Jeffrey H. Smith is a former CIA general counsel and currently a partner in the Washington law firm of Arnold & Porter.

Steve Smith is vice chancellor at the University of Exeter.

Christopher Spinosa is a Ph.D. candidate in the U.S. foreign policy program in the School of International Service at American University.

Bruce Stokes is adjunct senior fellow at the Council on Foreign Relations.

Strobe Talbott is a former U.S. deputy secretary of state and currently president of the Brookings Institution.

James C. Thomson, Jr., is professor in the Department of History and in the College of Communications at Boston University.

Walter Vanderbush is associate professor of political science at Miami University (Ohio).

William Wechsler served as special adviser to the secretary of the treasury, as director of transnational threats at the National Security Council, and as special assistant to the chairman of the Joint Chiefs of Staff.

Jon Western is Five College Assistant Professor of International Relations at Mount Holyoke College and the Five Colleges.